Structural Adjustment, the Environment, and Sustainable Development

Structural Adjustment, the Environment, and Sustainable Development

Edited by David Reed

WWF

EARTHSCAN
Earthscan Publications Ltd, London

First published 1996 by

Earthscan Publications Ltd.
120 Pentonville Road, London N1 9JN

Reprinted 1997

A catalogue record for this book is available from the British Library.

ISBN 1 85383 351 7 (paperback)
ISBN 1 85383 356 8 (hardback)

Printed and bound in Great Britain

email:earthinfo@earthscan.co.uk
Website:http://www.earthscan.co.uk

Earthscan Publications Ltd. is an editorially independent subsidiary of Kogan Page Ltd. and publishes in association with IIED and WWF-UK.

CONTENTS

FOREWORD

In 1992, WWF-International published *Structural Adjustment and the Environment*, based on case studies carried out by local institutes in Côte d'Ivoire, Mexico, and Thailand. The essence of this work was a historical analysis of the effect of macroeconomic reforms on the natural resource base in the countries concerned. A major conclusion, strongly contested by some critics at the time, was that environmental factors cannot be separated from social and economic factors and that, to be both efficient and effective, macroeconomic reforms must integrate social and environmental costs and benefits at the very outset of planning. Such integration is the essential tool of sustainability and sustainable development.

The work that is the subject of this publication took place between 1992 and 1995. The basic principles were the same in both projects: professional locally based research, creative engagement of governments and institutions in the learning process of analysis and policy formulation, and action-driven research, especially in capacity building and advocacy at the local level.

This publication attempts to take the sustainable development agenda one step further by answering three basic questions in the nine new countries: What are the country's major environmental assets and how has past development affected them? What are the assumptions, objectives, and impacts of current macroeconomic reforms? What alternative approaches are needed to guarantee environmental sustainability and economic growth? The answers to these questions vary considerably from country to country because sustainable development that integrates the social, environmental, and economic dimensions must be responsive to local and national conditions. Similarly, efforts to project environmental impacts into the future, one of the most challenging aspects of the research program, was carried out on a country-by-country basis. The general conclusions were the product of discussions with the many partners in this endeavor, whereas the recommendations are exclusively WWF's responsibility.

Our hope is that this publication will strengthen commitment to what the World Bank now calls mainstreaming the environment and social development. Moreover, we hope the analyses will stimulate adaptation of major economic reforms and interventions so that they become effective instruments of sustainable development.

WWF-International would like to acknowledge with thanks and appreciation the participation in and cofinancing of this work by BMZ (Federal Republic of Germany), CIDA (Canada), DANIDA (Denmark), Cooperation Française (France), DGCS (Italy), and the European Commission (DG8).

—KEVIN LYONETTE
Director, Sustainable Development
WWF-International, 1996

PREFACE

The writing of this book, and the research program on which it is based, have taken place during a period characterized by the integration and globalization of the world economy. The restructuring of the global economy and of national economies through structural adjustment programs has been driven by the promise that higher growth rates will translate into improved standards of living for individuals and the world community as a whole. Although traditional measures of economic growth do reflect the positive impacts of the outward oriented export-led growth model, voices protesting the social, human, and environmental costs of the restructuring process have challenged the viability of adjustment programs over the past 15 years.

This research program was motivated by an imperative to understand both the benefits and the costs associated with the process of global economic change and the role of structural adjustment programs specifically. It was driven by a conviction that only a rigorous, agnostic analysis of country experiences at both the local and national levels could help weigh the competing claims regarding the adjustment programs' impacts and the opportunities for developing countries as they have been integrated more deeply into the global economic order.

Readers with varying analytical perspectives and ideological convictions will react to this book differently. Some will view the study's endorsement of the need to continue, if not intensify, the adjustment process as a sign of cooptation by the prevailing economic forces of the period. Others will see the criticisms of adjustment's social and environmental costs, present and future, as a repudiation of the structural reforms and the premises on which they are built. If, in eliciting such reactions, this publication deepens debate about the impact of the emerging economic order on the planet's environment it will be welcome, for, in reality, debate and controversy were constant and healthy companions of this research project from its inception. For example, meetings of the project's international advisory committee echoed with competing views as members argued from their different institutional vantage points when reviewing results of the country studies and formulating recommendations; members of local research teams wrestled over differing analytical approaches as they tried to agree on the methodologies to be used in the study; macroeconomists, microeconomists, ecologists, and sociologists struggled to find common language and concepts as they tried to explain the complex yet interrelated outcomes of their research. Such debate was welcome because it forced all participants to transcend the boundaries of their professions, peer into the uncertain, and try to decipher new messages from the world unfolding around us.

As the project's technical director, I am privileged to have benefited from the experiences and opinions of dedicated professionals from five continents. First and foremost, I must thank the World Wide Fund for Nature-International core team, composed of Kevin Lyonette, Fulai Sheng, Tony Long, Alexander Wood, and Barry Coates, for their support and guidance and, in particular, the leadership of Kevin Lyonette in promoting a policy dialogue and forging partnerships with donors, governments, and nongovernment organizations.

The international advisory committee was indispensable at all stages of the implementation. Meeting in Washington and Brussels on three separate occasions, the committee brought together representatives of multilateral and bilateral development agencies, independent research institutes from the North and South, and nongovernmental organizations from the South. Its responsibilities included reviewing the proposed terms of reference for the nine countries before the research began, assessing and critiquing the country study results, and in light of the general conclusions derived from the research, suggesting recommendations for WWF's consideration.

In this context, I want to express particular appreciation to John D. Shilling for serving as the committee's convener and for reviewing many chapter drafts. I appreciate his good humor in handling the unenviable task of differentiating opinions made on his own behalf from those made when acting in an official capacity as a World Bank representative. Edith Kürtzinger, representing Germany's Federal Ministry for Economic

Cooperation, and Soe Lin, representing the policy branch of the Canadian International Development Agency, gathered the analyses and opinions of colleagues working in operations departments and therein greatly enriched our deliberations. I want also to express my gratitude to other members of the advisory committee who traveled far and often at great personal cost to contribute to our discussions. They are: Charles Abugre (Third World Network, Ghana), Cristovam Buarque (Governor of Brasilia, Brazil), Pablo Gutman (CLACSO, Buenos Aires), Jacques Loup (DIAL, Paris), Henrik Marcussen (Roskilde University, Denmark), Kirit Parikh (Indira Ghandi Institute of Development Research, Bombay), Michel Potier (Organisation for Economic Co-operation and Development, Paris), Atiq Rahman (Bangladesh Center for Advanced Studies, Dhaka), Youba Sokona (ENDA, Dakar), Marcel van Opstal (European Commission, Brussels), and Konrad von Moltke (Dartmouth College). Although the project could not have been implemented without them, their participation does not imply endorsement of the study's findings or recommendations.

Another vital partnership of this project was built with the Overseas Development Institute (ODI, London) and the Harvard Institute for International Development (HIID, Cambridge, Massachusetts). ODI and HIID provided technical and methodological support to the nine country teams throughout the project. Both institutes participated in joint seminars to develop research methodologies, review draft terms of reference for the local institutes, assess progress of the country teams, manage implementation problems, and write summaries of the research. James Winpenny and Elizabeth Cromwell, supported by ODI director John Howell, managed the African country studies in Cameroon, Mali, Tanzania, and Zambia on behalf of ODI. Theodore Panayotou, Jeff Vincent, and Anil Markandya represented HIID in supporting the research programs in El Salvador, Jamaica, Pakistan, Venezuela, and Vietnam.

Management and staff of the World Bank dedicated considerable time and resources to providing valuable input to this project. Ismail Serageldin, Vice President for Environmentally Sustainable Development, Andrew Steer, Director of the Environment Department, and Mohan Munasinghe, the Pollution and Environmental Economics Division Chief, created numerous opportunities to share work between our organizations and encourage a policy dialogue within the Bank. I want to thank Callisto Madavo and Andrew Steer for organizing internal seminars to review the country studies and the following Bank staff for their comments and advice on individual country reports: Ian Bannon, Robert Blake, Chantal Dejou,

Peter Dewees, Birger Frederiksen, Coby Frimpong, Randolph Harris, Victoria Kwakwa, Fred King, Francois Laporte, Philip Nouvel, Linda McGinnis, Jean Louis Sarbib, John Todd, Hasan Tuluy, and Steven Webb.

None of the partnerships and contributions mentioned above would have found resonance without the professionalism and dedication of the nine research institutes. I am humbled by the perseverance and skill with which each of the nine teams confronted and overcame daunting obstacles and difficulties particular to their own countries in carrying out their research tasks. I remain indebted to them for the kindness and patience with which they helped me take small steps to overcome my ignorance of their countries and peoples. Each of the following researchers made unique and invaluable contributions to this endeavor: *Cameroon*: Roger Tchoungui, Steve Gartlan, J.A. Mope Simo, Fondo Sikod, Augustin Youmbi, and Michel Ndjatsana; *El Salvador*: Deborah Barry and Herman Rosa of the Programa Salvadoreño de Investigación sobre Desarrollo y Medio Ambiente; *Jamaica*: Alfred Francis, Dillon Alleyne, and Ian Boxill of the Institute of Social and Economic Research, University of the West Indies; *Mali*: Alpha S. Maiga, Bino Teme, Bakary S. Coulibaly, Lassiné Diarra, Alpha O. Kergna, and Kalilou Tigana of the Institut d'Economie Rurale; *Pakistan*: Sajjad Akhtar, Akhtar Hai, Haroon Jamal, Shaukat Ali, M.M. Sajid Manzoor, Mohammad Ilyas, S. Iqbal Ali, Wasim Akhtar, and Samina Khalil of the Applied Economics Research Centre, University of Karachi; *Tanzania*: Mboya Bagachwa, Fanuel Shechambo, Hussein Sosovele, Kassim Kulindwa and Alexis Naho of the Economic Research Bureau, University of Dar es Salaam; *Venezuela*: Lourdes Yero, Cecilia Cariola, Mugues Lacabana, Francisco Javier Velasco, Arelys Caraballo, Victor Fajardo, Hercilio Castellanos, Francisco Herrera, Iokine Rodrigues, Chris Sharpe, Jorge Giordani, Yvan Laplace, Thais Maingon, Rita Pucci, Nelson Prato, Arnoldo Pirela, Luis Mata M., and Pablo Lacabana of the Centro de Estudios del Desarrollo, Universidad Central de Venezuela; *Vietnam*: Nguyen Quang Thai, Lea Anh Son, Nguyen Van Thanh, Nguyen The Hieln, Le Thi Kim Dung, Dang Huu Dao, Nguyen Van Vy, and Tran Kim Dong of the Institute for Long-term and Regional Planning; and *Zambia*: Christopher Mupumpila, Ventakesh Seshamani, Allast Mwanza, Emmanuel Chidumayo, and Inyambo Mwanawina of the Department of Economics, University of Lusaka.

The extensive experience and insights of Robert Goodland, David Kaimowitz, Pamela Hathaway, Isabel Lecha, Carter Brandon, Mark Renschler, Pamela Stedman, and David Schorr helped strengthen many aspects of the chapters I have written. To them I extend my deep appreciation.

I owe many thanks to Monica Chacon and Maria Boulos, my colleagues from WWF-International, whose managerial support kept the project turning smoothly during these three years. They coordinated the meetings of the international advisory committee, managed communications with the many partners in this endeavor, and oversaw editing and production of the text. Without them, the project would remain but plans on the drawing board. Tanya Lee's work transformed marked-up copy into finished text. Brian Schneiderman prepared the text, graphics, and layout for the publisher. I remain indebted to Sheila A. Mulvihill for her precision, rigor, and patience in editing the book.

—DAVID REED
Director, Macroeconomics for
Sustainable Development Program
WWF-International, 1996

INTRODUCTION

by David Reed

By the end of the 1980s, the development community was willing to acknowledge that macroeconomic reforms could have an impact on the natural resources of a country undergoing structural adjustment. Intuitively, it stood to reason that any country seeking to change relative prices throughout its economy, liberalize its trading relations with the rest of the world, and increase the contribution of the tradeable goods sector could not help but change patterns of production and consumption and, consequently, the management of its natural resource base.

Stiffly resisted, however, was the proposition that the relationship between instruments of macroeconomic reform and the natural resource base, not to mention specific environmental problems, could be analyzed with precision. Even more objectionable was the proposition that adjustment programs, already overburdened with conditionalities and complex reform activities, should include environmental objectives. It was argued not only that environmental concerns were of secondary concern compared with the economic crisis facing most developing countries but that correcting environmental problems required special instruments unrelated to those being used in adjustment programs.

This skepticism set the backdrop for the first World Wide Fund for Nature (WWF) study, *Structural Adjustment and the Environment*,[1] which examined the environmental impacts of adjustment programs in Côte d'Ivoire, Mexico, and Thailand. Although the research documented the complexity of linkages between macroeconomic instruments and specific environmental problems, that pioneering effort also underscored the high costs of continuing to ignore the environmental impacts of macroeconomic reforms. To help set the context for the study of structural adjustment and sustainability presented here, this introduction reviews some major conclusions of the initial study.

LESSONS DERIVED FROM THE FIRST RESEARCH PROGRAM

To begin, the development strategies pursued by the three countries created high levels of environmental degradation and generated unnecessary waste and loss of natural wealth. Structural adjustment programs did not move the countries to more sustainable development paths for two basic reasons: although price changes improved economic efficiency, higher production levels increased aggregate environmental impacts, and the economic reforms did not internalize environmental and social costs because requisite policy reforms did not accompany the economic corrections. There were strong grounds to believe that economic growth would have been stimulated, not stifled, had environmental and social costs been internalized in development strategies and adjustment programs.

Second, in seeking to document direct, immediate impacts of macroeconomic instruments on environmental problems, the three case studies generated less than categorical results. Linkages between monetary, fiscal, and exchange rate policies—the three principal instruments of macroeconomic reform used to varying degrees in the three countries—and specific environment problems proved indirect and complex. Although the environmental impacts of macroeconomic instruments tended to be more pervasive, sectoral reform programs had more direct, identifiable environmental linkages. The effects of the reform programs were mixed in each country, in some cases with positive environmental impacts and in others with existing environmental problems exacerbated. In no case study, however, could structural adjustment's impacts on the natural resource base be considered optimal because environmental concerns were simply ignored by designers of the reform packages.

Third, institutional factors strongly influenced the environmental impacts of adjustment policies. Economic reforms that should have generated positive economic and environmental outcomes were often undermined by institutional problems, such as weak managerial capacity and land tenure regimes. Failure to incorporate policy and institutional reforms before and during the adjustment process frequently offset potential price correction benefits.

Fourth, the relationship of adjustment policies, poverty, and the environment was complex. Causal links varied and they were often indirect. The recessions associated with adjustment programs tended to deepen poverty, in turn contributing to environmental degradation as the poor increased pressures on forests and other natural resources to survive.

Further, adjustment policies tended to reinforce the prevailing political economy in the natural resource sector. Privileged access to natural resources, an important source of wealth for elites, was frequently left intact under the adjustment programs. Moreover, governments tended to redistribute publicly held natural resources to the poor during adjustment programs to attenuate social discontent during the adjustment process rather than address the underlying causes of social inequality.

The three case studies concluded that macroeconomic stability is necessary for sound environmental management but is not sufficient to ensure long-term environmental sustainability. Lower inflation rates, increased savings, lower budget deficits, and improved trade balances were central to creating conditions for increased investment, a higher growth rate, employment creation, and poverty reduction. However, macroeconomic stability and increased economic efficiency would not and could not address other basic development issues, such as income inequality and cost internalization, which directly threatened the sustainability of the countries' development strategies. In light of the adjustment programs' shortcomings in addressing specific environmental impacts of the price corrections and government failure to implement complementary policy reforms, the study concluded that the economic reform packages in Côte d'Ivoire, Mexico, and Thailand came up short in placing the three countries on more sustainable development paths.

The earlier research also contributed to improving analytical methodologies for interpreting the economic reform programs' environmental impacts. An input-output model was constructed to determine the impacts of environmental controls on income distribution in Mexico. Macroeconomic modeling was used to determine "optimal" resource forest stocks and use in Côte d'Ivoire. To simulate the impacts of price changes and fiscal reforms on key environmental problems in Thailand, a 60-sector general equilibrium model was used. Each approach clarified understandings about the complex relationships between economic reforms and the environment and also provided new analytical methods for other researchers to use and improve in complementary studies.

The WWF study helped to change the terms of debate about adjustment programs' impacts on developing societies. It was no longer possible to deny the direct linkages between economic reforms, be they macroeconomic or sectoral, and the natural resource base and environmental problems in developing countries. Bilateral and multilateral donors found it difficult to ignore the potential environmental impacts of the economic reforms they were supporting. The World Bank, responding to the growing evidence, subsequently initiated and published its own research that examined the linkages between its policy-based lending operations and specific environmental problems in developing countries. Released in 1994, the Bank's *Economywide Policies and the Environment*[2] made important contributions to understanding the impacts of specific economic interventions on countries' natural resource bases. Many donors now require assessments of the potential environmental impacts of policy-based lending prior to their committing financial resources.

INFLUENCE OF THE FIRST WWF PROGRAM ON THIS SECOND STUDY

As with any ground-breaking endeavor, WWF's initial effort had a number of limitations, but they helped shape and give focus to this second study. First, there was a need to deepen understanding about the relationship between macroeconomic reforms and specific environmental problems in a wider range of developing countries. With this point in mind, the second study includes nine countries: Cameroon, Mali, Tanzania, and Zambia in Africa, El Salvador, Jamaica, and Venezuela in Latin America and the Caribbean, and Pakistan and Vietnam in Asia. By understanding how economic reforms affect the environment in more diverse societies, government and donor agencies as well as the informed public can predict more accurately the short- and medium-term impacts of adjustment on the major environmental problems of relatively similar countries. Further, their strengthened ability to anticipate such impacts increases the probability of preventing environmental irreversibilities and unforeseen consequences that societies—and some sectors of those societies in particular—might otherwise have to bear in the future.

Second, it was clear that the analysis of direct linkages between economic instruments and specific environmental problems told only part of the story of what was happening to the natural resource base of an adjusting country. The first study began analyzing the relation between specific economic instruments and specific environmental problems. It showed that changes in class structure, the breadth and depth of poverty, and institutional arrangements also had strong impacts on the rate and composition of natural resource use. In fact, those indirect impacts seemed at times to be as strong as, if not stronger than, the environmental impacts tied directly to specific economic reforms. For example, the poverty-environmental degradation nexus emerged as an important issue in the first study, but the causes, linkages, and impacts were not fully understood. Consequently, understanding economic reforms' impacts on social structures and therefore on the natural resource base became a primary objective of this second study.

Third, the impacts that economic reforms could have on the long-term economic viability of the adjusting countries cannot be ignored. Scores of studies document adjustment programs' correcting economic distortions and enhancing economic efficiency. However, economic efficiency is but one part of a far more complex equation that seeks to promote sustainability. In fact, if it were achieved at high social and environmental costs, economic efficiency could undermine long-term sustainability. If it is true, as the first study showed, that adjustment programs did enhance efficiency in the short run but did not necessarily help shift the economies toward a sustainable development path, what would be the impacts of the economic reforms on the prosperity, cohesion, and viability of the countries in the long term? It thus seems central to examine the long-term impacts of the economic reforms on the natural resource base, the social cohesion, and the productive capacity of individual countries long after the reforms were implemented.

Guided by these concerns, this second research program, while retaining the retrospective analytical focus of the first study, emphasizes assessing the long-term impacts of the economic reforms on the nine selected countries. Using an array of innovative methodologies, each adapted to the individual country's particular conditions, this study was designed to project future economic reforms to understand their potential contributions to and limitations on developing sustainable societies. Ultimately, this study was designed to identify policy failures that apparently led the countries into unsustainable development strategies and, in that context, to formulate policy options that would correct potential shortcomings.

STRUCTURE OF THIS STUDY

The urgent yet long-term challenge of reforming current development strategy and promoting sustainable development paths is extremely complex. Such change requires nothing short of reformulating the assumptions on which the current development enterprise is predicated and translating new standards of behavior into operational terms in quite different countries around the globe. This challenge also requires clarity and precision in both the analysis of present approaches to development and the articulation of what seem to be more viable alternatives. Thus the presentation of research results here tries to be explicit about the assumptions, analytical framework, and definitions of terms and concepts used.

With transparency and clarity in mind, the study is organized in three main sections. Part One's two chapters set a historical and conceptual context for the research project. The first chapter reviews the experience of structural adjustment, what is here called an instrument of global economic policy, as it facilitated the restructuring and integration of developing societies into the global market economy. This chapter also reviews salient challenges raised by critics about the viability of this instrument of global economic policy as it has facilitated the restructuring of developing societies and their relation to the world economy. Chapter 2 reviews the sustainable development concept that evolved parallel to, but largely isolated from, the economic restructuring taking place around the world. This chapter also presents the operational definition of sustainable development used in both the research and this publication.

Part Two summarizes the nine country studies. These case studies highlight adjustment program impacts on the countries' main environmental problems and examine the impacts of those reforms on the sustainability of each country's development strategy. Most studies conclude with specific policy recommendations to shift to more sustainable development paths.

Part Three steps back from the immediacy of the country analyses and draws out more general conclusions about the impacts of economic restructuring on developing societies. Chapter 12 summarizes the short-term impacts of structural reforms on the natural resource bases of the nine countries. Chapter 13 assesses structural adjustment's potential impacts on long-term sustainability. The last chapter's recommendations identify changes in structural adjustment programs and development policy required to ensure that future economic interventions help place developing societies on the path to sustainable development.

ENDNOTES

1. David Reed, ed., *Structural Adjustment and the Environment* (Boulder, Colo.: Westview Press, 1992).
2. World Bank, *Economywide Policies and the Environment: Emerging Lessons from Experience* (Washington, D.C.: World Bank, 1994).

PART ONE

1

AN INSTRUMENT OF GLOBAL ECONOMIC POLICY

by David Reed

THE EVOLVING DEBATE ON ADJUSTMENT

Attribution of Cause

Three sets of issues shaped the debate over structural adjustment during the past decade and one-half. The first emerged in the early 1980s, focusing on the principal causes of the economic crisis being experienced by so many developing countries. The initial controversy unfolded between advocates who cited adverse external economic conditions and those who stressed economic problems internal to individual developing countries as the main cause of the economic collapse. The "externalists" based their claims on the decades-long decline in the relative terms of trade, high real interest rates, and growing protectionism in Organisation for Economic Co-operation and Development (OECD) countries. The "internalists" offered abundant examples of the highly inefficient economic performance of individual governments, deeply ingrained economic distortions, and widespread financial mismanagement, to name but a few areas of policy and managerial failure. Between the debate's two poles was a full spectrum of opinions attributing relative importance to one set of causes or the other.[1]

This debate would have direct consequences for developing countries because conclusions drawn therefrom influenced the development assistance policies and priorities of multi- and bilateral development agencies over the following decade and one-half. To a large degree, the arguments of the internalists prevailed, at least among policymakers who were to become responsible for designing structural adjustment programs in the 1980s. Whatever external conditions may exist, they argued, the one domain in which most developing countries' governments had some degree of control over their economic future was the improvement of their own economies' efficiency and stability. By removing distortions, increasing internal economic efficiency, and creating a stable macroeconomic environment, governments could strengthen prospects for long-term productivity improvements, thereby helping to counterbalance adverse international conditions. Moreover, the internalists argued that by demonstrating their ability to stabilize and manage their economies more efficiently, governments would attract greater external assistance and more foreign direct investment.

But in Whose Interests?

As adjustment lending was being tested and applied more widely in the mid-1980s, the initial debate about the causes of developing countries' economic crises gave way to a second set of issues: Whose interests were actually being served by the economic restructuring process? Was the restructuring of scores of developing country economies being driven primarily by the internal needs of the adjusting countries themselves? Or were the needs and interests of the industrialized societies, the dominant forces in the international economy, determining the purposes and outcomes of those reforms? For example, was the developing economies' liberalization a means of generating higher levels of sorely needed foreign currency, or was it a long-awaited opportunity to subject those economies to the pressures and mechanisms of international market forces on which those small countries could have virtually no influence? By way of further illustration, was the privatization associated with many adjustment programs primarily a way of correcting fiscal imbalances in debt-strapped countries, or was it the means for facilitating penetration of foreign capital and its control over the emerging economies?

As with the initial debate about the causes of economic crises in the developing world, there were no clear-cut, definitive answers, then or now. On the one hand, no single set of indicators could reflect the complex costs and benefits to any country or the global economy from the adjustment process. On the other, by using different evaluation criteria, be they traditional measures of economic performance or human welfare indicators, observers could derive sharply contrasting conclusions about the main beneficiaries and losers from adjustment programs.

And What about Long-term Impacts?

Today, a third, equally important set of questions shapes the international debate on adjustment programs' impacts and continued viability. Rather than looking back or forward, today's issues focus on the future impacts of economic restructuring programs. Will today's efficiency gains result in a more productive, short-term allocation of resources but weaken the natural resource base and consequently the countries' productive capacity in the future? Will today's export-led growth strengthen those economic sectors tied to international markets but weaken the overall viability of local economies and undermine the ability of national policymakers to address their citizens' needs in years to come? Will these emerging economic relations increase disparities within individual countries and among regions of the world to unsustainable levels? Will economic restructuring help stabilize government expenditures and improve balance of payments liabilities now but at the cost of undermining the human potential and the productive capacity of future generations? Underlying these questions is concern for the impacts of macroeconomic reforms on the economic, social, and environmental sustainability of individual countries some 10, 15, perhaps 25 years from now.

When structural adjustment is considered in the context of these three sets of questions—the causes of developing countries' economic collapse, the interests served by adjustment programs, and the long-term consequences of economic reforms—it is not surprising that this policy tool has been and will remain the focus of intense debate for many years. For many governments and development agencies, it is a foregone conclusion that expanding economic growth through an outward-oriented development strategy remains the only viable option for seeking better living conditions for citizens of developing countries. For many others, however, improving traditional measures of aggregate economic performance alone has long ceased to be an adequate development strategy; the quality, the beneficiaries, and the costs of growth are equally important in determining the impacts of the economic reforms being implemented under structural adjustment programs.

This introductory chapter does not pretend to answer these questions. Its more limited objective is to present a historical context in which the evolution of structural adjustment can be understood more fully. The purpose of the overview is to identify the dominant political and economic influences that shaped this policy tool and that will continue to shape the future of developing countries around the globe. The review underscores the reasons why structural reforms were and continue to be urgently needed in many countries. It also brings into focus both the costs and benefits of the adjustment process as well as the distribution of those costs and benefits in developing countries.

THE ADJUSTMENT IMPERATIVE

The End of the Golden Age

As the World Bank's first structural adjustment loan, a $200 million program with Turkey, was being approved in 1980, the economic orthodoxy that dominated western economic planning in the postwar period was being challenged. Those challenges reflected fundamental changes that had taken place in the world economy, both among the industrialized societies of the North and between the industrialized North and the developing world. Since the 1940s, Keynesianism, coupled with its underlying social democratic ethos, dominated both analytical and prescriptive loyalties of policymakers. That policy framework encouraged an activist role of the state in economic affairs and, by relying on anticyclical government intervention, helped governments chart economic policy through periods of economic crisis for the better part of three decades. An integral part of this economic orthodoxy was maintaining harmony between labor and capital by cushioning workers from the worst impacts of economic fluctuations, providing minimal social services, and redistributing wealth through fiscal policies.

The economic difficulties experienced by industrialized nations during the 1970s revealed problems that the Keynesian analytical framework could not interpret satisfactorily and for which its policy prescriptions could no longer provide adequate remedies. For example, Keynesianism was unable to explain the simultaneous rise in inflation rates and higher unemployment levels that nagged industrialized societies during the 1960s and 1970s. Concomitantly, its traditional menu of anticyclical measures, combining stimulus packages, tax and trade reforms, and new investment incentives, failed to stabilize economies and pull them out of their doldrums.

The problems facing industrialized societies at the end of the 1970s were not simply the result of misguided policy, that is, a failure of Keynesianism; they were structural in nature. Since 1974, the industrialized world had tried to adjust to the fact that the 20 years of unprecedented growth following World War II, appropriately called the Golden Age, was ending.[2] The oil shock of 1974, coupled with the deepest global recession since the Great Depression, brought home the urgency of embarking on major structural reforms. Adjustments had to take place in relations among the industrial powers themselves. One such adjustment was the adoption of floating exchange rates to reflect the failure of the United States to control inflation and its declining economic power vis-à-vis the rising influence of Japan and the European Community. Adjustments also had to take place within individual industrial countries. One such major change was that governments sought to adjust the terms of the social contract between capital and labor largely by exerting downward pressure on wages, reducing social benefits, and modifying prevailing redistribution policies.[3]

The costs of adjusting industrialized societies to new global conditions were mild compared with the difficulties of many developing countries in the subsequent two decades. Initially, adjusting developing countries to emerging economic conditions, including response to the first major increase in oil prices, proved less disruptive than anticipated. In fact, despite the protracted 1974-75 recession in OECD countries, developing country "growth rates fell less than those of industrialized countries" during that same period.[4] This less than catastrophic result was due in large part to "substantial increases in official aid and other capital and [to] borrowing a significant part of the oil producers' recycled surpluses."[5]

By relying on external financing, many countries continued living beyond their means, thereby creating unsustainable economic conditions that would require future social and economic adjustments of far greater magnitude than those experienced in the industrialized societies. The first major problem was that although access to commercial lending helped stave off a sharp decline in living standards for many countries in the short term, borrowing governments acquired such levels of debt on unfavorable terms that they soon were unable to meet their financial obligations. The second major problem was the continuing decline in terms of trade, particularly for primary commodities. As a recent International Monetary Fund (IMF) study indicates, terms of trade for nonoil exports have declined 45 percent since 1986.[6] Despite improved export performance and trade policy reforms, many developing countries were even less able to meet foreign obligations than in the previous decade. Thus with the exception of a few countries (largely in East Asia), the process of adjustment, of aligning developing countries' living standards with real income levels, was postponed until the early 1980s, when further external shocks made structural reforms inevitable in scores of developing countries.

The Legacy of Supply-side Economics

The entry of the World Bank and the IMF into policy-based lending operations was preceded by efforts of developing countries themselves to adjust to the adverse economic conditions of the late 1970s. The magnitude of the emerging economic crises in developing countries, the difficulties governments encountered in implementing desired structural reforms, and the lack of financial resources prevented many developing countries from achieving their nationally defined adjustment program goals and obliged them to turn to the Bretton Woods institutions, the lenders of last resort.

As the World Bank moved somewhat reluctantly to expand its policy-based lending in the early 1980s,[7] a new economic orthodoxy gained the sympathies of political leaders in the industrialized countries. Supply-side economics, trumpeted by the Reagan presidency in the United States and the Thatcher government in the United Kingdom, heralded a direct challenge to the activist role of the state in economic affairs. The pantheon of supply-side economics included freeing market forces from excessive government regulation, reducing taxes, divesting state-owned enterprises, and ending the "crowding out" of the private sector by government intervention. Supply-side orthodoxy called for deregulation of labor markets, a weakening of government's redistributive functions, and a reduction in the scope of social safety nets.

The unabashedly aggressive ideological messages of supply-side economics emanating from the industrial powers in the early 1980s made acceptance of long-overdue economic reforms ever more difficult for many developing countries. The new economic doctrine was anathema to policymakers and public alike in many developing countries that relied on active government intervention to drive their development strategies. Governments had taken on a central economic function either because of the absence of a dynamic entrepreneurial class or as a means of ensuring economic sovereignty vis-à-vis former colonial powers. Consequently, accepting supply-side economics seemed tantamount to repudiating aspirations of national sovereignty and capitulating to the ideological agenda of the North.

To a large extent, the World Bank and IMF remained indifferent to the new economic orthodoxy. The primary motivation for promoting structural adjustment loans (SALs) was the fact that the Bank's traditional portfolio of development projects was seriously threatened by macroeconomic imbalances in most of its client countries.[8] Unless hemorrhaging of national budgets was halted abruptly, unless foreign debt obligations were significantly reduced, and unless foreign capital could be attracted back into the developing world, the viability of the Bank's project-level investments, totaling some $16 billion per annum, was clearly at risk.

Further, early adjustment program designers did not have to turn to supply-side economics or monetarist theory to write their own prescriptions for healing the ills of scores of distressed economies. Both the stabilization and the economic reform components of early adjustment programs were based on conventional policies that had evolved within the institutional experiences of the sister institutions over previous decades. Stabilization components were designed in accordance with IMF tenets that used fiscal, monetary, and exchange rate policies to redress government deficits and current account imbalances. Bank-sponsored structural reforms relied on traditional doses of trade liberalization, export-oriented growth, and sectoral reforms.

World Bank Intervention

The World Bank's initial effort to assess the impacts of the first generation of adjustment programs on developing countries' economic performance was carried out in 1986.[9] By the time the first review was completed, 38 SALs had been approved and 25 more were under preparation.[10] In addition to the macroeconomic restructuring programs, more than 40 sectoral adjustment loans had been approved by the Executive Board by 1987. In 1989, adjustment lending reached US$6 billion, thereby comprising 27 percent of the Bank's lending operations in that year.[11] The basic conclusion of the study was that the previous 5 years were not adequate to reach definitive conclusions about the effectiveness of policy-based lending. That study did lead the Bank to accept the fact that the adjustment process would take significantly longer than the 5-7 years originally anticipated and that Bank staff expectations were overly optimistic. From that basic conclusion flowed a number of complementary lessons: ownership and commitment by recipient governments were seriously lacking, adjustment loans included too many conditionalities and effectiveness requirements, and local institutional capacity did not correspond to the programs' ambitions. Transitional costs to the poor were acknowledged but were viewed as passing temporary concerns.[12]

Following that first review, changes in a second generation of SALs included: better sequencing of reform activities, more modest objectives that corresponded to local institutional capacity, and efforts to engender a deeper ownership of the reform program. In addition, protests from civil society in adjusting countries, coupled with research and lobbying by the United Nations Children's Fund (UNICEF) and nongovernmental organizations, raised the salience of adjustment's social impacts.[13] In response, the second generation of SALs included compensatory components to ease the burdens of economic reforms on low-income sectors.[14] The Bank and the Fund also placed greater emphasis on reforming social services delivery, including education and health care, to the poorest sectors of low-income countries.[15]

Twelve years after approving its first SAL, the World Bank had financed, in total or in part, 267 macroeconomic and sectoral adjustment programs in 75 countries.[16] By 1992, the Bank also completed its third and most inclusive assessment of the impacts of adjustment lending on 57 countries that had implemented adjustment programs of varying intensity.[17] Using standard measures of economic performance, the conclusions were categorical and as such stood in contrast to the Bank's earlier less conclusive reviews. It affirmed that middle- and low-income adjusting countries experienced rates of economic growth higher than those in nonadjusting countries. Specifically, the average growth rates in middle-income countries "were about 5 percent in 1986-90 and about four percentage points higher than would have been expected in the absence of adjustment."[18] In low-income countries, growth rates were "two percentage points above what would have been expected in the absence of adjustment lending, but they are below the levels necessary for rapid poverty reduction."[19] The study asserted that adjustment policies improved the status of the poor in the long run, but short-term dislocations generated higher than expected transitional costs for those groups. Further, private investment continued to lag behind improved economic policies and performance, particularly in low-income countries.

Bolstered by what the 1992 review considered positive economic results, the Bank reaffirmed its commitment to maintaining support for adjustment lending. The 1992 report recommended additional support to ensure proper incentives and conditions for private sector growth, greater attention to improving efficiency and equity of public sector spending, and more attention to poverty-reducing growth.[20] In short, the review emphatically encouraged the Bank to stay the course in maintaining its adjustment program. Recommendations from this review have guided design and implementation of the Bank's policy lending through the mid-1990s.

The Push Toward Privatization

While the economic results of the Bank-sponsored reform programs were becoming more evident, the impetus to reinforce the privatization components of adjustment programs began growing from outside the Bank. The collapse of the former Soviet Union and the centrally planned economy model, coupled with growing economic problems in developing countries, created fertile ground for privatizing state-owned enterprises. During the 1980s, privatization of state-owned enterprises and deregulation of labor markets had become two pillars of supply-side economics that industrialized countries, particularly the United States, exported to developing societies. For example, U.S. development assistance policy during that period explicitly established private sector development, with strong emphasis on privatization, as one of its major objectives. To this end, the United States Agency for International Development established private sector development and privatization as a primary policy objective, the U.S. government insisted that the newly created European Bank for Reconstruction and Development dedicate 60 percent of its resources to private sector development, again with strong emphasis on privatization,[21] and the U.S. government tried to change World Bank policy to include lending to the private sector, including financial support for privatization activities.

By 1990, these initiatives began showing results. Financial incentives transmitted through official development assistance, coupled with the growing fiscal burden of unproductive state enterprises on national budgets, encouraged middle- and low-income developing countries to revisit long-standing premises regarding the state's central economic role in development strategies. Within a relatively short time, privatization efforts included wholesale divestiture of state-owned enterprises to private companies (foreign and national), withdrawal of the state from national marketing boards and transportation systems, institutional restructuring, reductions in force, and a broad array of pricing and managerial reforms.[22] An integral part of the privatization drive was a direct effort to "deregulate" labor markets. In essence, that meant allowing the price of labor to shift to market levels rather than its being locked into socially oriented wage levels often established decades earlier through collective bargaining agreements. Eliminating "labor market rigidities" associated with privatization also included reducing the number of public employees and the scale and level of benefits.

The push toward privatization dovetailed with Bank and Fund efforts to reform fiscal policies of borrowing countries. From the Bank's perspective, privatization provided a unique opportunity to reduce bloated government payrolls, liberalize domestic markets, and challenge the privileges that had accrued to urban sectors over many years.[23] As countries began selling off insolvent and inefficient state-owned enterprises, not only did their fiscal and current account imbalances register improvements, but private direct investment began increasing as well, at least in middle-income countries. Enthusiasm within the Bank for privatization programs, with accompanying labor market reforms, increased in the late 1980s. By 1991, the number of World Bank loans with privatization components had risen to 74.[24]

A NEW GENERATION OF CRITICISMS

As the World Bank gained confidence in the economic benefits of its adjustment programs, new criticisms of the adjustment process began emerging. They built on, yet went beyond, those articulated in the mid-1980s, when, for example, UNICEF highlighted the negative impacts on the poorest, most vulnerable sectors of adjusting societies. The new criticisms challenged the impacts of adjustment on social sectors, economic sectors, and the environment and questioned the future viability of countries within the new global marketplace. Taken collectively, these criticisms asserted that adjustment programs increased the economic vulnerability of low-income countries, caused serious internal dislocations, diminished the prospects for long-term growth and development, and weakened the biosphere's environmental fabric. Several of the most salient issues raised by critics are summarized below.

Increasing Vulnerability to External Shocks and Pressures

Although adjusting low-income countries pursued demand-reduction programs, devalued currencies, and sought to expand production of tradeable goods, their ability to create a stable macroeconomic environment has been repeatedly weakened by declining terms of trade and susceptibility to fluctuations in international commodity prices and interest rates. With growing numbers of low-income countries competing to place similar products on stable or stagnant international markets, export-led growth has remained an illusory goal for countries dependent on primary commodities. Critics point out that the growing reliance of these countries on a narrow band of commodities, also being produced by a growing number of low-income countries (and often following World Bank strategies), has increased the countries' vulnerability to changes in international prices, increased supply, and weather.

Critics also say that support for export-led growth ignores the concern that many countries following this strategy over the past several decades are increasingly vulnerable to northern interests and influence. A recent OECD study on trade liberalization states the case:

> The contrast between trade liberalization theory and practice in the industrialized countries is striking. Whereas OECD Member countries unanimously endorse liberalization as an economic ideology, their trade practices point in the opposite direction. Formerly centrally planned economies and developing countries, which in the past have been seen as more protectionist, have been making major reform efforts. Their remarkable courage in undertaking economic adjustments is now threatened by the failure of the industrialized countries to undertake reciprocal measures. The industrialized countries are expected to gain most from a liberalization agreement because their economies are currently most distorted by protectionism. However, from a development and poverty-alleviation perspective, the former centrally planned and developing countries stand to suffer most from a continuation or, worse still, intensification of protectionism.[25]

Impacts on Industrial Policy

Although implementation of liberalization reforms and export-led growth strategies in low-income countries followed the logic of comparative advantage, critics claim that adjustment policies foreclosed all hopes of developing a national, albeit limited, industrial base. Many accept the widely known shortcomings of misguided import substitution policies in that they have led to inferior products, higher consumer costs, and weak international competitiveness. However, the pressing need to meet international financial obligations has led governments to shift investment resources to the tradeable sector and to implement trade reforms that have required dismantling tariffs, import quotas, and other nontariff barriers. These changes are consistent with prevailing economic orthodoxy, but critics stress the point that not only are valuable resources channeled into other sectors, but domestic industry is subjected to international competition in which its nascent industries simply cannot compete. Gradual reduction of protective barriers would provide a transitional period for infant industries to become more competitive rather than having to face stiff foreign competition overnight. The long-run consequence of the present policy is that, for the foreseeable future, the countries must forego prospects of developing an industrial base.[26]

Distributional Equity

The impacts of adjustment programs on distributional equity remain a contentious issue in both middle- and low-income countries. Early criticisms asserted that as aggregate output increased in many countries, entrepreneurial sectors, notably export-oriented sectors, profited handsomely; in contrast, the economic status of the overwhelming majority of workers and farmers deteriorated. Prompted by these claims, the OECD Development Centre launched a study in 1987 on adjustment's effects on distributional equity in six countries.[27] This early effort documented mixed results. In the two Asian countries, Indonesia and Malaysia, adjustment programs did not exacerbate distributional inequities despite fiscal retrenchments and recessions. The two Latin American nations, Ecuador and Chile, experienced a marked deterioration in income distribution under adjustment. Morocco and Côte d'Ivoire, the two African countries included in the study, experienced mixed results: the rural poor's economic status tended to improve relative to the urban poor's, whose conditions deteriorated.[28]

Despite adjustment's mixed impacts on income distribution in those six countries, many other voices continue to decry the negative long-term effects on class structure in countries undergoing adjustment. Critics point out that, even prior to 1980, the gulf was growing between the well-off and the poor in many developing countries. The recessions associated with adjustment, claim the critics, accelerated and aggravated that situation during the 1980s. The cumulative impacts of prolonged contractions only aggravated the economic status of the poor. As one specialized UN development agency stated,

> The worsening of income distribution is in large part the product of the sheer size of the macroeconomic losses that were sustained by these economies, together with the particular social and political mechanisms in force in each country. . . . But as long as economies cannot be shielded from large macroeconomic losses, and upper income groups cannot be made to share to any great degree in those losses, deterioration in income distribution is inevitable.[29]

"Deregulating" Labor Markets

Privatization and reduction in state economic functions, both integral components of the second generation adjustment package, have gone hand in hand with the elimination of "labor market rigidities." This "deregulation" of labor markets is built on the assumption that wages in many countries are being held at artificially high levels through collective bargaining agreements, and in the context of the international market, these excessive labor costs drastically reduce the competitiveness of domestic goods. Thus to increase competitiveness, the "deregulation approach" holds that wages must be lowered and nonwage labor costs restricted.

Critics hold that this "deregulation" is in reality a reregulation of labor under far more disadvantageous terms. As a recent International Labour Organization (ILO) study states in its analysis of adjustment programs' impacts on labor policy:

> What is clear is that the general trend in recent years . . . is that (a) capital is far more mobile, (b) management-organizational

options are more diversified, (c) the balance of negotiating power has shifted from labour to capital, and (d) many forms of conventional labor regulations are not so much right or wrong as potentially irrelevant or enfeebled. For example, to the extent that there is an erosion of the labour market and employment security because of increased external flexibility, national insurance-based social security income support becomes potentially anachronistic.[30]

Gender Equity

An emerging criticism of structural adjustment programs is the impact on gender equity in Africa. An ILO study states that "in no other region of the world are gender issues more critical to economic and social development than in sub-Saharan Africa." This is the case because "women have a prominent position in production, especially in the most populous sector of agriculture, but they lack control over resources and are discriminated against in markets for private and public goods and services."[31] Although critics assert that this point may seem extraneous to some macroeconomists, they believe that little progress in increasing productivity in the agricultural sector will be possible unless the socioeconomic status of women changes. The study concludes that "the basic problem is that the macro and sectoral measures taken so far in customary adjustment packages to liberalize markets and eliminate distortions do nothing to improve gender equity and reduce gender biases in markets; and may make them worse."[32]

Parallel studies reflect this criticism: "The problem with structural adjustment policies is not that they assume women are outside of development and need to be brought in . . . but that they 'are actually grounded in a gender ideology which is deeply, and fundamentally exploitative of women's time/work and sexuality'."[33]

Environmental Impacts of Liberalized Trade Regimes

Many criticisms of the impacts of structural adjustment on the environment focus on the negative environmental consequences of liberalized trade regimes. These concerns can be broken into three categories. First and foremost is the fact that liberalized trade discourages internalization of environmental costs. In the logic of competitive advantage, countries that lower the production costs for private enterprises can enjoy an advantage over competing nations by failing to internalize environmental costs associated with production and disposal of commodities and manufactured goods. The current trade regimes, notably the Uruguay Round of the General Agreement on Tariffs and Trade (GATT), typify prevailing trade practices that encourage the externalization of environmental costs. For example, GATT rules do not allow countries to distinguish between production processes that internalize environmental costs and those that pass such costs on to present and future generations. This policy failure of trade regimes thereby grants competitive advantage to those who do not internalize environmental costs.

A second example offered by critics of the antienvironmental bias of current trade regimes, again using GATT as a point of reference, is the fact that environmental standards can be attacked as nontariff barriers to trade that run contrary to the principles of enhanced international trade. Indeed, such attacks are occurring with increasing frequency under GATT, indicating that environmental regulations are high on the list of "obstacles" GATT seeks to reduce.

Critics also claim a third antienvironmental bias of current trade agreements, including GATT: they exert pressure that discourages nations' participation in international environmental agreements. For example, the Convention on Illegal Trade in Endangered Species (CITES) is predicated on the use of trade sanctions against nations that allow or encourage trade of endangered species. GATT's policy threatens to weaken enforcement of such international environmental agreements.[34]

Environmental Costs of Expanding Nontraditional Agricultural Exports

Stagnant or declining terms of trade for traditional agricultural exports (such as coffee, bananas, cotton, beef, and sugarcane) have led policymakers of African, Asian, and Latin American developing countries to shift resources to promoting nontraditional agricultural exports. This shift, or modernization of the agricultural sector, is a central feature of agricultural sector adjustments in scores of developing countries. Although the short-term economic benefits of these reforms are significant in many countries, analysts point out the growing environmental price tag associated with this policy change.[35]

The trade-offs between short-term economic growth benefits and the long-term environmental costs of promoting nontraditional agricultural

exports in Latin America are addressed by the Inter-American Institute
for Cooperation on Agriculture:

> The tendencies toward overexploitation of natural resources explain
> why the issue of sustainability and resource conservation has become
> a focus of attention in the [Latin America/Caribbean] region.
> However, there is a clear contradiction between policies and
> objectives. On one side, incentives are given for export expansion
> and a more intensive use of natural resources, while on the other, a
> new environmental and natural resource conservation policy is being
> advanced. This restates the contradiction between the short-term
> urgencies of the region's economies and the long-term sustainability
> problem affecting the structure of production.
>
> Furthermore, this contradiction between policies and objectives also
> seems to be implied in the activities of the financial multilateral
> organizations in the region. Both the World Bank and the Inter-
> American Development Bank are currently financing structural
> adjustment loans that have as a condition policies that foster
> economic liberalization and provide export incentives. Although
> both banks express a concern for environmental issues, it is clear
> that first priority is given to "get the prices right" policies. The
> requirement of environmental assessments on activities financed
> by the banks seems to be at present only an intent to save face.[36]

RESTRUCTURING THE WORLD ECONOMY

The merits of these criticisms must be the subject of constant review in
coming years to assess more accurately the benefits and costs of the
structural reforms being undertaken today. In particular, attention must be
given to understanding whether the criticisms elucidated above reflect
transitional costs incurred as existing economic structures are dismantled
and new ones put in place—or to the contrary, whether these concerns are
initial indicators of problems whose negative impacts will increase and
thereafter impose themselves with greater urgency on the development
agenda.

What must be stated unequivocally, however, is that adjustment of
developing country economies to the emerging international market system

was necessary and, in many cases, remains equally urgent today. Left uncorrected, the downward cycle of scores of national economies during the 1980s would have guaranteed, to varying degrees, a deepening of poverty, the collapse of social cohesion, and a weakening of the natural resource base. Failure to adjust would have guaranteed further marginalization from world markets and equally constrained access to international capital. Moreover, there is ample evidence, particularly when one considers counterfactual cases, that World Bank and IMF intervention has expedited the adjustment process and reduced the overall economic costs to developing countries as those societies made necessary and long-overdue adjustments to rapidly changing and often adverse economic conditions.

In reality, the question has never been whether to adjust economies to new economic realities; rather, it is the primary purposes, priorities, and processes of the adjustment programs that are being questioned. In that context, the issue remains whether adjustment programs adequately consider the particularities of individual countries and their differing functions in the emerging international division of labor. Moreover, distribution of economic reforms' costs and benefits remains a key determinant in the long-term acceptability and success of the current economic restructuring process.

An Instrument of Global Economic Policy

In conclusion, it is important to point out that while the international lending community has focused on correcting internal structural imbalances in individual developing countries, over the course of a decade and one-half, structural adjustment has become an instrument of global economic policy: the impact of structural adjustment has transcended the national context for which it was designed and has played a fundamental role in restructuring the world economy. Policy lending, coupled with new trade regimes, has been the driving force in realigning major sectors of the developing world and Central and Eastern Europe in their relations with the highly industrialized nations, opening new capital and commodity markets, altering the functions of the state, and changing the terms on which working people offer their labor. Under the mantle of structural adjustment programs, the basic reforms experienced in those two areas of the world include:

- shifting economies from inward-oriented to outward-oriented growth strategies through liberalized trade regimes;
- diminishing the role of the state in economic affairs, particularly as a direct economic agent;
- supporting privatization of major sectors of national economies;
- removing impediments to the international flow of capital and supporting the formation of domestic capital markets; and
- deregulating and reforming domestic labor markets.

Through the 15 years of adjustment experience, the developing world and the countries of Central and Eastern Europe have become fully enmeshed in the flow of international capital and goods. Those countries no longer claim to pursue alternative development models; they simply seek to improve their position vis-à-vis other competitors in the global marketplace. They no longer compete with and challenge the logic and priorities of the industrialized North; they now seek the maximum benefits from their new and quickly evolving relations with the centers of the international market system. The shift in developing country attitude is reflected, for example, in the fact that 78 of 107 participants in the Uruguay Round negotiations were developing countries representing an "enormous step forward in terms of the active and generalized participation of developing countries."[37] These changes are basic measures of adjustment's profound impacts in restructuring the global political economy.

Adjustment's Resilience

Structural adjustment lending has demonstrated its remarkable resilience over the past decade and one-half. It has withstood a wide range of criticisms delivered by many different messengers in many different forms. When necessary, architects of adjustment policy have nuanced and adjusted its focus and implementation process. When confronted with new economic orthodoxies, structural adjustment lending has demonstrated its ability to respond to, even absorb, aspects of popular economic policy and use them to further the objectives of the adjustment process. In short, as adjustment lending has been refined over the past 15 years, its effectiveness in restructuring local economies and integrating them more intimately into the global marketplace has also increased.

As stated at the beginning of this chapter, the intent here is not to reach a final reckoning of the costs and benefits of the 15 years of structural adjustment programs. The purpose is to illustrate why adjustment remains so controversial and why the impacts of adjustment lending are, for many reasons, so profound, so comprehensive, that its full costs and benefits will be known only in the next decade or beyond. What is clear, however, is that future generations will assess the long-term impacts of structural adjustment in the context of sustainable development, the new development paradigm. It is to that framework that this study now turns its attention.

ENDNOTES

1. An interesting exchange reflecting these two positions can be found in Chapter 2, "The Impact of Changes on the World Economy on Stabilization Policies in the 1970s," in *Economic Stabilization in Developing Countries*, ed. William R. Cline and Sidney Weintraub (Washington, D.C.: Brookings Institution, 1981). The internalist position is articulated by Stanley Black and the externalist position by the respondent, Sidney Dell of the United Nations Centre on Transnational Corporations. A final commentary on the chapter is offered by Ernest Stern, Vice President of the World Bank, who states: "Moralizing about the share of blame for instability that is attributable to the international community is not fruitful; what is needed are pragmatic policy options for developing countries to deal with stabilization problems" (p. 81).
2. See, for example, S.A. Marglin and J. Schor, eds., *The End of the Golden Age* (Oxford: Clarendon Press, 1990); and Angus Maddison, *The World Economy in the 20th Century* (Paris: Organisation for Economic Co-operation and Development, 1991).
3. Joyce Kolko, *Restructuring the World Economy* (New York: Pantheon Books, 1988), pp. 91-94.
4. World Bank, *World Development Report 1980* (Washington, D.C.: World Bank, 1980), p. 4.
5. Ibid.
6. Eduardo Borensztein, Mohsin S. Khan, Corman M. Reinhart, and Peter Wickham, *The Behavior of Non-oil Commodity Prices* (Washington, D.C.: International Monetary Fund, 1994), p. 1.
7. Paul Mosley, Jane Harrigan, and John Tage, *Aid and Power: The World Bank and Policy-based Lending* (London: Routledge, 1991), pp. 27-56.
8. Ibid., pp. 3-61.
9. World Bank, *Structural Adjustment Lending: A First Review of Experience* (Washington, D.C.: World Bank, 1986).
10. Ibid., p. 1.
11. World Bank, *Adjustment Lending Policies for Sustainable Growth* (Washington, D.C.: World Bank, 1990), p. 3.
12. World Bank, *Structural Adjustment Lending*, op. cit., pp. iii, 69-85.
13. Giovanni Andrea Cornia, Richard Jolly, and Frances Stewart, *Adjustment with a Human Face*, vol. 1, *Protecting the Vulnerable and Promoting Growth* (Oxford: Clarendon Press, 1987). The World Bank challenged the United Nations Children's Fund claim that adjustment programs "imposed fiscal austerity that compressed government expenditure on social services, particularly health and education." The Bank study states that "the data...do not support this hypothesis. There is no perceptible change in the ratio of central government expenditure on education and health to GDP in both IAL [intensive adjustment

lending] and NAL [nonadjustment lending] countries from the first half of the 1980s to the second half" (*The Third Report on Adjustment Lending: Private and Public Resources for Growth* [Washington, D.C.: World Bank, 1992], p. 59).

14. World Bank, "Summary of Discussions at the Meeting of the Executive Directors of the Bank and IDA, January 26, 1993," and "Implementing the Bank's Poverty Reduction Strategy: Progress and Challenges" (Washington, D.C., 1993), p. 3.

15. World Bank, Development Committee, "Social Security Reforms and Social Safety Nets in Reforming and Transforming Economies" (Washington, D.C., 1993), p. i.

16. World Bank, *Third Report on Adjustment Lending*, op. cit., pp. 72-76.

17. Ibid.

18. Ibid., p. 13.

19. Ibid.

20. Ibid., pp. 25-26. See also World Bank, *Structural Adjustment and Poverty: A Conceptual, Empirical, and Policy Framework* (Washington, D.C.: World Bank, 1990), pp. 149-81.

21. David Reed, *The European Bank for Reconstruction and Development: an Environmental Opportunity* (Washington, D.C.: World Wide Fund for Nature-International, 1991), p. 11.

22. John R. Nellis, "Reform of Public Enterprises," in *Restructuring Economies in Distress: Policy Reform and the World Bank,* ed. Vinod Thomas, Ajay Chhiber, Mansoor Dailami, and Jaime de Melo (New York: Oxford University Press, 1991), pp. 108-130.

23. Anne Maasland and Jacques van der Gaag, "World Bank-supported Adjustment Programs and Living Conditions," in *Adjustment Lending Revisited,* ed. Vittorio Corbo, Stanley Fischer, and Steven B. Webb (Washington, D.C.: World Bank, 1992), pp. 40-63. The authors note, for example, that in some countries, formal labor, especially in the manufacturing sector, bore a larger share of the adjustment burden than did other groups.

24. Christopher Adam, William Cavendish, and Percy S. Mistry, *Adjusting Privatization* (London: James Curray Ltd., 1992).

25. Ian Goldin, Odin Knudsen, and Dominique van der Mensbrugghe, *Trade Liberalisation* (Paris: Organisation for Economic Co-operation and Development, 1993), p. 16.

26. See, for example, Alicia Korten, "A Bitter Pill: Structural Adjustment in Costa Rica," Development Rep. No. 7 (Institute for Food and Development Policy, Oakland, Calif.).

27. Summaries of the studies were printed in "Adjustment with Growth and Equity," *World Development* (November 1991).

28. Ibid., pp. 1504-1505.

29. United Nations Conference on Trade and Development, *Trade and Development Report, 1990* (New York: United Nations, 1990), p. *III.*

30. Guy Standing, "Adjustment and Labour Market Policies," in *Towards Social Adjustment: Labour Market Issues in Structural Adjustment,* ed. Guy Standing and Victor Tokman (Geneva: International Labour Office, 1991), p. 44.

31. Ingrid Palmer, *Gender and Population in the Adjustment of African Economies: Planning for Change* (Geneva: International Labour Organization, 1991), p. 177.

32. Ibid., p. 178.

33. Peggy Antrobus, "The Impact of Structural Adjustment Policies on Women: The Experience of Caribbean Countries" (prepared for the UNDP/Programme on Women in Development, INSTRAW, 1988), p.1., quoted in Pamela Starr, "Banking on Women: Where Do We Go from Here?" in *Mortgaging Women's Lives: Feminist Critiques of Structural Adjustment,* ed. Pamela Starr (New York: Zed Books, 1994), p. 183.

34. Hillary French, *Costly Trade-offs: Trade and the Environment* (Washington, D.C.: World Watch, 1993); and Herman Daly, "The Perils of Free Trade," *Scientific American* (November 1993):50.

35. Lori Ann Thrupp, *Bittersweet Harvests for Global Supermarkets: Challenges in Latin America's Agricultural Export Boom* (Washington, D.C.: World Resources Institute, 1995), and *Challenges in Latin America's Recent Agroexport Boom* (Washington, D.C.: World Resources Institute, 1994), p.1.; and Susan C. Stonich, "The Promotion of Non-traditional Agricultural Exports in Honduras: Issues of Equity, Environment and Natural Resource Management," *Development and Change* 22 (1991) pp. 725-55.

36. Jorge A. Torres Zorrilla, *Agricultural Modernization and Resource Deterioration in Latin America* (San Jose, Costa Rica: Inter-American Institute for Cooperation on Agriculture, 1994), p. 21.
37. Organisation for Economic Co-operation and Development (OECD), *Integration of Developing Countries into the International Trading System* (Paris: OECD, 1992), p. 23.

2

SUSTAINABLE DEVELOPMENT

by David Reed

THE POLITICAL FOUNDATIONS OF SUSTAINABLE DEVELOPMENT

Structural adjustment evolved from a package of national-level economic reforms to an instrument of global economic policy over the past decade and one-half. Predating, then running parallel to, the evolution of structural adjustment was the emergence of sustainability as the new development paradigm. However, whereas structural adjustment was driven and shaped by the very centers of international economic power, sustainable development has emerged from public pressure, ultimately forcing itself onto the agenda of governments and international institutions.

Two international events mark the evolution of sustainable development over the past three decades, the Stockholm conference of 1972 and the Rio conference of 1992. Those two conferences are significant not because they represent radical departures from politics of the past or because governments fundamentally altered their policies thereafter. Rather, they acquire significance because they represent the formal institutional result of the public's demand that governments address the growing environmental crises. In this sense, the two conferences are the culmination of prior periods of international environmental struggles while also marking the beginning of new periods of political activity.

The Stockholm Conference

In this perspective, the United Nations Conference on the Human Environment held in Stockholm in 1972 acquired significance in that it reflected the mounting public distress in northern societies about the negative impacts of industrialization. In no uncertain terms, the Stockholm conference was driven by citizens in industrialized countries who were increasingly preoccupied with the cumulative impacts of stationary and mobile pollution. Prognostications of a planet rendered uninhabitable by industrial expansion were compounded by neo-Malthusian prophecies of population explosion in the developing world. *Silent Spring* (1962),[1] *The Population Bomb* (1970),[2] and *The Limits to Growth* (1972)[3] captured the general anxieties of the public in industrialized countries by expressing doomsday scenarios caused by a shrinking resource base, spreading pollution, and ever-expanding populations.

In many ways, the preparatory process for the Stockholm conference became a dress rehearsal for subsequent struggles between the industrialized North and developing countries of the South that continue to the present day. As conference organizers began seeking a consensual framework among the 113 participating nations, the environmental agenda of the industrialized societies collided head-on with the political perspectives and priorities of the developing world.[4] In contrast to industrialization problems of the North, developing countries identified the issue of poverty alleviation as their most urgent challenge to arresting environmental degradation. They highlighted the relation between impoverishment and the degradation of natural resources through soil erosion, deforestation, desertification, and diminishing water sources.

A tenuous compromise between the two perspectives was forged at the Preparatory Committee meeting held in Founex, Switzerland, in June 1971. One of the important concessions underlying the *Founex Report*[5] and the subsequent *Stockholm Declaration*[6] was acceptance of the developing countries' perspective that pollution caused by industrialization in the North imposed tangible constraints on their own development and industrialization options. A second important concession was acceptance of the South's view that poverty, not industrialization, was the overriding cause of environmental problems in the developing world for which economic growth would have to provide the principal answer. Moreover, their insistence on placing national sovereignty at the center of this compromise underscored developing countries' resistance to using future international environmental agreements to alter their own development paths, reduce development assistance, or condition financial transfers from the North.[7]

The formal statement of the conference, known as the *Stockholm Declaration*, established 26 principles of behavior and responsibility that were intended to serve as the basis for future legally binding multilateral agreements. The accompanying Action Plan for the Human Environment enumerated 109 recommendations in three areas: environmental assessment, environmental management, and supporting institutional measures. Implementation of those actions was intended to lay the institutional and legal foundation for global environmental monitoring and management. The conference also gave rise to the formation of the United Nations Environment Programme (UNEP) through a resolution of the UN General Assembly in 1972. The new agency was initially intended to coordinate environmental actions for the entire UN development system and to fund specific environmental programs of a global nature.

If the Stockholm conference were measured by its success in implementing the principles or recommended actions, it would be deemed a categoric failure. The principles have not become the basis of international law, the 109 recommendations have largely been overlooked, and UNEP has never acquired the functional status of being the UN agency responsible for coordinating the system's environmental activities. Indeed, UNEP has struggled consistently to gain comparable stature to the other agencies of the UN development system.

Rather, the significance of the Stockholm conference resides in its successfully crystalizing the underlying issues of global environmental politics leading up to 1972. The conference provided a forum for articulating the different agendas of the industrialized North and those of the developing countries, and it facilitated the forging of a compromise, albeit a fragile one, as the basis for future international environmental actions and accords.

Sharpening Global Environmental Tensions

In the subsequent 20 years, the evolution of the conceptual foundations of sustainable development was driven by the same two political forces that shaped the Stockholm conference—that is, public pressures exerted by a diverse but growing environmental movement and by tensions between North and South. The public-driven environmental movement was spurred by a multiplicity of environmental crises. Among them were localized disasters, such as the mass chemical contamination in Bhopal, India, and the Chernobyl nuclear accident in the Ukraine. Some environmental crises spread across regions of the world, such as acidification in the United States and Northern Europe and destruction of tropical rain forests in

Brazil, Asia, and central Africa. Other environmental problems acquired global proportions, such as stratospheric ozone depletion and greenhouse gas accumulation in the atmosphere. Public clamor for government action spawned a host of new international environmental conventions,[8] obliged multi- and bilateral development agencies to adopt new standards of behavior, and created new international financial incentives.[9]

The development cum environment agenda of the South, accepted as a matter of formality at Founex and Stockholm, fared less well in the real world politics of North-South power relations in the post-Stockholm period. The South's view on how to address its pressing development needs was captured in its demands for a New International Economic Order (NIEO). Dating back to the first United Nations Conference on Trade and Development meeting in 1964, followed by the Algiers Conference of the Non-Aligned Countries in 1973, the NIEO was formulated in 1974 at a special session of the UN General Assembly.[10] Premised on the assumption that the developing countries held considerable bargaining power over the North's access to oil and other basic commodities, the nonaligned countries felt they could force fundamental changes in North-South relations, including expanded trade opportunities, increased capital flows, accelerated technology transfer, even strengthened North-to-South income redistribution. The underlying objective of the developing countries in promoting the NIEO was to ensure their "national economic sovereignty" vis-à-vis the industrial powers.

This precedent-setting show of solidarity among fundamentally different developing countries collapsed without ceremony at the 1981 Cancun Summit when the leading industrial countries refused to give further consideration to their demands. Collapse of the NIEO was attributable in large part to sharply deteriorating economic conditions in scores of developing countries. The hard-earned Third World solidarity of the 1970s dissipated quickly as developing countries competed with each other to gain access to the limited, and urgently needed, capital resources of the industrialized societies.[11] One of the few meaningful accomplishments of this North-South dialogue in the post-Stockholm period was the agreement reached between European countries and their 69 former colonies in Africa, the Caribbean, and the Pacific (the ACP countries). The Lomé Convention, renewed through four consecutive negotiations, established preferential trade relations between the European Community and ACP countries, guaranteed agreed levels of development assistance, and promoted a wide range of social and human rights issues.

First Articulations of Sustainable Development

These two international pressures, growing public demand and conflicting North-South development perspectives, found their way, albeit unevenly, into two seminal formulations of sustainable development in the 1980s. The first statement was proffered in the *World Conservation Strategy* (WCS), published by the International Union for Conservation of Nature and Natural Resources (IUCN), UNEP, and the World Wide Fund for Nature-International (WWF-I) in 1980.[12] The WCS marked a significant departure from previous approaches to the development-environment nexus in that it sought to establish a "global framework for conservation" and affirmed the compatibility of promoting development objectives while "achieving conservation."[13] The WCS offered the first exposition of sustainability that effectively linked human welfare, now and in the future, to sustainable management of the planet's natural patrimony. The strategy set forth a carefully organized menu of requirements and action priorities for national governments that would help guide them in using their natural resource bases to promote human welfare while respecting the "carrying capacities of ecosystems."[14]

The major failing of the WCS was that this ethically grounded, morally persuasive statement disregarded the political realities of the North-South divide. The moral high ground established by the WCS was undermined by its political naiveté and inability to come to grips with the international political economy. As a consequence, the WCS was received as a compelling if somewhat visionary statement, but one that failed to mobilize international political support and consequently proved unable to generate enduring practical and programmatic influence.

The WCS, as the *Founex Report* before it, did provide a strengthened conceptual foundation for the next articulation of sustainable development offered by the World Commission on Environment and Development (WCED), also known as the Brundtland Commission, in its 1987 report, *Our Common Future*.[15] The Brundtland Commission's contributions to establishing sustainable development as the standard for international development were threefold. First, the WCED effectively established the present generation's responsibility for safeguarding future generations' development options and opportunities by protecting the planet's environment and natural resources. Second, it placed the alleviation of poverty in developing countries as the central axis around which global sustainability would revolve. Third, it recast the pursuit of sustainability in the context of the international economy by recognizing the need to reorder patterns of international trade and flows of capital and to ensure greater developing world influence in these economic relations.

The biggest weakness of the Brundtland Commission report lay not in its analytical contributions but in its prescriptions. Its highly ambiguous proposals sent the message to governments and development agencies alike that "growth as usual" policies would remain the linchpin for promoting sustainable development practices. In this regard, the commission asserted that a 3-4 percent growth rate in the industrialized nations was the pivotal economic requirement on which poverty alleviation in the developing world depended.[16] In turn, the WCED called for the world economy to expand "by a factor of five or ten," ultimately translating into an annual per capita income rise of 3 percent in all countries, North and South.

The WCED also called for "changing the quality of growth," and it recognized the need to redistribute wealth in order to alleviate poverty. However, those potentially radical propositions were diluted by its overall message that the transition to a sustainable world would not require fundamental changes in the current distribution of wealth, consumption patterns, standards of living, or the character of growth in the North and South. Further, the WCED did not offer an accurate or complete portrayal of the political relations and struggles, international and national, that needed to be addressed in order to move the world society to a sustainable development path. However, where the *World Conservation Strategy* had failed, the Brundtland Commission achieved remarkable success in establishing sustainable development as the standard against which the behavior of governments and international institutions would measure their policies and activities. Moreover, *Our Common Future* cemented the conceptual and political foundation on which the United Nations Conference on Environment and Development (UNCED), the Rio conference, was to be erected.

The Rio Conference

The formal accomplishments of UNCED, held in 1992 and also known as the Earth Summit, were, in some ways, considerable. Global conventions on climate change and biodiversity were signed; the "Earth Charter," a set of principles to be respected by governments and people, was agreed upon by 178 governments; an action program to promote sustainability, called Agenda 21, was adopted; and an institutional mechanism within the UN system, notably the Commission on Sustainable Development (CSD), was created. To this list can be added the fact that the Earth Summit was the culmination of a protracted and intense period of awareness raising among policymakers at the highest level.[17]

UNCED can be viewed as the moment when the international community formally embraced the concept of sustainable development as the standard for measuring development objectives and performance in both the North and South. Reflecting a southern perspective, the UNCED approach attempted to emphasize basic development needs within a framework that included environmental issues. However, the conceptual framework of sustainable development emerging from UNCED, while giving greater attention to changing North-South economic relations, ultimately did not alter the basic "growth as usual" prescription articulated a few years earlier by the Brundtland Commission. This attitude was particularly evident in the approach promoted by northern countries that posited "growth as usual" and technological innovations as the strategic pillars of sustainable development.

As with the Stockholm conference, the Earth Summit did not fundamentally alter the current development approach; nor did it significantly enhance the political conditions required to shift the world to a sustainable development path. International economic incentives remained virtually intact,[18] power relations between North and South were unaffected, and economic disparities continued to grow.[19] The Earth Summit assuaged the domestic political concerns of leaders vis-à-vis their respective publics while leaving basic economic and social relations unaffected. In short, UNCED produced ample verbal agreement but postponed for the indefinite future the actual making of commitments and the undertaking of structural reforms required to promote sustainable development.

Another significant shortcoming of UNCED influenced the international development agenda in the years that followed. Although UNCED proclaimed to have forged the vital linkage between the economic and environmental dimensions of sustainable development, it significantly downplayed the third pillar of sustainability, namely, the social dimension. That neglect fueled the convocation of successive international summits under the mantle of the United Nations to reaffirm the rightful place of such concerns on policymakers' agendas. Those summits began in 1994 with the Summit on Human Rights in Vienna, followed in quick order by the Population Summit in Cairo in 1994, the Social Summit in Copenhagen and the Women's Summit in Beijing in 1995, and the Habitat II Summit in 1996. Given UNCED's relative lack of attention to social issues, it is not surprising that the official declarations agreed upon during those successive international conferences focusing on social issues give scant attention to the central role of the environment in supporting all aspects of the human enterprise.

One final historical note is in order. Although the evolution of sustainable development as the new development paradigm has been driven by public pressure and the North-South political struggle, the conceptual foundations of sustainability have been enriched over the past two decades by contributions of a new intellectual order. The hallmark of that intellectual effort is the breaking down of rigid disciplinary boundaries that have separated the natural and social sciences. The works of Nicholas Georgescu-Roegen, K. William Kapp, Kenneth Boulding, and Herman Daly, among many, have posed fundamental challenges to the postwar development enterprise in two fundamental areas.[20] First, these scholars assert the intractable physical constraints that the natural environment imposes on the prevailing economic growth paradigm, which is predicated on unlimited resources and unrestricted environmental sink functions. Second, they explore the implications of those constraints by challenging the basic assumptions of trickle-down economics and the perspective that growing poverty can be addressed without a global redistribution of wealth. These authors' challenges to mainstream development thinking have yet to be answered, if even accepted, by policymakers on national and international levels.

AN OPERATIONAL APPROACH TO SUSTAINABLE DEVELOPMENT

Toward an Operational Definition

These political forces and international struggles have shaped the definition of sustainable development used in this study. In general terms, the definition is based on the framework set forth in *Caring for the Earth*, a joint publication of the IUCN, UNEP, and WWF-I.[21] Sustainable development is people centered in that its aim is to improve the quality of human life, and it is conservation based in that it is conditioned by the need to respect nature's capacity to provide resources and life-supporting services. In this perspective, sustainable development means improving the quality of human life while living within the carrying capacity of supporting ecosystems.[22]

This definition of sustainable development is a normative concept that embodies standards of judgment and behavior to be respected as the human community seeks to satisfy its needs of survival and well-being. The definition embraces the three basic components—the economic, the social, and the environmental—that constitute the foundations of sustainable development. These components are intimately interdependent and consequently require that efforts to promote development support all three of them.

The economic component of sustainability requires that societies pursue economic growth paths that generate an increase in true income, not short-term policies that lead to long-term impoverishment. It further requires that societies generate an optimal flow of income while maintaining their basic stock of capital. Capital, in this context, includes man-made capital, human capital, and natural capital. To avoid unrealistic and even self-defeating growth strategies, sustainable economics requires identifying where man-made capital, human capital, and natural capital are substitutable and where they remain complementary. Sustainable economics requires a differentiated approach to growth in that many developing areas of the world urgently need to increase their productive capacity, and at the same time and with equal urgency, the industrialized societies need to reduce their consumption of natural resources and use those resources more efficiently.[23] Economic sustainability also requires internalizing all costs, including the societal and environmental costs associated with the production and disposition of goods, thereby implementing the full cost principle.

The social dimension of sustainable development is built on the premise that equity and an understanding of the human community's interdependence are basic requirements of an acceptable quality of life, which is, ultimately, the aim of development. For a development path to be sustainable over a long period, wealth, resources, and opportunity must be shared in such a manner that all citizens have access to minimum standards of security, human rights, and social benefits, such as food, health, education, shelter, and opportunities for self-development. Social equity means ensuring that all people have access to education and the opportunity to make productive, justly remunerated contributions to society. Interdependence of the human community implies an understanding that stark social inequities threaten the stability and long-term viability of the human enterprise. Interdependence also implies recognition that the human community's standard of living is ultimately related to the size of the human population to be sustained by the planet's environmental resources and infrastructure. Moreover, the social dimension of sustainable development demands the active political participation of all social sectors and the accountability of governments to the broader public in making basic social policy regarding, among other issues, social equity and population size. It requires drawing on local populations' knowledge and experience and strengthening social groups' capacity to shape and manage their own lives.

The environmental dimension of sustainable development is predicated on maintaining the long-term integrity and therefore productivity of the planet's life-support systems and environmental infrastructure. Meeting this standard requires investing in the biosphere's infrastructure to ensure the continuity and quality of environmental goods and services on which all life depends. Environmental sustainability requires the use of environmental goods in such a way as not to diminish the productivity of nature or the overall contribution of environmental goods and services to human well-being. Application of the precautionary principle should become an integral feature of all development programs to ensure that these activities do not result in either human harm or ecological irreversibilities.

These three components of sustainable development should converge in such a way as to generate a steady stream of income, ensure social equity, pursue socially agreed upon population levels, maintain man-made and natural capital stocks, and protect the life-giving services of the environment.

Reforming National Development Strategies

Achieving sustainability will require behavioral changes on all levels of the human enterprise, from international relations down to community-level development activities. While recognizing the interrelations of the global, national, and local levels, the focus of this study is primarily on the requirements of promoting sustainable development policies at the national and international levels. The empirical analysis and scenario-building presented in Part Two focus primarily on the policies and practices of individual nations for the main reason that the nation-state remains the basic, yet clearly not the exclusive, unit of decision-making, standard-setting, and public administration. Although the emerging international economic regime is swiftly eroding the state's sphere of influence, it is on the national level that basic development strategies are formulated and implemented and, in that context, that basic choices are made regarding human welfare and natural resource management. It is also on the national level that correcting unsustainable policies and practices is most urgently needed.

Consistent with the definition of sustainable development offered above, correcting deficient national development strategies requires addressing the three pillars of sustainability—that is, the economic, social, and environmental dimensions. Far from inclusive, the elements listed below constitute some of the more important requisites for shifting to national sustainability strategies in the context of the rapidly changing world order. This list is tailored to developing countries, including the nine covered in this research project. Transition to sustainable development strategies in the industrialized world is equally urgent, but the specific reforms required to make that transition differ from the points listed below.

The economic component

- Sound macroeconomic management: pursuing prudent fiscal policies, maintaining the international balance of payments in the long run, contracting manageable levels of international financial obligations;
- Poverty-alleviating growth: pursuing labor-intensive economic policies to maximize employment generation for the poorest, most vulnerable sectors; applying monetary and fiscal incentives to strengthen productive and marketing opportunities for small farmers and businesses; distributing national productivity gains to increase productive opportunities for the poorest sectors; strengthening economic and social incentives for associative and cooperative enterprises of the poorest sectors;
- Agricultural production: reversing policy biases against the agricultural sector; strengthening domestic food security; increasing the share of public investment in agriculture for land improvement, watershed management, afforestation, and extension services.
- The role of the state:
  - As an economic agent: adapting the role of the state to areas in which it performs more efficiently than the private sector and in which it facilitates optimal participation by the private sector;

o As manager of the public well-being: strengthening the administrative, regulatory, and standard-setting functions of government in
areas in which the defense of public interest and welfare is required;
o As guarantor of social development: providing social and environmental goods and services and equitable social conditions.

- Cost internalization: eliminating distortions in existing pricing
structures to include environmental and social costs in order to achieve
true efficiency; incorporating these costs into development project
feasibility considerations; taking into account the costs of resource
depletion and degradation in the calculation of GDP in the system of
national accounts and reinvesting those capital costs to ensure a constant
stream of benefits; reflecting in the balance of payments the environmental costs associated with the international trade of goods and
services.

The social component

- Distributional equity: institutionalizing mechanisms for redistributing
wealth, productive assets, and future investments to ensure both
participation of the poor in income-generating activities and their access
to social wealth and productive resources;
- Social services: providing basic amenities of shelter, sanitation, and
clean water; improving social infrastructure to guarantee education,
training, health care, and population services; ensuring equal access
of the poor to legal assistance, credit and financial services, and
employment opportunities;
- Gender equity: providing equal opportunities for women to engage in
income-generating activities, education and training, and health care
programs; establishing equal legal status for women to ensure rights
to property ownership and access to credit;
- Population stabilization: fostering population stabilization and adaptive
strategies and providing family planning services to ensure a population
that does not exceed the carrying capacity of a country's ecosystem;
- Political accountability and participation: establishing transparent,
accessible mechanisms by which governments are held accountable to
the general public on national social, environmental, and economic
development matters; ensuring consultation and participation of all
sectors in national development policy formulation and implementation
and in specific development activities and projects.

The environmental component

- Sustainable resource use: limiting consumption of renewable natural resources to regenerative rates; ensuring nonrenewable resource consumption rates that do not exceed the provision of substitutes;
- Sink functions: decreasing the discharge of atmospheric contaminants, water pollutants, and toxic wastes to ensure emissions that do not exceed the environment's absorptive capacity;
- Natural capital: establishing regulatory and market-based mechanisms to ensure that the total stock of natural capital is constant over time; establishing national policy and implementation plans to increase the quantity and quality of natural capital;
- Precautionary principle: refraining from pursuing activities whose negative, potentially irreversible impacts are not fully known owing to limited current knowledge;
- Institutional framework: establishing clear, enforceable legal and regulatory standards for the private sector in order to protect and help manage the country's environmental patrimony.

Changing International Development Patterns

If proposed reforms for promoting sustainable development were to focus exclusively on the national level, they would ignore the basic trends of integration and globalization that characterize the emerging international economy. Those trends endow private capital and the international marketplace with far greater influence in shaping national development processes while national governments watch their own influence decline proportionately. The driving force behind agreement on recent regional and global trade regimes is the compelling argument that the gateway to world prosperity is expanded trade and easier access to markets.[24] Although economic growth generated by the globalized world economy will continue to provide economic benefits for some social sectors, those benefits are not and will not be accessible equitably to all sectors or all countries. Nor will those benefits necessarily accrue to future generations. What is certain is that in order to ensure the transition to sustainability on a global level, three additional changes in the human enterprise, addressed briefly below, are urgently required.

The first reform is a fundamental change in the intensity of use of environmental goods and services on a global level. International debate on this issue was initially enjoined when the Club of Rome released the results of a global modeling exercise in 1972.[25] *The Limits to Growth* examined the long-term prospects for the human enterprise in consideration of disturbing trends in industrialization, environmental deterioration, depletion of nonrenewable resources, human population growth, and expanding poverty. The 20 years since its publication have demonstrated that exhaustion of many energy and mineral resources has not become the main environmental constraint challenging the short-term viability of the human enterprise. Rather, the major environmental constraints are the limited absorptive capacity of environmental sinks, the depletion and degradation of soil productivity, and the consumption of both renewable and nonrenewable resources at unprecedented rates. These and other factors have converged to erode the very conditions required for economic production and human survival. Lack of clean water, fresh air, and uncontaminated, nondepleted soils have combined with growing population pressures to generate deteriorating standards of living and societal instability in virtually all countries and regions of the world.

The principal response of policymakers to those growing constraints has been to look to resource substitution and technological innovation as ways of forestalling potential dislocations caused by such constraints.[26] In relying on technological changes and substitution of resources, policymakers obviate the need to undertake fundamental alterations in the prevailing economic growth model. Without undervaluing the significant contributions brought by technological innovation in recent years, the planet's weakening environmental infrastructure, the accelerating consumption of environmental goods and services, and the ever-growing pollution demand a revisit to the premise of limitless growth underlying the current economic growth strategy. A sustainable development strategy would replace the current unlimited growth framework with a world moving toward individual societies' and the community of nations' making basic choices about the scale and quality of economic growth, the level of human population, and the distribution of wealth and resources.

The second level on which sustainable development demands fundamental change regards establishing equitable relations between northern societies and the developing societies of the South. This relationship is currently characterized by stark disparities in the distribution of wealth, as reflected, for example, in the fact that the 23 high-income countries have a combined GNP of more than US$18.3 trillion but the combined income of more than 160 developing countries is approximately US$4.7 trillion.[27] The per capita income of the 23 high-income countries averaged US$22,160 in 1992; yet 1.3 billion people live in absolute poverty, and over 3.1 billion had yearly incomes of less than US$310.[28] Accompanying the inequitable distribution of wealth is the skewed resource consumption between North and South wherein, for example, the average northerner uses 5,101 kilograms of oil (or energy equivalent) per year and a southern counterpart in low-income countries consumes just 338 kilograms per year.[29] Moreover, barely one-fifth of the world's population consumes 70 percent of all energy, 80 percent of its wood products, and 75 percent of all metals.

Quantitative comparisons provide useful indications of the levels of inequality between North and South. Alone, however, quantitative analysis does not capture the full band of disparities between these two parts of the world in that they do not reflect, among other points, differences in their (in)ability to influence the world's economic and political affairs. This point is poignantly reflected in the fact that by the year 2000, the developing world will contribute more than 50 percent of the world's annual output.[30] Yet the present distribution of wealth and international economic decisionmaking arrangements in no way reflect the South's growing economic contribution or its urgent economic and social needs. A fundamental shift in the distribution of resources and opportunity from the North to the South is required to address the growing disparities and the growing sources of social instability.[31]

The third fundamental change regards addressing the intensified pressures that growing populations are placing on their countries' natural resources and productive capacities. Population growth rates of up to 3 percent per year simply exceed the economic growth rates of many countries, condemning the growing populations to declining standards of living. Confronted with this reality, a far more comprehensive effort is required to empower women to control their own lives and profit from educational and health services, productive resources, and opportunities. In addition, countries must move to implement adaptive strategies to avoid overtaxing the productive capacity of agricultural lands and other consequences.

Neither operational mechanisms nor the political will to create such mechanisms for promoting sustainability on a global level exists today. In fact, the evolving economic system, current development strategy, and ideology have consistently generated outcomes that run contrary to these

three requisites of sustainable development. Little hope can be taken from
the somewhat cynical response that it may be necessary to wait until the
impacts of the current development strategy, including more severe
environmental degradation, untenable social inequalities, and demographic
crowding, are dramatically manifested before an ecological restructuring
of our economic system finds a more attentive public audience.

ADJUSTMENT POLICY IN THE CONTEXT OF SUSTAINABLE DEVELOPMENT

One further linkage between sustainable development and structural
adjustment must be identified. Here the conceptual and strategic statements
of the World Bank are important because that institution has played and
continues to play a central role in shaping, implementing, and coordinating
the adjustment process in scores of developing countries. As pointed out
in the preceding chapter, the basic contours and characteristics of
adjustment programs were dictated primarily by the requirements of capital
accumulation on a global scale during this historical period. However,
depending on the capacity of national governments, the Bretton Woods
institutions have played a major role in shaping the way in which countries
have responded to the evolving world economy. Thus their publications
are used here to reflect the role of sustainable development in restructuring
national economies in response to the new demands and opportunities of
the evolving world economy.

From their initial design to the present, structural adjustment programs
have had no pretense or specific aim of encouraging sustainable
development reforms on an international level. For example, they had no
intention of strengthening the biosphere's sustainability, reducing natural
resource consumption levels, enhancing the global sink function
performance, or rebuilding the planet's environmental infrastructure.

The purpose of adjustment programs, moreover, has not been to address
the disparity between North and South. Economic restructuring programs
have not sought to change basic patterns of consumption or use of natural
resources by the industrialized and developing countries. Designers of
adjustment programs did not set goals to alter terms of trade between North
and South or change the conditions under which developing countries
would have access to the northern markets. Nor was there any intention to

redistribute productive assets or wealth from the rich to poor nations through the economic restructuring programs.

In no uncertain terms, sponsors and designers of adjustment programs intended only to effect reforms on the level of national economies. This single-minded purpose is clearly set forth in the World Bank's Operational Manual Statement of 1982: "Structural Adjustment Lending (SAL) is non-project lending to support programs of policy and institutional change necessary to modify the structure of an economy so that it can maintain both its growth rate and the viability of its balance of payments in the medium term."[32]

A high degree of consistency and continuity is apparent in the Bank's formulations if one traces objectives of structural adjustment beginning with this formal statement and continuing through the following 15 years. This consistency is reflected in the initial justifications of policy-based lending, subsequent policy iterations, and the Bank's evaluations. In short, adjustment lending sought "to support policy changes for short-term stabilization and longer-term growth. It thus supports policies to bring domestic demand into line with resource availability and policies to increase economic efficiency and flexibility."[33]

Over the course of those years, the Bank has nuanced its basic objectives of adjustment lending in two ways. The first was to add "sustained" or "sustainable" as a qualifier to the growth objective. This change occurred in the early 1990s with the release of a World Bank evaluation of adjustment programs, *Adjustment Lending Policies for Sustainable Growth*.[34] Not only did "sustainable growth" find its way into the title of that publication, but sustainability references surfaced in many expressions, including "sustained adjustment,"[35] "sustainable reductions in the public sector deficit,"[36] and "sustainability of the balance of payments situation."[37] However, the references did not establish a direct conceptual linkage to the framework of sustainable development that evolved during the 1980s and that was formally agreed upon by governments at UNCED in June 1992.

In 1992, the World Bank injected a second nuance into its structural adjustment lending objectives statement. As stated in *The Third Report on Adjustment Lending*, adjustment policies are designed to "shift an economy to a new, sustainable and *poverty-reducing* growth path" (emphasis added).[38] By the 1990s, it was apparent that the public's protests regarding structural adjustment's negative impacts on the most vulnerable sectors of adjusting societies were not going to disappear. Not only were these problems enduring in character; their negative impacts threatened the viability of the economic reform programs and social cohesion, particularly in low-income countries. Faced with growing public discontent and its admitted difficulties in alleviating poverty, senior management again elevated poverty reduction to the level of the Bank's primary objective.[39] Subsequent Bank strategy and publications, including those dealing with structural adjustment, have reflected that new clarity of purpose.

The Bretton Woods institutions (BWI) have responded to the social dimensions of adjustment policies,[40] they recognize the political dimension of policy-based lending,[41] and they accept the mixed impacts of adjustment lending on the environment of adjusting countries.[42] Recognition of these impacts, however, has not led the World Bank to alter the definition of the objectives of its policy-based lending programs. From the outset of these programs some 15 years ago, the Bank has viewed any improvement in developing countries' social, political, and environmental fabric as contingent on improving a country's macroeconomic performance. The underlying BWI approach to adjustment lending is that restoring aggregate growth in adjusting countries is the sine qua non of addressing the social, political, and environmental problems besetting adjusting countries. In this framework, raising countries to a "higher growth path" will provide more resources for alleviating poverty, providing social services, strengthening management of natural resources, supporting redistribution policies, and so on. The accuracy of these assumptions are examined in light of the nine country research programs presented in Chapters 3 through 11.

ENDNOTES

1. Rachel Carson, *Silent Spring* (Boston: Houghton Mifflin, 1962).
2. Paul Erhlich, *The Population Bomb* (New York: Ballantine Books, 1990).
3. Donella Meadows, Dennis Meadows, Jorgen Randers, and William W. Behrens III, *Limits to Growth* (New York: Universe Books, 1972).
4. The communist countries withdrew from the preparatory process on the grounds that "pollution was the product of capitalism, and consequently a problem from which they did not suffer" (Tony Bretton, *The Greening of Machiavelli* [London: Earthscan, 1994], p. 37).
5. Panel of Experts Convened by the Secretary-General of the United Nations Conference on the Human Environment, *Environment and Development: The Founex Report on*

Development and Environment (New York: Carnegie Endowment for International Peace, 1972).

6. Stockholm Conference, *Only One Earth: An Introduction to the Politics of Survival* (London: Earth Island, 1972).

7. Bretton, op. cit., pp. 35-50.

8. Most of these conventions were regional agreements that included the Oslo Convention to control maritime dumping, the Helsinki Convention to control pollution in the Baltic Sea, the Paris Convention to control land-based pollution sources of the North Sea, the Mediterranean Action Plan to address Mediterranean maritime pollution, and the Basel Convention on the Transboundary Movements of Hazardous Waste.

9. See, for example, Gareth Porter and Janet Brown, *Global Environmental Politics* (Boulder, Colo.: Westview Press, 1991); J. McCormick, *The Global Environmental Movement* (London: Bellhaven Press, 1989); and David Reed, "The Global Environment Facility and Non-governmental Organizations," *American University Journal of International Law and Policy* (Fall 1993):191-213.

10. Tamas Szentes, *The Transformation of the World Economy: New Directions and New Interests* (London: Zed Books, 1988), pp. 98-101.

11. Joyce Kolko, *Restructuring the World Economy* (New York: Pantheon, 1988), p. 258.

12. International Union for Conservation of Nature and Natural Resources (IUCN), United Nations Environment Programme, World Wide Fund for Nature-International, *World Conservation Strategy* (Geneva: IUCN, 1980).

13. W.M. Adams, *Green Development: Environment and Sustainability in the Third World* (London: Routledge, 1990), p. 47.

14. IUCN, op. cit., p. i.

15. World Commission on Environment and Development, *Our Common Future* (Oxford: Oxford University Press, 1987).

16. Ibid., p. 51.

17. For one of the more thoughtful summations of the Rio conference, see Johan Holmberg, Koy Thomson, and Lloyd Timberlake, *Facing the Future* (London: Earthscan, 1993).

18. Replenishment of the Global Environment Facility (GEF) at approximately US$2.1 billion was agreed upon in principle at the Rio conference. The GEF is an important and innovative multilateral mechanism for addressing global environmental problems; as such, it represents a change in the international financial incentive structure that will encourage environmentally beneficial development activities. Its innovative features notwithstanding, the GEF's actual and leveraged resources play a minuscule role in altering global capital flows, both private and public.

19. United Nations Development Programme, *Human Development Report 1994* (New York: Oxford University Press, 1994).

20. Works of these scholars include: Nicolas Georgescu-Roegen, *The Entropy Law and the Economic Process* (Cambridge, Mass.: Harvard University Press, 1971); K. William Kapp, *The Social Costs of Private Enterprise* (New York: Schocken Books, 1950), *Towards a Science of Man: A Positive Approach to the Integration of Social Knowledge* (The Hague: Matinus Mijhoff, 1961), and *Social Costs, Economic Development and Environmental Disruption*, ed. John Ullman (Lanham, Md.: University Press of America, 1983); Kenneth Boulding, *Beyond Economics: Essays on Society, Religion and Ethics* (Ann Arbor: University of Michigan Press, 1970); Herman Daly, *Steady-state Economics* (Washington, D.C.: Island Press, 1991); and Herman Daly and John Cobb, *For the Common Good* (Boston: Beacon Press, 1989).

21. International Union for Conservation of Nature and Natural Resources, United Nations Environment Programme, and World Wide Fund for Nature-International, *Caring for the Earth* (London: Earthscan, 1991), p. 4.

22. Ibid., p. 10.

23. An early formulation of this position can be found in Kapp, *Social Costs*, op. cit., p. 141. A more recent exposition is offered in Robert Goodland and Herman Daly, "Ten Reasons Why Northern Income Growth Is Not the Solution to Southern Poverty," in *Population,*

Technology, and Lifestyle, ed. Robert Goodland, Herman Daly, and Salah el Serafy (Washington, D.C.: Island Press, 1992).

24. See, for example, Daniel McGraw, ed., *NAFTA & the Environment: Substance and Progress* (Chicago: American Bar Association, 1995); *Agenda 21: Programme of Action for Sustainable Development* (New York: United Nations, 1992); and Patrick Low, ed., *International Trade and the Environment* (Washington, D.C.: World Bank, 1992).

25. Meadows et al., op. cit.

26. See World Bank, *World Development Report 1992: Development and the Environment* (Washington, D.C., 1992), for the most recent recitation of this thesis. A challenge to the thesis can be found in David Reed, "Review of *World Development Report 1992*," *International Environmental Affairs* 4 (1992):367-71.

27. Pamela Stedman, *Setting a New Mandate for the Bretton Woods Institutions, Meeting the Challenges of Sustainable Development in a Changing Global Econqmy* (Washington, D.C.: World Wide Fund for Nature-International, 1995), p. 19.

28. United Nations Development Programme, *Human Development Report 1992* (New York: Oxford University Press, 1992), p. 36.

29. World Bank, *World Development Report 1994: Infrastructure for Development* (New York: Oxford University Press, 1994).

30. Stedman, op. cit., p. 30.

31. World Commission on Environment and Development, op. cit., pp. 50-51. The WCED offers a simple, persuasive argument for the need to redistribute global wealth although the means and mechanisms for effecting wealth redistribution are conspicuously missing from its recommendations. A more inclusive policy statement regarding the imperative for redistributing wealth is presented in Goodland and Daly, op. cit., p. 128.

32. World Bank, Operational Manual Statement No. 3.58, Annex II, 1982.

33. World Bank, *Adjustment Lending: An Evaluation of Ten Years of Experience* (Washington, D.C.: World Bank, 1988), p. 10.

34. World Bank, *Adjustment Lending Policies for Sustainable Growth* (Washington, D.C.: World Bank, 1990).

35. Ibid., p. 2.

36. Ibid., p.1.

37. Ibid., p. 5.

38. World Bank, *The Third Report on Adjustment Lending: Private and Public Resources for Growth* (Washington, D.C.: World Bank, 1992), p.1.

39. Lewis Preston, "The World Bank's Increasing Commitment to Poverty Reduction" (Opening remarks at the press conference on Implementing the World Bank's Strategy to Reduce Poverty: Progress and Challenges, Washington, D.C., April 28, 1993); and James Wolfensohn (Address to the Board of Governors of the World Bank Group, Washington, D.C., October 10, 1995).

40. World Bank, "The Social Impact of Adjustment Operations: An Overview" (Washington, D.C., 1995).

41. Ernest Stern, "Evaluation and Lessons of Adjustment Lending," in *Restructuring Economies in Distress*, ed. Vinod Thomas, Ajay Chhibber, Mansoor Dailami, and Jaime de Melo (New York: Oxford University Press, 1991), pp. 4-5:

"Underestimating the Political Factor

"Taken together, these lessons hold a moral for economists. It is that we at the World Bank—and everyone else, I believe—underestimated the political difficulty of protracted adjustment. Economists here and elsewhere often tend to believe that we need only do our analysis, reach our conclusions, and write a report; the rest will follow. We do not have much experience with the political processes of change. We fail to give full weight in our own thinking to the fact that structural adjustment means a major redistribution of economic power and hence of political power in many of the countries undergoing this process.

"Such a shift is not neutral. It does not happen easily or by itself. The politics of change is one of the reasons adjustment has taken a great deal more time than expected in some countries and one of the reasons some adjustment efforts have not been sustained.

"I do not believe that the World Bank can do very much about this process except to understand the problem. Hiring political scientists to tell us what will or will not work in a country is not the solution. Those judgments are properly the country's responsibility.

"Nevertheless, in working out adjustment loans and time frames for policy change, we need to give due attention to the political difficulty of adjustment. We should not say that because the politics are difficult the time has to be very protracted. Rather, we should take the difficulty as part of the judgment to be made about the adequacy of both the government's commitment and its capacity to bring about the specific change and achieve its objectives in the time agreed. We need to recognize that either the commitment or the pace of its implementation may be less than required."

42. World Bank, *Economywide Policies and the Environment: Emerging Lessons from Experience* (Washington, D.C.: World Bank, 1994).

PART TWO

INTRODUCTION

by David Reed

ORGANIZATION OF THE RESEARCH PROGRAM

An operational premise of this study was that local researchers were to remain agnostic about possible effects of adjustment programs and causalities of environmental problems until all evidence had been gathered. It should be made clear, however, that organization of the research program was not a value-free endeavor. Specifically, each aspect of the project's organization and implementation required weighing a series of trade-offs that could influence, to one degree or another, the emphasis and potential outputs of the research. Lest the reader harbor doubts, this introductory note summarizes the major issues that had to be resolved.

At the project's outset, two quite distinct organizational approaches were open. The first option was to contract with one preeminent research institute to carry out the studies in all nine countries. This option would have encouraged greater commonality in methodological approaches as well as a higher degree of comparability among the nine countries. It would have facilitated centralization of information and thereby encouraged cross-country analyses and comparisons. However, given the innovative character of the research being proposed and the existing geographic distribution of experts specializing in this field, it was probable that a central research facility based in a northern industrialized society would be chosen. Thus although strengthening some aspects of the research effort, this approach would not help build the analytical capacity of research institutes in the developing world.

The second option was to obtain the services of research institutes in each of the nine countries. Although limitations to this approach were clear (for example, it would diminish comparability and methodological continuity), the advantages were persuasive. Local researchers would have greater sensitivity and understanding of history, local conditions, and social relations. They would have access to local information sources and could conduct household surveys and local case studies more effectively. Even more significant was the importance of strengthening local capacity to continue similar research efforts in the future. Moreover, this approach opened the door to encouraging an on-going policy dialogue between researchers and their countries' respective policymakers in coming years. For these and other reasons, WWF contracted with the most capable and experienced research institutes in the nine countries included in this study.

This option generated additional support requirements to ensure successful implementation. First and foremost, WWF had to ensure adequate technical and methodological support for each institute as it undertook this innovative research activity. To this end, WWF contracted with the Overseas Development Institute (ODI) and the Harvard Institute for International Development (HIID) to provide such regular technical advice and guidance as the local teams required. ODI supported the four African institutes and HIID the Asian and Latin American/Caribbean institutes.

Second, this approach also required formation of local advisory groups to serve as fora for discussing implementation problems and reviewing conclusions. These groups were composed of academic experts, well-placed government officials, and representatives of local nongovernmental organizations (NGOs). They would also serve as the springboard for initiating and thereafter sustaining a policy dialogue with government policymakers once the research was completed and the results released.

Further, to help guarantee that the research met the highest analytical standards, WWF formed an international advisory committee composed of representatives of the World Bank, the European Commission, the German Ministry of Development Cooperation, the Canadian International Development Agency, the Danish International Development Agency, the French Ministry of Development Cooperation, and the Organisation for Economic Co-operation and Development. Also included were experts from developing country research institutes and NGOs. This advisory group met with representatives of the nine research institutes on two occasions to review the proposed terms of reference for each country and the preliminary conclusions of the studies. They then met separately to propose recommendations for WWF's consideration.

COMMON METHODOLOGICAL CHALLENGES

Local research teams faced several methodological difficulties as they began to analyze the impacts of adjustment polices on their countries' respective natural resource bases. First, with the exception of Venezuela, each research institute experienced problems in obtaining consistent data on the economy and the environment over an extended period. The challenge was greatest in Vietnam, where the entire economy was shifting from a physical accounting system to a system of national accounts based on monetary values.

The second problem was isolating the impacts of structural reforms on the environment from what would have happened had those reforms not been implemented. Separating the "with reforms" from the "without reforms" scenarios was further complicated by the fact that adjustment programs were implemented in an interrupted on-again, off-again way in several countries. Here it must be pointed out that absolute isolation of the two scenarios was impossible, as is true in many similar analytical efforts. Economic crises, environmental problems, and social dislocations beset each country prior to implementing structural reforms, and such factors inevitably influenced, to one degree or another, the environmental impacts of the macroeconomic reforms.

A third common problem was that of developing methods for projecting probable environmental impacts of macroeconomic reforms for the long term. In some cases, developing economic models helped researchers predict probable environmental impacts as the economic reforms take hold in coming years. In other cases, more modest scenario building exercises proved most reliable.

Regardless of the specific analytical techniques employed, the analytical processes were similar. The research teams reconstructed basic relationships between economic development and the emergence of environmental problems over past decades. Changes during the adjustment phase relative to historical trends were analyzed and the probable causes of those changes identified. In addition, each country was asked to verify the accuracy of the causes through local case studies. Depending on the circumstances, some institutes examined particular economic sectors;

others analyzed the impacts and causes on a community level. Researchers then used case study results to correct and refine the analytical framework for each country. As a final step, the research teams constructed scenarios of future economic growth patterns and, in the framework of those projected economic trends, identified probable environmental impacts.

The reader will recognize the differences among the nine summary reports. They reflect the basic organizational decisions made at the outset of the project that placed local capacity building and local perspective on a somewhat higher scale of importance relative to methodological similitude and analytical comparability. Responsibility for the focus and quality of the research activities' outputs rests exclusively with WWF, the sponsoring organization.

3

CASE STUDY FOR CAMEROON

This chapter is based on a study conducted and written by Roger Tchoungui, Steve Gartlan, J.A. Mope Simo, Fondo Sikod, Augustin Youmbi, and Michel Ndjatsana, with support of James Winpenny of the Overseas Development Institute. This summary was written by James Winpenny.

This study's objective is to improve understanding of the ways in which economic policies can affect people's behavior toward the natural environment. It documents the principal economic adjustment measures taken since the late 1980s and traces their potential environmental impact in the agricultural and forestry sectors through case studies in four contrasting but representative regions—the North-West, Far North, East, and South. Implications are drawn and recommendations made for the pursuit of sustainable development in agriculture and forestry.

BACKGROUND

The Setting

The Republic of Cameroon is roughly triangular in shape with a base of some 700 kilometers and a height of 1,200 kilometers. It lies between 2 and 13 degrees north latitude and between 8 and 16 degrees east longitude in west-central Africa. It covers an area of 475,000 square kilometers; of this, 466,464 square kilometers are land and 8,536 are water. It has a coastline of 402 kilometers on the Gulf of Guinea (see Figure 3.1).

Cameroon's population was estimated at 12.2 million in 1991, with an average 1980-90 growth rate of 3.2 percent. It is expected to grow to 20.2

Figure 3.1 Cameroon

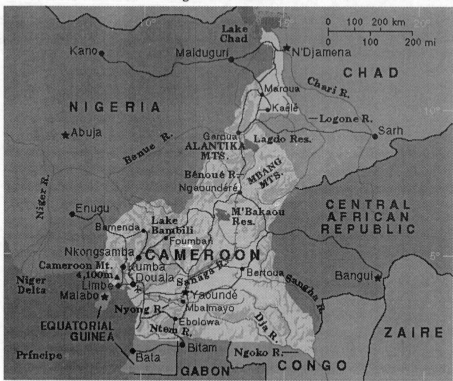

From *Picture Atlas of the World* CD-ROM, © National Geographic Society, 1995

million by the year 2010, an increase of 60 percent in 18 years. Until the mid-1980s, Cameroon enjoyed rapid growth, as conventionally measured; since then it has slowed down and most recently contracted. The GDP growth rate was 5.1 percent in 1965-80 and 2.3 percent in 1980-90. In the most recent period, 1988-92, the negative rates of growth of GDP (-5 percent) and GDP per capita (-8 percent) have been the worst in Africa.

One-quarter of GDP originates in agriculture, one-third in industry and mining, and the remainder in "services." Gross domestic investment is about 12 percent of GDP; 79 percent of the labor force is employed in agriculture, 7 percent in industry and mining, and 14 percent in services. Cameroon's principal exports are petroleum, coffee, cocoa, bananas, timber, rubber, cotton, gold, and some other metals. The economic base is well diversified.

Many of Cameroon's human development indicators are those of a middle-income developing country, although slippage has occurred to the point at which it now qualifies for International Development Association lending terms. Prior to the recent devaluation, its income per capita was about US$860 (US$2,400 in purchasing power parity terms). Life expectancy at birth is 55.3 years; 55 percent of the population has access to safe water and 78 percent to sanitation. The adult literacy rate is 57 percent. Overall, Cameroon was ranked 124th out of 173 in the Human Development Index of the United Nations Development Programme (UNDP).

Methodology

Structural adjustment programs (SAPs) are undertaken in response to pressing economic problems. Environmental objectives rarely feature in their conception or design. Any environmental effect is usually an unintended by-product.

So far, little attempt has been made to incorporate environmental aims into SAPs. Reasons may include:

- The relevance and impacts of adjustment on the environment are still poorly understood.
- The urgency of the economic and social problems being addressed by SAPs drowns out environmental considerations.
- Incorporating new environmental features in SAPs would complicate programs that are already problematic enough. SAPs have had a mixed record, many African countries have applied adjustment weakly and half-heartedly, and many SAPs have been too complex.

However, understanding the adjustment-environment link can serve useful purposes:

- Uncovering trade-offs and conflicts among economic, social, and environmental aims, which can help in designing future SAPs or compensatory/complementary projects (e.g., if adjustment encourages the production of an erosive crop, its support price can be adjusted or taxed or antierosion measures introduced). The trade-off may be acute (e.g., the need for export revenue may lead to pressures for timber exports or mass big game tourism) or it may be minor, and a major gain in environmental aims could be achieved with a relatively small sacrifice in economic terms.
- Identifying "win-win" policies that fulfill both economic and environmental goals (e.g., increasing logging concession fees, promoting exports of tree crops, raising energy prices).

The main methodological problems encountered in this study are the following:

- The difficulty of isolating the impacts of adjustment from those of underlying social and economic trends. By definition, adjusting countries are suffering economic and social problems before SAPs are formally introduced. Adjustment cannot be blamed for preexisting economic problems or for the growth in underlying poverty. This point is especially applicable where adjustment has been weak and/or flawed.
- The intervention of exogenous factors. During the course of adjustment, Cameroon has been affected by important changes in national policies and fluctuations in international commodity and financial markets.

There is growing interest in the use of computable general equilibrium (CGE) models, which enable alternative policy scenarios to be tested for their possible effects on natural resources and the environment. However, these models have a huge appetite for data, are often based on outmoded structural features and behavioral relationships, and are rarely calibrated in sufficient detail to display environmental factors. A suitable model for Cameroon was not available.

The approach followed in this study was eclectic. Researchers identified links between adjustment and the natural environment that seemed plausible on a priori grounds, based on their knowledge of adjustment, environmental processes, and local circumstances. These were tested by the use of time series evidence reinforced by field surveys and local professional opinion. The analysis conducted from a macro perspective was complemented by a review of the issues at the grass roots level in four different but important regions, namely, the fertile farming area of the North-West Province, the populous but semiarid Far North Province, the cocoa-producing area of the East Province, and the forestry economy of the South Province.

The method used, like any other, was greatly constrained by the supply of data and their quality. Evidence on environmental status and trends is imperfect in all countries, and Cameroon is no exception. Intuitive and impressionistic views are difficult to match with robust, quantified evidence. Data are patchy, impressionistic, and sometimes anecdotal, and they were culled from various sources. The results of the study should be regarded as suggestive rather than definitive. They identify promising lines of inquiry and, in some cases, suggest provisional conclusions based on the data at hand. Further research along these lines is desirable.

THE ENVIRONMENT

Salient Features

Cameroon extends south from Lake Chad, through Sahel and Sudan savanna into semi-deciduous and gallery forest into the dense, humid evergreen forest zone. These bands of vegetation run roughly parallel to the southern edge of the Sahara. The parallel zones are broken by elevation changes into altitudinally determined distinct vegetational communities, with submontane and montane forest and subalpine grassland on the highest peaks. Periods of climatic desiccation have led to the isolation of the montane massifs, which display high levels of endemism. The coastal forests functioned as refuges during these periods and in consequence have high biodiversity as well as endemism. The wetlands of the Chad basin and the marine and coastal habitats are also important.

Cameroon has exceptionally high biological diversity and high levels of endemism. Some 260 species of mammals, 848 species of birds, 542 species of fresh and brackish water fish (17 percent endemic), and 9,000 species of plants have been recorded, of which at least 156 plant species are endemic, including 45 on Mount Cameroon. Plant and mammal endemism is highest in the moist evergreen forest belt along the coast.

Major Environmental Problems and Their Causes

Mature forests are being lost at a rate of about 100,000 hectares per year. Currently, the increase in land dedicated to permanent (plantation) agriculture is about 8,000 hectares per year. In contrast, between 75,000 and 95,000 hectares are cleared each year for slash-and-burn farming. This activity is compatible with sustaining forest resources as long as the fallow periods are long enough to allow the forest to recover. Unfortunately, with increasing population pressure, the fallow periods are being shortened. The results are soil depletion, erosion, and environmental degradation.

Soil erosion is a serious and increasing problem in the intensively farmed areas of the West, North-West, and North provinces. Much of the problem derives from the fact that the increased need for farming land has forced people to work increasingly steep slopes. In the western highlands, these new lands are used principally for farming roots and tubers on the steep, highly erodible slopes. Terracing and other soil conservation practices need to be introduced to minimize runoff. In the northern provinces, planting cotton tends to lead to degraded soils because the ground surface is left open to wind after harvest.

Soil washed from the fields is carried down by streams and rivers. Eventually, much of this sediment reaches the sea, where it is deposited as mud or clay. The most serious result of this process is the silting of dams that were constructed to help control river flows (e.g., Bamendjim, Mbakaua) and those that provide direct power for hydroelectricity (e.g., Edéa, Song-Lolou); the effective life of the dam may be reduced one-third to one-half.

Because of the low levels of industrialization, industrial pollution is not yet a serious problem in Cameroon. Industrial wastes are discharged into waterways or the sea or are piled in dumps. The discharge of these wastes is uncontrolled, and the legislative system that regulates industry is ineffective in this matter.

Forty-five percent of Cameroonian farmers use fertilizers, pesticides, or fungicides, especially on crops for export. There is much waste and mismanagement, and many farmers do not understand the optimal application of these inputs.

Most logging activity in Cameroon is extremely selective, not because of environmental concerns or legislative constraints but because of economic considerations. The high costs of transport and labor make it uneconomic to transport all but the highest quality and most valuable wood from southeastern Cameroon. The amount extracted per hectare can be as low as 2 or 3 cubic meters.

Ecologically, logging is problematic. In the tropical forest canopy, the crowns of trees tend to be joined with a network of lianas. It is impossible to fell a forest giant without damaging adjacent trees. As much as 30-50 percent of the remaining trees can be destroyed or fatally damaged, and the soil can become so impacted as to impede regeneration. In other areas nearer Douala, such as the Littoral, logging is less selective and forests have already been logged several times since the colonial period. Logging in the coastal forests is likely to do more ecological damage because these forests are old growth and are rich in *Caesalpiniaceae*. The main damage from selective logging is to biodiversity; the sink and ecological service functions of the remaining vegetation may not be much reduced. Industrial plantations still maintain a foliage that processes carbon dioxide in the same way as intact forest. Secondary forest performs similar climatic functions and will protect against soil erosion just as well as intact forest.

Logging provides access to forest areas, which farmers tend to invade until the forest is transformed into farms and agricultural land. Roads and tracks also give access to hunters. Hunting and trapping are common subsistence and commercial activities, often carried out with dogs and homemade shotguns. The latter are dangerous, frequently inflicting wounds on the hunters themselves. This type of hunting is illegal although universal. Illegal commercial hunting is carried out in a similar way, although with more modern weapons obtained from gendarmes or the military.

During the economic crisis, the exploitation of natural resources has increased. Applications for licenses to trade in parrots *Psittacus erythracus* have doubled in number over the past year. It is certain that the legal CITES (Convention on the International Trade in Endangered Species of Wild Flora and Fauna) quota of 16,000 birds is far exceeded by illegal and irregular exports. Trading in reptiles, amphibians, primates, tropical fish, and frogs and other bird species as well as in the dried skins of snakes and lizards is potentially lucrative.

The Environmental Impacts of Past Development Policies

In the decade prior to the mid-1980s, Cameroon achieved relatively high growth, as it was then conceived and measured. This growth was based mainly on earning economic surpluses (rents) from the exploitation and export of natural resources, both renewable and nonrenewable. In effect, the surpluses were devoted to the creation of a domestic industrial base, expansion of the country's social and economic infrastructure, and support of a growing public sector.

The aggregate rate of investment in this period was high. Industrial output grew rapidly, as did spending on infrastructure and the public service. However, subsidies to loss-creating public enterprises and the increasing recurrent costs of public services of all kinds absorbed rising portions of the central budget.

Rents extracted by exploiting Cameroon's natural resources were not used to create sustainable development. Conventional measures of economic performance created the illusion of success and concealed the extent of resource depletion that was occurring. Even without the economic difficulties from the mid-1980s onward, Cameroon was launched on an unsustainable economic trajectory, with the environmental consequences described earlier.

The conclusion of a recent poverty study on the early period of high economic growth is that growth alone is not sufficient to reduce poverty. This period failed to maximize income opportunities for the poor from agricultural growth. There was an undue stress on industrial promotion based on uneconomic investments and a tendency to favor capital-intensive methods over labor-intensive ones. Investment in human resources in rural areas lagged as part of a general urban bias in the choice of public investments and expenditures. The bias against rural areas was highlighted as a basic factor.

Environmental Policies and Sustainability

The political setting for environmental policy can be described as centralist, hierarchic, and geared to the collection and distribution of natural resource surpluses (rents). Cameroon's natural environment is viewed as an opportunity for revenue rather than as interdependent resources to be managed over the long term. Not surprisingly, the characteristic policies are not coherent, they are motivated by revenue and control objectives, and they do not provide the basis for rational management. There are many competing offices and agencies.

In April 1992, the Ministry of the Environment and Forests (MINEF) was formed with a mandate to develop a national comprehensive strategic plan to protect the environment and conserve natural resources. Protection and conservation of the ecosystem to ensure long-term economic and social benefits are to be emphasized. It marks a shift away from the previous perception of the environment as an asset for short-term income generation.

In Cameroon, environmental concern and awareness were virtually nonexistent a decade ago. The government lacked an environmental policy, and there was little evidence of such concerns in the published 5-year development plans prior to 1986. However, the sixth plan (1986-91) did foresee the need for development of a national policy on the environment and rational management of the national territory. Such concerns have increased dramatically over the past 5 years, partly reflecting the momentum of international activities.

With the support of the World Bank and the Food and Agriculture Organization of the United Nations, Cameroon developed a Tropical Forest Action Plan (TFAP) in 1988. The plan called for high-level political support for the conservation, protection, and sustainable management of forests and the related natural resource base. However, the TFAP was prepared primarily by forest technicians focusing on forest exploitation. It met with mixed reviews both locally and internationally and has had almost no impact on the forest industry or on the status of Cameroon's forests. There has been virtually no progress toward sustainability.

Cameroon is also a member of the International Timber Trade Organisation (ITTO) and is a signatory to its convention, which commits member states to achieve sustainability in the logging industry by the year 2000. Such a commitment has far-reaching implications and will require a significant reform of current practices and development of a permanent forest sector.

Cameroon's new Minister of Environment and Forests took part in the 1992 Earth Summit (the United Nations Conference on Environment and Development, UNCED) in Rio de Janiero. The preparation process for UNCED helped to develop a national capacity for environmental planning. A national commission (NATCOM, the National Commission on the Environment) was set up to prepare the national report for the summit. A draft report under the sponsorship of UNDP and the government of Canada was discussed at a national seminar held in December 1991. Following this seminar, the Cameroon national report for Rio was finalized, containing an up-to-date review of the environment.

After Rio, the impetus for environmental change grew stronger, and there was an increasing awareness of the importance of involving nongovernmental organizations (NGOs) in order to be effective in these areas. A UNDP multidisciplinary mission in which various UN agencies and interested bilateral donors drew up a potential environmental plan and policy for Cameroon took place between September 7 and October 9, 1992.

As a result of this gathering momentum, a National Environmental Action Plan is currently being drawn up; it follows a series of regional public meetings between government and interested parties, including NGOs. A round table held on October 14, 1993, included a statement from the Minister of Planning that environmental concerns would be specifically included in future government planning projects.

This growing permeation of environmental concerns in government policy is not reflected in the contents of the structural adjustment program. The only explicit environmental feature of the SAP is concerned with the reform of the forestry sector through the formulation of a new Forestry Code. The proposed legislation was submitted to Parliament in December 1993 and was debated, altered, passed, and signed by the President as law

No. 94/01 of January 20, 1994. The decrees of implementation for the law, which will define its modalities of operation, are still being drawn up. Alterations to the draft law made by the National Assembly seriously weakened it.

Part of the process of political liberalization is the marked increase over the past 3 years of indigenous NGOs with environmental advocacy as one of their main functions. Their existence will create further impetus for the development of a sound environmental policy at the grass-roots level.

Long-term Environmental Trends

The destruction of mature forests, their degradation by selective logging, and eventual reversion to secondary growth, unless arrested, will cause the loss of most of the forested area over the next generation. This would be of major concern to Cameroon's rich stocks of biodiverse fauna and flora. An example of the potential cost to humankind of reduced biodiversity is the discovery that a chemical constituent of a liana found in Korup is effective in the treatment of the AIDS virus in vitro. Tests are currently under way to see if it could be an effective treatment in vivo for the human population. Even in the testing phase, it is a valuable commodity. If proved clinically effective, it could become one of Africa's most important cash crops.

The preservation of biodiversity depends heavily on Cameroon's protected area system, which includes seven national parks and nine wildlife reserves. Many are being threatened by various local factors (e.g., illegal settlements, seismic exploration, clearance for farming, hunting, logging concessions). Most of the protected areas are suffering from neglect of management and policing, and all will be degraded in the long term unless local populations are able to capture more of the benefits of conservation.

As background to the formulation of the new forestry policy, an exercise in land use planning has been undertaken for the 30 percent of the national territory that includes nearly all the dense humid tropical forest—most of it in the South Province.[1] The study took into account the land requirements of the likely population in the year 2020 and made assumptions about both farmland per capita and fallow periods. Even in this currently lightly populated region, an estimated 32 percent of the forested area would be required for human occupation, 43 percent for working forests, and 17 percent for various kinds of protected areas.

The Economy

Economic Performance and Structural Adjustment since 1985

Until 1985-86, the economic growth of Cameroon was strong, by conventional measures, resting on the production and export of natural resources and latterly on the expansion of the petroleum sector. However, in 1985-86, petroleum revenues dropped owing to the simultaneous reduction in prices and lack of exploitable sites. At the same time, the terms of trade for crop exports declined. The situation was aggravated by the fact that most of the export income was expressed in U.S. dollars, whose exchange rate against the CFA franc fell about 40 percent after June 1985.

The slowing down of the economy exposed serious deficits in public finance and the balance of payments. The budgetary deficit was funded by a reduction of state deposits in the banking sector, a build-up of internal arrears on payments, and an increase in foreign indebtedness. The balance of payments deficit was funded by an increase in foreign debt, the repatriation of external bank assets, and the build-up of a debit balance with the French Treasury.

GNP fell in 1986-87, owing to a fall in the export earnings of agricultural produce and oil. The deflationary effects of the worsening terms of trade were offset by an increase in the budget deficit, which rose to 8.7 percent of GNP. The first measures to tackle the budget were announced in the Finance Law of 1987-88, promulgated in June 1987, which aimed at cutting public spending.

The persistent weakness in primary commodity markets and its effects on public revenue frustrated attempts to halt the deterioration of the economic and financial situation. The results were a build-up of arrears on payments by the state and growing illiquidity in the payments system.

The government resorted to a series of adjustment and reform programs in concert with the International Monetary Fund (IMF) and the World Bank. Three Stand-by Agreements were made with the IMF in September 1988, November 1991, and March 1994. An SAP was approved by the World Bank in 1989 and renewed in essentially the same form in 1994.

In view of the increase in effective value of the CFA franc, the measures taken can now be judged as too late and too weak. The currency increased in value about 30 percent in real terms from 1984-85 (July-June) to 1991-92. The problems caused by this increase were compounded by a sharp drop in the terms of trade. As the tradeable goods sector suffered a cost-price squeeze, public revenues fell, domestic arrears built up quickly, and the banking system found itself increasingly insolvent.

Over this 7-year period, real GNP fell 30 percent, and real income per capita fell 50 percent. The current external deficit has averaged 6 percent of GNP. Foreign debt tripled to more than 60 percent of GNP, and debt service ratio rose strongly to over 42 percent. Arrears on foreign payments have recurred.

Devaluation of the CFA franc took place in January 1994, long after the start of the other adjustment measures. Other key fiscal and structural measures agreed upon with the IMF were not implemented on time. These delays caused a shortfall in non-oil-based revenue for the state, preventing compliance with other program obligations. A revised program was developed in June 1994 with the IMF, but at the time of writing, no official agreement had been reached.

There is no evidence that environmental considerations influenced the overall design of the adjustment programs or the choice of specific measures, apart from forestry reforms. The completion of a forest policy review and the formulation of a Forestry Code count as practically the only environmental bonus from the adjustment period.

Economic and Social Impacts of Recent and Current Adjustment

The choice of SAP measures dictated the impacts of adjustment on different social groups. Until 1993, civil servants were among the few relative gainers from adjustment. The first to suffer were cocoa and coffee farmers in 1990, whose output prices were reduced and whose support services (e.g., extension, input subsidies, credit, marketing systems) were drastically scaled down. Soon afterwards, social services (e.g., education, health) were squeezed. Public servants did not feel the pinch until January 1993 (in fact, they continued to benefit from artificially cheap imports). But in January and November 1993, their benefits were sharply reduced, leaving the total public service wage bill 60 percent of what it was at the beginning of the year.

Because the exchange rate was not part of the adjustment process until January 1994, adjustment had to take the form of deflation—a fall in nominal prices and incomes—which has been painful. The urban elite and public servants have been better able to defend themselves and have suffered the least. Politically weaker groups (e.g., farmers) have suffered most. By the end of 1993, however, most sections of society were experiencing economic hardship.

With the devaluation of January 1994, the burden of adjustment is likely to shift. Producers of tradeables and import substitutes and consumers of nontradeables should benefit. Consumers of tradeables and producers of nontradeables should suffer. The former group will include many farmers and manufacturing firms; the latter will include most urban consumers. The poor and/or landless rural population will have mixed fortunes: supplies (including food) that they buy may cost more on balance, but their employment prospects should improve.

At the time of writing (September 1994), the devaluation (from CFA franc 50 to 100 per French franc) had had little immediate impact on production and exports. Over 1993-94, the economy of Cameroon continued its decline (-11.2 percent). The secondary sector (i.e., manufacturing) shared in the decline owing to the loss of domestic purchasing power, the lack of new investment, and transitional difficulties of the liberalization program. Likewise, services, including transport, continued to decline.

The initial inflationary effect of the devaluation on retail prices appears to have stabilized at a level some 32 percent higher than previously. So far, little change has been registered in the alarming state of public finances. The one sector showing signs of revival is primary production. The increased competitiveness of Cameroonian products, coupled with increases in world prices (e.g., of coffee) have stimulated activity, especially in the second half of 1994. However, this has not yet had any clear-cut effect on exports.

Surveys of manufacturing and agroprocessing firms point to a lift in confidence that may soon work through to output and employment. Imports have fallen more sharply than expected, although the drop is depressing fiscal receipts.

Environmental Impacts of Recent and Current Adjustment

The following adjustment measures with potential direct environmental effects are summarized in Table 3.1:

- The reduction of official purchasing prices of coffee, cocoa, and cotton by about 50 percent in 1988-89. Its purpose was to increase the competitiveness of these basic exports and to eliminate the losses sustained by the official marketing boards. In practice, this measure, combined with the others described below, led producers to reduce output and lessen plantation maintenance, in some cases to cut down trees and plant food crops, in other cases to plant food crops on marginal land.

- The curtailment and suspension of support services to rural producers (e.g., input subsidies, provision of free materials, extension services). The purpose of these measures was to conserve revenue. One effect

Table 3.1 Adjustment Components and the Environment

Adjustment Components	Environmental Impacts
Cuts in farmer support facilities (e.g., fertilizer subsidies, extension services)	Discouragement of more intensive farming, diversification, conservation, and agroforestry
Reforms in marketing systems for export crops	Increased incentives to plant new coffee and cocoa trees and restore existing plantations at expense of foodcrops, environmental risks of increased profitability of cotton
Reforms in rural credit	Farmers hampered by collapse of credit in purchase of cash inputs (e.g., labor, fertilizer)
Devaluation	Planting new areas to export crops, restoring existing plantations
Redundancies and salary cuts in public service and parastatals	Widespread impoverishment and environmental encroachment by new and underresourced farmers
Enactment of new Forestry Code	Positive effect on sustainable forestry use if implemented in robust form; in present form, effect greatly diluted
Cuts in Forestry Service	Logging unsupervised, forest rent not collected, degradation of forests accelerated
Increase in price of commercial fuel	Increased use of fuelwood and forest encroachment
Less public spending on health and education	Increased impoverishment because of reduced productive ability, decline in environmental education

was to discourage the use of agrochemicals. Farmers in some areas used little or no fertilizer. Those who did (40-50 percent of all farmers) were hit both by the withdrawal of the subsidy and (after January 1994) by the doubling of the cost of fertilizer imports from Nigeria. The effective withdrawal of extension services in some areas (e.g., cessation of North-West Development Authority [MIDENO] activities in the North-West) was a blow to diversification, conservation, the spread of agroforestry, and the adoption of more intensive production methods.

• Reforms in marketing arrangements for export crops. These reforms were intended to reduce the fiscal burden of unprofitable marketing boards and improve incentives for the production of tradeable crops. The production and marketing of nontraditional export crops and arabica coffee have been fully liberalized. This change principally affects West and North-West Provinces and transfers powers from the former National Produce Marketing Board to cooperatives. The latter are increasingly being run by their members and world prices publicized through a new Arabica Marketing Information System.

For robusta coffee and cocoa, liberalization of marketing began in August 1994. Both the reference price system and fixed marketing margins have now been abolished, and reference prices have now doubled. For cotton, liberalization will proceed more gradually; for the time being, the guaranteed producer price is up 50 percent.

These reforms should eventually ensure that producers keep a greater share of the world prices by eliminating or reducing the share absorbed by the Marketing Board's overhead costs. At a time of low world prices and reduced official purchase prices, the marketing reforms in arabica coffee had little apparent impact. But given a recovery in prices, such as occurred in 1994, magnified by the devaluation, producer incentives are greatly sharpened. The restoration of plantation production and its extension onto new land or at the expense of food crops can be expected.

• Reforms in rural credit institutions. The main impact of the reform of the financial system on rural producers has been through the demise of the National Fund for Rural Development (FONADER). The fund's decay was well advanced before its formal end; hence there was no dramatic change in the supply of rural credit. In some regions, credit agents based in cooperative unions exist to collect repayments, but there is currently great confusion about where the funds should be paid. In effect, rural credit is in a state of abeyance in most areas. This situation seriously hampers producers in their purchase and use of cash inputs.

- Devaluation of the CFA franc. The purpose of devaluation was to provide an alternative to internal deflation, which was reaching intolerable levels, and to provide a sharper incentive for the production of tradeable goods by changing price relativities. This measure helped to reverse the impacts of the earlier reduction in the purchase prices of export crops, and in the case of coffee, its effect was magnified by the sharp increase in the world prices in the first half of 1994. Farmers appear to be responding by restoring the capacity of existing plantations and planting new areas. Initially, potential benefits to cocoa producers appear to have been captured by middlemen, but gains should eventually reach producers.

- Redundancies and salary cuts in the public service, including parastatals, public cooperatives, and agricultural extension and forestry services. In 1993, there were sizable cuts in the salaries and benefits of public servants. Taken with the increased cost of living following the devaluation of 1994, these cuts drastically reduced living standards in the public service. Many public servants have taken up farming to supplement their incomes.

  In rural areas, many of the redundant village extension workers added to environmental risks by encroaching on marginal land or hunting or cutting trees in forest reserves.

- Implementation of the new Forestry Code. The code only recently (1994) came into effect, in a watered-down form. Its aim is to improve incentives for concessionaires to manage Cameroon's tropical forests sustainably. The government is under some pressure to restore the code to the form in which it was presented to the Assembly before it was modified.

  The main issues in dispute are transparency, accountability, and the scale and length of concessions. It is desirable that the terms of concessions should be clearly set out so that companies can bid knowing what is expected of them and their performance can be monitored against clear criteria. In the original draft of the code, concessions were to be for areas of at least 500,000 hectares for a minimum of 25 years. This condition was considered an incentive for concessionaires to use their areas sustainably. The Assembly reduced the limits to 200,000 hectares and 12 years. The code also contains a proposal to create an Office National du Bois to act as a parastatal for selling logs.

  The structure of forestry taxation has several purposes. The area tax is aimed at making concessionaires use all their areas. The stumpage tax varies according to species, size, etc. The export tax is intended to be an incentive to domestic processing. Theoretically, any remaining natural "rent" will be captured in the fee during the bidding process.

- Curtailment of the Forestry Service. The decline in the general effectiveness of the Forestry Service is not wholly attributable to adjustment, but the recent cuts in government spending have aggravated the Service's operational problems. The case studies show that little of the revenue due from logging concessions is being collected, and logging practices are not being properly monitored. Hence the "rent" from forests is not being collected by government, and this failure, together with the absence of controls on logging practices, increases the incentive for unsustainable rates of extraction.

- An increase in the official price of commercial fuel (a substitute for fuelwood). The purpose of this measure was to reduce the public subsidy on commercial fuel and increase incentives for fuel economy. However, from the environmental point of view, an unfortunate side effect has been to increase incentives for the use of fuelwood for heating and cooking, leading to increased deforestation.

- A reduction in public spending on health and education. This resulted from the overall fiscal stringency and the failure to implement special programs to protect these key social sectors. Evidence from rural areas shows that the standard of service in both health and education has declined. The longer-term effect of declining health on the environment is difficult to predict without more field work. Declining educational standards—especially when associated with reduced rewards for educational attainment—leave parents with an incentive to remove their children from school to help with farm and household duties. In effect, the opportunity cost of labor is reduced, and other things being equal, it spurs labor-intensive methods.

The growing attention to environmental education in schools (e.g., on the perils of soil erosion) is also likely to have suffered a setback.

Four Case Studies

Examination of the impacts of adjustment from a national or top-down viewpoint was complemented by a review of the circumstances of four regions of Cameroon that represent different socioeconomic and geographical conditions.

Farming Systems and Society in North-West Province

The province has a population of 1.2 million, with an economy devoted mainly to small farming in humid, fertile, hilly conditions. Coffee is widely grown for export. A range of food crops is grown partly for subsistence but increasingly for sale. Livestock are raised and the forests are used for various purposes.

The case study concentrates on the Kilum Massif, the second highest mountain in West Africa, and one of the most densely populated areas of Cameroon. The mountain is now a protected area, with a population of 100,000 and a forest area supporting much biodiversity and a number of rare and threatened species. The natural environment is retreating in the face of encroachment by small farmers, bush fires, illegal felling of trees for firewood, and heavy grazing and browsing by goats and sheep.

In the past few decades, the population of the entire region has increased owing to improved transport links with the rest of the country and the improved market access they have brought. However, cultivation methods have changed little, and no real progress has been made toward the use of intensive methods instead of continuing expansion of the farmed area through shifting cultivation. The typical farm is worked by the family, mainly using hand tools and little fertilizer. Men clear the land for food and cash crops such as coffee, Irish potatoes, beans, maize, and oil palm. Women till, weed, harvest, gather fuelwood, and collect water, in addition to childcare and household duties. The fallow period has gradually been shortened in the face of population pressure, to the point at which it is threatening future yields.

Structural adjustment has had various impacts, mostly negative from the social and environmental viewpoints. Reductions in the local price of coffee caused neglect of coffee plantations and a shift of land use into food crops. Much of the newly farmed area was on erodible slopes.

As part of adjustment, reforms were made in the coffee marketing system, beginning with the arabica grade, with the aim of making pricing more transparent and linking the farm gate price explicitly to world market levels. This reform, added to the effects of the January 1994 devaluation and the sharp increases in world prices early in 1994, is renewing interest in coffee production. Meanwhile, other aspects of adjustment have tended to weaken farm support services, such as extension, credit, seeds, and other agricultural development activities of projects like MIDENO. In this respect, adjustment runs counter to the clear need to encourage the intensification of farming using sustainable agronomic packages and techniques.

The increasing impoverishment of the rural population, together with the decline in government social spending, has lowered the quality of both education and health care, and there are signs of reduced school attendance and more recourse to traditional medicine. The shift in the relative attractiveness of coffee and food crops has led to some changes in the customary division of responsibilities between men and women, with men taking more interest in profitable food crops, and more recently, women taking up coffee planting in response to the 1994 prices.

Farming in the Far North

The Far North region is located in the narrow strip of land that extends to Lake Chad in the Sudano-Sahelian transition zone. This semiarid area is made up of 7 percent of the country's land area but contains 17 percent of the population. Thus the population density is 2.5 times the national average.

This is one of the poorest regions of Cameroon. Ninety percent of the population is rural. More than one-half the population is illiterate and only 3 percent has any education beyond primary school. Ninety percent of the water comes from wells. The region has suffered recurrent cholera and meningitis, and infant mortality is higher than the national average.

Agriculture dominates the regional economy. Subsistence crops include sorghum, millet, maize, groundnuts, and niebe, some of which are also traded. Cotton, the leading cash crop, is sold to the parastatal National Cotton Development Authority (SODECOTON). Onions are also produced under irrigation. The region contains 35 percent of the national livestock herd. Animals are an integral part of most farming operations, but there are also pastoralists who migrate over large distances with their herds. Livestock are regarded as a store of wealth and a mark of status.

Certain environmental stresses are evident. The high and growing pressure of population on a fragile land resource limits fallowing and threatens soil erosion and loss of fertility. Competition for land between a growing sedentary farm population and the pastoralists has similar effects, in addition to localized overgrazing. The region contains important national parks (e.g., Waza) and protected areas that are suffering encroachment, and relations between wildlife and the human population are becoming problematic. Elephants from Waza are apt to roam into adjacent areas, seriously damaging farms and households.

Farming techniques are generally primitive, with the exception of those used by some cotton and onion farmers. Little use is made of fertilizers or pesticides except on cotton. Although cotton plants are rotated and are fertilized and strict measures are taken to avoid disease, the fields are completely cleared of trees and all residues burned. The sustainability of cotton in the overall farming economy can be questioned.

The monopsony position of SODECOTON buffered cotton farmers from the fluctuations in world prices and the deflationary squeeze on tradeable goods before 1994. Even after the purchase price was reduced in 1988, this crop was still relatively profitable, with a secure market outlet and ensured supplies of inputs and advice. However, the fall in price did lead to some shift of resources into other crops. Given the conditions in which these are grown and the background of growing rural impoverishment and scaled-down government support services, this shift carried environmental risks. They should be weighed against the sustainability of cotton production, which is itself debateable. On balance, adjustment did nothing to hasten agricultural sustainability in this region and probably set it back.

In a separate study of fuelwood, it was found that wood accounts for 90 percent of energy use in the region, and 95 percent of all wood used is for fuel.[2] The apparent deficit between consumption and local production is growing, suggesting imports from other regions. Further, the average distance traveled to collect wood is large and is growing. The institutions for the collective management of forests are weakening under the strain of population pressure and impoverishment. Inevitably, there is serious encroachment on local forests and wildlife habitat.

Cocoa Producers in East Province

East Province is large (109,000 square kilometers) and is relatively lightly populated (about 0.5 million). Three-quarters of the area is covered with dense semideciduous forest. Almost one-half the land area is unpopulated. This province contains the Dja Wildlife Reserve; other areas may soon be protected with the support of the Global Environment Facility (GEF).

Cocoa is the main cash crop, produced mainly on smallholdings using family labor. During the 1980s, the crop was promoted by various rural development funds, infrastructure development, cooperatives, and credit programs. However, since 1988, support has dwindled to the point at which plantations are neglected and output has fallen sharply.

Food crops are grown for subsistence, mainly by women, on the same farms as cocoa. The low population density adds to the government's problems in providing health and education services. The supply of government officers and services is thin, and there is evidence that school attendance has been falling recently and that the population's health is poor and health services deteriorating.

The province's main environmental problems are deforestation, the degradation of dense primary forest into secondary and tertiary growth, the loss of valuable timber species owing to selective logging, encroachment on protected areas, and the threats to certain wildlife species (e.g., gorillas, chimpanzees, elephants).

Adjustment has affected cocoa producers in various ways, mostly negative so far. The purchase price of the crop fell sharply in 1988, leading to widespread neglect and even abandonment of cocoa farms as producers turned to food crops, hunting, and fishing. The sale of government vehicles deprived farmers of visits by extension officers and other agents. Rural credit systems collapsed along with vital rural development projects. Agrochemicals necessary for phytosanitary control are more costly and inaccessible, leading to deterioration of plantations. Merchants buying the cocoa have taken advantage of the growers' disorganization by striking hard bargains.

Resources have shifted from cocoa to food crops, hunting, and forest exploitation. Forests have been cleared for food crops. Hunting has increased in forest areas. The number of licensees for forest exploitation has risen, as has recorded sector output. The reduction in civil service hiring, plus staff reductions in rural projects, credit agencies, and the extension service, has led many people, especially the young, to live directly off the land by hunting as well as by clearing land for farming. These new farmers have little in the way of support services.

By the end of the cocoa season in August 1994, there was little sign of any change in either production or exports compared to the 1992-93 season. Any effects of devaluation, together with the liberalization of markets, are likely to be felt from now on, but the market is likely to remain disorganized for awhile.

Forestry in South Province
Cameroon's forests are among the richest and most varied in Africa. They comprise 17.5 million hectares of humid tropical forest, much of it in

South Province. Apart from their substantial value to the forest dwellers, about 30,000 people owe their livelihoods directly or indirectly to the forest, and wood and wood products account for about 7 percent of the country's exports. Unlike agriculture, industry, and mining, value added in the forestry sector held up well during the recent traumas of adjustment. It did so partly because its profitability was sustained and its attractiveness relative to other economic activities increased, as shown in the increased number of small licenses awarded.

Deforestation is going on apace, at an estimated rate of 100,000 hectares annually. This results from the interaction of selective logging and primitive small-farming techniques. Commercial loggers rarely extract more than two or three of the more highly valued trees per hectare, but in the process they cause widespread destruction to other vegetation. Further, their roads and trails into the forest allow the penetration of small farmers, who complete the degradation with their slash-and-burn methods.

Following the formulation of a Tropical Forestry Action Plan in 1988, certain of its key elements were incorporated into the SAP when it was adopted in 1989. The basic principle is sustainable management of the forest, taking account of the interests of the various stakeholders. The Permanent Forestry Estates will be developed as working forests, with the logging concessionaires becoming responsible for their sustainable management. On the other hand, the National Forestry Estates would be developed principally with the interests of the local populations in mind. The key principles were incorporated in a new Forestry Code, which was debated by the National Assembly in 1993 but which emerged seriously compromised.

Although the government is nominally a joint partner in logging concessions, in practice it has obtained little of the economic rent from timber exploitation. The element of the current forestry tax that varies according to the volume of trees felled has been stymied by the failure of the Forestry Directorate's computer; for the past 3 years, concessionaires have calculated their own taxes.

Officials in the Forestry Service lack their own vehicles and depend on the concessionaires they are monitoring for transport to forest areas. In addition, there is widespread corruption both in the Forestry Service and among politicians involved in the award of concessions. For these reasons, the public share of forest exploitation is small, a mere 800 million CFA francs (US$1.6 million) for the whole South Province, the main logging area.

Conclusions

Until 1994, the absence of exchange rate adjustments led to a severe squeeze on the farming sector, which penalized the production of tree crops such as coffee and cocoa. This in turn led to the neglect of plantations and a switch of land and other resources to the production of annual food crops. On balance, the environmental impacts of this process were probably negative.

The eventual incentive effect of devaluation, followed soon after by sharp increases in the world prices of coffee, was weakened by the disorganization of marketing systems, the collapse of rural credit, and a weakening of all rural support services, particularly extension. The use of agrochemicals and other tradeable inputs in agriculture was also discouraged by the ending of subsidies and the devaluation. Some of these effects preceded adjustment and some were inevitable, but the design of the SAP made them worse. These internal contradictions of the SAP have hampered the reflux of resources into export tree crops and reduced the potential environmental benefits that might have occurred.

General deflation prior to 1994 and the specific measures to reduce government spending programs and reform parastatals caused widespread impoverishment. Many people took up farming, and unemployed youths returned to the countryside to hunt and trap. Their inexperience, plus the weakening of farm support services, led to the adoption of unsustainable and degrading farm practices.

The SAP continued the bias of incentives toward extensive rather than intensive farm cultivation. The use of new land was effectively free, apart from the cost of clearance, and the more intensive use of existing land was penalized by the increased costs of inputs, the shortage of credit, and the scaling down of extension advisory services. Hence the cultivated area continued to expand onto marginal and potentially erodible land. Where uncultivated land was scarce, as in the North, farmers tried to intensify production, but they were without sufficient means to do so. The result was a tendency to degrade the land.

An important element of the SAP was the formation of a new forestry policy and Forestry Code aimed at fostering the sustainable exploitation and management of forests. The eventual shape of the code is still being debated within government, but when it is in place and is effectively monitored, it will have major benefits for Cameroon's forests. Meanwhile, the degradation of forests has worsened under adjustment. Cutting trees has become more profitable than activities related to other exports, whose selling prices were reduced. The collection of concession revenues and policing of logging practices have practically stopped because the Forest Service has been seriously weakened. The exploitation of forests may have become even worse as concessionaires anticipated the imminent enaction of the Forestry Code.

The social repercussions of adjustment were intended to be offset by various actions to be undertaken by the World Bank and other donor agencies. In practice, the weakness and inefficacy of adjustment alienated some donors, and many complementary programs failed to materialize. The conclusion to be drawn is that social and environmental programs intended to offset adjustment measures should be contained within the initial design of the SAP and not left to separate or subsequent programs. Otherwise, the growth of poverty, the continued decline in health status and literacy in rural areas, and the withdrawal of resources from environmental awareness programs are likely to aggravate environmental abuse.

Interpreting adjustment-environment links requires an understanding of the crucial role of women as cultivators, especially of food crops, and as gatherers of fuelwood. There is evidence that extension and other farmer support services are neither oriented toward women nor sympathetic to their needs. Moreover, legal and customary practices deprive women of secure rights over land use except through their male relatives. These factors militate against the more intensive and productive use of land. Marginalizing women worsens the potential environmental harm from adjustment.

SUSTAINABLE DEVELOPMENT

Development Scenarios

All the evidence indicates that Cameroon has well-diversified resources with major potential. This statement applies to its natural resources, climate and hydrological assets, fauna and flora, soil fertility, mineral reserves (e.g., offshore petroleum, natural gas at Kribi, bauxite at Minim Martap, iron ore at Sangmelima), etc. It has relatively good infrastructure and communications and plentiful high-quality human resources.

Unfortunately, all these resources, without being fundamentally wasted, seem never to have been developed efficiently, even during the prosperous years (1960-85), when economic performance was less spectacular than that of some other countries that are not so well endowed. The situation became acute with the advent of the difficulties in 1985-87.

Appropriate adjustment measures have been taken, but they have been too few and too late. The result is a long and far-reaching recession and a situation that is continually deteriorating: all the key indicators are in a bad state, from the chronic state budget deficit and the worrying instability of the cumbersome and inefficient public sector to the neglected capital, the diminishing production capacity, and the impoverishment that is damaging the education and health sectors.

The recent devaluation of the CFA franc has opened up the possibility of new initiatives, but efforts to control the inflation recorded in the first months have been compromised by the speculative price increases of August-September on essential products such as salt, sugar, and palm oil.

For the foreseeable future, much depends on the political will of Cameroon's authorities to implement a series of complex reforms in the face of stiff resistance from powerful interest groups. The leadership needs to be resolute in resisting the temptation to postpone the reforms or to change course.

Particular attention must be paid to management of the reform program, and the functions of coordination, administration, and monitoring must be a continual priority. Then and only then can the credibility of the initiatives to be taken stimulate the private sector to make the necessary investments for the definitive reversal of the negative trends observed today. It is the private sector, both domestic and foreign, on which the hopes of growth are pinned.

Important uncertainties remain in both the economic and political domains while democratization proceeds. This circumstance makes projections and scenario building unusually problematic. Another difficulty arises from the reliability of the data used. Even when statistical data are available, they may be unreliable or biased.

One set of projections examined are those of the World Bank's country economic model. These forecasts are based on a 3 percent growth of nearly all the variables and do not take into account any expected changes in the structure of the economy. They also assume the successful implementation of current adjustment policies.

It is imperative that the restructuring of the Cameroonian economy be pursued to redress the deficit in the balance of payments, reduce inflation, and revive growth. There is no sustainable scenario that excludes economic stabilization and adjustment.

Requisites for Sustainable Development

Agriculture and forestry are the two sectors on which this study focuses. Because of the importance of agriculture for income, employment, public revenue and exports, the sector bears a heavy responsibility for the sustainable development of the whole economy. The agricultural growth rate should therefore be somewhat greater than the population growth rate. Because of impending limits on cultivable area and the pressure of population, cultivation methods should become more intensive, and agronomic packages, farming techniques, and land conservation and enhancement should all be more widely adopted. To this end, research, dissemination, and extension efforts should be doubled. Systems of rural credit need to be reestablished or improved. The recent damage to farm support services, the victims of adjustment measures, needs to be reversed.

The law governing land tenure and property rights needs to be reassessed and procedures simplified. At present, most cultivators are subject to traditional laws and customs that underpin traditional land uses. Modern formal legislation exists that is intended to cater to migrants, acquisition of land by "outsiders," purchase of land for public purposes, etc. The application of this legislation in areas governed by traditional systems is a source of confusion, uncertainty, and—frequently—abuse. In addition, the procedure for registering formal title is prohibitively costly and time-consuming. An important objective should therefore be to clarify the respective spheres of application of modern and traditional law and to simplify procedures.

In forestry, the government's announced policy is prohibition of the export of unprocessed wood, to begin soon. The aim is to stimulate domestic timber processing and add more value to the raw timber. Implementing this policy would forfeit fiscal revenues for the government in the short to medium terms. Both export and domestic markets for the new processed products would need to be developed and a radically new type of investor attracted. The industry would need to turn its attention to new types of wood, presently overlooked in favor of high-value species.

The need for managing the forest estate in a sustainable fashion would become more urgent in view of the likely requirements of the domestic processing industry. Experience elsewhere warns of the waste and inefficiency likely if a domestic wood processing industry is allowed to grow in an overindulgent regime.

Implications for Adjustment and Development Program Design

The following actions are recommended to complement measures at the sectoral levels:

- preparation of a land use plan (including urbanization plans) and creation of regulations and structures for the effective implementation of these plans;
- enactment of comprehensive environmental laws and creation of conditions for their effective implementation;
- completion and effective implementation of a National Environmental Action Plan and improved interministerial coordination on environmental matters; and
- clarification and simplification of legislation relating to property to give the rural population sufficient security to encourage investment in farm improvements, tree planting, and adoption of more intensive agricultural practices and to encourage development of a market in land.

Recommendations on the design of future structural adjustment programs are:

- explicit incorporation of environmental aims and indicators in SAPs;
- reform of forest legislation (including wildlife laws), preferably the restoration of the terms of the original Forestry Code;
- promotion of mutual rural credit funds, offering loans on appropriate (short, medium, and long) terms, with guarantees from all or groups of members;
- protection of recurrent budgets of the Forest Service, park guards, and agricultural extension and other key farmer-support services by earmarking revenues, making budgetary guarantees, or implementing sectoral programs or projects closely synchronized with the SAP;

- when the national fiscal position allows, subsidization of the use of commercial substitutes for fuelwood and of fertilizer, in both cases justifying the subsidy by the presence of external benefits (or avoidance of external costs) from the greater use of these products;
- development of social and environmental programs intended to offset certain negative impacts of adjustment, ideally within the original SAP rather than left to separate or subsequent programs, but if not possible, then closely synchronized with the SAP;
- adjustment programs containing a balance of measures, including action on the exchange rate if necessary to improve SAP chances of success and to avoid disproportionate hardship on particular groups such as farmers, with consequences for the environment; and
- exercise of great care in the sequencing and balancing of SAP components to avoid internal contradictions, for example, gradual reforms in marketing arrangements, credit agencies, and systems for supplying farm inputs without causing a damaging decline in the level of services.

Prospects for Adoption of Sustainable Development Policies

The government and international agencies have to recognize certain constraints in implementing the above reform agenda.

The government has the political task of elevating environmental issues to their rightful place amid the many other pressing political, social, and economic problems to be addressed. The people need to be persuaded of the importance of seemingly remote and exotic issues, such as the conservation of forests and wildlife, even though many are oppressed by jobs, growing poverty, declining public services, and other bread and butter issues.

Politicians will be reluctant to forfeit a source of patronage, such as might happen if forestry policies became more transparent. The prospects for new subsidies or environmental programs are bleak until the budget deficit is eliminated (this point is relevant to the strong environmental case for subsidies on commercial cooking and heating fuels and on fertilizer). Improving the level of policing forests and other protected areas in the face of local encroachment would also be unpopular and difficult. In any case, some of the relevant public services (e.g., forestry, wildlife, extension) are seriously demoralized.

Nor should the political and constitutional obstacles to environmental policy be underrated. New legislation would have to be passed by the recently elected Assembly, which has shown in its treatment of the Forestry Code that it relishes its new independence. Moreover, several reforms discussed here would entail the devolution of powers or the transfer of responsibility to local communities, with constitutional and political implications. The empowerment of NGOs, also desirable in many cases, would be a further forfeit of power by central government.

For their part, international agencies have to face difficult and delicate decisions. They need to persuade the government to adopt an environmental agenda without subverting or further complicating the urgent task of economic reform, which is the precondition of sustainability. They have to attract local support for environmental programs with global as well as local significance. This endeavor, to which the GEF is applying itself, means capturing tangible benefits for locals. The international agencies need to be generous in their offer of local rather than offshore costs and of finance for recurrent as well as capital items. They need to be ready to work with NGOs and to be flexible in their cooperative efforts.

ENDNOTES

1. This planning exercise is an ongoing project of Canadian assistance to inventory all the forests of Cameroon (ONADEF/ACDI Inventory of the Forest Resources of Cameroon).
2. Bonifica Consultants, *Schema d'Amenagement de la Zone Soudano-Sahelienne: Bilan Diagnostique* (Milan: Bonifica Consultants, 1990).

4

CASE STUDY FOR MALI

This chapter is based on a study conducted by the Institut d'Economie Rurale. The study was coordinated by Alpha S. Maiga and carried out by Bino Teme, Bakary S. Coulibaly, Lassiné Diarra, Alpha O. Kergna, and Kalilou Tigana, with support of James Winpenny of the Overseas Development Institute. This summary was written by James Winpenny.

This study's purpose is to document and analyze recent changes in Mali's natural environment, consider the causes and the role of structural adjustment in the observed effects, and make recommendations on how policies should be reformed if sustainable development is to be achieved. The analysis conducted from a macro perspective is complemented by a review of the issues at the grass-roots level in three different but important regions.

Mali is one of the world's poorest countries. Its population of about 8.7 million is growing at a rate of about 2.7 percent annually, and current income per capita, after the recent devaluation, is only US$200. According to the 1987 census, 80 percent of the population is rural.

Mali covers an area of 1,240,000 square kilometers and lies between 1 and 25 degrees north latitude and 3 and 12 degrees west longitude. The northerly three-quarters of the land falls in the Saharan and Sahelian zones, with less than 600 millimeters of rainfall. Thirty percent of the land is desert and a further 21 percent is Sahelian. The southern part is in the Sudano-Sahelian, Sudanian, and Sudano-Guinean zones, with a semihumid climate and a dry season from November to May. The extreme South, representing 6 percent of the territory, includes some dense forest. Altogether, about one-quarter of the total area is arable.

Environmental problems impinge on the livelihoods of the majority of the population, in particular, desertification, increasing aridity, overgrazing

Figure 4.1 Mali

From *Picture Atlas of the World* CD-ROM, © National Geographic Society, 1995

in many areas, soil erosion and depletion, unsustainable intensive farming, and devegetation. Although the population is small in relation to the land area, the quality of land is generally poor, and there are many obstacles, not least climate and poverty, to developing a more productive and sustainable agriculture.

Agriculture is the mainstay of the economy, providing one-half GDP, a livelihood for over 80 percent of the population, and three-quarters of export revenues from cotton and livestock. Millet, rice, and other coarse cereals are widely grown, and many farmers and householders keep livestock. Compared to agriculture, other sectors are minor. Some agroprocessing and light industry cater to the modest domestic market, and some gold is mined. Adventurous tourists visit the historic Saharan trading cities, but the country is not prepared for major tourist traffic.

Mali's social indicators are discouraging. Apart from its extreme poverty, society is largely illiterate (83 percent), with a primary education enrollment rate of only 23 percent (17 percent for girls). The crude death rate (18.7 per 1,000) and infant mortality rate (166 per 1,000) are high, and basic health services are limited in their coverage.

Serious adjustment efforts began in 1988 following earlier half-hearted episodes. Apart from restoring macroeconomic balance in the fiscal and monetary areas, the program aimed at rebalancing government spending (capping payroll costs, favoring social sectors, directing more toward operations and maintenance), reforming parastatals (including privatization and restructuring), and improving private incentives across the board. The cotton sector was specifically targeted for reform and the cereals market was liberalized. Measures were also taken to improve the efficiency of education and public health services.

Economic performance has shown some improvement. In the 1980s, year-to-year fluctuations in GDP were large owing to climatic changes, events in neighboring countries, and changes in international terms of trade. Average growth in the first half of the 1980s was about 2 percent. By comparison, growth in 1988-92 was 3 percent, not enough to reverse the net decline in income per capita witnessed in the 1980s.

The overall fiscal deficit has been reduced slightly, but it is still 9.5 percent of GDP (1993). This situation lies at the heart of the country's macroeconomic problems. One reason for the disappointing progress of adjustment is that the exchange rate of the CFA franc remained unaltered until the devaluation of January 1994, and in the meantime, the real exchange rate became seriously overvalued.

Beginning in 1991, the political system in Mali moved toward a multiparty democracy, which was established in June 1992. Reaction to the repression of the past has been vigorous, and in asserting their new democratic freedoms and rights, the people have made it difficult for the new government to take the necessary strong actions to continue reforms and control the economy.

THE ENVIRONMENT

Salient Features

Mali is traversed by the River Niger, the interior delta of which is an important wildlife habitat and agropastoral resource. A large part of the River Senegal also flows through Mali. With the exception of the area covered by the Office du Niger (ON), the resources of these two major rivers are generally underutilized.

According to a 1982 census, about 40 percent of the total land area was occupied. Five percent was being cultivated, 8 percent was under fallow, 4 percent was classified forest, and the remainder (about one-quarter of the whole) was used as rangeland and pasture. Mali's predominantly rural population is heavily at the mercy of its climate. Over the last 40 years, there is evidence of increasing aridity, although whether this is part of a long climatic cycle or a permanent shift connected with global warming is disputed.

Major Environmental Problems and Their Causes

The increased desiccation over the last few decades, aggravated by shorter, more intense droughts such as those of the early 1980s, has increased pressures on rangeland. Herders in search of better pasture have migrated south in recent years, where they have added to the competition for land and grazing. One of the paradoxical consequences is the lessened interaction between animals and farmers on particular pieces of land: because animals are taken off fields before cultivation begins, their dung is not available, thus reducing the long-term capacity of the soil.

The traditional agricultural system depends on shifting cultivation with long fallow periods. This practice is being strained because of growth in the rural population and pressures to reduce the fallow period. More and more land is coming under permanent cultivation, and commercial cropping is extending into distinctly marginal areas. The exhaustion of soil fertility, the degradation of land, and soil erosion are increasing problems. One estimate is that soil erosion causes annual losses equal to 4-16 percent of agricultural GDP.

The Institut d'Economie Rurale (IER) and the Dutch Royal Tropical Institute have estimated that over one-half the land area in the southern zone of Mali is at or over the limits of its carrying capacity with present techniques. The level of exploitation in 7 of the 13 administrative districts (*cercles*) is considered high or excessive. The southern zone supports a disproportionate share of the country's population and agriculture, including all its cotton cultivation.

In the irrigated areas under ON control, sustainability is threatened by increasing salinization and waterlogging. The underground water table is near the surface in many parts. Neglect of drainage works is the principal cause, coupled with profligate water management. In addition, the incidence of water-related diseases such as bilharzia is increasing in areas of irrigated farming.

Mali depends on fuelwood for 90 percent of its energy needs; yet its forests are being depleted without being renewed. In the Bamako district, annual consumption is about 1.5 million cubic meters, none of which is produced locally. In the southern zone, the situation is much easier, with consumption representing only about 40 percent of annual growth. However, the national fuelwood deficit is one of the main causes of forest loss, estimated at 300,000 hectares annually. Other factors are the extension of the cultivated area (both permanent and in shifting cultivation) and the spread of uncontrolled bush fires.

Major hydraulic works interfere with wetland regimes, many of which are important wildlife habitats.

Environmental Impacts of Past Development Policies

Two particular features of past development strategies have left their mark on Mali's environment. The first is the development of the country's water resources to increase its agricultural potential and make farming less vulnerable to climatic changes. Rivers were dammed and irrigation networks created, particularly in the rice-producing zone of the ON. These hydraulic works have seriously modified local landscapes. Although the benefits to local rice farmers should not be overlooked, on the debit side, these works altered the water regime for downstream users (e.g., farmers and herders relying on seasonal floods) and disrupted wetland habitats (of concern to both wildlife and human populations). The incidence of water-related diseases has also increased in these areas.

Second, the development of cotton as a cash export crop in the southern region has been a conscious government strategy over the past 30 years. With the guarantee of a secure and generally remunerative market by the parastatal Compagnie Malienne pour le Developpement des Textiles (the Malian Textiles Company, CMDT), plus support with extension, credit, and input services, the area planted to cotton has expanded dramatically. The introduction of animal traction complemented this trend.

Cotton production has substantially increased the cultivated area and markedly reduced the fallow period. One recent official study found that in the northern and central parts of Mali-Sud, virtually all cultivable land was being used.[1] In these areas, the theoretical optimum cycle is 5 years' cultivation followed by 25 years' fallow, whereas the actual fallow period is much less in nearly all areas. Degradation is compounded by the inclination of farmers to invest their profits from cotton in the acquisition of livestock, adding to the pressure on pastures.

Environmental Policies

Mali has no environmental policy in the strict sense, but it has a history of concern about the potential of its land, on which 90 percent of its population depends and which accounts for the largest single portion of national income and most foreign exchange. Agricultural development policies and projects necessarily have a strong environmental aspect when most of the rural population depend for their livelihoods on the condition of their local habitats.

In particular, authorities have long been concerned with food security, drought, and potential desertification. Mali is a member of two regional institutions aimed at combatting drought and desertification, the Institut du Sahel and the Inter-State Committee for Drought Control in the Sahel. At the national level, the top organization is the Ministry of Rural Development and the Environment. Reporting to it are several technical services organized on a sectoral basis, such as the directorates of agriculture, livestock, cooperative action, plant protection, water, and forests. The IER is another such body, responsible for agronomic research.

These hierarchical government services are complemented by a dozen externally funded agencies organized on a regional basis, such as the ON, the Office of the Upper Valley of the Niger, and the Office of Integrated Development of West Mali. The integrated textile conglomerate, Compagnie Malienne pour le Developpement des Textiles (CMDT), may also be regarded as such, though it has some private French equity. At a lower level are the numerous nongovernmental organizations (NGOs) concerned with local poverty relief and rural development.

The overriding objective of government has been improved food security for a dirt-poor population living in an uncertain climate with a meager land resource. Hence the emphasis of development efforts has been to reduce the importance of climatic uncertainty by building hydraulic structures; extending irrigation; increasing agricultural productivity by supplying inputs, credit, and farmer support services; encouraging cash crops (notably cotton) to improve and diversify farm incomes, etc. Over time, the single-minded aim of food security has yielded to a more complex concern for productivity, diversification, and better land management.

The improved management of natural resources was never far from the minds of government, but until recently, it was considered in the context of increasing production. This view is changing with the realization that inattention to environmental factors is threatening the sustainability of important resource systems (e.g., rangelands, forests, lands used for rice and cotton production, the interior delta). Recent research efforts have produced estimates of the national costs of soil erosion and the potential costs of soil nutrient depletion in cotton cultivation. Conflicts over land (and water) in the South between cultivators and pastoralists and over shortening fallow periods will affect future production unless they are resolved. In short, environmental concerns are merging into concerns for production in an economy in which rural development will remain the driving force for the foreseeable future.

There has been a recent movement to devolve powers and responsibilities to local organizations, symbolized by the village associations (AVs). This is part of the process of democratization now under way at the political level. In principle, the devolution of responsibility for such areas as care of local forests, management of irrigation systems, and livestock-arable conflicts should be a positive element in developing environmental policy.

Long-term Environmental Trends

The most serious trend is increasing aridity. Evidence from the past 30-40 years seems to point to reduced average precipitation punctuated by severe drought episodes in each successive decade. The crucial 600 millimeter rainfall shifted significantly southward in this period. Much disputed is whether this is a long-term trend or the downswing of a secular climatic cycle. Equally controversial is human responsibility for the apparent desertification. Whatever the causes, increased aridity has aggravated the degradation of marginal land under cultivation and has forced livestock herders to move south in search of pasture.

If unchecked, the current trend of deforestation, estimated at about 300,000 hectares annually, would lead to the disappearance of forests in 15-20 years. Current agricultural practices have extended the cultivated area to most of the cultivable land in the South, the area of greatest potential and densest population, and shortening fallow periods signal the risk of declining future yields. In other parts of the country, there is also evidence of land degradation and soil erosion.

The Dutch government financed a study of the Fifth Region, a rice-growing area in the south-center of the country, using quantitative programing methods to assess the long-term carrying capacity of the land under current farming practices and crop mix. It concluded that agriculture could not support the expected population increase over the next generation except at reduced levels of income per capita.

THE ECONOMY

Development Strategy

Until the early 1980s, Mali pursued a *dirigiste* development policy in which resources were channeled into the creation of manufacturing and processing industries, often in public ownership, with protection against imports. Foreign trade as well as internal crop marketing were closely controlled and dominated by parastatals. The public sector increased its share in the economy and recurrent costs absorbed a growing slice of the budget.

Over the past 10 years, the government has retreated from this strategy, which imposed unsupportable economic and budgetary costs. As a result, little diversification has occurred in sources of income, employment, and foreign exchange. The economy remains highly vulnerable to climate, international terms of trade, and events across its borders.

As the largest sector, agriculture bore many of the costs of the earlier strategy, both directly (e.g., taxes, adverse internal terms of trade, bias against exports) and indirectly (e.g., neglect, diversion of spending and investment, channeling of resources into other areas). Subsistence farming failed to become an efficient system that can support growing populations. Cotton, rice, and livestock were targeted by development programs, and they have responded, although each has increasing problems of sustainability.

Economic Performance and Structural Adjustment

Over the decade 1980-90, average growth in GDP was 3 percent, slightly above the population growth rate (2.6 percent). The GDP growth rate in the latest period, 1988-93, has been maintained at about 3 percent. However, the averages conceal great annual variations, owing mainly to climatic factors and changes in world commodity prices. Economic performance in the early 1980s was particularly affected by the serious drought from 1982 to 1985. GDP actually contracted in 1983, 1985, and 1991.

The growing structural problems noted above led the government to attempt partial adjustment measures in the early 1980s. In agriculture, some reforms were begun in the cereals market, and more discipline was applied to the management of public finance. The adjustment effort faltered in 1985-87 as a reaction to the severe drought and the fall in the world price of cotton. Talks with the International Monetary Fund and the World Bank resumed in 1987, and a program of adjustment measures was agreed upon in 1988 and 1989.

The objectives of adjustment were the usual ones of restoring greater fiscal and monetary discipline, containing the public sector payroll costs, reforming parastatals, simplifying the tax system, and improving private incentives, especially for export. Adjustment was supported by a series of International Development Association credits, beginning with a sectoral focus (successively, public enterprises, education, and agriculture) and broadening into a full structural adjustment loan in 1991.

In the absence of devaluation before 1994, internal adjustment was pursued to reduce the real exchange rate and improve competitiveness. Domestic marketing and prices are now fully liberalized, and trading has been simplified and freed by the removal of trading monopolies, rationalization and reduction of tariffs, and removal of nontariff barriers.

Up to summer 1994, 29 public enterprises had been restructured, liquidated, or privatized and performance contracts introduced for important entities still remaining in public hands. Under a voluntary departures program, 4,000 or more civil servants have left. The producer price of cotton is now explicitly linked to the world price, and performance contracts have been drawn up between farmers and the parastatal CMDT and the government. The pricing and marketing of cereals have been successfully liberalized. However, little has been accomplished in reforming education.

Economic and Social Impacts of Adjustment

In a comparative international perspective, Mali's adjustment effort is considered weak, by the Global Coalition for Africa, for example.[2] The main reason for this weak performance, until January 1994, was the absence of devaluation, which led to the increasing overvaluation of the CFA franc. This situation led to a squeeze on Mali's tradeable sectors, just the opposite of normal adjustment goals. Agriculture was a principal victim. The competitive position of the main export crop—cotton—was weakened while that of domestic rice was undermined by artificially cheap imports. The internal terms of trade of farmers vis-à-vis urban producers and consumers is likely to have deteriorated for these reasons, though the available evidence is inconclusive.

Although adjustment improved the government's fiscal position, the deficit remained high (9.5 percent of GDP in 1993), thus limiting the government's ability to fulfill its goals in the education and health sectors or to contribute counterpart funding to essential development projects. Specifically, the financial position of agencies in the cotton and rice sectors was weakened by their growing noncompetitiveness, which was related to the exchange rate, and in the case of cotton, by the effort to shield producers from external competition.

Employment in the formal sector fell for three main reasons. Industry was squeezed by artificially cheap imports from neighboring countries. The public service dismissed several thousand staff, and 29 public enterprises were liquidated, restructured, or privatized, with consequent layoffs. As already noted, the tradeable sectors were unable to expand and absorb this unemployed labor. For such reasons as these, there has been practically no diversification of the economy during adjustment.

In social terms, the general level of poverty probably increased during adjustment. Although some increase in hardship may have been unavoidable, the design and implementation of the program have most likely aggravated its extent and duration. Until 1994, the rural sector, on which 90 percent of the population depends, bore the brunt of adjustment. However, the unemployed from the formal and urban sectors added to poverty both in urban areas and among their rural dependents. Since devaluation, the potential for growth in the tradeable sectors has improved, but until these effects work through, a further increase in hardship can be expected among consumers as prices rise. Meanwhile, all social programs, plus actions to compensate vulnerable groups, have suffered from the continuing fiscal crisis.

Environmental Impacts of Adjustment

The following measures appear to have had the greatest potential impacts on the use of Mali's natural resources and environment.

Exchange Rate Policy

The absence of exchange rate adjustment until January 1994 depressed agricultural terms of trade and deprived the sector of resources. In the case of cotton, the leading cash crop and export earner, producers were protected from the decline in the CFA franc-denominated income from this crop by the actions of the CMDT. Hence cotton has remained an attractive crop to farmers, especially because it continues to have a guaranteed market and credit supply, thanks to the CMDT. But rice producers had no such buffer against import prices, and cheap imports seriously reduced the profitability of rice cultivation before 1994.

Devaluation reduced the immediate threat of cheap imports to domestic rice producers and potentially increased resources available for this sector (e.g., for much-needed drainage and rehabilitation of irrigation systems). In cotton, if increased export earnings are passed through to farmers, existing trends—toward unsustainable extensification and intensification—are likely to continue.

Devaluation led to an increase in the export of livestock to neighboring countries, especially Côte d'Ivoire, because franc-zone producers are now more competitive relative to European Union sources. In the short term, this situation has relieved pressure on Mali's pasture. However, it is to be expected that livestock numbers will recover in the course of time and will even increase over the previous level, reflecting their greater profitability.

Liberalization of the Cereals Market

The attempt to allow domestic cereal prices to reflect international levels is largely successful. However, this has coincided with increasing exchange rate overvaluation; hence it had the perverse effect of depressing CFA prices to producers, especially of rice and wheat.

Privatization of Rice Marketing and Input Supply

The ON is being reformed with a view to reducing its losses and making it more streamlined and efficient in its core services to farmers. The range of services offered to rural producers is drastically reduced. Now the office is limited to operating and maintaining the irrigation system up to the edge of farmers' fields and to advising the farmers. Marketing and input supply are left to private merchants.

There are preliminary signs that the distribution of benefits has shifted away from farmers toward merchants in the purchase of rice. The higher cost of imported inputs, and in many cases, their inferior quality will discourage diversification and intensification unless compensated by improved crop prices.

Increased Costs of Farm Credit

In 1994, positive interest rates were charged on some farm credit. In theory, they would discourage the purchase of inputs such as labor, equipment, and fertilizer. They may also induce more short-term decisions regarding production and investment that could discourage conservation. In practice, not all farmers—and certainly not the poorest—previously received credit; hence the change would not affect them directly.

Impacts on Resource Use

From the environmental point of view, the following decisions are important:

- whether to extend the cultivated area (which in Mali's case would normally be onto inferior or marginal land) or to farm existing areas more intensively;
- whether more intensive farming is done in a sustainable manner or in an exploitative way; and
- to what degree pastures, woodlands, wetlands, and other common property resources are used.

Adjustment has affected the following incentives directly:

- the price of crops realized by the farmer;
- the cost of agrochemicals and other inputs; and
- the cost of credit.

Adjustment has also changed the cost and supply of labor, although not in a straightforward way. Because growing urban unemployment is accompanied by net migration from rural to urban areas, the effect on the farm labor balance is ambiguous.

Measuring the impacts of adjustment measures is rendered more difficult by:

- growing poverty in both rural and urban areas;
- the continued lack of clarity over land tenure and property rights and the responsibility to manage communal resources; and
- deterioration in public services, especially health and education, and failure to provide programs to protect vulnerable groups.

Before any conclusions are set forth, the case study material is presented to illustrate how the regions perceived these measures.

Three Case Studies

The grass roots impacts of adjustment were assessed in three detailed case studies of regions representing different farming regimes: the cotton district of Koutiala, the rice-growing area around Niono in the ON zone, and the arable-livestock regime of the Sikasso region.

Cotton Cultivation in Koutiala
The zone under study has an area of 23,000 square kilometers and a population of about 455,000 distributed in 45 villages. Compared with the rest of Mali, this zone is relatively favored with infrastructure, is densely populated, and contains land with good potential. In line with the growth of general prosperity owing to cotton cultivation, agroprocessing enterprises have sprung up.

The CMDT is a joint venture of the Mali government and the French company Compagnie Francaise pour le Developpement des Textiles (CFDT). It is a large vertically integrated company that effectively has a monopoly position in the cotton sector and has diversified into other crops and related agroprocessing. The CMDT is the major buyer of raw cotton; is a source of advice, credit, and inputs; and manufactures textiles and processes cottonseed oil and much else. Over time, it has delegated the provision of farm inputs and other materials, finance, and the collection and payment for cotton to the AVs. Private merchants are now heavily involved in the supply of farming inputs.

As part of structural adjustment, the CMDT was required to focus on its core functions, cotton and textile production, and shed its ancillary enterprises.

In this region, the area of land under cotton rose from 14,000 hectares in 1960 to 63,000 hectares in 1993; its yields rose from 263 to 1,256 kilograms per hectare. However, yields have been on a plateau since the mid-1970s. The profitability of cotton led farmers to increase greatly the area cultivated, extending onto marginal land. There is evidence of farmers' occupying and working land in excess of their real needs in order to forestall its use by others. Almost no fallowing is practiced in this region. Where it exists, the cycle is little more than 1-2 years.

The environmental effects are evident in land degradation and soil erosion owing to overcultivation, insufficient fallow, and the use of marginal land against a backdrop of increasing aridity. Fertilization alone cannot offset the depletion of soil nutrients, and antierosion measures are inadequate. Certain localized problems are caused by the use of inappropriate motorized equipment.

Recent droughts and civil unrest in the North have caused a southerly migration of people and their herds into this zone, and they have added to the competition for land. The attraction of cotton can be explained by the reliability of the market and its relative profitability. Cotton price movements abroad were buffered by the CMDT, in contrast to cereals prices, which were liberalized and are therefore more volatile. Cotton has both a secure market outlet and well-organized marketing, credit, and input supply systems. Yet since 1994, the cost of inputs has increased sharply, and interest-free credit has been abolished.

In a nutshell, the Koutiala region has enjoyed growing prosperity for several decades based on cotton cultivation. But there are serious doubts whether this regime is sustainable. The land shows signs of growing exhaustion and degradation, as cultivable areas are occupied and fallow periods shortened. Yields of cotton have long since ceased to increase.

The CMDT shielded producers from the worst effects of adjustment prior to 1994, and cotton has remained attractive relative to other crops, especially because liberalization has introduced uncertainty into the cereals market. The growing privatization of input supply, the recent devaluation, and the abolition of credit subsidies all raised the costs of production and discouraged wider application of fertilizer.

Rice Production in the Niono Region

This region falls under ON influence. Since the early 1970s, the region has absorbed an increasing number of people and generated growing employment. Thanks largely to the office's efforts, the region has made the transition to intensive rice cultivation through the introduction of double cropping in the 1980s along with other land conservation techniques. With little increase in the cultivated area from 1973 to the present, paddy production has increased from 91,000 to 245,000 tons.

This apparent success conceals growing environmental concerns. Waterlogging and salinization are becoming serious problems. When the Office du Niger was created, groundwater was at a depth of 30-50 meters. Now, as a result of the lack of investment in drainage and the over-application of water, it is 1 meter or less. Surveys in one area near Niono showed that three-quarters of the soils were affected by salinization. Erosion and the corresponding siltation of water courses are leading to the need for substantial rehabilitation work on certain irrigation systems. According to local professional opinion, the continuing rise in average yields may conceal an underlying depletion of soil fertility disguised by the spread of double cropping. A rise in the incidence of water-related diseases (e.g., malaria, bilharzia) has also been reported.

Rice marketing reforms began in 1985-86, but full liberalization had to wait until 1993. The functions of the ON are now limited to hydraulic works, maintenance of structures, management of water, and advisory services. The office was divested of other peripheral activities: the purchase and milling of rice, the sale of rice, new rehabilitation projects, agricultural credit, the supply of farm materials, seed production, transport, livestock, training, etc. In keeping with the move to decentralize official services, irrigation user groups are being encouraged to take over maintenance costs, management, and farmers' land tenure improvement.

Marketing rice, among other functions, is now in the hands of the AVs, and input supply is passing to private merchants. The price of rice has been freely determined since 1985. Although most farmers are content with the reforms, there are transitional problems. Private buyers are sometimes able to exert monopsony powers against farmers at the expense of prices. The entry of private input suppliers has led to some adulteration of fertilizer and pesticides, and the sale of substandard and unreliable material. Input subsidies have been abolished.

In 1992-93, domestic production came under serious threat from massive imports of rice, stimulated by the growing overvaluation of the CFA franc. This situation was partly responsible for the recent financial difficulties of AVs and the resulting sharp fall in credit granted for input supplies.

Livestock and Agriculture in the Sikasso Region

Sikasso is located in a relatively productive farming region in the South, and its population has gained from the migration of farmers and pastoralists from the North. The current population of the study area is about 900,000. It is in the heart of cotton country, and the livestock population has rapidly increased. It has done so partly because herds migrated from farther north and partly because cotton profits were invested in animals, which are becoming part of farming operations. In the entire southern region, the number of cattle increased from about 1.19 million in 1970 to 2.01 million in 1983. Although recent comprehensive data are not available for Sikasso, the number of draught animals in that region increased from 18,500 in 1976 to 73,000 in 1980.

Cattle numbers increased for several reasons. Cattle are a source of prestige and a store of wealth and savings. They are traditional forms of dowry as well as barter. Working animals provide draught, increasingly used in land clearance and preparation and in other farm operations. Manure is important for soil fertilization in a region where the use of chemical fertilizer is seriously suboptimal. The export of cattle on the hoof to neighboring countries is a regular occurrence, which has received a fillip from the 1994 devaluation—exports doubled in the first half of 1994.

Cattle are implicated in the environmental pressures noted earlier: the extension of cultivation onto marginal lands, the degradation of pasture, the compaction of soil, etc. However, the relationship has several aspects. The large increase in cotton acreage was facilitated by the increased number of draught animals. Animals occupy land, both directly for grazing and indirectly for the cultivation of fodder crops (currently only about 2 percent of the total land area is given to cultivation of fodder crops), and thus crowd out other crops and force free-range animals onto marginal land. Viewed purely as providers of meat, milk, and calves, the cattle herd is unproductive, and the pastures of Koutiala and Sikasso are, respectively, overgrazed and near their carrying capacity. On the other hand, draught power and manure are essential to agricultural intensification.

With regard to trends in land use in the Sikasso region since 1980, the area under cotton appears to have expanded steadily, quite separate of what was happening to food crops. From 1982 to 1986, the area under food crops increased dramatically, then fell sharply in 1987. This change is explained mainly by the response of maize producers to the incentives in the Project Maize campaign, which tied maize prices to those of other cereals and guaranteed a market outlet. The liberalization of prices in 1987, as part of the general freeing of the cereals market, caused a sharp reaction amongst producers that also coincided with increased fertilizer prices.

Shifts in the relative importance of different crops, principally cotton and cereals, appear to have increased the total area cultivated rather than using the same land for other crops. The price of fertilizer is an important factor here. Fertilizer became more expensive relative to export crop prices after 1987, and surveys show that most farmers' application of fertilizer is suboptimal. Improved production incentives tend to result in an expansion of the cultivated area.

The conclusions to be drawn about the determinants of cultivation trends in the Sikasso region are similar to those in the neighboring Koutiala region. The output of different crops and land use respond to changes in relative prices, but these changes tend to lead to extensification. The clearest impacts of structural adjustment have been to deflate the maize boom in 1987 (in the liberalization of the cereals market, which was an immediate precursor of formal adjustment) and effectively to cap the price of cotton until 1994. Maize and cotton are, in different ways, environmentally problematic. The supply of farm inputs has been freed, but apparently without reducing the price of fertilizer, whose quality is much more variable. Devaluation has clearly increased the price of all imported inputs, including fertilizer.

Introducing livestock into this equation further complicates the picture. The increase in livestock is partly explained by the increased supply of fodder crops made possible by the greater freedom granted to private merchants to purchase and trade in the agricultural supply sector. Fodder and animals are integral elements of a sustainable mixed farm regime, but in the circumstances of southern Mali, animals and crops are in potential competition for land, and increases in either tend to add pressures on marginal land.

Conclusions on Adjustment-environment Linkages

The following conclusions are summarized in Table 4.1 (references to adjustment are principally to the period before 1994):

- Adjustment did not clearly affect the basic profitability of cotton to the farmer. The CMDT buffered the decreasing competitiveness of Malian production until devaluation came to the rescue. The greater profitability of cotton is likely to have increased incentives to farm new land. The greater availability of animals for land clearance and preparation is another factor.

Table 4.1 Adjustment-environment Linkages

Adjustment Measures	Environmental Impacts
Exchange rate	Predevaluation, squeezed producers, especially rice; postdevaluation boost, especially to cotton, increased pressures to expand area; increased export of livestock, relieving pressure on pasture in the short term
Liberalization of cereals market	Depressed prices, especially of maize
Reform of Office du Niger (rice)	Greater responsibility of farmers for operations and management, including drainage
Abolition of input and credit subsidies	Increased costs of purchased inputs and discouragement of intensification
Liberalization of farm input supply	Encouragement of fodder production, with mixed environmental effects; lower quality of inputs

- Growing rural poverty, a deterioration of the ratio of output to input prices, and recently, the devaluation have reduced the demand for fertilizer and pesticides. However, the use of animal manure, related to the growing number of animals in the cotton zone, has partly helped to maintain soil fertility and crop yields up to now. The CMDT has maintained the supply of credit to its producers.

- For farmers without access to animal manure, the increased cost (and diminished quality) of chemical fertilizer and the abolition of fertilizer subsidies are another factor biasing production decisions toward the extensive mode. The recent abolition of credit subsidies in the rice area also raises the cost of all purchased inputs.

- Underlying the above producer responses is the problem of land tenure. New land can be farmed at little cost other than that of clearance and preparation. In fact, leaving land fallow is discouraged by current official attitudes.

- Where extensive development was not possible (e.g., because of land constraints) the continued profitability of cotton encouraged greater intensity of production. Serious concerns have been expressed about the long-term decline in soil fertility from intensive cotton monoculture. The above-mentioned effects on the price of fertilizer have aggravated this problem.

- The greater freedom allowed to private operators in the farm supply sector has facilitated the growth of fodder production. In the long term, this is highly desirable, but in the short term, it has probably added to the competition for land by permitting more animals.

- Reforms in the rice sector, specifically divesting the ON of many peripheral functions, will increase the responsibility of farmers themselves for the proper management and care of their irrigation systems, which is the first step in solving growing problems of salinization and waterlogging.

- The exchange rate policy has affected rice more than cotton or other crops. Growing overvaluation led to a build-up of imports in the early 1990s, which seriously undercut local producers. This bias deprived the sector of resources that might have been applied to urgent remedial and extension work to the irrigation network and to the acquisition of more fertilizer and other inputs. Devaluation released this import pressure and will allow margins to expand, but by the same token, it has increased the cost of fertilizer.

SUSTAINABLE DEVELOPMENT

Development Scenarios

Mali's future should be considered in the context of trends since 1980. On the economic front, growth has barely kept up with population and has been irregular. Macroeconomic adjustment has been weak, with little progress in tackling the budget deficit. Inflation has not been a major problem, although the inflationary impact of the 1994 devaluation will need to be contained by strong measures. Investment has fallen, the industrial sector has been squeezed, unemployment has risen along with net rural-urban migration, and the informal sector has had to take the strain. The economy is scarcely more diversified now than it was in 1980, or even in 1973, if the growth of the service sector is regarded as a residual.

Some social indicators have improved, although recent economic stagnation, impoverishment, and cuts in spending on key social programs do not bode well for the future. The underlying natural rate of population increase continues and has been disguised only by past net migration. Mortality and food intake have improved. Public spending on health and education has declined. Female education and literacy levels remain deplorable.

With or without adjustment, it is unrealistic to expect major changes in Mali's economic performance and social indicators. The country lacks the natural, human, and economic endowments to make a significant breakthrough in development for the foreseeable future. Meanwhile, it has to solve difficult current problems even to maintain its modest progress, notably the budget, public sector performance, and issues of sustainability in its key agricultural sectors: rice, cotton, livestock, and coarse cereals.

These needs are the justification for assuming little or no structural change on any future scenario. The growth of GDP will hinge mainly on the performance of the agricultural sector, which is subject to evident constraints. To provide a framework for considering policy changes, a target growth rate of 4 percent to the year 2010 is considered; it would enable a 1 percent increase in average income per capita. A second scenario, entailing expansion of the agroprocessing sector, is also considered, but because of the current size of the sector and the constraints under which it operates, expansion is considered complementary to, rather than an alternative to, growth in the primary sectors.

Requisites for Sustainable Development

Experience of land conservation policies in the Sahel shows that recommended practices need to be based on farmers' felt needs, to fit into their production system, and to offer tangible benefits to the parties involved. Responsible participation of the intended beneficiaries is more desirable than the top-down authoritarian tradition favored by some agencies. Practices that have proved successful elsewhere should be tried in different regions. The use of trees and vegetation should be fully integrated into conservation practices. Integrated nonsectoral policies appear to work best.

There is no real prospect of diversification to diminish the importance of cotton. If this crop is to support future growth under the first scenario, its cultivation will need to become more intensive, productive, and sustainable because farming new land is not a long-term option.

Studies of cotton production in the South have exposed the risks of depleting soil nutrients through prolonged monoculture of this demanding crop.[3] In general, farmers do not use sufficient fertilizer to offset the underlying decline in soil nutrients fully, and the application of manure and crop residue is inadequate to maintain soil structure.

In the long term, diversification, better crop rotations, improved soil conservation, and the spread of antierosion techniques to maintain and enhance soil fertility are needed. More and better fertilization is also needed, but so too is a shift toward organic means such as manure, compost, and crop residues. Despite the cogent fiscal objections, there is a case for subsidizing fertilizer as an incentive to increasing its use in intensively farmed and high-potential areas (e.g., Koutiala, Sikasso, Dioila). Property rights should be modified to increase producers' incentives to implement the above measures. Animal husbandry practices need to be better integrated into farming and farming should be intensified.

In the rice-growing areas farther north, there is scope for enlarging the irrigated area, especially through small-scale schemes. Some of the investment could be contributed in kind by local beneficiaries, including women. The need for investment in drainage on existing irrigation schemes is becoming urgent; otherwise, yields will decline. Investment in public health in irrigated areas needs to be restored to combat the growth in water-related diseases. Water bodies in irrigated areas should be more fully exploited for aquaculture. Currently, irrigated rice farmers in the ON region do not enjoy property rights that encourage them to invest in a more sustainable system.

The future for livestock will increasingly be as part of a mixed farming regime in sedentary farming areas. The successful development of fodder crops for stall-fed animals points the way, with animals contributing draught power and manure to intensive mixed systems. In contrast, pastoralists are going to be increasingly squeezed out of the regions of greatest agricultural pressure. Control of both the quantity and quality of livestock will be required, although this will be difficult to achieve.

Mali's forests, although not lacking commercial potential (e.g., for construction), should be viewed mainly as resources available for the benefit of local people. Arresting the present trend of deforestation will require people's willingness to take responsibility for managing and safeguarding their local forests. This step entails the dissemination of information and awareness locally, local involvement in decisions about managing and replacing forests, and the integration of trees into arable and livestock regimes. Afforestation will demand better control of livestock and the substitution of fodder for natural forage.

The protection of fauna and flora from the present degree of exploitation could be achieved partly by extending the national network of wildlife reserves to the southern areas, where none exists at present. It is also desirable to bring hunting under the control of local associations under the aegis of village authorities.

Implications for Adjustment and Development Program Design

The following general and parallel actions are recommended:

- A National Environmental Action Plan should be completed and effectively implemented and interministerial coordination on environmental matters improved.
- Clarification and simplification of legislation relating to property should give the rural population sufficient security both to encourage investment in farm improvements, tree planting, and the adoption of more intensive agricultural practices and to encourage the development of a market in land.
- Full implementation of political decentralization should give greater powers and responsibilities to local authorities, village associations, etc., and the powers and responsibilities for the management of common property resources should be clarified.

The following actions are recommended with specific reference to future adjustment programs:

- Structural adjustment programs (SAPs) should contain a balance of internal and external adjustment measures, including action on the exchange rate if necessary. Otherwise, their success will be jeopardized and the onus of adjustment will fall on particular groups, such as farmers, with potential harm to the environment.
- The timing and complementarity of SAP components should be managed to prevent different elements from interfering with the others' success. Reforms in prices, marketing, credit, input services, etc. should be undertaken consistently to avoid giving conflicting signals to farmers and to maximize incentives to engage in sustainable agricultural development.
- Environmental goals and indicators should be explicitly included in the SAP.
- The recurrent budgets of public services critical to the environment should be protected for the services of agricultural extension, forestry, conservation, and antierosion officers and other key farmer support services. This protection could be effected by earmarking revenues, guaranteeing budgets, or implementing sectoral programs or projects closely coordinated with the SAP.
- In the above context, high priority should be attached to restoring subsidies on the use of commercial substitutes for fuelwood and of fertilizer as soon as the national fiscal position allows.
- SAPs should provide for the continuation or introduction of key social and environmental programs that would otherwise be neglected. Apart from environmental conservation and antierosion and antidesertification programs, basic health and education programs should have the resources to continue. Ideally, funding for these programs should be covered by the original SAP rather than being left to separate or subsequent programs. If this arrangement is impossible, such programs should be closely coordinated with the SAP.

Prospects for Sustainable Development Policies

There are a number of serious constraints on the ability of the government and people of Mali to implement the above reform agenda. One of the most basic tasks is to elevate environmental concerns to their appropriate place in a society that is poor, has serious macroeconomic problems to overcome, and is undergoing a political transition to a democratic and decentralized regime. In the current political climate, small vocal groups find it easy to challenge government authority.

Tackling the budget deficit is a fundamental and urgent precondition to any kind of progress. The dilemma is that in the short term the necessary actions worsen the social and environmental problems noted earlier. This possibility increases the importance of reordering public spending priorities and developing new and environmentally friendly revenue sources (e.g., capture of resource rents, new levies on resource depletion, countervailing export taxes after devaluations).

On the other hand, most Malians live close to nature, environmental problems in their various guises do affect most of them intimately, and they would need little persuasion of the importance of these problems. Further, the movement to decentralize political responsibilities is potentially helpful to local environmental managers.

External donors, agencies, and NGOs can assist in several ways. They should continue their level of support and develop a realistic attitude to the adjustment timetable. They should consider increasing their local cost and recurrent cost support in view of the government's difficulties in meeting its own commitments to projects. Further, sustainability should become their constant criterion in judging what actions to take.

ENDNOTES

1. Institut d'Economie Rurale and Royal Tropical Institute, *Profil d'Environment: Mali-Sud* (Netherlands: Bamako and Royal Tropical Institute, 1993).
2. Global Coalition for Africa, *1993 Annual Report* (Washington, D.C.: Global Coalition for Africa, 1994).
3. F. van der Pol, *Soil Mining: An Unseen Contributor to Farm Income in Southern Mali* (Amsterdam: Royal Tropical Institute, 1992).

5

CASE STUDY FOR TANZANIA

This chapter is based on a study conducted and written by Mboya Bagachwa, Fanuel Shechambo, Hussein Sosovele, Kassim Kulindwa, and Alexis Naho of the Economic Research Bureau of the University of Dar es Salaam, with support of Elizabeth Cromwell of the Overseas Development Institute. This summary was written by Elizabeth Cromwell.

This study attempts to address a question: "Under what conditions will 'sensible' economic policies have unintended social, economic, and environmental consequences?"

The social and environmental impacts of structural adjustment in a given situation are "complex, ill-defined, and difficult to bound."[1] Quantitative measurements can be attempted using modeling exercises, but these are difficult to construct, run, and interpret in the kind of data-constrained situations typical in many African countries. This study therefore uses a conceptual model that allows a mixture of techniques to be used to analyze policy-degradation links, combining general equilibrium modeling, regression analysis, and ground-truthing using published surveys and secondary data.

The conceptual model is designed to identify the most important price and nonprice factors determining the response of producers and consumers to structural adjustment. As set out in Figure 5.1, these factors are categorized by the three key levels of decisionmaking in the policy process that they influence: political economy, policy delivery, and response determinants. For the purpose of analyzing individual environmental problems, the conceptual model can be used in a bottom-up fashion to trace the factors determining a given rate of degradation, as illustrated in later figures.

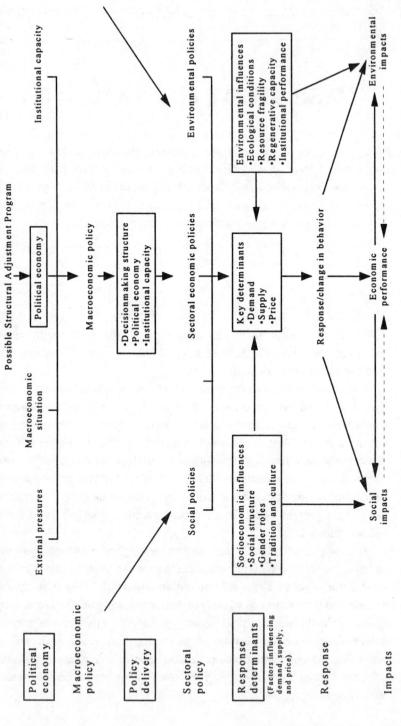

Figure 5.1 Structural Adjustment and Sustainable Development: Framework for Analysis

Possible Structural Adjustment Program

"Political economy" means the decisionmaking process that determines the choice of macroeconomic measures. "Policy delivery" is the process that translates macro policy into sectoral and regional policies and legislation. An important part of this study is the analysis of the filters that distort macroeconomic policies as they are translated into sectoral, regional, and legislative policies.

"Response determinants" are the many factors that determine how micro-level actors will respond to the prescribed sectoral, regional, and legislative policies. These decisions are typically made on the basis of demand, supply, and price factors. In Figure 5.1, the "Key Determinants" box includes those factors that can be considered to determine decisionmaking most directly. A given response is likely to cause a range of economic, social, and environmental impacts, and the strength of the linkages between response and impact will be influenced by broader socioeconomic and environmental influences.

BACKGROUND

State of the Economy and the Environment

Tanzania is a country of contrasts, from the seafaring traders of the coastal strip and island of Zanzibar, to the vast wildlife-studded plains of the Central African Plateau in the interior, to the densely populated agricultural areas around Mount Kilimanjaro in the North and in the Southern Highlands (see Figure 5.2).

Although there are abundant mineral resources of iron ore, coal, and precious metals, they have been little exploited so far. The population is still primarily rural and agricultural, relying on a wide range of crops, including maize, beans, rice, wheat, cassava, coffee, cotton, tea, sisal, tobacco, and cashew nuts for 85 percent of employment and 60 percent of GDP. However, only one-fifth of the country has a secure annual rainfall of more than 750 millimeters, so rain-fed agriculture is precarious. Together with poor soils over much of the plateau, this condition has produced intense population concentrations of up to 200 people per square kilometer in the favorable agricultural areas around Kilimanjaro.

Thus the majority of the country is still covered by sparsely populated grazing lands and woodlands; only 5 percent is cultivated. In addition, Tanzania is renowned for its wildlife, and 25 percent of the country has

Figure 5.2 Tanzania

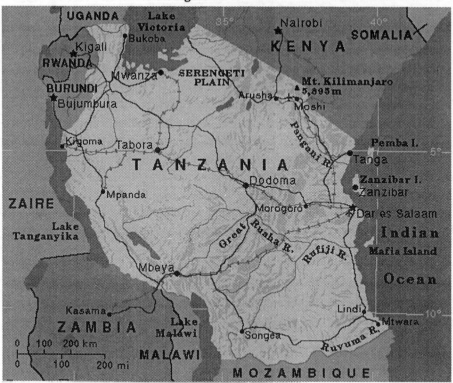

From *Picture Atlas of the World* CD-ROM, © National Geographic Society, 1995

been demarcated as national parks, game reserves, and game controlled areas. Mount Kilimanjaro, Ngorongoro Conservation Area, Selous Game Reserve, and Serengeti National Park have been classified as World Heritage Sites.[2]

In the 1960s and 1970s, Tanzania's socialist government tried to implement radical policies of self-reliance (the famous Arusha Declaration of 1967), including extensive compulsory villagization (*ujamaa*), nationalization, and price controls. This effort produced considerable achievements in the social sector and economic growth of 5 percent per year between 1965 and 1976; however, performance faltered in the late 1970s. This change was partly the result of the world economic downturn, partly the result of regional events (the acrimonious breakup of the East African Community [previously linking Tanzania with Kenya and Uganda], a war with Uganda, and two severe droughts) and, with hindsight, partly the result of the development policies pursued at the time. *Ujamaa* was contentious, and inefficient state transport and marketing caused agriculture to stagnate. Industrial development had been overemphasized at the expense of agriculture, and government intervention in the economy had been excessive.

All this produced a gloomy outlook by the 1980s. Although official inflation was less severe than in some other African countries, much of the economy was operating via the parallel market network, and here the real purchasing power of the minimum wage declined 90 percent during the 1980s. Earlier investment in social infrastructure meant that Tanzania ranked thirty-fourth in the United Nations Development Programme's Human Development Index, but in GDP per capita terms, the country was the second poorest in the world. Sixty percent of the population was living below the poverty line, a high proportion of them in the rural areas.

At the same time, the natural resource base was coming under threat. Probably best known is the loss of wildlife: 290,000 elephants (60 per day) were lost because of poaching and despoliation of habitat during the 1980s. As a result of population concentrations, continuous clearing for agriculture, and a 90 percent dependence on fuelwood, wood resources were also being lost at an alarming rate (25 percent of the forest area between 1980 and 1993). This loss in turn exposed the fragile soils to wind and water erosion, resulting in rates of soil loss of 55 tonnes per hectare per year in the worst affected areas. In addition were localized problems of coastal erosion and pollution from dynamite fishing, sand quarrying, and uncontrolled development plus growing urban pollution. Urban planning had been a low priority during the villagization era, but with urban expansion of about 10 percent per year, problems increased: by the late 1980s, 75 percent of urban households still had no piped water, 12 of Tanzania's 19 major towns still had no sewage systems, and two-thirds of urban refuse remained uncollected.

The growing economic problems resulted in a move toward more market-oriented policies from the early 1980s onward, aided by a change of political leadership in 1985. Further political liberalization took place in June 1992, when the Constitution was amended to allow political parties other than Chama Cha Mapinduzi to operate (CCM has ruled since Independence). Multiparty elections were planned for 1995.

Environmental Policy

The 1970s strategy for ensuring food and export crop production centered on large-scale production-oriented agricultural parastatals. In addition, at the village level, *ujamaa* disrupted established rural resource use practices and accelerated degradation.

With the introduction of structural adjustment in the 1980s, national economic policy now focuses on restoring growth; although it recognizes environmental problems, it does not contain practical measures to deal with them. A result is marked policy conflicts between structural adjustment and sectoral policies. For example, in the forestry sector, maximizing timber exports is promoted on the one hand and sustainable management of the nation's forest resources on the other.

Tanzania has had a National Environmental Management Council (NEMC) since 1983. The NEMC produced a National Conservation Strategy in the mid-1980s based on the World Conservation Strategy; after the 1992 United Nations Conference on Environment and Development, it was modified to become Tanzania's National Conservation Strategy for Sustainable Development. This development continues the historical emphasis on top-down, centralized natural resource management. The policy statement has not yet been ratified. The Ministry of Tourism, Natural Resources and Environment has prepared a National Agenda 21 Framework.

There are many institutions with environmental responsibilities, including the NEMC, 10 ministries, 24 parastatals, and 50 nongovernmental organizations (NGOs); however, most remain centralized in their management, and there is little coordination among them. Environmental legislation has been geared toward control, and enforcement has been poor—with too few staff and resources and fines eroded by inflation. The ambiguity of current land law is a major problem. Private land ownership was abolished at Independence, although individuals' customary usufruct rights continued to be recognized, but with *ujamaa*, much customary land was transferred to collective village ownership. On top of this situation, with the recent economic liberalization, there has been a de facto shift toward commercialization of land (including government auctions of periurban plots), although this has no legal backing as yet.

Structural Adjustment

At first, Tanzania tried its own recovery programs: the National Economic Survival Program in 1981 and the Structural Adjustment Program (SAP) in 1983. However, neither mobilized sufficient external resources. Therefore a donor-sponsored Economic Recovery Program (ERP) was agreed upon in 1986; it continues to the present, with modifications in 1989 (the Economic and Social Action Program, ESAP) to include rehabilitation of physical infrastructure and measures to mitigate the social impacts of adjustment. Tanzania now depends heavily on aid: official development assistance accounts for 75 percent of GDP and external debt equals 285 percent of GDP.

The overall aim of the ERP was to achieve sustainable growth in real income and output. To this end, it attempted to encourage production of food and cash crops through better prices, improved product and input marketing, and an increased government budget for agriculture. It planned to increase industrial capacity utilization by liberalizing raw material imports and to carry out the maintenance of transport infrastructure that had been deferred during the crisis period. The balance of payments deficit was to be reduced by devaluation, export incentive schemes, and foreign exchange liberalization. On the domestic front, the budget deficit was to be brought under control, as was money supply and thus inflation.

According to World Bank figures, prices for agricultural exports such as coffee and cotton increased some 25 percent in real terms between 1990 and 1993. However, in practice, continued inflation negated the nominal increases in food crop agricultural prices, and marketing reform failed to improve producers' margins. Credit continued to be extended to the marketing institutions, confounding efforts to control the money supply. Few of these or any other state enterprises were privatized (although some 15 percent of the civil service was made redundant) because virtually none was a going concern, and in any case, few of Tanzania's existing private sector operators had sufficient capital to purchase those enterprises.

Despite this less than perfect record, agricultural output and exports increased significantly, and between 1983 and 1987, the supply of food crops marketed through official channels increased 100 percent. Industrial imports also increased. And between 1986 and 1992, per capita income increased 6 percent in real terms. Nonetheless, problems with deteriorating infrastructure and poor social services delivery remained.

The ESAP has also had a mixed impact. Industrial capacity utilization and output had increased, although not to match 1976 levels or sufficient for long-run sustainable growth. The value of nontraditional exports increased 24 percent per year between 1986 and 1990, to some US$202 million. In acknowledgment of Tanzania's adjustment efforts, aid has increased significantly.

Yet producer prices for food crops have not improved in real terms, but input prices have increased dramatically (fertilizer prices around 300 percent during 1990-92). The state marketing structure has been largely dismantled, but this change has produced substantial gaps in areas where private traders are unwilling to travel.

Formal sector job creation actually fell from 5 percent per year between 1970 and 1980 to less than 2 percent per year between 1984 and 1992. At the same time, minimum wages fell in real terms, as described earlier. In the social sector, primary school enrollment fell from 100 percent in 1980 to 66 percent in 1987, and the number of people per doctor increased from 17,500 to 26,200.

ADJUSTMENT-ENVIRONMENT LINKAGES: ANALYSIS

This section examines the effects of structural adjustment on Tanzania's two major environmental problems: deforestation and soil erosion. For each problem in turn, what is known about the major trends in degradation is first set out. Then the extent to which structural adjustment seems to have exacerbated these trends and the differential impacts of adjustment on rich and poor are examined.

Deforestation

Some 43 percent of Tanzania's land area is covered by upland and lowland evergreen forests and *miombo* woodland, but about 2 percent of this area is being lost each year. The data for clearly identifying trends over time are lacking, but anecdotal evidence suggests an increase over time. The loss is the result of clearance for small-scale and commercial agriculture; felling for domestic and agricultural fuelwood, charcoal, building poles, and exports; low rates of reafforestation (see Figure 5.3); and a lack of monitoring and implementation capacity.

Figure 5.3 Deforestation in Tanzania: Conceptual Map of Causal Factors

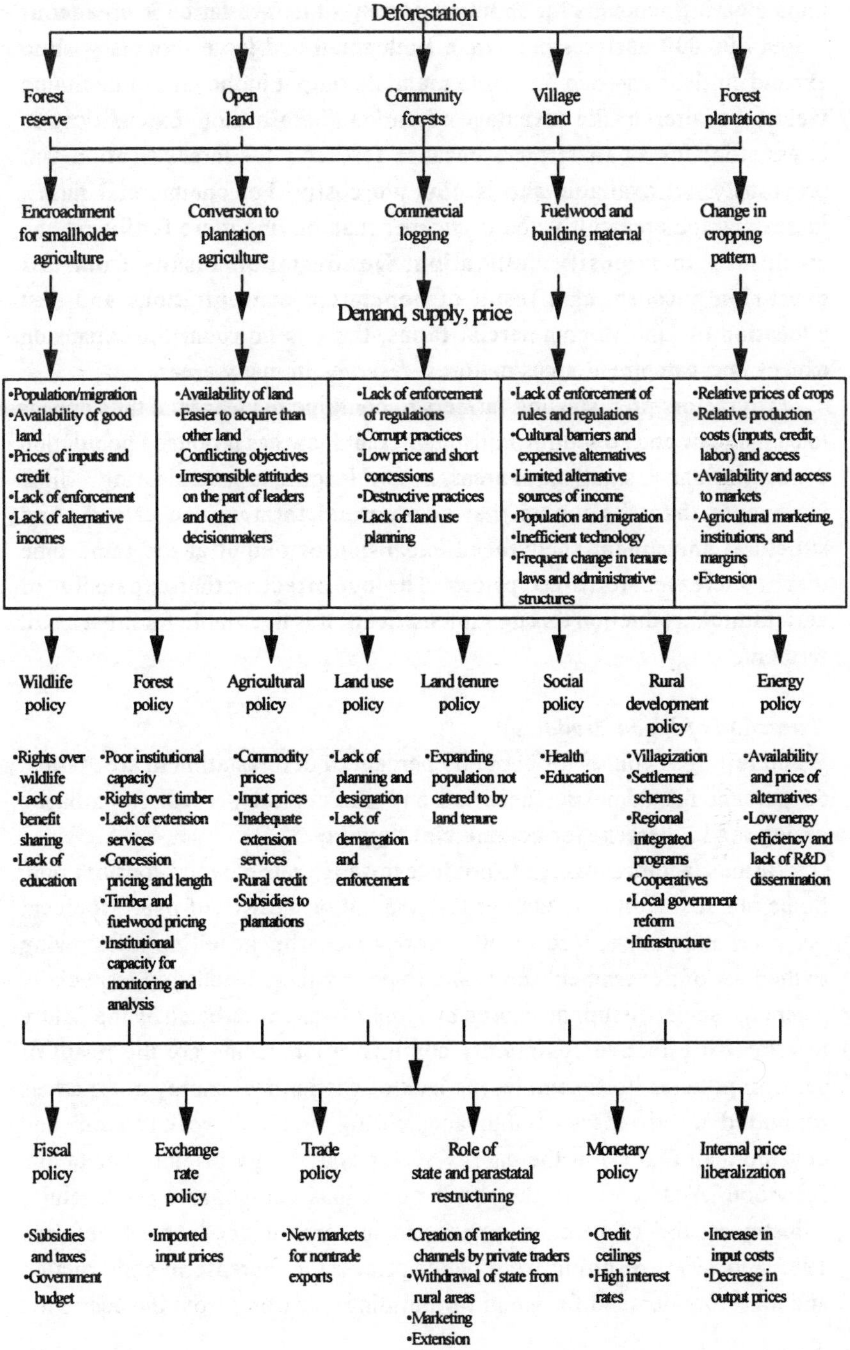

Deforestation

Forest reserve | Open land | Community forests | Village land | Forest plantations

Encroachment for smallholder agriculture | Conversion to plantation agriculture | Commercial logging | Fuelwood and building material | Change in cropping pattern

Demand, supply, price

•Population/migration •Availability of good land •Prices of inputs and credit •Lack of enforcement •Lack of alternative incomes	•Availability of land •Easier to acquire than other land •Conflicting objectives •Irresponsible attitudes on the part of leaders and other decisionmakers	•Lack of enforcement of regulations •Corrupt practices •Low price and short concessions •Destructive practices •Lack of land use planning	•Lack of enforcement of rules and regulations •Cultural barriers and expensive alternatives •Limited alternative sources of income •Population and migration •Inefficient technology •Frequent change in tenure laws and administrative structures	•Relative prices of crops •Relative production costs (inputs, credit, labor) and access •Availability and access to markets •Agricultural marketing, institutions, and margins •Extension

Wildlife policy | Forest policy | Agricultural policy | Land use policy | Land tenure policy | Social policy | Rural development policy | Energy policy

•Rights over wildlife
•Lack of benefit sharing
•Lack of education

•Poor institutional capacity
•Rights over timber
•Lack of extension services
•Concession pricing and length
•Timber and fuelwood pricing
•Institutional capacity for monitoring and analysis

•Commodity prices
•Input prices
•Inadequate extension services
•Rural credit
•Subsidies to plantations

•Lack of planning and designation
•Lack of demarcation and enforcement

•Expanding population not catered to by land tenure

•Health
•Education

•Villagization
•Settlement schemes
•Regional integrated programs
•Cooperatives
•Local government reform
•Infrastructure

•Availability and price of alternatives
•Low energy efficiency and lack of R&D dissemination

Fiscal policy | Exchange rate policy | Trade policy | Role of state and parastatal restructuring | Monetary policy | Internal price liberalization

•Subsidies and taxes
•Government budget

•Imported input prices

•New markets for nontrade exports

•Creation of marketing channels by private traders
•Withdrawal of state from rural areas
•Marketing
•Extension

•Credit ceilings
•High interest rates

•Increase in input costs
•Decrease in output prices

Land Clearing

Land clearing accounts for about 40 percent of deforestation in area terms (about 400,000 hectares per year). Both small and large farmers wish to expand cultivation—the former to maintain output in the face of declining yields, the latter to take advantage of market liberalization. Extensification is essential for small farmers because fertilizer for intensification was previously not available and is now too costly. For commercial farms, increasing the area cultivated is cheaper than buying more fertilizers and machinery to intensify cultivation. Deforestation results from this expansion because, as a result of population concentrations and past allocation of land to commercial farms, there is no room for expansion except into catchment areas or forest reserves in many areas.

Two factors predisposing farmers to continue to clear land thus appear to be land law and structural adjustment. Land law has produced population concentrations in small-farm areas, in turn leading to land clearing, which is cheaper than the inputs that commercial farmers can afford. And structural adjustment encouraged expansion of output at the same time that it increased fertilizer prices. The net effect is that expansion of agricultural production through intensification is not viable for most small farmers.

Extraction of Wood Products

Wood felling accounts for about 60 percent of deforestation in area terms: 55 percent for domestic fuelwood and charcoal, 4 percent for tobacco curing, and 2 percent for commercial logging.

Various factors converge to produce this high rate of wood consumption. Some are sociocultural, such as the population growth of over 3 percent per year, and poor enforcement of Forest Department felling rules owing to the lack of government funds and to poor village leadership, especially where the social disruption caused by *ujamaa* was exacerbated by the failure to establish effective community administration. Some are the result of sectoral policies, for example, the lack of economical energy alternatives for both domestic energy and tobacco curing, owing to weak research and development (R&D) in the energy sector and energy pricing that favors fuelwood. And some are the result of various components of structural adjustment: the 13 percent increase in the area under tobacco between 1985 and 1991, resulting from better prices; the increase in construction and therefore demand for wood for building, resulting from the economic upswing; and external market liberalization, leading to a dramatic increase in timber exports, from 2,500 tonnes in 1986 to 33,000 tonnes in 1989.

Reafforestation

About 50 percent of the farmers interviewed for this study have planted trees, but they do so only when population pressures force them to stem on-farm soil degradation. Government reafforestation replaces only about 0.5 percent of the area lost each year. This situation is partly the result of a longstanding lack of funding, which has been exacerbated by the SAP; between 1974 and 1990, funding declined from 0.35 percent of the overall government budget to just 0.05 percent. However, it also reflects uncertain land tenure arrangements.

Soil Erosion

The quantification of soil erosion remains problematic and few data exist, other than the extreme losses of 55 tonnes of productive soil per hectare per year recorded in the Kondoa eroded area in central Tanzania. Nonetheless, 63 percent of farmers interviewed for this study consider that soil erosion is a problem in their areas. The main causes of soil erosion are land clearing for agriculture (as discussed above), poor farming practices, and cultivation of erosive crops (see Figure 5.4).

Farming Practices

Ox plows or tractors are used on only 30 percent of the cropped area, and usage has declined in recent years. However, 90 percent of small farm households have adopted some kind of soil conservation measures, commonly contour plowing.

Only 30 percent of farmers use organic manure because crop-livestock systems are not integrated, and only 15 percent use chemical fertilizer. Further, application rates are low (20 kilograms per hectare), and the number of households using fertilizer has declined 30 percent in the last 5 years.

Thirty percent of households use improved seeds, but of these, 30 percent use 1 kilogram or less, and the number of households using improved seeds declined 60 percent between 1985 and 1991.

Several factors account for this deterioration in farming practices. Poor agricultural extension (as few as 6 percent of the farmers contacted are

Figure 5.4 Soil Erosion in Tanzania: Conceptual Map of Causal Factors

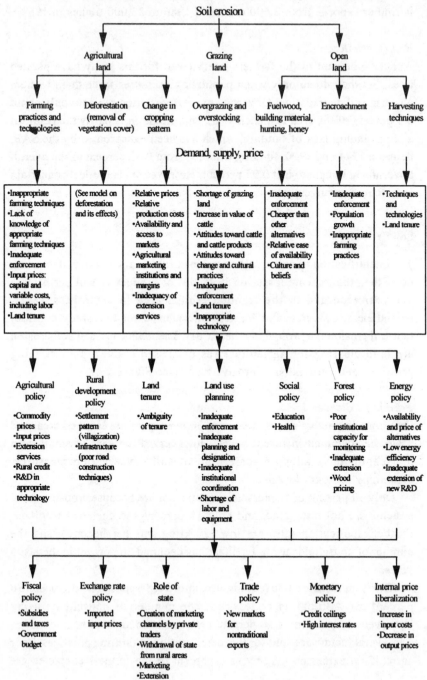

aware of agents' visit schedules) is a long-standing problem owing to underfunding and poor links with research. Poor village leadership is also a problem: leaders do not always adhere to agreed-upon bylaws concerning grazing and encroachment, thus encouraging ordinary villagers to do the same.

Access to improved technologies, especially chemical fertilizers, is also a factor. Prior to structural adjustment, 70 percent of the fertilizer was allocated preferentially to the "Big Four" southern maize-growing regions at the expense of the rest of the country. Since structural adjustment began, access has been limited by price because the 80 percent subsidy on fertilizer was removed and credit is harder to obtain for both farmers and potential input traders. According to a regression analysis conducted as a part of this study, in Tanzania, there is a strong negative correlation between fertilizer price and quantities used.

Cropping Patterns

Since structural adjustment began in 1986, there has been a 17 percent increase in the area planted to the nine major food and cash crops grown in Tanzania. Using Barbier's[3] categorization of "erosive" and "nonerosive" crops, about 80 percent of this increase was in heavily or lightly erosive crops: maize, sorghum, cassava, cotton, and tobacco.

This change can be attributed to various factors. Clearly, the long-term decline in rainfall and its consistency have encouraged drought-tolerant crops, such as cassava and sorghum, which are erosive. In addition, market liberalization as part of the adjustment process has encouraged the planting of maize; it has also encouraged cash crops for export, and cotton—which is highly erosive—is Tanzania's main export crop in terms of area cultivated.

The influence of price changes is more difficult to determine. In real terms, producer prices increased between 50 and 90 percent for the major cash crops but fell 10-30 percent for the major food crops; the decline was most marked for erosive crops. Thus for food crops, there may be a negative relationship between producer price and area cultivated (i.e., the area increases as real prices fall) and vice versa for cash crops; this point needs further investigation.

In addition, the regression analysis shows that for maize, rice, sorghum, and cassava (i.e., the food crops), the area cultivated increases as yields decline and vice versa for cotton and tobacco (i.e., the cash crops).[4] The increase in fertilizer prices, which will have adversely affected yields for many crops, may thus also have affected the area cultivated.

The Influence of Structural Adjustment

In Tanzania, rates of soil erosion and deforestation have been affected by structural adjustment to the extent that it increased the cost of fertilizer and reduced the availability of credit with which to buy it, changed the erosive-nonerosive balance in the cropping pattern and increased timber extraction through internal and external market liberalization, and reduced spending on afforestation.

But ongoing sectoral policies, unrelated to structural adjustment, have also been influential. They include the ending of *ujamaa*, thus ending incentives to mechanize; poor agricultural extension and poor enforcement of Forestry Department felling rules; ambiguous land tenure, which provides no incentive to conserve natural resources for either small or commercial farmers; and inappropriate energy pricing and energy R&D.

Longstanding sociocultural factors (e.g., population growth, attachment to ancestral lands, poor village leadership) have also been influential, although less so, as have underlying environmental conditions, such as uncertain and declining rainfall, and the low rate of regeneration of indigenous tree species compared to exotics.

With regard to the differential impacts of structural adjustment on the rich and the poor, the increase in fertilizer prices and the reduction in credit availability have hit smaller farmers harder because they are on poorer land that is more in need of fertilizer, which they are less able to afford. One result is increasing cultivation of marginal areas, with its associated deforestation and erosion problems. Commercial farmers and timber traders are now able to benefit from the strong market for plantation crops and timber exports, leaving society as a whole to meet the costs of this unsustainable exploitation of natural resources.

SUSTAINABLE DEVELOPMENT: FUTURE SCENARIOS

The following scenarios were based on estimated changes in key economic, social, and environmental indicators if current adjustment programs continue without modification and, alternatively, if "more sustainable" policies are introduced. (Accurate modeling was not possible owing to the lack of data.)

If Current Adjustment Programs Continue

According to the latest plan, the share of the government budget allocated to natural resources management will remain static, and strict limits will be placed on the size of the overall budget; however, stronger efforts will be made to rehabilitate the social infrastructure. Increased outputs of food and export crops will continue to be encouraged, as will better use of industrial capacity.

Deforestation is likely to increase owing to continued land clearing for agriculture, the effects of economic growth on demand for timber, and the continued lack of R&D on energy alternatives. In turn, soil erosion is likely to increase, causing siltation and therefore affecting water and hydropower availability. Declining water quality, increased air pollution, and reduced biodiversity (because protected areas will be increasingly encroached on) can also be expected.

With regard to poverty, Tanzania can expect an increase in GDP per capita *but* increasing income inequality owing to the concentration of economic power resulting from liberalization. On past evidence, this change will force people in both urban and rural areas to adopt environmentally unfriendly livelihood strategies (natural resources are the only resources to which the poor have access because they are public goods that are poorly protected). Rural poverty, in particular, is likely to increase in the short term owing to the removal of fertilizer subsidies, possibly leading to overexpansion of cultivation and thus soil erosion.

With regard to environmental costs and benefits, it is clear that benefits accrue in the short term only; in the long run, everyone loses from the overexploitation of natural resources. Short-term gainers will include: (1) large-scale producers (e.g., industrialists, farmers, miners, timber companies), who can profit from internal and external market liberalization by extracting natural resources below true cost; (2) the tourism sector, which gains from devaluation, foreign exchange liberalization, and better availability of service goods domestically; (3) the rich, who are now able to import whatever they want (including, e.g., luxury cars, which would add to urban pollution) and to buy periurban land; and (4) the government, which has offloaded many of its direct costs (e.g., agricultural marketing and subsidies, social services), leaving others to pick up the resulting indirect environmental costs. Losers will be: (1) small-scale producers, who cannot afford fertilizer, cannot capitalize on the new market opportunities because they are on poorer and more remote land, and will lose out on some resources (e.g., irrigation water, periurban land) to big irrigation schemes, large industrialists, etc. in the newly powerful private sector simply because of their size; (2) all rural dwellers, who will witness the large-scale merchants' cutting fuelwood for towns; and (3) the poor, who will suffer from increased urban pollution without receiving any benefits.

Under Alternative Policies

The situation is different if "more sustainable" policies are pursued. On the negative side, economic growth is likely to be slower, official development assistance considerably lower (because donors would withdraw support for noncompliance with structural adjustment conditionalities), and inflation higher than under a continuation of structural adjustment. On the positive side, in the short run, unemployment is likely to be lower, income distribution more equitable, and gross fixed capital formation and tax revenue as a percentage of GDP higher. The balance of payments deficit and debt-service ratio as a proportion of GDP would probably be little changed.

The secondary effects on social indicators are likely to be broadly positive, with lower population growth and child mortality and higher caloric intake. With increasing per capita income, the number of criminal offenses may fall. Reflecting higher social expenditures, school enrollment and access to clean water are likely to improve.

With regard to environmental resources, energy consumption, freshwater withdrawal, and atmospheric pollution are likely to increase less rapidly, the threats to biodiversity should lessen, and the rates of deforestation and soil erosion are likely to fall.

Trade-offs

There are different winners and losers under these two scenarios.

Promoting Growth

This strategy focuses on privatization and increasing capacity utilization. On the social side, unemployment is likely to increase, thus poverty, thus crime. On the environmental side, unsustainable rates of natural resource extraction are likely.

The alternative is to allocate a proportion of government resources to unemployment, poverty, crime, and environmental degradation. Doing so is likely to reduce economic growth (because strict controls discourage firms and because the public sector is often a less efficient economic actor than the private sector and crowds it out) and will not reduce the budget deficit.

Social Services Expenditures

On past evidence, reducing expenditures lowers the quantity and quality of social services. But increasing expenditures will require cuts in funding for other sectors and will therefore reduce their performance without reducing the budget deficit.

The Balance of Payments Deficit

Encouraging exports in order to reduce the deficit may lead to unsustainable rates of natural resource extraction. But encouraging sustainable natural resource extraction increases costs to firms and reduces export earnings, thus increasing the deficit and reducing Tanzania's ability to import, with a damaging effect on economic growth.

Privatization

Privatization increases the economic power of wealthy individuals, whose interests may not coincide with the nation's. Privatization cannot be reversed, but an alternative is to increase government's capacity to regulate and monitor the private sector.

Inflation

Freeing market prices may increase inflation, causing consumers to suffer, eroding the confidence of the business community, and causing difficulties for government budgeting. Reducing inflation requires restricting credit and the money supply, but doing so reduces the availability of working capital to the private sector and therefore their output. It also reduces government expenditures, with possible increased unemployment (through retrenchment) and cuts in social services.

RECOMMENDATIONS

Based on the above analysis, suggestions for policy changes that could encourage more sustainable development in Tanzania are set forth below.

Activities That Could Be Integrated into Existing Structural Adjustment Programs

Agricultural policy changes would:

- guarantee agricultural price stability to provide incentives for investment in soil conservation and tree planting; and
- retain subsidies on farm implements because the benefits (i.e., intensification of production) outweigh the budgetary costs.

Trade policy changes would:

- reduce import taxes on agricultural equipment to encourage its use;
- increase tariffs on imports of polluting diesel vehicles and generators; and
- increase tariffs on imports of intermediate inputs for high-polluting industries.

Public expenditure changes would:

- increase revenue instead of cutting expenditures (e.g., introduce the value added tax, widen the tax base, end discretionary tax exemptions, increase compliance through improving revenue service incentives); and
- increase cost sharing and cost recovery in health and education.

Changing the Objectives of Future Structural Adjustment Programs[5]

- Generate broad-based support for structural adjustment: encourage participation of the private sector, professional organizations, opposition parties, NGOs, students, journalists, and trade unions.
- Increase government accountability: openly provide information about the state of the environment and about the potential environmental impacts of planned programs and projects.
- Mitigate the adverse effects of structural adjustment: provide assistance programs for "losers" (e.g., credit for small-scale producers and traders)

and introduce compensatory measures to generate employment and redistribute income.

- Integrate social objectives: improve health and education levels, improve rural infrastructure, support small-scale off-farm enterprises, and implement Tanzania's fledgling population policy.
- Integrate environmental conservation: increase investments in natural resource management, introduce environmental impact assessment and social impact assessment for all SAPs and projects; control exploitation of natural resources to prevent overexploitation in response to market prices that may not reflect long-run environmental opportunity costs.

Sequencing of Structural Adjustment

The appropriate pacing of structural adjustment depends on the conditions prevailing at the start of the adjustment process. The Tanzanian economy was heavily state controlled, with serious market and policy distortions and weak design and implementation capacity. Thus a relatively long time was needed to move to a market economy. Luckily, Tanzania had sufficient time because the country's political leaders were able to generate and sustain support for the process.

With regard to sequencing individual components, in retrospect, Tanzania may have been wrong to begin with price reforms (e.g., exchange rate, tariffs, domestic prices) before moving to institutional and structural reforms. One result was a significant loss of potential export earnings because institutional barriers to exports had not been removed (it may have been better to remove the institutional barriers at the same time as liberalizing external trade). Another result was an acute banking crisis because 90 percent of the loan portfolios of commercial banks consisted of loans to the (effectively bankrupt) state cooperatives, marketing boards, and parastatals. These enterprises should probably have been restructured *before* the financial sector was liberalized.

It may also have been wrong to begin with economic reforms and leave social sector restructuring until later because structural adjustment became most unpopular and unnecessary suffering resulted.

Policies to Pursue in Parallel with Structural Adjustment[6]

- Agricultural extension: promote crop rotation, longer fallows, use of manure and farm implements, and tree planting.

- Land tenure: provide titles to land and security of tenure for small farmers, transfer control of land use from the national to the village level (to increase the effectiveness of enforcement), extend village control to common lands, increase the cost of leases, and enforce observation of leasehold boundaries more strictly.
- Forestry: enforce adherence to felling rules more strictly, increase fees for forest products, and improve collection rates.
- Wildlife: control access to protected areas and use of resources within them more strictly, establish buffer zones between population centers and protected areas, increase the involvement of local communities in wildlife management, and use tourism revenue to improve physical and social infrastructure in communities around protected areas.
- Credit: provide credit for private fertilizer traders and for small farmers to buy fertilizer.
- Energy: conduct more R&D on nonwood energy sources (e.g., solar, wind power, biogas) and on energy-efficient domestic stoves and charcoal kilns, provide credit for households to purchase energy-efficient domestic stoves, enforce fuel emission controls and power plant pollution regulations more strictly, and promote afforestation of water catchment areas (to protect hydroelectric power supplies).
- Industry: enforce pollution and waste controls and work-safety regulations more strictly and increase penalties for emissions.

Limiting Factors

According to this study, the two main factors constraining Tanzania's implementing more sustainable development policies are domestic weaknesses in policy design and implementation capacity and dependence on (not always effective) international aid. A major fear of many Tanzanian development workers is that international aid will be cut off, as happened before in the country's history, if alternative policies that are implemented do not conform with the free-market orientation of the current SAP.

ENDNOTES

1. R. Mearns, "Environmental Implications of Structural Adjustment: Reflections on Scientific Method," IDS Discussion Paper No. 284 (Institute of Development Studies, University of Sussex, Brighton, 1992).
2. United Republic of Tanzania, "Draft National Environmental Action Plan: A First Step" (Ministry of Tourism, Natural Resources and Environment, Dar es Salaam), p. 8; and International Union for Conservation of Nature and Natural Resources, *Masterworks of Man and Nature: Preserving Our World Heritage* (Patonga, Australia: Harper-MacRae, 1992).
3. E. Barbier, "The Role of Smallholder Producer Prices in Land Degradation: The Case of Malawi" (Paper presented at the European Association of Environmental and Resource Economists Annual Meeting, Stockholm, June 11-14, 1991).
4. This analysis is not relevant for coffee because it is a tree crop.
5. In mid-1995, a number of these objectives were part of structural adjustment discussions.
6. In mid-1995, a number of these elements were being considered for inclusion in sectoral policies.

6

CASE STUDY FOR ZAMBIA

This chapter is based on a study conducted and written by Christopher Mupimpila, Venkatesh Seshamani, Allast Mwanza, Emmanuel Chidumayo, and Inyambo Mwanawina of the Department of Economics of the University of Lusaka, with support of Elizabeth Cromwell of the Overseas Development Institute. This summary was written by Elizabeth Cromwell.

This study attempts to identify the conditions under which "'sensible' economic policies will have unintended social, economic, and environmental consequences." The approach was to use a conceptual model rather than a formal modeling exercise. The conceptual model combines general equilibrium modeling, regression analysis, and ground-truthing using published surveys and secondary data. It is the same approach used in the Tanzania country study, and the reader is here referred to Chapter 5's introductory material. Figure 5.1 and the accompanying text set forth the framework for analyzing structural adjustment and sustainable development.

BACKGROUND

State of the Economy and the Environment

Zambia is known as one of Africa's last great "frontier" territories. It has many species of wild animals, and 40 percent of the country is set aside for wildlife as national parks and game management areas. At 10 people per square kilometer, one-half of whom live in mining towns in the Copperbelt, land pressure should not yet be an issue, and indeed only 3.5 percent of cultivable land is currently cropped. The climate is good for a

Figure 6.1 Zambia

From *Picture Atlas of the World* CD-ROM, © National Geographic Society, 1995

wide range of cash crops, including maize, wheat, sugar, cattle, tobacco, and cotton as well as small grains, legumes, and cassava. Forty-five percent of all southern Africa's water resources are within Zambia's borders, including part of the largest dammed lake in the world, Lake Kariba, which is a major source of hydroelectric power. Zambia also has massive mineral resources: it is the fourth largest producer of copper in the world and has lead, zinc, and coal as well. Although the country is landlocked, the jointly owned Tanzania-Zambia railway is supposed to guarantee access to the ports of the East African coast, and road links to the South African ports are good.

But this potential has not been successfully exploited. Copper production fell one-third between 1975 and 1990 owing to falling world prices, poor management, and unreliable external transport. The hydroelectric plants are characterized by poor maintenance, frequent breakdowns, and low-capacity utilization. Agriculture has been bedeviled by inefficient state input supply and marketing, low prices, and archaic land tenure arrangements that have created problems of overcultivation in some areas. Poaching for trophies has pushed the rhino population to the brink of extinction and culled elephant numbers 90 percent since 1960.

Thus environmental problems have emerged, including deforestation, loss of wildlife, water pollution in urban areas, and loss of soil fertility. The economic and social impacts are also severe. Government deficits equal to 20 percent of GDP became the norm during the late 1970s and early 1980s, foreign debt was 300 percent of GDP at its peak, inflation ran to 3-digit levels, and economic growth was negative for a number of years (at the same time that population was increasing 3 percent per year).

Although initially prosperous because of its copper wealth, the relatively high wages in the mining sector set the trend elsewhere in the economy. In Zambia, inequality has always been marked: as early as 1970, the top 7 percent of the population received nearly 25 percent of all income. Poverty is a rural as well as an urban phenomenon, with 50-60 percent of the total population living below the poverty line. Of late, real wages have been seriously eroded by inflation.

Zambia did not anticipate the global collapse in copper prices in 1974-75 and subsequently failed to diversify and manage the national budget effectively. The United National Independence Party (UNIP), which ruled from Independence until 1991, instead used the state machinery to control economic activity, create jobs, and act as a source of political patronage. Further, the country's massive debt burden confounded policy initiatives for restoring macro balance and economic growth.

Implementation of a donor-funded structural adjustment program (SAP) began in 1983 and has continued intermittently to the present, with a serious break between 1987 and 1989. In 1991, multiparty elections were held for the first time in 19 years, and the winners, the Movement for Multi-party Democracy (MMD), have stated that implementing the SAP is a priority.

Environmental Policy

For many years, there was no real consideration of environmental issues in policy planning because of the perception of Zambia as a frontier territory. Serious conflicts over resource use began to emerge only when the economy deteriorated in the late 1970s. During the UNIP era, the economic strategy of widespread state control meant that for many resources, the same institution was responsible for both exploitation and control (e.g., Zambia Consolidated Copper Mines for minerals, the Forest Department for timber). In addition, UNIP's policy of humanism (roughly, people-centered socialism) meant that it was politically difficult to enforce some environmental regulations—removal of squatters from protected areas, for example.

Following the example of the World Conservation Strategy, a National Conservation Strategy (NCS), completed in 1985, became the accepted basis of environmental policy in Zambia. It resulted in a new environmental protection law, a new Ministry of the Environment and Natural Resources (MENR), and a National Environmental Council. The NCS was recently updated to form Zambia's National Environmental Action Plan, which was ratified in 1994. Despite this development, serious conflicts still occur between the MENR and other ministries concerning implementation of environmental policy. For example, following a recent appeal by the MENR to remove squatters from Zambia's Forest Reserves, the minister for the Copperbelt area refused to comply, quipping, "I cannot see any forest here. All I can see are cassava, groundnuts, and cabbage forests."[1]

Structural Adjustment

Zambia has had a mixed relationship with its international donors. It first received International Monetary Fund (IMF) funding in 1975, but until 1983, compliance with donor conditions was poor. Between 1983 and 1987, Zambia made significant headway with economic deregulation, but relations with the IMF were broken in May 1987 and a New Economic Recovery Program initiated on the theme of "Growth from Our Own Resources." The program was similar to the SAP in its objectives, but its strategy was a return to economic control. It also involved a unilateral limitation on debt repayments to 10 percent of export earnings. Relations with the IMF resumed in July 1989 (running the economy had been made virtually impossible by the suspension of external aid); since then, structural adjustment has continued—albeit with a period of policy volatility preceding the 1991 multiparty elections.

The overall aim of Zambia's SAP is to restore macroeconomic balance and growth by:

• reducing state control of the economy;

- reducing food subsidies to control the budget deficit and encourage a return to the land as a means of increasing agricultural production and exports;
- reducing import dependence (especially the overdependence on imported capital equipment of much of the industrial sector); and
- diversifying exports away from copper.

Privatization of the 80 percent of the economy controlled by the government has been slow, but external and internal trade is now fully liberalized. The final steps toward complete liberalization of agricultural marketing that were taken in 1993 caused considerable disruption as private traders failed to move into all areas.

Food subsidies were finally removed in late 1991 as one of the incoming MMD government's election pledges. Earlier attempts in 1986 and 1990 had provoked riots, and the subsidies were subsequently reinstated. A move in the mid-1980s from universal price subsidies to the distribution of maize coupons to the urban poor was widely held responsible for the increase in malnutrition recorded in the late 1980s: maize meal prices increased 160 percent in the 12 months preceding July 1989. There was no significant return to the land.

Trade liberalization policy contributed to a flood of imports, particularly of consumer goods, with which local agriculture and manufacturing cannot compete. This situation, together with civil service retrenchment since the MMD came to power, reduced the share of formal sector employment from 27 percent to 9 percent between 1974 and 1990.

Export diversification is insignificant, partly because of the difficulties facing domestic agriculture and manufacturing. At the same time, copper exports have fallen substantially owing to a reduction in production caused by poor maintenance and the exhaustion of some reserves.

At the macro level, foreign exchange liberalization has contributed to domestic inflation and the continuation of a large balance of payments deficit and has made control of the budget deficit more difficult. The MMD introduced cash-based budgeting into the government system at the beginning of the 1993 financial year, and this severe step appears finally to have stamped out the deficit.

Economic performance was hampered by a severe drought that destroyed Zambia's 1992 harvest and necessitated massive food imports. Thus economic growth remained negative for most of the 1980s and early 1990s, and real per capita GDP also fell. One result was an increase in poverty and inequality that moved Zambia from middle-income to least-developed country status, sliding between 1987 and 1992 from thirty-ninth to fifteenth poorest country in per capita GDP terms. This drop had an added effect on social indicators, pushing Zambia—according to United Nations Children's Fund (UNICEF) statistics—from the forty-seventh to the seventeenth highest under-5 mortality rate between 1990 and 1992. The first year for which a positive rate of growth of GDP was recorded was 1993.

ADJUSTMENT-ENVIRONMENT LINKAGES

This section examines the extent to which structural adjustment affected Zambia's three main environmental problems: loss of wildlife, deforestation, and urban water pollution. For each problem in turn, what is known about the major trends in degradation is first set out. Then the extent to which structural adjustment may have exacerbated these trends and the differential impacts of adjustment on rich and poor are examined.

Loss of Wildlife

The loss of big game species in Zambia has accelerated during the SAP period; for example, between 1960 and 1985, elephant numbers fell 3 percent per year from 270,000 to 75,000, but between 1985 and 1993, they fell 9 percent per year to just 22,000.

Figure 6.2 shows the factors believed to influence the rate of wildlife loss in Zambia. Some factors that are influential in other countries can be discounted. Poaching for meat has never been a substantial cause of loss of big game in Zambia; neither has legal safari hunting nor pest control (only about 280 elephants per year were shot for the latter purpose between 1966 and 1977).

The main cause of big game loss is poaching for trophies. In some respects, structural adjustment has encouraged this activity. The increase in urban unemployment and erosion of farm incomes resulting from structural adjustment have clearly increased incentives for poor people to collaborate with the organized poaching gangs. It is also the case that public spending reductions have reduced the effectiveness of national parks administration.

Figure 6.2 Loss of Wildlife in Zambia: Conceptual Map of Causal Factors

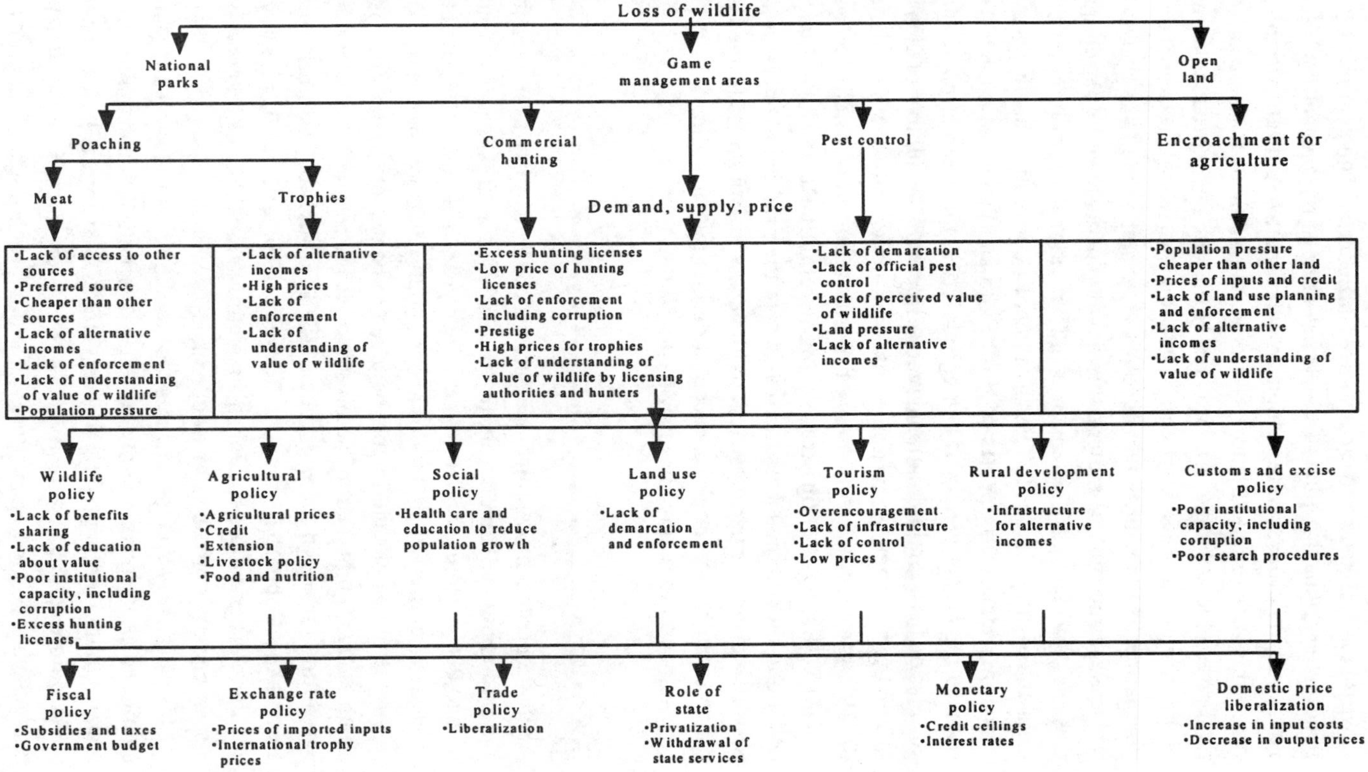

Loss of wildlife

National parks | Poaching | Trophies | Commercial hunting | Game management areas | Pest control | Encroachment for agriculture | Open land

Meat | Trophies

Demand, supply, price

- Lack of access to other sources
- Preferred source
- Cheaper than other sources
- Lack of alternative incomes
- Lack of enforcement
- Lack of understanding of value of wildlife
- Population pressure

- Lack of alternative incomes
- High prices
- Lack of enforcement
- Lack of understanding of value of wildlife

- Excess hunting licenses
- Low price of hunting licenses
- Lack of enforcement including corruption
- Prestige
- High prices for trophies
- Lack of understanding of value of wildlife by licensing authorities and hunters

- Lack of demarcation
- Lack of official pest control
- Lack of perceived value of wildlife
- Land pressure
- Lack of alternative incomes

- Population pressure
- cheaper than other land
- Prices of inputs and credit
- Lack of land use planning and enforcement
- Lack of alternative incomes
- Lack of understanding of value of wildlife

Wildlife policy
- Lack of benefits sharing
- Lack of education about value
- Poor institutional capacity, including corruption
- Excess hunting licenses

Agricultural policy
- Agricultural prices
- Credit
- Extension
- Livestock policy
- Food and nutrition

Social policy
- Health care and education to reduce population growth

Land use policy
- Lack of demarcation and enforcement

Tourism policy
- Overencouragement
- Lack of infrastructure
- Lack of control
- Low prices

Rural development policy
- Infrastructure for alternative incomes

Customs and excise policy
- Poor institutional capacity, including corruption
- Poor search procedures

Fiscal policy
- Subsidies and taxes
- Government budget

Exchange rate policy
- Prices of imported inputs
- International trophy prices

Trade policy
- Liberalization

Role of state
- Privatization
- Withdrawal of state services

Monetary policy
- Credit ceilings
- Interest rates

Domestic price liberalization
- Increase in input costs
- Decrease in output prices

But non-SAP factors have also been influential. The continued failure to enforce antipoaching laws reflects a decline in funding for the National Parks and Wildlife Service, which predates the SAP; it fell two-thirds in real terms between 1975 and 1990, hovering at about 0.4 percent of the total government budget. And it is likely that the low reproductive rate of elephants means that numbers have now fallen below a sustainable population. Thus the decline will continue, in part owing to natural factors.

At the same time, some positive developments have to be set against these negative factors. The reduction in international trophy prices resulting from the signing of the CITES agreement (Convention on International Trade in Endangered Species of Wild Flora and Fauna) in the late 1980s reduced the attractiveness of smuggling ivory: there is a strong negative correlation between international ivory prices and the number of elephants in Zambia.[2] Further, a revision of national parks and wildlife policies in the 1980s to introduce community benefit sharing from wildlife resources (ADMADE, the Administrative Management Design program) cut collaboration with poachers in areas where the program is operating. The SAP also played its part: restrictions on access to foreign exchange were a major incentive to convert kwacha to dollars by smuggling ivory. These restrictions were removed as part of the SAP.

Deforestation

About 45 percent of Zambia's land area is covered by dry evergreen forest and miombo woodland, but during the 1980s, this area was lost at a rate of 900,000 hectares, or 2.6 percent, per year. This figure represents an increase over pre-1980s rates of about 680,000 hectares per year.

Figure 6.3 shows the factors believed to contribute to deforestation in Zambia. Over 90 percent of deforestation is the result of land clearing for agriculture (although the proportion felled for fuelwood is locally higher around the Copperbelt towns). Between 1980 and 1990, clearing for commercial agriculture and for shifting cultivation (*chitemene*) contributed almost equally to the loss of wooded land.

It seems likely that most of this loss was the result of rural households' continued predisposition toward extensive cultivation, combined with inappropriate land laws. The former reflects a historical lack of concern about deforestation in a land where trees were plentiful. The latter has two dimensions. First, the majority of small farm households has remained on the 27 million hectares of Reserve Land (customary land) that covers

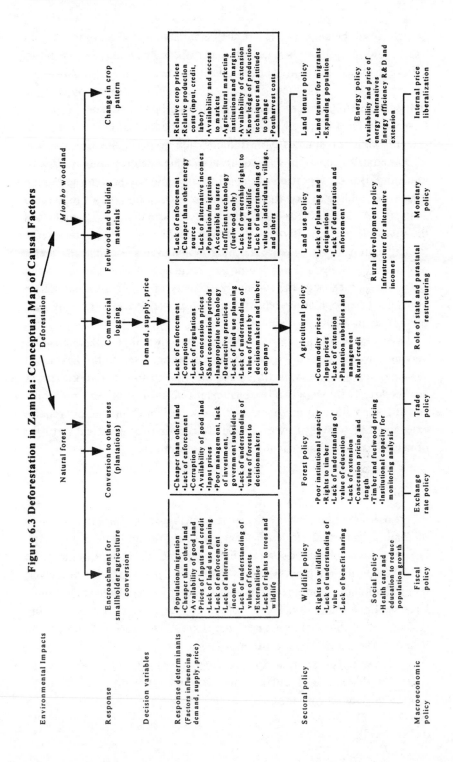

Figure 6.3 Deforestation in Zambia: Conceptual Map of Causal Factors

36 percent of the country because the demarcation of small farm plots on Trust Land (43 million hectares of nontribal land covering 58 percent of the country) has been slow. The result is overcrowding, the effects of which are exacerbated by the poor soils covering much of Zambia outside the fertile Southern Province. Second, there is no private land tenure on either Reserve or Trust Land, a situation that has produced an unwillingness to preserve natural resources typical in common property situations.

The contribution of the SAP to this accelerated deforestation is difficult to distinguish. A proportion of the urban unemployed has returned to the rural areas, adding to existing population pressure; this study's regression analysis shows a positive correlation between urban unemployment and the area under maize cultivation. However, population pressures may serve to limit deforestation in some farming systems: in the *chitemene* areas, recent studies show a *reduction* in the frequency of land clearing when the population exceeds the sustainable density of 2.4 persons per square kilometer (the population density is now 6 per square kilometer in most rural areas in Zambia).[3]

By the same token, the SAP-induced reduction of fertilizer subsidies may not have increased the rate of land clearing. Even in the heyday of subsidization in Zambia, fertilizer use was limited to about 10 kilograms per hectare. There were two reasons: extensive cultivation was traditional and still feasible, and the poor soils that cover much of Zambia require extensive fallowing even with regular applications of chemical fertilizer because fertilizer alone cannot maintain soil fertility.

Urban Water Pollution

Figure 6.4 shows the factors believed to contribute to urban water pollution in Zambia. Industrial effluent has increased significantly in recent years. For one Copperbelt public sewage treatment works, the volume of industrial effluent entering the plant is almost double its design capacity. However, mining pollutants—another important source of urban water pollution— have declined markedly: the dissolved copper level in a river passing through one Copperbelt town declined from 19 parts per million in 1970 to less than 0.10 parts per million in 1990.

As shown in Table 6.1, urban access to public water supplies and sewage facilities deteriorated during the early SAP period but improved substantially in recent years.

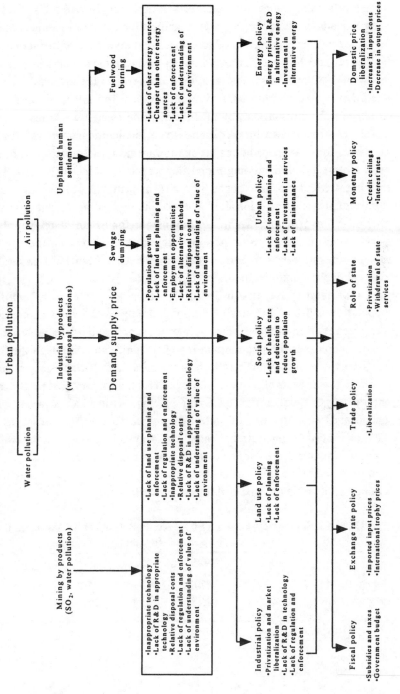

Figure 6.4 Urban Pollution in Zambia: Conceptual Map of Causal Factors

Despite being connected to these facilities, many households still face long periods without running water, and public sewage treatment plants have become increasingly unable to handle the volume of effluent, both industrial and human. For example, in one treatment plant in Lusaka, between 1983 and 1991, the fecal coliform level in the effluent entering the plant increased from 0.04 to 49 million per 100 milliliters and from 0.009 to 0.23 million per 100 milliliters in the treated water leaving the plant. The result is a marked increase in the incidence of waterborne diseases; for example, cholera epidemics are now an annual occurrence, with 800 people alone dying in one Copperbelt town in 1992.

One particular aspect of the structural adjustment process may have contributed to this deterioration. The decline in funding for the Ministry of Local Government, which is responsible for urban water supplies, accelerated during the SAP period: prior to the mid-1980s, the decline was about 5 percent per year in real terms, but between 1983 and 1990, the real decline doubled to about 10 percent per year.

Other factors are also influential. About 60 percent of Zambia's population is urban dwelling. With population growth over 3 percent per year, the required annual expansion in water supply and treatment facilities just to keep pace with population growth is significant. Although the SAP has brought about a modest return to the rural areas, it has not yet fully reversed the impacts of past economic policies that encouraged rural-urban migration. Official policy on water pricing, which keeps prices low, encourages wasteful use of water, thus exacerbating the pressures on facilities. Further, institutional capacity for town planning remains weak; Zambia's town planners failed to anticipate the massive rural-urban influx that followed rescindment of the pass laws at Independence, and they have not been able to keep pace with urban growth since.

Table 6.1 Urban Households with Access to Public Water Supply and Sewage Facilities (percent)

	1985	1988	1990
Piped water	48	44	57
Sewage system	27	26	49

Source: Government of Zambia, Central Statistics Office.

Poverty and the Environment

The formal sector employment declined from 24 percent of the labor force in 1980 to 10 percent in 1990 as a result of civil service retrenchment and contraction in the manufacturing sector. The informal sector has been unable to absorb all the unemployed.

Rural incomes have also declined. This situation reflects a long-term neglect of the agricultural sector, but the more recent removal of fertilizer subsidies has affected large numbers of farmers, and the withdrawal of state marketing services has led to the collapse of markets in many areas.

Food subsidies have not been replaced by effective safety nets for the truly poor; for example, the donor-funded Programme Urban Self-Help (PUSH) provides small rations and requires women to work to obtain theirs despite the fact that their time is already overburdened. Begging and street children have appeared for the first time in Zambia's history (although their presence is partly the result of the more permissive political atmosphere since the 1991 multiparty elections).

This increase in poverty (which predates the introduction of adjustment measures) may have forced people to look for alternative sources of income; many of these alternatives are natural resource intensive. Charcoal production now employs about 45,000, and Lusaka alone consumes 5 million bags per year, contributing significantly to deforestation. Home beer brewing (always an important source of income in rural and periurban areas) is also thought to have increased; there is a ready market because the price of commercial beer has increased sharply since liberalization. Home brewing requires large quantities of fuelwood for the 5-day process. Consumption of wild foods, traditionally used only during famines, has also been increasing. Because fuelwood and clean water are now found farther from settlements, women are spending more time collecting these resources—requiring an extra 2 days per month, according to one estimate.[4]

Distribution of Costs and Benefits

Most of the immediate environmental costs of the economic recession, which adjustment has yet to reverse, have fallen on rural dwellers, especially women. The long-run loser is the Zambian nation itself as its public goods of forest resources, soil wealth, wildlife, and plant diversity are permanently eroded. If urban dwellers have seen any change under the SAP, it is a modest improvement in their environment because a return to the rural areas eases population pressures and social infrastructure (e.g., public water supplies) is extended.

SUSTAINABLE DEVELOPMENT: FUTURE SCENARIOS

Table 6.2 shows the likely changes in key economic, social, and environmental indicators under two scenarios: if current SAPs continue without modification (the table includes both the World Bank's projections and projections of this study's model[5]) and if alternative "more sustainable" policies are effected.

If Current Adjustment Programs Continue

The World Bank predicts increased domestic investments, thus increasing economic growth and tax revenues. However, the authors of this study believe that these predictions are based on overoptimistic assumptions relating to mineral production and prices, growth in nontraditional exports, levels of foreign investment and aid, and debt servicing. In addition, the World Bank projections do not allow for the negative impacts of certain aspects of the SAP, namely, the insistence on cash-based budgeting in the public sector; the speed of external trade liberalization, which has put domestic manufacturing under severe pressure; and the speed of agricultural market liberalization, which left many farmers without a market for their produce in 1993.

Even if the World Bank's attempts to promote increased agricultural exports succeed, the resulting expansion in cultivation would not exceed available cultivable land. However, it should be pointed out that such an increase is unlikely to improve real GDP significantly because trade in agricultural raw materials has low value added and Zambia is a price-taker in international commodity markets.

Another sector that the World Bank is promoting as a new source of foreign exchange is wildlife tourism. However, given the fact that a majority of Zambians now live in poverty, there are criticisms of increasing public spending on tourism development instead of improving the welfare and

Table 6.2 Future Scenarios: Model Results

	2000 Business As Usual[a]	2000 Business As Usual[b]	2010 Alternative Policies
Economic			
GDP growth (constant percent)	6.10	3.00	3.20
GDP per capita (constant percent)	286.00	254.00	248.00
Tax revenue (percentage of GDP)	18.00	20.00	24.00
Domestic investment (percentage of GDP)	26.00	22.00	25.00
Social (percent)			
Population growth	3.20	3.20	3.20
Environmental (percent)			
Deforestation	<1.00	<1.00	1.00
Biodiversity loss	<0.05	<0.05	0.05
Water pollution	NA	NA	NA

Source: Provisional estimates from the first run of the Computable General Equilibrium Model to Measure the Effects of Structural Adjustment on Ecology and Development in Zambia.
NA = not applicable.
a. World Bank.
b. Model projections.

productive capacity of the people. On the other hand, some progress has been made in sharing the benefits of increased tourism revenue at the local level, as in the ADMADE program.

The authors' projections for key indicators under a continuation of current SAP policies suggest more modest performance: lower domestic investment and, consequently, lower economic growth, together with increasing public resistance to the SAP. In turn, a likely result is reduced donor assistance because the lack of support will mean that the government is unable to meet the SAP conditions.

For the environment, continuation of current SAP policies means less investment in commercial agriculture but also an expansion of small-scale shifting cultivation as farmers attempt to maintain production in the face of declining inputs. Movement of unemployed urban families back to rural areas will add to this expansion. However, the net effect on deforestation will not exceed the sustainable felling rate.

Loss of wildlife is assumed to be inversely correlated to the level of funding for the National Parks and Wildlife Service. The model predicts that even under the funding constraints imposed by cash budgeting, poaching will not exceed the sustainable rate of offtake.

Although the immediate effect of the SAP on the social sector has been to exacerbate some existing trends toward poverty and inequality, it is hoped that these negative impacts can be mitigated by the desire of both government and donors alike to incorporate sustainable human development and poverty alleviation in future SAPs. Accordingly, it is the government's intention that plans for future SAPs will be evaluated according to their likely social as well as economic outcomes. However, success with this objective depends on two factors: (1) that the planned social programs are implemented (few have begun so far) and (2) that the World Bank's assumptions concerning growth (and therefore the resources available for redistribution) are valid.

If Current Sectoral Policies Continue

As shown earlier, non-SAP sectoral policies as well as structural adjustment itself have a significant impact on patterns of natural resource use. Thus it is important to remember that continuation of these policies without modification may counteract or exacerbate the SAP impacts.

Without a change in energy policy to subsidize electric cooking equipment, households will continue to rely on fuelwood, thus exacerbating deforestation. Currently, only 56 percent of electrified households use electricity for cooking because stoves cost too much.

Introduction of the ADMADE program in the Department of Wildlife, on the other hand, may reduce wildlife poaching through its emphasis on involving local communities in wildlife management and sharing revenue from wildlife utilization with them.

Similarly, if the policies set out in the recently ratified National Environmental Action Plan are implemented, mining and industrial water pollution are expected to decline (although water pollution from domestic sewage is not included in the plan).

Under Alternative Policies

The model shows that higher levels of investment will be required to achieve acceptable rates of economic growth under the alternative policy scenario. This condition has implications for monetary and fiscal policies and for trade policy as well: to generate sufficient internal investment capital, the current trade liberalization policy will have to be modified to include some degree of protection for domestic manufacturing. Because the aim of the alternative policy scenario is to improve the quality of life of the Zambian people rather than simply to restrain demand, it is not expected to attract additional donor funding; it is outside the donors' definition of structural adjustment. As a result, reliance on tax revenues will increase significantly.

Trade-offs

There is a clear trade-off between social welfare and economic efficiency. It is assumed that greater economic efficiency is achieved by moving to a market economy. This statement implies a reduction in state participation in the economy, food subsidies, and free health and education. However, there are risks associated with making these reductions. For example, the private sector is too small and too fragile to take on some government roles, notably, agricultural marketing. In the short term, this transition has produced a collapse in farm incomes and widespread wastage of the 1993 harvest. The obvious instability also jeopardized the long-run growth in agriculture that is critical to Zambia's return to growth. The picture is similar in manufacturing: the rapid liberalization of external trade caused a collapse of the manufacturing base in the face of foreign competition and resulted in unemployment. It also proved impossible to eliminate food relief altogether owing to the high levels of poverty in Zambia; in the short run, donor-supported programs are distributing cheap food, but the longer-run question is how food support can be paid for from domestic resources.

RECOMMENDATIONS

Based on the above analysis, suggestions for policies that could encourage more sustainable development in Zambia are set forth below.

Reorienting Current Structural Adjustment Programs

- Make the assumptions behind program targets more realistic, so that targets are achieved and thus public support for the SAP is maintained.
- Reduce the political and social costs of the SAP by slowing down the speed and scope of reform.
- Increase donor funding so that SAP implementation is not weakened by underfunding.
- Develop a partnership with donors, government, and the public to generate support for the SAP.
- Incorporate long-term development planning as well as short-term financial budgeting in SAP programing.
- Improve the efficiency of government and clearly define its role in the economy (government corruption has meant that the poor perceive the SAP as opening new opportunities for the rich and powerful to enrich themselves further at the expense of the poor).
- Increase tax revenues (introduction of the Zambia Revenue Authority has improved collection, but the tax base remains narrow).

Developing Alternative Structural Adjustment Policies

- Adopt the principle of sustainable development in economic policy formulation.
- Integrate poverty alleviation into the SAP (the disbursement of social funding should not be deferred because of budget constraints).
- Integrate the National Environmental Action Plan into the SAP.
- Increase the role of local communities and nongovernmental organizations in implementing SAP policies.

Policies to Pursue in Parallel with Structural Adjustment

- Macroeconomic policies

o Attract foreign and domestic investment: promote political stability, efficient government, and economic policies that interest the private sector.

o Form, retain, and support human capital; encourage child spacing; and improve education.

- Agricultural policies

  o Increase research resources devoted to finding alternatives to shifting cultivation.

  o Improve the supply of agricultural inputs to encourage agricultural intensification.

  o Introduce freehold tenure in the communal sector, redemarcate old state farms, speed up demarcation of virgin land, and attach environmental conditions to land occupancy.

- Other natural resource policies

  o Reduce import duties and sales taxes on electric stoves to encourage use of electricity in preference to fuelwood.

  o Raise the price of raw wood to reflect the true environmental costs of deforestation.

  o Continue the ADMADE program.

  o Rehabilitate the sanitation and water supply infrastructure.

ENDNOTES

1. *Zambia Daily Mail*, June 6, 1994, p. 5.
2. N. Leader-Williams, S.D. Albon, and P.S.M. Berry, "Illegal Exploitation of Black Rhinoceros and Elephant Populations: Patterns of Decline, Law Enforcement and Patrol Effort in the Luangwa Valley, Zambia," *Journal of Applied Ecology* 27:1055.
3. P. Stromgaard, "Field Studies of Land Use under *Chitemene* Shifting Cultivation, Zambia," *Geografisk Tidsskrift* 84:78-85.
4. World Bank, *Beneficiary Assessment of the Social Reserve Fund* (Lusaka: Study Fund, 1992).
5. Computable General Equilibrium Model to Measure the Effects of Structural Adjustment on Ecology and Development in Zambia, funded by the Research Council of Norway under the Ecology and Development Program through the Agricultural University of Norway. Complete details are given in Appendix 3 of the full country report.

7

CASE STUDY FOR EL SALVADOR

This chapter was written by Deborah Barry and Herman Rosa of Programa Salvadoreño de Investigación sobre Desarrollo y Medio Ambiente and is based on a study by them, with support of Anil Markandya of the Harvard Institute for International Development.

Environmental degradation, which in the past had given El Salvador a reputation as one of the worst cases in the Western Hemisphere, accelerated sharply during the years of the civil war and economic reforms, delivering the country into a period of postwar reconstruction and development with significant environmental handicaps that threaten to undermine the very peace and economic stability so fervently pursued.

Over the past 15 years, the civil war, the drop in world prices for agroexports, and the implementation of stabilization and adjustment policies together effected major changes in the economy and patterns of human settlements. Although the specific impacts of each factor cannot be easily separated, all three appear to have reinforced changes in the same direction. Thus in a relatively short period, the country witnessed a major break from the past: economic growth and dynamism historically rooted in the agricultural sector shifted to commerce, services, and industry as the new foci of economic growth and profitability. At the same time, the precipitous decline in rural economic activity and subsequent breakdown in rural livelihoods fostered a surge in the migration of the rural poor and investment in the burgeoning but totally unplanned and unregulated urban landscape of El Salvador.

The dimension of these changes and their repercussions on the natural resource base of the country are only barely becoming understood in the postwar period. This study reveals that the degree and dynamics of environmental degradation have reached a point at which the capacity to renew the most basic natural resource for any development option—water—is rapidly being lost. Past problems of deforestation and soil erosion now combine with widespread sedimentation and contamination of the sources of water, limiting both its sink and supply functions. Although these problems have worsened considerably, the country has lost its capacity to monitor, assess, prescribe policy, and enforce the laws and measures necessary to counter the land degradation and water contamination, elements critical to the sustainability of any development option.

ENVIRONMENTAL OVERVIEW

Population and the Environment

Reflecting a widely held view, the 1979 World Bank's country economic memorandum (CEM) for El Salvador regarded rapid population growth as "the country's most fundamental long-run problem, given the country's size and natural resource base."[1] The central recommendation of stepping-up family planning programs was followed in the eighties with U.S. Agency for International Development (USAID) encouragement and financing, thus increasing the use of contraceptives. Owing largely to this factor, the national fertility rate dropped 38 percent between 1978 and 1993 and further drops are expected.

More significant for its short-term impact on population growth was the large-scale outmigration that occurred at the end of the seventies and through the eighties as the political and economic situation deteriorated and accelerated with the outbreak of civil war. As a result of this outmigration and the drop in fertility rates, population grew at a much lower rate than anticipated. The 5 million figure given by the 1992 census means that annual growth in 1977-92 was just 1.2 percent. As the war began to wind down, outmigration began to decrease, and the current population growth rate is now an estimated 2.2 percent. With that rate unchanged, the population will reach 6.0 million by the year 2000 and 10.3 million by 2025. In addition, in the medium term, it is possible that the rural population will drop below its present levels if the urban population continues to grow at a faster rate.

A spatial rendering of population by municipality shows an increasing concentration of the population in the southern and southwestern parts of the country. Although an internal migration pattern established before the seventies, this massive dislocation occurred in a relatively short time. Of particular relevance is the concentration of 30 percent of the population in the municipalities of the San Salvador Metropolitan Area (SSMA) that together comprise 6.6 percent of the national territory.

Current Dynamics of Environmental Degradation

The concentration of population and rapid urbanization have established a new dynamic of environmental degradation more damaging than in the past. Today the country awakes from a period of civil conflict to a postwar situation considerably different than 20 years ago. Current patterns of urban settlement and agricultural production have produced a degree of land degradation that if unchecked will soon limit the country's capacity to provide and renew the water resources needed for its future development. Below are the principal environmental problems that affect the country at the national level:

- Growing urbanization is contaminating the major river systems and is pushing them to their limit as a sink. With surface waters used primarily as a sink, they are currently limiting supply.[2]
- Unplanned and hazardous urbanization is also interfering with the natural recharge capacity of groundwater, today the principal source of supply.
- Expansion of agriculture on steeper slopes and fuelwood harvesting in the mountainous rural areas, particularly the North, have radically reduced the natural capacity for regulation of surface waters. Increased levels of erosion and sedimentation of rivers also negatively affect the surface water supply, groundwater recharge, and hydroelectric generation.
- With high levels of rainfall concentrated in less than 5 months per year, water availability varies drastically from season to season, seriously limiting a continuous and expanding supply for the immediate future.

Pattern of Human Settlement and Groundwater Aquifers

Rapid urbanization and an increased concentration in rural areas are occurring in or near the last significant areas of forest cover, mostly shade coffee plantations that act as a close substitute for tropical forests, thus maintaining the tropical hydrological functions intact. These coffee-covered volcanic mountains and surrounding areas are part of a hydrogeological formation that captures, channels, and restores the groundwater aquifers (currently supplying more than 90 percent of potable water) that run along the southern corridor of the country. This region represents a fragile ecosystem that depends on adequate land use conditions to guarantee high levels of infiltration of rain water through the porous volcanic rock into underground reserves. Both rapid deforestation and voracious "urban cover" (i.e., replacing coffee with asphalt and cement) contribute to diminishing recharge capacity while the population concentrates and increases the local demand for water.

Urbanization-related Contamination and Sedimentation of Surface Waters
Owing to rapid, massive, and unchecked urban growth, the increase in contamination and sedimentation of surface waters has reached the point of imposing serious limitations on supply for domestic and productive consumption and is decreasing hydroelectrical energy generation at a faster rate than expected. Because of San Salvador's unique geographic location relative to the country's surface waterways, the SSMA currently contributes to contamination of over 60 percent of the surface water resources, of which 90 percent are contaminated.

The SSMA resides within the Acelhuate River watershed, which then empties into the reservoir of the principal hydroelectric dam, which in turn harnesses the flow of the Lempa River, the country's principal river (see Figure 7.1). Totally untreated urban sewage, industrial waste, and high levels of sediment from land movement for urbanization flow from the SSMA into the Acelhuate River, which empties directly into the reservoir, creating serious problems of siltation of the dam floor. Three other rivers receiving high levels of agrochemical runoff, urban sewage, and industrial waste also empty into the reservoir. Besides contaminating the reservoir, these materials continue downstream to the coast, where fragile ecosystems are impacted negatively.

With surface waters nearly at their threshold as a sink and declining trends in health indicators, increasing pressure is put on the use of groundwater sources. However, unchecked rates of pumping, together with destructive changes in surface land use, are setting a pattern for the systematic destruction of the ecosystem's regenerative capacity.

Figure 7.1 El Salvador

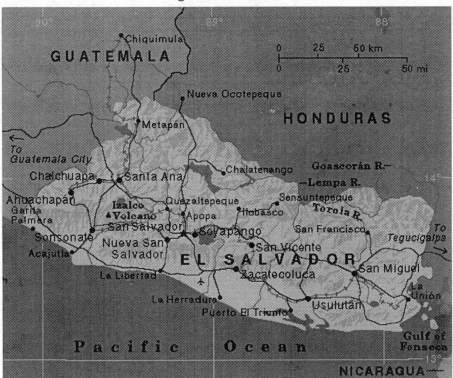

From *Picture Atlas of the World* CD-ROM, © National Geographic Society, 1995

Small-producer Hillside Agriculture

Expanded deforestation and erosion-prone agricultural practices on steeper slopes, particularly in the northern highlands, are contributing to the loss of capacity to regulate surface water flows and absorption for both agricultural purposes as well as year-round human consumption. More widespread erosion as a result of cultivation on steeper slopes in these upper watersheds is now increasing sedimentation of rivers, in turn limiting the supply of surface water for urban consumption and also contributing to damsite siltation.

Approximately 65 percent of the land is of a nonarable soil type, and 85 percent of all agricultural producers farm less than 5 hectares, mostly on those poor soils. Depending on the crop, 60-80 percent is cultivated on steep slopes; the area planted to corn has grown continuously. Often grown in association, corn and beans have highly degrading effects on these marginal lands. The situation is aggravated by the practice of total clearing and burning of vegetation before planting in addition to the high-level use of agrochemical inputs and the near disappearance of fallow periods.

Although the land reform program of the eighties had a positive temporary impact on land distribution, a recent study by Seligson and others indicates a return to previous practices: an increase in *minifundismo*, an overall decrease in the average size of agricultural plots, and possibly a return to the prereform number of producers renting land.[3] As a result, deforestation, erosion, and sedimentation, particularly in the northern highlands, are increasing. The sharp decline in rural wages, a crucial component of rural livelihoods, together with a tendency to decrease yields for hillside agriculture have most likely driven the spatial extension of basic grains production and also forced the rural population into other depredating livelihoods, such as extremely small-scale fuelwood gathering and commercialization.

The immediate and most evident impacts are a loss of biomass energy (i.e., fuelwood) for human use, lumber for construction, and topsoil for agricultural production. However, the downstream effect of upper watershed degradation is far more widespread and serious: a decrease in the capacity for human "harvesting" of soils and water. The compacting and drying out of soils reduce productivity and decrease local year-round water supplies (lessening surface recharge), eliminating local water sources for human consumption. At the same time, this situation produces a subsequent increase in sedimentation of the major river systems, downstream flooding, siltation of hydropower reservoirs, and with the increased flow of sediments, major ecological changes in coastal ecosystems.

THE UNSUSTAINABILITY OF PAST DEVELOPMENT

The Early Role of Agroexport Production

Agroexport production has been a dominant practice in El Salvador since colonial times. The shifts in land use for agroexports, from indigo to coffee and eventually to sugar cane and cotton in some areas, have taken their distinctive tolls on the soils of the country, which originally supported a dense tropical forest cover with high levels of biodiversity.

Given the scale on which indigo was cultivated, large expanses of the country were deforested because it entailed clearing and burning. Indigo became the main export crop in the 1870s, but with the advent of artificial dyes, it declined rapidly and was replaced by coffee as the major export. Coffee plantations are seen today as providing the most important remaining forest cover and one of the least ecologically destructive agricultural systems in El Salvador. Yet their creation entailed large-scale deforestation. In addition, expanded coffee production caused major social dislocation when it drastically altered the land tenure pattern.

Economic Diversification in the Fifties and Sixties

In the fifties and sixties, an attempt was made to move from the traditional export-led model based almost exclusively on coffee toward a growth model that added two new elements. The first was agroexport diversification based on cotton expansion. The second was an industrialization drive based on the promotion of intraregional trade of manufactures and the creation of the Central American Common Market (CACM).

Cotton Expansion

Cotton production began to increase in El Salvador just before World War II, propelled by the invention of pesticides against human disease vectors and cotton pests and by the scarcity of cotton during the war. Although the area planted to cotton doubled between 1948 and 1951 (when it reached 30,000 hectares), the biggest push came in the sixties through construction of the Litoral Highway (begun in 1958). This road and the secondary ones branching from it led to a large increase in cotton areas in the early sixties, and most of the remaining forests were destroyed. Cotton expansion also had a highly destructive environmental impact owing to its effects on soil fertility and to the notoriously excessive use of pesticides. From 1965 through the 1970s, cotton growers applied more pesticides per land unit than anywhere else in the world, poisoning soil, water sources, and aquatic ecosystems. Levels of DDT in mothers' milk were among the highest in the world. Compared to coffee, the cotton boom was short lived. Production and exports peaked in 1963-64 and fell sharply thereafter, largely because of the increasing cost of controlling resistant pest species.

The Industrialization Drive of the Sixties

Based largely on the production of light industrial consumer products, import substitution made an important contribution to the economic growth in the sixties, with manufacturing output doubling between 1960 and 1967. In addition, while the value of cotton exports was falling and that of coffee exports stagnated, the export of manufactured goods, mostly to the rest of Central America, was rising rapidly.

Despite its initial success, this import-intensive industrialization scheme had three basic weaknesses:

- its ultimate dependence on the foreign exchange provided by the region's traditional agroexporting sectors;
- the tendency to deepen regional imbalances in industrial development and trade, with a particularly sharp contrast between El Salvador and Honduras; and
- its limited impact in terms of employment creation.

Failed Attempts at Agrarian Transformation and Economic Diversification during the Seventies

As the industrialization drive faltered, traditional agroexports regained prominence in the economy of the seventies, particularly with sharply increased international prices for these products. Thus the combined area planted to coffee, cotton, and sugar cane rose 41 percent between 1971 and 1978.

During the seventies, there were also attempts to diversify the economy through the development of tourism and the promotion of industrial exports based in the expansion of assembly operations in duty-free industrial parks (free zones). In the end, those efforts failed owing to the increased political instability toward the end of the decade.

One element of the political instability was the failure to introduce changes in the rigid agrarian structure that had become more polarized as the historical pattern of concentration in land ownership continued unabated. As shown in Table 7.1, the number of farmers with access to more than 1 hectare of land was reduced one-third between 1961 and 1971. Overall, there was an 8 percent reduction in the number of farmers with access to any land at all. At the same time, the peasants' demand for

Table 7.1 Farmers with Access to Land, 1961 and 1971

Land Access	1961	1971	Percent Change
More than 1 hectare	118,687	78,267	-34.1
Less than 1 hectare	96,456	119,350	+23.7
Total	215,143	197,517	-8.2

Source: Mitchell Selgison, "Treinta Años de Transformación en la Estructura Agraria de El Salvador," Universidad Centroamericana José Simeón Cañas (UCA), Realidad, *Revista de Ciencias Sociales y Humanidades*, No. 41, San Salvador.

agricultural land was increasing with rural population growth at 3.4 percent per year, faster than in previous decades. Opposition to any changes in the land tenure system, combined with the closed nature of the political system, paved the way for the 12-year civil war that broke out in 1980.

Reforms under the Civil War, the Eighties and Early Nineties

In 1980, following a coup and the rapid reshuffle of civil-military juntas, a land reform program was decreed. In addition, the government took over the marketing of coffee and sugar exports. These reforms that expanded the role of the state in the economy gave way in the mid-eighties to a different type of economic reform that had the opposite effect. In both cases, the U.S. government through USAID played a decisive role in terms of political, financial, and technical support. With the advent of a new government in 1989, an economic reform program closely following the blueprint of International Monetary Fund (IMF)-World Bank adjustment programs began to be implemented. Further, under the United Nations-brokered Peace Accords of 1992, a major political reform and a land transfer program benefiting excombatants in the civil war were launched.

Taken together, these reforms are changing El Salvador in significant ways. Political reform seems to be removing an important obstacle to development. Land distribution programs, seen basically as a political expedient rather than as a serious development effort, are having mixed results. On the other hand, the economic reform, while allowing for fairly high economic growth rates and postwar recovery, is not adequately tackling, and may be even worsening, the serious problems that the country faces both socially and environmentally, as discussed below.

ECONOMIC REFORM: CONTEXT AND OVERALL PERFORMANCE

The economic reform has gone through two basic stages. The first, in 1985-88, was basically a stabilization package that had fiscal adjustment and exchange rate devaluation as its basic components. The second stage of economic reform, the structural adjustment phase proper, began immediately after a new government came to power in June 1989. Three relevant aspects of El Salvador's economic reform are:

- The economy was affected by major shocks during the eighties from factors largely unrelated to the economic reform, such as the civil war, high levels of external aid, large-scale outmigration that in turn led to a massive inflow of remittances, and falling international prices of the main export products.
- USAID played a major role in launching both stages of economic reform. The second stage was also implemented with heavy support from multilateral organizations (i.e., the IMF, the World Bank, and the Inter-American Development Bank [IDB]).
- The structural adjustment reforms were launched in a context of foreign exchange abundance (i.e., the Dutch disease syndrome) from remittances, aid, and greater inflows of private and official capital.

Economic Decline During the Early Eighties

With the deepening political crisis at the end of the seventies and the breakout of the civil war came a massive flight of private capital and significant disruption of economic activities. As a result, the economy plunged into a deep recession (see Figure 7.2). In constant 1990 colones, GDP dropped 29 percent during 1979-82 and private consumption 35 percent. In contrast, public consumption fell only 9 percent during that period while defense-related expenditures increased. Public finances deteriorated sharply and the public deficit rose from 1 percent of GDP in 1979 to 9.2 percent in 1981.

The Role of U.S. Economic Aid and Remittances

The civil war also attracted massive economic and military assistance from the United States in an attempt to strengthen the Salvadoran government and the military against the challenge of the guerrilla movement. The disbursements of economic aid increased rapidly from about US$11 million

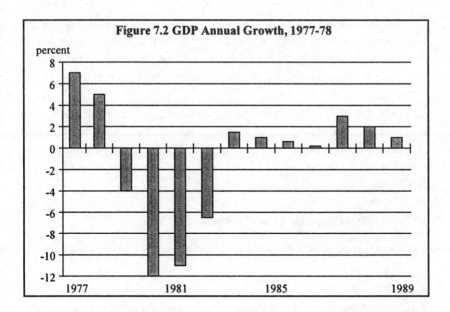

Figure 7.2 GDP Annual Growth, 1977-78

per year in 1978-79 to US$248 million by 1983.[4] The availability of these funds was key in arresting the drop in GDP and in supporting government finances.

Together with official aid, remittances became an additional extraordinary source of foreign exchange for the Salvadoran economy until they became the main source of foreign exchange. Because only a small fraction came through formal channels, the level of remittances was severely underestimated by the Central Bank in the eighties, thus introducing serious miscalculations in some balance of payments items (e.g., imports, private capital outflows). For 1987, the Central Bank reported about US$180 million in remittances,[5] whereas for the same year, the World Bank made a conservative estimate that was three times higher (US$557 million).[6] For 1993, the Central Bank published a figure of US$824 million in remittances, which seems a more realistic estimate.[7] Thus in the nineties, the Central Bank finally came to terms with the magnitude of the problem.

The First Stage of Economic Reform

The Role of USAID
The call for substantial economic reform in the eighties came from USAID as Duarte was taking office in mid-1984 with an economic plan that contradicted USAID proposals. Although the new government proposed

an inward-looking strategy and the consolidation of the 1980 reforms (e.g., land reform, nationalization of the banking system and of foreign trade of the main agroexports), USAID proposed an export-led growth strategy based on nontraditional exports to extraregional markets and fiscal austerity.

In the end, USAID prevailed, using its substantial economic assistance as leverage. Thus in January 1986, the government launched what can be considered the first stage of economic reform: a stabilization program that included as its central measure an exchange rate devaluation and a severe fiscal adjustment.

Inflation, Fiscal Adjustment, and Institutional Collapse

The most immediate impact of the first phase of economic reform was rising inflation. As speculation on the devaluation mounted in 1985, the exchange rate in the black market soared and so did the inflation rate. In the face of renewed inflation, public expenditures fell sharply in real terms during 1985-88. Although the drastic fiscal adjustment that took place in this first stage of the economic reform was rather successful in reducing the overall public sector deficit, it also devastated the institutional capacity of the government across the board. The area referred to in the public accounts as "development of natural resources" was hit particularly hard (see Figure 7.3), despite the fact that it represented only a small fraction

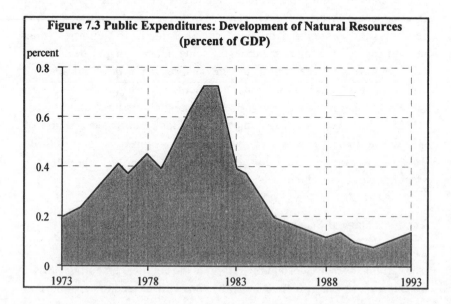

Figure 7.3 Public Expenditures: Development of Natural Resources (percent of GDP)

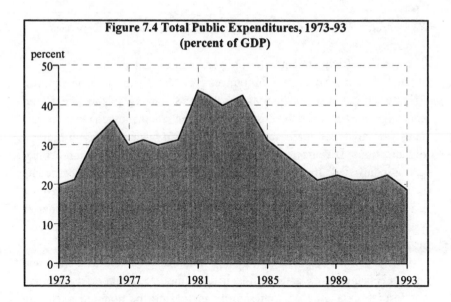

Figure 7.4 Total Public Expenditures, 1973-93 (percent of GDP)

of the total (See Figure 7.4). This institutional impact is discussed in the section on "Economic Reform and the Environment."

The Structural Adjustment Stage of Economic Reform

The Roles of USAID, the World Bank, the IMF, and the IDB

With this heavy USAID support, the structural adjustment reforms began under the Cristiani government, well before the first stand-by agreement with the IMF and approval of the first structural adjustment loan (SAL) from the World Bank. By that time, the government had already implemented significant reforms, such as internal price liberalization, exchange rate liberalization, and far-reaching tax reforms. In addition, trade and financial liberalization (including privatization of previously nationalized banks) were implemented.

The Cristiani government sought its first agreement with the IMF to improve its standing in the international financial community. This was successful. The Paris Club members rescheduled El Salvador's bilateral debt 1 month after the IMF approved its first stand-by operation. The World Bank also approved the first SAL in February 1991 and approved other loans thereafter. The IDB, on the other hand, considerably expanded the scale of its operations. In this way, the World Bank assumed the leadership role in advising and supervising the economic reform in El Salvador, and the IDB assumed the major supporting role.

The Foreign Exchange Bonanza, Trade Liberalization, and Economic Growth

The structural adjustment reforms were carried out in the context of a foreign exchange bonanza. Remittances grew sharply through the eighties. Private capital inflows increased after 1989 owing to the liberalized exchange market, a relatively stable exchange rate that made local interest rates attractive, and increased the confidence of business and multilateral organizations. Disbursements of official loans also increased and official grants continued. In addition, debt servicing was reduced because the reform program allowed rescheduling the bilateral debt and forgiving US$465 million owed to the United States. As a result, foreign exchange was much more available in 1989-93 than in 1984-88 despite lower export levels (see Figure 7.5).

In this context of a foreign exchange bonanza, the liberalized exchange market became quite elastic; that is, it accommodated an increased demand for foreign exchange without sharply increasing the nominal exchange rate[8] despite a surge in imports from 1989 onward (see Figure 7.6). Thus the most immediate impact of trade liberalization in this "Dutch disease" context from 1989 onward is a sharp increase in registered imports; the import level in 1993 was 90 percent higher than 5 years earlier.

With a stable exchange rate and no import constraints, the economy began to grow under structural adjustment at a much faster pace than

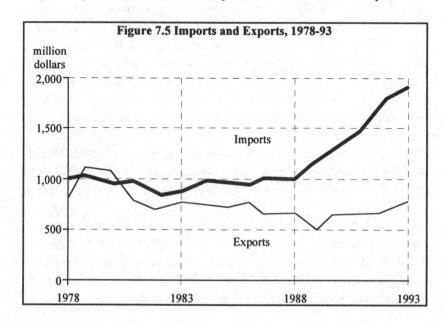

Figure 7.5 Imports and Exports, 1978-93

million dollars

Imports

Exports

1978   1983   1988   1993

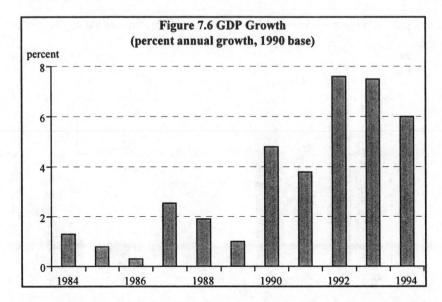

Figure 7.6 GDP Growth
(percent annual growth, 1990 base)

before this phase. The average annual growth rate jumped from 1.2 percent during 1984-89 to 5.9 percent during 1990-94. Growth rates have been significantly higher since 1992, with the formal ending of the civil war and a substantial increase in available credit from commercial banks that began to be reprivatized that same year.[9]

ECONOMIC GROWTH, THE BREAKDOWN OF RURAL LIVELIHOODS, AND THE ENVIRONMENT

Private Consumption-led Growth under Structural Adjustment

Although the structural adjustment reforms in El Salvador ("Dutch disease" and postwar recovery) have been highly expansive, the pattern of growth established was not export led, as proponents of the reforms might have envisioned. Consumption, in fact, has played a far more important role, to the extent that the consumption increase exceeds the total GDP increase by a wide margin (see Figure 7.7).

Private consumption is particularly important. During 1990-94, it grew two-thirds. At the same time, public-sector consumption decreased one-third. The private consumption increase exceeded the total GDP increase by nearly 50 percent during 1990-94 (see Table 7.2), whereas increased investments and exports each represent only about one-fourth the total

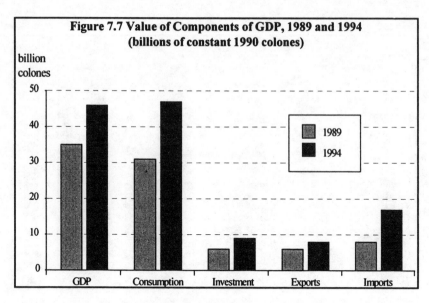

Figure 7.7 Value of Components of GDP, 1989 and 1994
(billions of constant 1990 colones)

GDP variation. In other words, growth in this period was basically led by private consumption rather than by exports or investment.

Given this central role of private consumption in the pattern of growth, economic sectors such as commerce and internal demand-driven industry also appear as the main contributors to the high growth levels achieved during the period (see Table 7.3). Commerce, with an average annual growth rate of 10.1 percent, contributed 32 percent to GDP growth achieved during 1991-94. In contrast, agriculture, which in 1990 still represented 17.3 percent of GDP (almost the same as commerce in that year), contributed only 7 percent to GDP growth owing to its low average growth rate during the same period (2.6 percent).

Economic Growth, Urbanization, and Environmental Degradation

As discussed above, the economy has been growing at fairly high rates under structural adjustment, and the most important contributors to that growth are commerce, industry, and services in general—economic activities that are highly concentrated in the SSMA and its surroundings. In the absence of even minimal regulatory capacity, concentration in the SSMA of population and of the most dynamic economic activities is a major source of environmental degradation.

The boom in the commercial and services sector is changing the predominant patterns of land use in several SSMA zones. For example,

Table 7.2 GDP by Expenditure, 1989 and 1994

	Value in constant 1990 colones (billions)		Total Variation, 1989-94 (percent)	Total Variation/ GDP Variation, 1989-94 (percent)
	1989	1994		
Consumption	31.4	46.5	48	132
Private	25.5	42.6	67	149
Public	5.8	3.9	-33	-17
Investment	6.0	9.0	49	26
Exports	5.5	8.1	49	23
Imports	8.1	17.2	113	80
GDP	34.8	46.3	33	100

previous high-income residential areas in the western part of San Salvador are being converted to commercial, financial, and services establishments. To compensate for that change and meet increased demand (real and speculative), new high-income residential areas and shopping centers have been developed in the South, in areas previously designated as ecological reserves for essential groundwater recharge. This development process is also being fostered by the liberalized and reprivatized banking system because it provides increasing credit to the highly dynamic construction sector.

Table 7.3 Sectoral Growth Rates and Contribution to Total GDP Growth, 1990-94 (percent)

Sector	Distribution of GDP		Average Annual Growth	Contribution to GDP Growth
	1990	1994		
Commerce	18.1	21.0	10.	31.9
Industry	21.5	22.6	7.	26.6
Construction	3.5	3.9	9.	5.5
Financial	2.3	2.6	9.	3.7
Agriculture	17.3	15.1	2.	7.0
Other	37.3	34.8	4.	25.3
GDP	100.0	100.0	6.	100.0

Internal migration from rural areas has increased the demand for shelter near the SSMA, where commercial developers have responded by promoting miniplots (the so-called *lotificaciones*), where shelters are established and basic grains cultivated. Fuelwood is the main energy source for this large population.

With these developments, coupled with the concentration of population and economic activities in the SSMA, the urban environment is affected seriously in several ways. Rapid deforestation of areas surrounding the SSMA is caused by the growth of housing projects and fuelwood harvesting. Previous norms regulating where and how construction was permitted (e.g., to protect aquifer recharge and avoid contamination, maintain the physical integrity of volcanic slopes, provide adequate green space per square meters of construction) have suffered wholesale violation, now a common practice.

The provision of potable water for the SSMA is acute: the basic grid for delivery is outdated and the institutional support systems are ill equipped and weak, not to mention the limited permanent water sources throughout the dry season. As mentioned above, the volume of untreated domestic and urban waste from major urban centers is creating widespread health problems (rivers passing through urban areas are the equivalent of open sewage systems), is contaminating downstream sources and aquatic bodies (otherwise usable for recreation and tourism), and is beginning to limit supply. Sedimentation in surface waters is also limiting the supply, a problem related to erosion from hillside agriculture. In addition, as the number of motor vehicles increases exponentially (in part, related to dropping import barriers), congestion and air contamination are also increasing significantly in the SSMA.

Poverty and Environmental Degradation in the Rural Economy

In contrast to the urban economy, the rural economy has remained largely depressed under structural adjustment. Thus there is no significant change in the massive loss of rural livelihoods that has occurred since the eighties owing to the war, dropping international prices of agroexports, and economic policies. The loss in rural livelihoods was so severe that it was a major driving force for increased outmigration to the urban centers.

Cotton production fell to near extinction in the eighties. Grown mostly in conflict areas, cotton was affected by the civil war in the early eighties. Later on, rising costs of chemical inputs and falling international prices played a major role in its demise. Coffee, the main agroexport, was largely spared by the civil war because it was grown mostly in nonconflict zones. Yet it was seriously hit by sharp drops in international prices. Although the area planted to coffee did not change significantly, production fell as plantations deteriorated.

Apart from unfavorable world prices, the World Bank argued that economic policies penalized coffee production in the eighties by depressing domestic prices beyond what would be warranted by the drop in world prices. Comparing real world prices in 1973-75 with those in 1985-87, the Bank found that they had been 13 percent higher in the latter period; yet real domestic producer prices had been 52 percent lower, owing mainly to exchange rate appreciation.[10] It should be added that the drop in domestic prices referred to by the World Bank was compensated for by a sharp drop in real wages for harvest and permanent agricultural workers because minimum wages were not adjusted for inflation.[11] By 1989, real minimum harvest wages for coffee had fallen to 27 percent of the 1978 level.

The fact is that the decline in agroexport production had a serious impact on temporary rural employment. By the 1988-89 harvest season, harvest employment for the two major export crops (coffee and cotton) had fallen 70 percent from the peak level of 1979-80. Cotton accounts for the larger part of those employment losses. This change is more a function of the overall decline in the area planted to cotton, a decline that continued after the war. As a major crop, cotton has reached near extinction.

Real prices of basic grains, the other basic component of rural livelihoods for small farmers with access to land, also show significant drops; in 1989, corn and bean prices were less than 50 percent of their 1978 levels. The drop in real prices for basic grains and in harvest wages and employment during a prolonged period (since the eighties) constitutes a significant breakdown in rural livelihoods; together with the war, it was the principal impetus for the stark increase in rural-urban migration. The breakdown also increased the use of survival strategies that depredate the environment, for example, wood gathering and wildlife trafficking (e.g., parrots, iguanas, tucans, papagayos), both of which have increased considerably in the North.

Access to land is another rural livelihood determinant. Despite the land reform of the 1980s, recent studies (although suffering from problems with earlier data) indicate a return to prereform practices. Added to the increasing cultivation of poor to extremely poor lands, *minifundismo* and the number of producers renting land appear to be on the rise. At the same time, the area planted to corn continues to expand, moving into overused grazing lands and onto higher slopes fit at best for forestry. All these trends are causing more widespread erosion in the upper watershed and consequent sedimentation of El Salvador's major rivers. The implications for agricultural production as the basis for sustaining rural livelihoods are extremely negative because both the small plot size and nonownership of land appear to dictate eventual decreasing returns in production. Other problems for rural livelihoods accentuate land degradation. One is the highly skewed access to financial inputs or official credit. Only 12-20 percent of small producers obtain credit for their production.[12] Even then, the credit packages exclude the introduction of soil conservation techniques.

Established trends show a serious breakdown in the principal rural livelihoods of El Salvador and therefore in living conditions of the rural poor. Two ameliorating factors are remittances and, since 1989, a minimal recovery in harvest employment and a recovery in coffee production. Nonetheless, rural poverty is so pervasive that 88 percent of the rural population lived in poverty in 1992, according to a World Bank study (see Table 7.4). With such pervasiveness of rural poverty and the breakdown in rural livelihoods, rural survival strategies are a major factor in land degradation that leads to extensive and higher levels of erosion, sedimentation of major rivers and dams, and the general loss in the capacity of water resources.

Table 7.4 Poverty Levels, 1992
(percent)

	Rural	Urban	National
Nonpoor	12.3	44.8	31.6
Poor[a]	87.7	55.2	68.4
Structural poor	49.1	24.1	34.0
Ascendant poor	32.0	12.2	20.2
Descendant poor	12.3	44.8	31.6

Source: World Bank, "El Salvador: The Challenge of Poverty Alleviation," Rep. No. 12315-ES (Washington, D.C., 1994).

a. Structural poor = income below poverty line and at least one basic need unmet; ascendant poor = income above povery line with at least one basic need unmet; descendant poor = income below poverty line but with their basic needs met.

ECONOMIC REFORM AND THE ENVIRONMENT: THE INSTITUTIONAL DIMENSION

The two stages of economic reform had different institutional impacts. The drastic fiscal adjustment during the first stage led to near collapse of the country's capacity to deal with environmental issues. During the second stage—the structural adjustment phase proper, from 1989 onward—the key external actors (USAID, the IDB, and the World Bank) attempted to reintroduce the environment into the reform process, including institution building.

The Demise of the National Institutional Capacity During the First Stage

Previous high levels of public spending and a focus on strengthening national capacity during the seventies allowed for considerable institution building across a relatively broad spectrum of expertise and professional specialization relevant to natural resource planning and management. The most important institutional development was the creation of the Directorate for Renewable Natural Resources (DGRN) in 1968. Through it, El Salvador developed a considerable capacity to monitor and research environmental developments as well as to design policy proposals. Although the political situation weakened enforcement, the DGRN implemented some of the most effective and sophisticated environmental projects carried out by any Central American government agency.

During the eighties, most of this capacity was lost, owing mainly to budget cuts, and by 1988, real spending was down to 16 percent of the 1978 level (see Figure 7.8). The impact of these cuts on the DGRN was severe. As the beginning of the budget crunch was felt, the institution was slowly but surely dismembered. Some programs fled to other institutions in search of funding. Most monitoring and studies were suspended. At the same time, for political reasons, program efforts concentrated in areas affected by the land reform, passing over the urban areas and the remaining rural areas.

Although external project funding began to substitute for central government support of much of DGRN activity, the costs for running the institution became impossible to sustain. As real salaries plummeted and

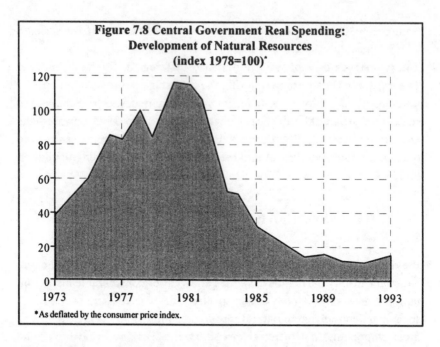

Figure 7.8 Central Government Real Spending:
Development of Natural Resources
(index 1978=100)*

*As deflated by the consumer price index.

internal political strife developed, high-level professional staff and competent managers began to leave the institution, leading to its virtual collapse.

Key institutions related to resource management problems in the agricultural sector were also affected when real government spending dropped to 29 percent of the 1978 level by 1988. Institutions related to urban development also suffered deterioration, with real spending in 1988 down to 38 percent of the 1978 level. The National University's Biology Department exemplifies the destruction of the national capacity for generating basic information and research required for natural resource monitoring and management. Once an institution of academic excellence enjoying as many as five Ph.D.s on staff, this depository of independent research capacity was demolished economically and later, politically.

The Roles of USAID, the World Bank, and the IDB

USAID, the Front Runner

As the second phase of economic reform, structural adjustment proper, was being launched with its support, USAID began to introduce new conditionality and policy proposals linked with environmental concerns. With encouragement from USAID, the presidents of Central American countries began the process of creating the Central American Commission on Environment and Development (CCAD) in 1989. Each country created a National Commission for Environment (CONAMA), to be a decisionmaking body representing the relevant ministries. An Executive Secretariat for the Environment (SEMA) would be located in the ministry in which most interest in the environment existed. In El Salvador, SEMA began to function in 1991 and was located within the Ministry of Agriculture and presided over by its minister. SEMA's mandate was to coordinate policies and strategies established by CONAMA, which consists of 14 ministers and is coordinated by the Minister of Agriculture.

SEMA's main purpose was to coordinate environmental activities carried out by different ministries, which were often perceived as duplicative or even conflicting. SEMA was also expected to establish environmental norms and policies to be elaborated in consensus with public and private institutions, nongovernmental organizations, and other related parties. Further, SEMA was to channel financial resources to the different actors in the environmental scene and catalyze actions that would confront a wide gamut of environmental problems in El Salvador.

SEMA's development, as an exercise in institution building, is less than successful. One of its major organizational weaknesses stems from the fact that the institutional arrangement gave it: (1) no participation in the national-level planning process; (2) no authority or regulatory capacity with respect to administration; (3) therefore no basis on which to carry out intersectoral or interagency coordination; and (4) no organic institutional relationship with specialized research or monitoring bodies, which, in any event, were almost totally destroyed by the time of SEMA's creation.

A first look at SEMA reveals that it was relatively successful in carrying out the initial mobilization of international funding related to environmental interests.[13] However, CONAMA has been virtually non-functional, and SEMA in practice operated as a high-level, semipermanent government counterpart to international agencies. It had no national counterpart institutional capacity with which to design, plan, and/or carry out plans of almost any kind. Despite its initial capable professional staff, with some of the highest salary levels in the government, little effort was put into seriously updating information on current environmental conditions.

Although housed in the Agriculture Ministry, SEMA had little relation to the World Bank's agricultural sector reform, which concentrated on revamping the research and extension center (CENTA, described in the following section), the most important governmental institution relating to rural policy impacts. Similar developments are seen in the energy and water sectors, in which reforms (i.e., privatization and cost pricing for resource use) are being carried out without consideration or coordination with SEMA.

The incoherence of the institutional reforms is further evidenced by the fact that with the installation of the new government, SEMA was transferred to the Planning Ministry just when this ministry is supposedly being dissolved under the guidance of the state modernization reforms. Internally, SEMA has suffered from a wholesale turnover of staff while in search of its role. It has also been plagued by the need to answer for the administrative and financial management under the previous government, which is currently an encumbrance.

In addition to supporting SEMA, USAID created three other instruments for dealing with environmental policy and issues: (1) a business sector environmental foundation (SALVANATURA) to mobilize support for and involvement in environmental reforms, education, biodiversity protection, and a cleanup industry; (2) the Enterprise for the Americas debt reduction plan; and (3) an environmental project named PROMESA.

Owing to a late start and difficulties in operations, it is too early to evaluate PROMESA. In general, USAID's environmental agenda has helped to create initial awareness within government structures and private enterprise. However, legal reforms and public institution building have resulted in accumulated failures and, at best, weak and partial advances. Many government responses to USAID conditionalities cannot be considered more than pro forma compliance with formalities, and the lack of political will seriously to include environmental concerns as inherent to economic and social policy has left SEMA without a relevant role.

The World Bank

The World Bank was largely absent from El Salvador during the eighties, and when it reappeared with its first SAL in February 1991, not a single reference to the environment was made. Not until the appraisal report for the second adjustment loan of September 1993 is the subject of environmental concern explicitly introduced. A natural resources management study was not carried out until the end of that year.

With this late timing, the Bank's overall approach to environmental questions has been one of supporting the existing measures, approaches, and processes already established by USAID and the IDB with the Salvadoran government rather than one of innovation. To date, the Bank's only additional contribution is within the framework of agricultural reform, a hybrid loan approved in March 1993; known as PRISA, it is part of a series of loans supporting agricultural reform.[14]

PRISA was intended to finance the reform and strengthening of the Ministry of Agriculture and CENTA, the Agricultural Research and Extension Center. The goal was to strengthen the institutional capacity directed toward small and medium-size agricultural producers, principally those dedicated to the traditional cultivation of basic grains.

Despite its objectives, the reform process has had serious negative impacts on the institutional capacity to meet these goals. CENTA has been broken up and reassembled by outside experts along the lines of World Bank institutional prototypes in other countries. The unfolding reform has been plagued with poor human resources management, a lack of sensitivity to the local reality of small producer clients, and inappropriate location of extension services that resulted from inadequate diagnosis of small producers' problems. In turn, these shortcomings have led to a program with highly dispersed goals, further undermining its effectiveness in the field.

In summary, the result is a weakened and almost ineffective research and extension agency, a climate of disincentives leading to an inability to attract national experts and managerial personnel, and problems with the extension methodology, thus seriously limiting the agency's impact in the field. Because most internationally funded programs and projects addressing rural land degradation have basic components that depend on this extension system, their prospects are also seriously handicapped.

The Inter-American Development Bank

Unlike the World Bank during the eighties, the IDB maintained an ongoing funding relationship that concentrated on infrastructure (e.g., roads and bridges, energy, irrigation and water) and health. Although all infrastructure and, particularly, energy projects are of extreme environmental importance, they are not interpreted as such in the Bank's institutional approach to lending. Environmental impact statements are required for large-scale investment projects, but the projects' relationship to the country's overall environmental condition and needs are not at the heart of Bank planning.

However, the IDB, together with the Organization of American States (OAS), has supported the Salvadoran Environmental Project, which has two major components. The first is design and implementation of an environmental information and management system within the public sector; it includes a geographical information system, an environmental information system, and a system for environmental impact evaluations. The second and largest component of the project is investment in the upper watershed of the Lempa River. Originally conceived of in relationship to the problems of dam siltation, there appears to be a tendency to delink these problems and concentrate on resource conservation projects, particularly soil conservation related to increasing agricultural production.

This is perhaps the environmental investment project with potentially the most strategic importance for the country, given the central role of the Lempa upper watershed to El Salvador's water and energy balances.[15] The major subcomponents of the project will address soil conservation, agroforestry systems, protected areas, and environmental education within the project area. However, the project suffers continued delays owing to weakened institutional counterparts, and it runs the risk of limits on its original strategic scope of setting up the capacity for assessing the environmental impacts of infrastructure development projects.

COMMENTS AND RECOMMENDATIONS

The social and economic changes that have taken place over the past 20 years in El Salvador have catapulted the country into a situation of extreme environmental degradation. Yet the institutional capacity to monitor and interpret the current environmental damage and trends was virtually destroyed.

These concerns have not been included in the economic reform process or in the political reforms promoted by the Peace Accords of 1992. Nonetheless, the postwar era provides an excellent opportunity to reconsider this problem while some international donor interest is still focused in this region. A renewed and continued effort should be made to recommend modifications in the current scheme of institutional and environmental reforms/modernization that would establish adequate national capacity to develop policies, programs, and projects with a perspective of stopping and eventually reversing the present trends that threaten the renewability of El Salvador's natural resources and the environmental systems that support them.

Several recommendations are derived from the results of this research:

1. Develop a comprehensive monitoring capacity, baseline data, and a system of environmental indicators as well as the capacity to integrate environmental concerns into mainstream economic and social policy formulation.

The implications of the collapse in the national capacity to monitor the state of natural resources and the environment in general have not been considered seriously by national policymakers or by their counterparts in the international bodies that provide technical assistance in financial management and economic indicator monitoring. Although existing information is fragmentary, outdated, and highly unreliable, the country has no system for keeping the most basic resource use records and following even rudimentary environmental indicators.

In this sense, there is an urgent need to reorient international cooperation to help develop a permanent national capability regarding monitoring equipment, baseline studies, and interpretation skills. The centers of economic decisionmaking and planning need to develop the capacity to determine linkages between the patterns of environmental degradation and economic and social development in order to derive realistic policy proposals. The needed institutional setup should go beyond the executive institutions and should involve the national academic institutions. In general, there is a need for developing a sustainable institutional setup capable of providing up-to-date information on the state of the environment in all its facets.

2. Redefine the role of hillside agriculture as a provider of environmental services.

Agricultural strategies are usually justified in terms of maximizing exports, generating foreign exchange, ensuring food security, or reducing rural poverty. Rarely is it considered that the agricultural sector (including forestry) has a significant bearing on the capacity to provide environmental services, such as groundwater recharge, regulation of surface water flows, control of soil erosion and sedimentation, preservation of fisheries, etc. On the contrary, agricultural development under a logic of providing foreign exchange, employment, or foodstuffs has often resulted in highly negative environmental impacts. Such was the case for pesticide-intensive cotton production in the flatlands of the coastal zones of El Salvador—and is still the case for basic grains and livestock production on hillsides.

Thus there is a real need to address the problems of hillside production in order to reverse its current negative environmental impacts. To do so demands a reconceptualization of the role of hillside agriculture and the mobilization of the substantial investments required to establish sustainable livelihoods (thus reversing the poverty trends), decrease rural-urban migration, contribute to food security, and last but not least, provide water to the country.

Below are some basic elements of the needed framework:

- There is an urgent need to carry out a major study on current conditions of and trends in the country's water resources, given current patterns of land degradation and contamination.

- A major policy shift is needed to introduce soil conservation techniques, ecologically sound agricultural practices, and the restoration of vegetative cover in hillside agriculture on a massive scale that is sustainable over the long haul. These actions would also serve as a buffer against the current loss of the last reserves of biodiversity.

- There must be a coherent policy directed toward the coffee-producing sector to increase the area planted to shade coffee nationally and promote a shift to organic production. The policies adopted should include incentives for small agriculturalists to grow shade coffee and measures to enhance the sustainability of both the cooperatives and the small producers, changes that require their further participation in processing and commercialization.

- Although land policy remains a major problem, a major shift is required from a focus on land tenure to a radical reform in land use. El Salvador urgently needs to establish a national policy for land use regulation based on sound information and analysis. The policy would incorporate different levels of mechanisms for resource use in order to guarantee the environmental balance necessary for water replenishment as the priority and to guarantee the sustainable management of soil resources.

- These measures all point to the need to reorient the relationship of the state apparatus to the territory based on social and environmental criteria. For El Salvador, this means including the watershed as a working territorial definition for institutional focus by all extensions of the state in the field. This same criterion needs to be incorporated in the current state reforms promoting decentralization.

3. Regulate urban development to safeguard the country's environment. Rebuild and strengthen the institutional capacity related to the monitoring, planning, and regulation necessary for the future.

The speed, scale, and style of urbanization that has taken place in El Salvador are contributing to country-wide environmental problems that must be analyzed as such. The measures needed are numerous. They include the following:

- Carrying out a major diagnosis and review of the principal urban areas of the country, particularly the San Salvador Metropolitan Area, and determining the local, regional, and/or national environmental impacts of current trends in urbanization.
- Revamping and strengthening the institutions necessary to guarantee a sustainable capacity to monitor, interpret, and regulate urban development. The capacity to enforce land use regulation needs to be a major priority.
- Generating the necessary baseline and interpretive studies as supports for determining scientifically sound criteria for a comprehensive land use regulation policy.
- Implementing a full pricing scheme for urban domestic and industrial water consumption or sink use based on studies and recommendations that consider low-income consumers.
- Directing specific attention to energy resource problems, ranging from substituting fuelwood for household and industrial use to developing a national energy strategy. For a more rational balance of thermal, geothermal, and hydropower sources, hydropower needs to play a larger role based on more socially inclusive and environmentally sustainable practices.

ENDNOTES

1. World Bank, "Economic Memorandum on El Salvador," Rep. No. 2287-ES (Washington, D.C., 1979).
2. In 1994, the process of natural dilution of contaminants was using up to as much as 85 percent of surface resources. If unchecked, the major rivers will be totally saturated in a few more years.
3. Mitchell Seligson et al., "El Salvador Agricultural Policy Analysis," Tech. Rep. No. 133 (prepared for Agricultural Policy Analysis Project, Phase II [APAP II] and United States Agency for International Development, El Salvador).

4. Economic assistance provided through USAID in 1981-93 reached US$3 billion, according to Central Bank figures (FUSADES, *Cómo Está Nuestra Economia?* San Salvador, September 1992 and August 1993).

5. Banco Central, *"Revista Trimestral: Octubre-Diciembre,"* San Salvador, 1994.

6. World Bank, "El Salvador Country Economic Memorandum," Rep. No. 7818-ES (Washington, D.C., 1989).

7. Banco Central, *"Revista Trimestral: Enero-Marzo"* (San Salvador, 1994).

8. For example, when the government authorized exchange houses in mid-1990, the exchange rate was about 7.75 colones per dollar, and since 1993, it has remained fixed at about 8.75.

9. According to the International Monetary Fund, private sector credit that grew 8.2 percent in 1991 expanded 27.7 percent and 17.1 percent in 1992 and 1993, respectively. Expansion continued in 1994: 21.0 percent through May ("El Salvador: Staff Report for the 1994 Article IV Consultation and Midterm Review under the Stand-By Arrangement," 1994). These are much higher rates than the Central Bank programed.

10. "El Salvador Country Economic Memorandum," op. cit.

11. Yet the World Bank's report on poverty alleviation states that about 20 percent of rural workers reported earnings below the minimum wage in 1992 ("El Salvador: The Challenge of Poverty Alleviation," Rep. No. 12315-ES [Washington, D.C., 1994], p. 19).

12. Food and Agriculture Organization of the United Nations, El Salvador, *Credito para el Pequeño Agricultor de Escasos Recursos en Areas de Laderas, Frágiles y de Altas Pendientes* (1993).

13. Nearly US$300 million in project funding has been identified and is in some stage of project elaboration or implementation.

14. Medium- to long-term recommendations were to become part of a loan in 1995. Referred to as Land and Agricultural Services, it would concentrate on land management support services, land use, subsidies, land markets, and land-related transfers/conflict resolution under the Peace Accords.

15. It is also important because of the total investment, US$33 million.

8

CASE STUDY FOR JAMAICA

This chapter is based on a study conducted and written by Alfred Francis, Dillon Alleyne, and Ian Boxill of the Institute of Social and Economic Research, University of the West Indies, with support of Anil Markandya of the Harvard Institute for International Development. This summary was written by Anil Markandya, with assistance of Abdul Shibli.

Sustainable development paths attempt to ensure that the welfare of future generations is at least no lower than that of present generations. And despite current inequities in the distribution of world resources, it should be possible for countries like Jamaica to follow sustainable paths of development. Their doing so, however, will require developed and developing countries to share the costs of appropriate policies.

The question of what constitutes a sustainable development path cannot be determined on objective grounds, and there has to be some compromise between environmental damages and economic returns, both now and in the future.

An important issue is private firms' frequent concern with private instead of social costs. Under the circumstances, a regulatory framework may be necessary, especially when market-based solutions are inadequate. Further, sustainability must incorporate both improvement in the human condition and environmental protection and conservation. However, this approach was not incorporated in the many structural adjustment programs (SAPs) pursued over time. One of the difficulties in linking structural adjustment and sustainable development is the paucity of environmental data; further, it is not always possible to establish a direct link between environmental degradation and economic reform. However, it is important to ensure the following: (1) the environmental problems should be shown to exist after particular policies came into being; (2) other explanations for the problems must be ruled out; and (3) a consistent pattern in which certain policies are linked to certain types of environmental problems must be apparent. The implication is that environmental damage is often indirect and unexpected.

PAST ECONOMIC REFORMS AND STRUCTURAL ADJUSTMENT POLICIES

Jamaica's major economic resources are mining, agriculture, and tourism. It is not surprising that exploitation of these resources is the principal cause of pollution. Despite its physical beauty, however, the island is subject to natural disasters: floods owing to heavy rainfall, hurricanes, and earthquakes.

Jamaica's physiography is especially significant because it is an island. For example, islands have more endemic species than continents, and they experience wave action on all sides. This fact suggests that their problems are complex and the pressures of population growth and small markets quickly become economic constraints. Jamaica was traditionally a plantation economy, exporting sugar and bananas. In the 1950s, bauxite production was added to the traditional agricultural outputs, and the country became the world's leading bauxite exporter. After independence from Britain, Jamaica pursued a strong import substitution strategy.

In the relatively favorable climate of that time and with the emergence of tourism as a booming new industry, Jamaica experienced high growth rates; in 1970, GDP grew 1 percent and in 1973, 9 percent. However, growth came to an abrupt halt after the oil crisis of 1973. The economy did not adjust well to that shock. Output fell continuously throughout the decade, so that GDP was 21 percent lower by 1980 compared to 1973. Over the 1980s, the economic growth rate was low, barely enough to keep up with population growth.

Despite the fact that government revenues were falling, there was a major expansion in social services. Huge deficits resulted: by 1980, the deficit was 17 percent of GDP, compared to a balanced position in 1970. The persistence of these deficits resulted in pressures on prices and on the exchange rate. The government responded by tightening import controls even further, but to no avail; the external account deficit rose to 17 percent of GDP in 1981-82 from only about 1 percent in the mid-1970s. The financial crisis necessitated a change in policy.

Figure 8.1 Jamaica

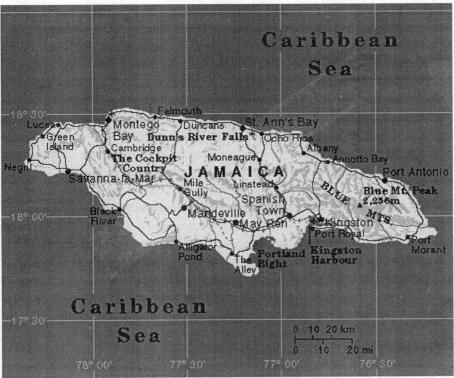

From *Picture Atlas of the World* CD-ROM, © National Geographic Society, 1995

Although Jamaica has been criticized heavily for its social spending policies of the 1970s, they resulted in a major improvement in important social indicators, such as primary school attendance, infant mortality, and life expectancy at birth. It should be noted that the development policies of the 1960s and 1970s paid little attention to the environment. Bauxite production plants, for example, emitted large amounts of dust and red mud.

In terms of sustainable development, the government did not channel the rents from bauxite into investments that would yield an income stream to replace that coming from this exhaustible resource. The bauxite levy was used largely to finance consumption, although its rationale was that it would finance capital development.

One consequence of this unstable economic situation was that the country could not finance its external account deficit and had to seek help from the International Monetary Fund (IMF) through a 2-year stand-by facility in 1977. But it had to be abandoned when Jamaica failed to satisfy the performance criteria. In 1978, a 3-year Extended Facility Agreement was signed for $240 million. The agreement required several stringent measures, such as reductions in government expenditures and domestic credit and devaluation of the currency. It too was suspended when all the requirements were not met.

The new government that came to power in 1980 changed the focus. It shifted from state control to deregulation of prices and imports. By establishing free zones for garment manufacturing and large-scale agriculture, the government encouraged exports. A reform program adopted in 1981 required a reduction in domestic demand through fiscal and monetary discipline. The IMF provided Extended Facility and Compensatory Facility Agreements, which encouraged considerable external private capital flows as well. Unfortunately, in the severe economic recession of the early 1980s, Jamaica could not meet its current account targets that had been set, and again the program was suspended in 1982. It seemed that nothing could break the cycle of macroeconomic failure. The government deficit remained large, and the massive devaluations did not avoid balance of payments crises.

In 1984-85, the government implemented another adjustment program with IMF support. This one was more successful owing largely to a more favorable external environment—a fall in oil prices, a rebound in the demand for bauxite, and a growth in tourism. Thus aided, the economy achieved moderate economic growth, decreased inflation, and a stronger balance of payments in 1986-88. At the same time, government expenditures began to rise, and again inflationary pressures began to build. In 1987, the government had to resort to a new stand-by agreement with the IMF. There is clearly a pattern here: the economy is marginally viable in a favorable external economic climate, but in these circumstances, social pressures increase the need for government spending. In addition, the country needs external support from the IMF in adverse weather conditions.

In September 1988, Hurricane Gilbert exacerbated the fragile economic situation. In the aftermath of the disaster, the country needed assistance to rehabilitate the economy. However, there are some signs that the measures taken then and subsequently are more consistent and durable. Increasing government revenues through a broader and fairer tax system was a key part of the reforms, as were restraints on government expenditures. Economic deregulation measures have been more aggressive and have included a major privatization program. Some of the positive economic indicators are a decline in inflation, improvement in the external current account, an increase in net private capital inflows, and a modest recovery in GDP growth.

An important issue here is constraint of the external debt. The debt problem emerged in the late 1970s owing to a combination of circumstances; among them were reduced investment inflows, oil price increases, expansionary fiscal policies, and subsequent balance of payments deficits. Total medium- and long-term debt grew 10 percent annually between 1980 and 1992 and 23.8 percent between 1980 and 1988. The structure of the debt limited successive governments' obtaining debt relief because Jamaica owes much of its debt to bilateral and multilateral agencies. In 1992, 37.3 percent was owed to multilateral agencies and 51.1 percent to bilateral agencies. The magnitude of the debt is evident from the fact that the ratio of debt service to exports was 17 percent in 1980, 33.6 percent in 1985, and 42.6 in 1986. Although the ratio has declined, it was still 40 percent in 1992. As a consequence of the debt, sustainable development options have been limited:

- The noncessional debt limits the resources available for development and creates balance of payments crises when regular foreign exchange inflows decline.
- Much of the focus of economic planning has been on meeting debt obligations, given the threat of default, to the neglect of long-term development issues.
- The reduction in public sector spending in the past 10 years is partly a function of debt repayments. Direct environmental consequences followed some cuts, for example, in agricultural extension services.

Any scenario that considers Jamaica's future development will have to consider debt relief. The impacts of adjustment programs on the welfare of various groups are particularly important here because improving the human condition is closely related to good environmental practices and the ability of people to relate environmental concerns to their daily lives. Although the largest cuts in government expenditures are in investment, those in public expenditures have had considerable consequences for available social goods; education, health, housing, and public transportation were subject to higher costs, reduced supply, and lower quality. The main support program for the poor was the food program, which targeted the very poor. Yet this was not enough to maintain food consumption at past levels.

Between 1971 and 1991, spending on social security and the water supply declined, housing expenditures remained static, and health and education rose. However, all items fell relative to their levels in the late 1970s. These declines are indicative of a worsening in the welfare of the poorest members of society. Moreover, the decreased spending will have implications for the natural environment, either directly (e.g., water quality) or indirectly (e.g., education and training).

Some indicators of the quality of life in Jamaica, such as life expectancy, infant mortality, and mean years of schooling, have improved uniformly over the two decades. But others, such as the perinatal mortality rate, which had been falling, rose between 1990 and 1991, and hospital admissions for malnutrition increased as a share of all hospital admissions. Further, moderate malnutrition among children under 4 years increased between 1989 and 1991.

Other indicators of social welfare are overall consumption and employment-unemployment levels. In spite of lower real income in 1971-91, *per capita* consumption for the poorest (the lowest 20 percent of the population) rose. The same is true for the next quintile. In terms of unemployment, the levels have always been high, but there are signs of a decline in recent years. For all males, the rate was 14.3 percent in 1972; by 1980, it had risen to 17 percent and remained in the upper teens until 1987, when it fell to 12.8 percent. In the 3 years 1991-93, it has been about 9 percent.

POPULATION CONCENTRATIONS AND HUMAN SETTLEMENTS

In Jamaica, as in other island countries, population concentrations and the environment are closely related. Pressures of the human population on lowland urban areas have been intense, and they have been aggravated by the lack of land and housing facilities for low-income households. Squatting has emerged as a major social and environmental issue, and in 1989, some 8.3 percent of the population occupied land illegally.

In the past decade, poverty and unemployment have affected rural-urban migration, leading to overcrowded squatter settlements and the shortage of drinking water and sewerage facilities in these areas. In addition, there has been the resurgence of gastroenteritis and typhoid fever in the 1990s. Part of the cause is that Jamaica has no comprehensive settlement policy. Current problems in the urban areas include urban sprawl and housing shortages, even considering a bias toward urban areas in the provision of social amenities. Although the rural population has experienced little growth, urban growth has been considerable owing to the search for jobs and better social facilities. In the intercensal period, for example, annual internal migration was 24,500, an 8 percent increase over previous intercensal periods. Population growth and urban concentration have also affected solid waste management. It is estimated that in 1992, municipal and ship-generated waste was some 7,941 tons per day. Fifty percent of it came from the urban centers of Kingston and St. Andrew, Montego Bay, and Clarendon. Adjustment has affected the government's capacity to deliver efficient social services, among them waste disposal. The government's draft action plan points out that significant construction and upgrading of waste management facilities are required for both public and private sectors.[1] In addition, sewage facilities are generally inadequate; perhaps the most serious evidence of this situation is pollution of the Kingston harbor.

Apart from solid waste disposal, air pollution is a serious problem in Spanish Town, Kingston, and Montego Bay. Among the sources are emissions from oil refineries, chemical processing plants, cement and bauxite-alumina plants, and municipal dumps' burning garbage. Pollution of surface- and groundwater is also serious. Contamination results from deforestation of watersheds, improper disposal of solid and liquid wastes, and use of agrochemicals. These problems are aggravated by the expansion of illegal human settlements, which have no access to reliable water systems or waste disposal systems.

Water Contamination

The Centre for Nuclear Sciences, in an all-island study of ambient water quality between November 1990 and April 1992, found that water quality in some areas exceeded U.S. Environmental Protection Agency (EPA) standards by far.[2] This is a landmark study because of its coverage and the implications for public health and environmental quality. In terms of human influence, water is contaminated from point sources, watershed and industrial discharges' draining from mining activities, and from nonpoint sources, agricultural and urban runoff, landfills, land development, atmospheric deposition, and recreational activities. Between November 1990 and April 1992, 10 basins were sampled, including well and river sampling sites.

The sites are significant because they cover areas of tourist activity, industrial effluence, agricultural areas in coffee production, and human settlements. Unfortunately, it was not possible to disentangle the several factors affecting surface- and groundwater quality in these areas. The EPA guidelines for fecal coliform in drinking water and surface water were exceeded in 70-80 percent and 50 percent of the samples, respectively.[3] The basins most affected were the Dry Harbour Mountain, Carbaritta, and the Great River basins, where every sample had coliform present and some far in excess of the EPA-recommended level for surface water. Nitrates, phosphates, sodium, and fluorides were also present in some samples. Sodium was found in some wells used for irrigation, and the worst phosphate cases were found in wells in Kingston and the Rio Cobre basins.

Water contamination in Kingston harbor is a major environmental concern. The main sources are:

- bacterial contamination from malfunctioning sewage treatment plants and industrial discharge;
- waste from the Kingston and St. Andrew Corporation (KSAC) slaughterhouse that receives little treatment and is funneled into storm drains emptying into the harbor; and
- waste from the Rio Cobre, which accounts for an estimated 32 percent of the harbor's total biological oxygen demand.

Given the water quality problem, much more in-depth analysis is needed to identify specific sources of contamination in order to formulate public policy. One difficulty is the lack of clear guidelines on waste disposal and sanctions against companies and individuals who disregard the guidelines. But the problem is much broader owing to staff reductions in the monitoring organizations, poor incentives, and the general inefficiency of the public sector.

External Migration

Of considerable importance in the dynamics of Jamaica's population is migration. Population growth declined from 2.0 percent in 1983 to 1.0 percent in 1990-92, partly because of migration. The waves of migration began in the early twentieth century, when an estimated 80,000 Jamaicans left to work on the Panama Canal. Another 50,000 went to work in Cuba between 1919 and 1922. In recent times, Jamaicans have gone to England, the United States, and Canada.

With regard to migration trends, the number fluctuated widely over time. For example, 12,100 and 24,300 persons migrated in 1975 and 1980, respectively; then there was a considerable decline in 1981-83. After 1984, the number rose again, reaching 38,900 in 1988. The pattern of migration may be cyclical, reflecting economic and social conditions at home and migration policies abroad. The projections for population growth, given current growth trends, show a decline in growth rates by the year 2000.[4] The estimated population growth rate using a median variant is 1.5 in 1995 and 1.3 percent in 2000. The estimates also suggest that crude birth and death rates will continue to decline. It should be noted, however, that barriers to future migration to the United States and Canada and further internal migration may contribute to the emergence of population control as a major problem.

Environmental Impacts of Past Development Policies and Practices

The 1960s were a period of considerable economic growth, but they brought dissatisfaction because income inequality continued to increase while unemployment remained as high as 25 percent. The domestic economy was largely characterized by a strategy of import substitution industrialization, which favored capital over labor.

During the 1970s, the strategy changed to an emphasis on government intervention, income distribution, and a reduction in income inequality. The early period of democratic socialism brought increased government expenditures on the social sector, especially in education and health. They were manifested in increased health and education status, reduced malnutrition rates, and higher real wages, especially for women. This expanded government activity coincided with increased fuel costs, and it gave rise to budget deficits and balance of payments instability. Despite the introduction of the bauxite levy and internal attempts at adjustment, the macroeconomic imbalances could not be managed in the short run. Exchange rate instability, inflation, and high unemployment levels, together with a mounting foreign debt and capital flight, forced Jamaica to rely heavily on multilateral and bilateral support.

Involvement of the IMF and to a less extent, the World Bank, helped to focus the adjustment effort on stabilization. Many of the adjustment packages were abandoned, however, because the burden might have caused social instability.

The change of government after 1980 oriented development policy toward exports, large- as against small-scale agriculture, and private sector participation in the economy. But despite considerable inflows from the IMF-World Bank group, the economy stagnated and the economic structure continued to center around the bauxite-alumina, tourist, and banana sectors, all of which depend heavily on price fluctuations abroad. In terms of sustainability, it is fair to say that after the 1970s, there was always a recognition that the social sector was vital to overall development. Often, however, policy goals of successive governments redounded slowly to the poor and unemployed youth.

The consequences of a development approach that did not explicitly incorporate environmental considerations are as follows:

- Low stumpage prices on government-owned land were often well below replacement costs, aggravating deforestation. For example, land prices in coffee-growing areas do not account for the social damage from watershed destruction.
- Trade barriers and subsidies, especially on agricultural inputs, may have encouraged overuse of chemical pesticides.
- The production of bauxite and coffee in particular was allowed to continue, given the exigencies of foreign exchange—but without proper guidelines on the levels of environmental damage to be allowed. The same statement can be made for tourism and manufacturing.
- Fuel costs were not linked to environmental damage initially or to fuel conservation; thus the high fuel prices directly affected wood consumption. Kerosene was later subsidized in an attempt to encourage its use.

What are the implications of this review of macroeconomic policy for questions of sustainability? It is evident that the economy is fragile and lacks resilience in the sense that external shocks result in major economic disruptions. The costs of these disruptions fall heavily on vulnerable groups, although the evidence does suggest that they have been cushioned against some of the worst declines in real incomes. Nevertheless, certain groups have had to face declines in income and the quality of life. A development path that requires such change is not sustainable.

In response to the question of what comprises a sustainable path, it is suggested that social policies have to be contained with efficiency considerations. For example, a striking feature of the Jamaican government prior to the external shocks in the 1970s and structural adjustment policies in the 1980s was its commitment to reducing income inequality and creating greater social justice in society. The government strategy was one of democratic socialism, which focused on developing a mixed economy with increasing government participation in many sectors, including a major expansion of social services, especially those related to health and education. Given its heavy dependence on bauxite, from which income was unstable, and with the benefit of hindsight, one can say that a shortcoming of the government strategy was its failure to invest the returns from bauxite mining and alumina production in diversifying the economic base and developing alternative and sustainable sources of government revenue to fund its ambitious social program.

CASE STUDIES OF ECONOMY-ENVIRONMENT LINKS

This section discusses the environmental impacts in four sectors: bauxite/alumina, coffee, tourism, and cement.

Bauxite/alumina

The bauxite sector is central to the Jamaican economy in terms of both its earning potential and its contribution to government revenues. However, this capital-intensive industry provides relatively little employment, with benefits largely accruing to the multinational corporations and the government. Its inputs (bauxite, limestone, caustic soda, etc.), processes, and output technologies all pollute the environment. Loss of agricultural productivity in and around mined land, pollution of water bodies, and the burden of red mud are the main impacts that need to be mitigated. The mining companies have the technology for mitigating most of the impacts, but the government is often reluctant to pressure them to do so in the fear that the companies will reduce operations, with consequent loss of export revenues and government income. In recent years, however, the government has begun to take a stronger line on the environmental impacts of bauxite mining. It appears from preliminary reviews that the environmental problems could be solved without major effects on the overall viability of the industry and its contribution to the national economy.

In many respects, the key issues here do not relate to the environment but to the role of an exhaustible resource in an economy that is seeking a path of sustainable development. The user cost of producing bauxite—

that part of the income from sale of the product to be invested if consumption is to be maintained at its present level after the mineral is exhausted—is between J$15.7 million and J$125.3 million at 1986 prices. At the same time, the government's bauxite levy in 1974 was about J$168 million. Thus the levy would have been more than enough to cover user costs. But it was not used for investment purposes; instead, it mainly financed consumption. Thus the government was not pursuing a sustainable development strategy relative to this mineral.

The bauxite industry is a major earner of foreign exchange, which is critical to sustainable development. At the same time, the industry is a major polluter of the island's air, land, and water resources. Some aspects of the alumina plants' polluting activities can be easily corrected in such a way as to yield net financial benefits to the operating companies and to internalize the social costs of its operations. The cost of alumina dust at the port has been successfully tackled by the Alpart refinery, and it is recommended that similar approaches be adopted by the other refineries at the ports of shipment.

The red mud dilemma is a matter of the greatest urgency. In treating the disposal of red mud, the developed countries have adopted a more environmentally acceptable approach than Jamaica's. The government should ensure that steps be taken to improve the companies' red mud disposal immediately. Further, as a matter of priority, the government should support research on transforming red mud from waste into useful commodities. It is even suggested that with research, red mud might be used for housing construction. A general recommendation is that wherever possible, technological approaches should be encouraged to sustain production that is environmentally sustainable.

The issue of taxing bauxite has to be linked to the fact that it is a nonrenewable resource. For this reason, the heavily criticized bauxite production levy is justifiable from several points of view. First, some adjustment to private costs have to be made for the use of a diminishing asset. Second, revenues received from bauxite should be part of the general revenues used in relation to the broader issue of sustainability, which is consistent with a holistic approach to development. And third, environmental damage and the consumption of natural resources should be accounted for in GDP. Social accounting to include environmental costs of production should be part of the data collected by official environmental agencies.

Coffee

Since the 1970s, Jamaica has come to depend on the foreign exchange earned from coffee, and the clearing of land has increased for its cultivation. It is estimated that there are more than 20,000 coffee farmers, most of whom have small farms. The increased land clearing has affected the environment. In the Blue Mountains, it has reduced natural forestry and degraded water quality. In addition, hillside coffee cultivation often leads to a loss of the protective cover of topsoil, resulting in mud- and landslides in heavy rains. The extensive use of pesticides and other forms of crop spraying has also increased with intensified cultivation. It is clear that environmentally sound practices are necessary to avoid further damage.

Tourism

The Jamaican tourism industry has exploded since the early 1970s. It is now the largest source of foreign exchange earnings in Jamaica. The importance of tourism is reflected in the Tourist Board Budget, which increased 300 percent between fiscal years 1979-80 and 1992-93. The major tourist areas are Negril, Montego Bay, and Ocho Rios. In 1986, there were 1,560 hotels, and the number had increased to 1,758 in 1992. Despite this growth in tourism, its socioeconomic and ecological implications have not been carefully assessed.

The industry has developed as a series of tourist enclaves of wealth surrounded by poverty. Housing and other facilities have not been made available to adjoining communities, a situation that has given rise to squatter settlements, which contribute to unsanitary conditions. Within these areas are large numbers of unemployed and underemployed youth who seek to make a living by providing various services to tourists. In extreme cases, these efforts can result in the harassment of tourists. A visible source of enclave tourism is the deteriorating infrastructure in Ocho Rios, Montego Bay, Port Antonio, and other popular tourist areas.

The development of all-inclusive tourism ensures that the visitor is provided with a variety of services without necessarily interacting with the community. As a result, small businesses and taxi owners no longer derive business from the tourists. Problems also arise from the fact that many hotels do not allow adjoining communities to use their beaches freely. Other problems include the blasting of coral reefs to provide channels for small craft and for boating basins. In addition, many hotels are without proper sewage treatment facilities, and raw sewage is often dumped in ocean waters; the result is fecal coliform and other bacterial contamination of the surrounding water.

In general, the environmental problems associated with the growth of tourism in Jamaica are the destruction of reefs, water pollution, and poor sewage disposal. These problems cannot be tackled in a piecemeal fashion but have to be solved by planning and regulation. There is need for private parties and the government to invest in infrastructure for communities adjoining the tourist areas. Such infrastructure as roads, schools, and public parks help forge an alliance between those within and outside the industry and encourage better environmental practices. Lack of affordable housing in communities adjoining tourist areas creates the growth of squatter communities along with population growth.

To organize the activities of the informal economy while controlling harassment of tourists, effective regulation of vendors is needed in these areas, perhaps through licensing. For this system to be effective, vendors must be afforded the opportunity to advertise their goods and services through or with the assistance of the hotels and the Tourist Board.

All-inclusive hotels avoid harassment and crime against tourists, but they reduce the income of small operators. The dumping of effluents into rivers and lakes may have been a major contributor to poor water quality in some river basins. It is recommended that all who propose to build hotels should be required to conduct an environmental impact assessment study and gain National Resources Conservation Authority (NRCA) approval before they are permitted to build. In Negril, for example, the results of the study should be discussed within the community where the hotel is proposed in order to ensure full community participation in the development of such an environmentally sensitive area. This broad participation is especially necessary when state monitoring institutions have been weakened by budget cuts and cannot monitor such activities effectively.

The NRCA has developed a fee structure that sets out both the changes for use of harbors and other public facilities and the penalties for environmental damage by firms. In the hotel industry, this regime has to be more seriously enforced, with fees tied realistically to social damage. Public beaches that have been neglected and allowed to deteriorate with overuse, for example, the Hellshire beach, raise serious property rights issues. Although the government has sought to privatize some beaches, most are regarded as common property under state control. Realistic user charges will have to be imposed to raise money for beach facilities and the regulation of their use. In this way too, the beaches will no longer be used as dumps for the disposal of personal and industrial garbage. The government's approach to environmental problems in tourism has been after the fact rather than preventive. Contributing to the situation is the lack of advance planning on expanding these areas and a lack of the necessary infrastructure to handle a growing population attracted by perceived wealth in these areas. Overall planning with consideration of the environment will have to become part of the expansion process if tourist areas are to remain viable.

Cement

Carib Cement Company (CCC), established in 1952, is the only cement producer in Jamaica. Between 1952 and 1988, it operated three wet kilns, three wet slurry mills, and three open circuit mills. Most of the company's production is now consumed by the local market, and the remainder is exported to the Caribbean market. In 1989, production reached 400,000 tons, and an increase will have major environmental impacts. The plant emits a wide variety of pollutants although operations are regulated by law. The Mining Act of 1947 requires the lessee to restore every acre of land, as far as is practicable, so that it may be put to productive use. The act also sought to prevent human harm from any lessee activities. Other laws, the Underground Water Authority Act of 1962 and the Quarries Control Act of 1984, also seek to protect the environment. Despite this legislation, only recently has there been an effort to reduce pollution. Air pollution is mainly dust and water pollution mainly thermal. Analysis of air emissions shows that dust levels are far beyond international standards, adversely affecting area residents. It is estimated that the company spills some 301,000 gallons of industrial effluent per day into the Kingston harbor. This contribution to thermal pollution causes oxygen depletion in the water, with consequent destruction of fish and other aquatic organisms.

Increased environmental awareness and complaints from adjoining communities and the press have prompted the company to move forward. Following meetings with the affected community, CCC formulated a pollution mission statement. But even with the steps taken so far, pollution levels are still high. However, a new filter is expected to reduce dust emissions in the near future, and impact assessment studies have been commissioned to determine how CCC operations have affected the environment.

For solid waste, the company now has several dumps, and a new air-cooled power plant is expected to reduce thermal pollution. Although progress is being made, the plant's technology is outdated and the company wants to upgrade equipment. Absent an assessment of the effects of internalizing environmental costs on the company's profitability, CCC estimates additional capital costs of 10 percent of annual expenditures. Maintenance costs are expected to be relatively low. If the planned changes are implemented quickly, it is possible that pollution from the plant will be reduced to tolerable levels. But there is a clear need for stringent enforcement of NRCA air and water quality standards. Polluting companies should be required to show how and when (i.e., over what time) they will reduce pollution levels. If a company continues its polluting activities, then property rights should be vested in the affected community, which should also be compensated for any damage. In case of extreme pollution, the company should be made to suspend its activities.

ENVIRONMENTAL INSTITUTIONS

Prior to the NRCA, environmental institutions in Jamaica were weak in several ways. First, there was no ministry or overarching office to determine major environmental issues, and many ministries were involved in monitoring different aspects of the environment. And second, apart from institutional fragmentation, organizations were badly weakened by the reduction in public expenditures and by layoffs in the public sector.

This situation affected these parties' capacity to monitor and guide environmentally sound development strategies. Those affected are in the private and public sectors and in the international donor-financed program. This plethora of interested parties lacking coordination but with converging interests often duplicates efforts. Further, when one government body refuses to grant permission for a project on environmental grounds, another may do so.

The NRCA's replacing the Natural Resource Conservation Department is a step in the right direction. The NRCA has the power to impose environmental fines and fees. Although it is advisory to the Ministry of the Public Service, it lacks the influence to override decisions of other ministries with which it has a coordinating role. The government of the day can easily emasculate the NRCA in terms of its functions or the level of funding necessary to its effectiveness. Ultimately, government commitment to sustainability becomes absolutely necessary.

Some scholars approach the problem of environmental protection through market-based strategies, for example, selling pollution rights and allocating property rights. This approach does not suggest a lack of institutional arrangements; instead, clear institutional arrangements must be backed by incentives and sanctions. In recent years, the World Bank's focus on institutional strengthening has recognized this point. For example, in regard to new stumpage rates, the Bank states:

> The implementation of these [environmental] instruments has fallen behind in part because the departments responsible for collecting these royalties, fees, and fines have had little incentive to do so, as all revenues are consolidated into the central budget, and because the real value of the payments has been undermined by inflation.[5]

The relation between fees and true social costs will have to be fully examined. Too often fees for the use of public facilities bear no relationship to social costs, and collection efforts often exceed returns.

CONCLUSIONS

Jamaica's development strategies over the past two decades have had significant impacts on present environmental problems. These problems were aggravated in recent years by massive public cuts in both recurrent and capital spending in order to reduce the budget deficit and at the same time service the external debt. The productive sectors emphasized over the past decade are also the offending sectors in terms of environmental degradation. The major sources of environmental degradation are:

- Bauxite/alumina production, effectively under the control of international aluminum companies, has caused dust pollution and the problem of red mud disposal.[6] Insufficient land restoration affects the productivity of farm lands and the salinity of water in the area owing to the volume of water needed in production.
- Cement production releases dust into the atmosphere, a health hazard in adjoining areas.
- Coffee production uses fertilizer that leaches into rivers and destroys watershed areas. Although evidence is not conclusive, it is suggested

that coffee cultivation in the Blue Mountains has affected rainfall patterns over time owing to deforestation.

- Unorganized and unplanned human settlements along rivers and in adjoining river basins have polluted both surface- and groundwater. The lack of a coherent low-income housing policy and the inability and often unwillingness of government to monitor and organize squatter communities have contributed to the situation.

- Industrial discharge into rivers and drains has also polluted both surface- and groundwaters. Many of these are hotels and manufacturing enterprises located along rivers. Pollution of the Kingston harbor by effluents discharged directly into the harbor or by way of the Rio Grande is a case in point.

- The tourist sector is also a significant source of pollution not only from hotels but from the rural population they attract (internal migration) and the subsequent development of squatter communities nearby. Part of the problem is that the hotels operate without offering the adjoining communities opportunities to share in the benefits of the sector.

- The level of poverty in some communities, coupled with deficit reduction and reduced spending on social services, has affected environmental practices. (It is here argued that increasing poverty and inequality is inconsistent with sustainability.) The lack of empowerment owing to falling real incomes and employment opportunities is another source of degradation. Further, inflation affects deforestation, especially in the countryside, where wood is an alternative fuel source.

- Natural disasters should not be forgotten. Jamaica experiences hurricanes and earthquakes, potential sources of both environmental and human destruction.

- Solid waste disposal, congestion, and illegal sand mining are causing major environmental problems in urban areas. Many dumps are nonfunctional but continue to be used. In some cases, solid waste is disposed of on isolated public beaches and in gullies, causing floods. The number of old cars in urban areas has increased owing largely to a fairly liberal import policy in recent years; air pollution is an immediate effect. The impacts of sand mining on erosion and flooding are vast. But for the dispossessed youth, it is an important source of income. The fact that is often occurs in well-known areas reflects the impotence of government bodies to monitor and regulate these activities.

RECOMMENDATIONS

Given the issues raised with respect to economic reforms and the environment, a number of recommendations can be made:

1. Environmental planning and macroeconomic policy should be integrated in public policy. The National Resources Conservation Authority recommendations cannot merely address existing problems but should be an integral part of development options. Thus the national action plan should not be an appendage to the budget and other policy documents but should be a part of budgetary policy.

2. Development strategies must include not only growth but sustainability. This statement means that improvement of the human condition is also linked to good environmental practices.

3. There is clearly a need for institutional strengthening of the public sector in terms of both efficiency and coordination of activities. Institutional fragmentation, which characterizes institutions dealing with the environment, does not permit effective monitoring and control of pollution.

4. The polluter pays principle is one way of initially reducing pollution levels, and it should be applied along with user fees. These payments are also a potential source of revenue for the central government. This change would have to be made in such a way that distributional considerations are not neglected. For example, raising utility rates to reduce the public deficit would not be wise because obtaining alternative fuels may be environmentally harmful.

Increasing user charges and fees may not reduce the level of pollution from all sources, and in some cases, punitive legislation may have to be enacted and implemented. For example, dumping raw sewage by hotels and firms into rivers and onto deserted beaches cannot be reversed by application of the polluter pays principle.

5. Although a wholesale incentive structure is not being advocated here, it is clear that for cement manufacturing and tourism, an incentive structure can be developed to encourage firms to install "green" technologies. Some feel that because most of this technology is imported, it may work against local development of technology.

IMPACTS OF CURRENT AND PLANNED ADJUSTMENT PROGRAMS

If current trends continue, the natural resource base and social infrastructure will be affected in the following ways:

- The public sector will increasingly lose its capacity to regulate industrial activity and enforce environmental standards. Unplanned settlements and industry are already in place in the residential areas of such urban centers as Kingston and Montego Bay.
- Exhaustible mineral resources will be depleted more rapidly and mass tourism will intensify in a deteriorating environment. Already many local people have deserted some public beaches and parks owing to pollution.
- Reliance on voluntary compliance with regulations by the private sector and nongovernmental organizations will increase along with an increased emphasis on their responsibility for environmental protection. In addition, reliance on foreign sources of financing for environmental development will also increase.
- Continued reductions in social spending, especially in health and education, housing, and public transportation, will affect future generations. Continued reliance on the traditional sectors without significant diversification will mean further economic instability and macroeconomic imbalance.
- Continued stagnation may mean further expansion of the informal sector, which is characterized by job instability and little or no worker protection.
- The present situation clearly suggests that in a period of reduced capital inflows from either private or multilateral agencies, a huge debt burden, and reduced public expenditures on the social sector, poverty and inequality will continue to increase.

DEVELOPMENT CHOICES

At the institutional level, it is clear that considerable restructuring must take place. Many agencies are governed by old legislation that does not reflect new developments. These changes would mean the allocation of more funds to environmental and related agencies. At the same time, public policy at all levels should include environmental considerations directly.

- The polluter pays principle should be enforced in order to cap pollution levels in the major industries. User charges can improve environmental management, contribute to government revenue, and achieve distributional objectives. Clearly, user charges and fees should be progressive.
- Much of the traditional economic approach to public sector cuts assumes that when public expenditures decline, governments become efficient. But usually they do not. Given the environmental responsibility of the government, the issue now is how to improve efficiency in government operations. Future public sector reforms should not threaten the capacity of public institutions to perform their environmental functions.
- A sustainable response to economic incentives is premised on well-defined property rights. The Land Use Commission was recently formed to assist in developing a national policy on land use and to complete the land titling process.

The recent World Bank report on environmental management in Jamaica[7] suggested higher tax rates on hillsides and unsuitable coastal lands. However, because many hillside farms are small holdings by the poor, a more appropriate strategy is improving farm practices.

- The structural reform package should include a program of targeted environmental and community projects to accelerate adoption of the new economic incentives. Wherever possible, these projects should be designed to further community participation in the benefits of economic reform and improve environmental management. One example in the tourist sector is small-scale ecotourism projects.
- Because short-term objectives to reduce public expenditures and increase foreign exchange earnings to service the public debt often supersede longer-term issues of sustainability, policy sequencing is critical to successful reform. Thus liberalizing prices and granting property rights in the absence of cultivation regulations (e.g., for coffee) will not lead to sustainable output. At the same time, public sector cutbacks in the absence of institutional reorganization will not help to provide basic environmental services.

In addition, the short-term debt repayment objectives of stabilization programs must be consistent with and not constrain the adjustment objective of sustainable development.

- The environmental issues raised also have a global dimension. Developing countries may be motivated to develop environmentally acceptable products if there is a premium for such products abroad. It would seem then that the World Bank should support a program of international recognition for products/production and processes/firms that are environmentally acceptable. The program could also be introduced at the national level, with institutions like the National Resources Conservation Authority offering incentives to firms whose products are environmentally acceptable.

- This study was greatly hampered by the lack of a readily available and consistent database on key environmental indicators. Many such indicators as the levels and sources of harmful effluents in major rivers are vital for long-term economic planning. The study by the Centre for Nuclear Sciences on water quality is an example of how data can capture the extent and urgency of environmental problems.[8] For this reason, it is suggested that *The Economic and Social Survey of Jamaica,*[9] produced by the Planning Institute of Jamaica, include timely and necessary environmental data.

- Lending agencies need to review carefully the development strategies they have encouraged in developing countries. Many of these policies have contributed to environmental degradation in the name of stabilization. By their theoretical and methodological ideas and policies, these agencies are implicitly part of the environmental degradation and must take some responsibility for the lack of sustainability of past policies pursued in Jamaica.

ENDNOTES

1. Jamaica National Environmental Plan (draft), Kingston, May 28, 1992, p. 16.
2. M. Davis et al., "Some Recent Results from an Island-wide Survey of Ambient Water Quality" (Centre for Nuclear Sciences, University of the West Indies, Jamaica, 1993).
3. Ibid.
4. United Nations, *World Population Prospects, 1988* (New York: United Nations, 1988).
5. International Bank for Reconstruction and Development (IBRD), *Jamaica: Economic Issues for Environmental Management* (Washington, D.C.: IBRD, 1993).
6. Canada and Ireland have dealt more successfully with this waste product.
7. IBRD, op. cit.
8. Davis et al., op. cit.
9. Planning Institute of Jamaica (PIOJ), *The Economic and Social Survey of Jamaica* (Kingston Mall: PIOJ, annual).

9

CASE STUDY FOR VENEZUELA

This chapter is based on a study conducted by the Centro de Estudios del Desarrollo of the Universidad Central de Venezuela under the direction of Lourdes Yero. The research team was composed of Cecilia Cariola, Miguel Lacabana, Francisco Javier Velasco, Arelys Caraballo, Victor Fajardo, Hercilio Castellanos, Francisco Herrera, Iokine Rodrigues, Chris Sharpe, Jorge Giordani, Yvan Laplace, Thais Maingon, Rita Pucci, Nelson Prato, Arnoldo Pirela, Luis Mata M., and Pablo Lacabana, with support of Anil Markandya of the Harvard Institute for International Development. This summary was written by Anil Markandya.

ECONOMIC POLICY AND STRUCTURAL ADJUSTMENT

The economy is characterized as mixed, meaning that the government role has been interventionist, but the private sector is also large. Oil has always been the dominant sector, and until the late 1970s, revenues from oil exports allowed private and public savings to finance enough investment to maintain moderate economic growth and relatively full employment. From about 1975, oil revenues increased sharply; instead of helping the country, however, they proved to be more a problem than a blessing. Large capital-intensive projects were undertaken, many of them economically unsound, and the country borrowed heavily abroad. Real exchange rate appreciation from the increased capital inflow made it difficult for other sectors to operate effectively. By 1983, exchange control was necessary and although it was gradually eliminated, the effort to stabilize the currency deteriorated as the debt burden increased and oil revenues did not owing to price decreases.

A structural adjustment program (SAP) became "necessary," and at the beginning of 1989, newly elected President Carlos Andrés Pérez initiated a macroeconomic SAP, dubbed the *paquete* shortly after. The policies included:

- deregulation of the prices of many essential commodities;
- increases in minimum urban and rural wages and in public workers' salaries;
- elimination of the multiple exchange rate system and a shift to floating currency, immediately devaluating the bolívar 150 percent in 1989;
- elimination of interest rate controls and attempts to establish positive real rates (i.e., the difference between the nominal rate payable and the rate of inflation);
- increases in prices and tariffs for electricity, fertilizers, etc. to reflect international prices;
- a reduction in the direct taxes on firms and a shift to a value added tax (application of the latter, however, was patchy and was eventually suspended at the consumer level);
- a move away from general to more targeted subsidies, with food, education, day care, etc. selectively funded;
- a reduction in tariff protection for a wide range of goods and elimination of permits, licenses, etc. in several areas;
- elimination of several direct foreign investment controls;
- renegotiation of the international bank debt with US$20 billion in liabilities discounted and/or deferred in various ways; and
- the signing of agreements with the International Monetary Fund (IMF) and the World Bank for financial assistance for balance of payments and sectoral structural financing (at the same time, external finance was also obtained from other multilateral institutions and the international capital market).

Privatization became an important accompaniment of the SAPs in several Latin American countries. In Venezuela, the justification for privatization is especially strong because the government, as the direct recipient of oil revenues, was able to invest in several sectors that may be more efficiently organized in the private sector (e.g., hotels, banks, cattle ranches, mines). In some cases, the state became the owner only when state loans to the private sector were not paid. However, some of these enterprises soon became a major drain on the public budget; they were responsible for more than US$20 billion in foreign debt, and the deficit reached 9 percent of GDP when social spending was declining. This

Figure 9.1 Venezuela

From *Picture Atlas of the World* CD-ROM, © National Geographic Society, 1995

situation meant that the social and environmental sectors were being starved while state enterprise deficits were being financed.

The privatization programs of 1989-93 were designed to reverse these trends and improve public services. By the end of 1993, approximately US$2.3 billion of assets were privatized. Most of it was accomplished in 1991 and early 1992; by mid-1992, serious political and social conflicts were beginning to appear. For the remainder of the decade, the government plans to accelerate privatization to retire a substantial part of its internal and external debt.

The program is a partial success in terms of the amount privatized, but it lacks a deeper vision. All the privatizations completed to date have been justified by the argument that the companies involved are inefficient, generate losses, and impose a fiscal burden or render low quality services. Selling off these state-owned enterprises for these reasons alone will not guarantee a final coherent outcome of the privatization process. Although this approach could lead to more efficient services and improved fiscal performance, it will not help forge a state that is clear about its objectives and scope of activities.

A shift of enterprises to the private sector can result in better regulation if the framework is right and if (as is often the case) the government finds it difficult to enforce regulations against itself. On the other hand, there is a strong temptation to sweeten the package being privatized by exempting it from some of the more burdensome environmental regulations. The main part of the privatization program until now has included the national telecommunications company, the CANTV, and the national airline, VIASA. Given the type of activity involved, the environmental impacts of these changes of ownership are not significant. State enterprises with important environmental impacts—the oil companies and the Guayana region consortium of state enterprises, for example—have not yet become part of the privatization program. Having received the mining concessions, private companies, including foreign ones, have recently begun operations that can be expected to have significant environmental impacts, especially those related to gold and diamond mining (which increased 105 percent and 271 percent, respectively, in this period).

Until 1993, considerable success appeared to have been achieved in arresting the deteriorating macroeconomic indicators. Market-oriented reforms accompanied by fiscal austerity coincided with an important increase in world oil prices (and thus in Venezuela's oil revenues) that turned economic indicators around and achieved substantial economic growth. Nevertheless, since the *paquete's* beginning, despite what some macroeconomic indicators showed, social, political, and military unrest increased (including violent social protests, several aborted coups d'état, and President Pérez's being expelled from office in 1993). The SAP was accompanied by a compensatory social program (CSP) almost from the start, but its effects were not strong enough to compensate for the economic deterioration that was being strengthened by the adjustment process.

Reform difficulties were evident by the end of 1993 in the commercial banking crisis and in 1994 by the foreign exchange market crisis. The former arose from the bank's financial speculation and resulted in widespread illiquidity and insolvency. The latter is related to the former and reflects the capital flight that took place as investors became aware of the impending banking crisis in a climate of growing social unrest and political instability. With a liberal free exchange rate in operation, such a flight could not be arrested. The consequences of these developments are now evident, and important changes have affected the SAP policies. The rapid devaluation process culminated in strong exchange control, partial price controls, and the deprivatization of an important part of the banking system (owing to their becoming state-owned banks and given the sizable state aid to back deposits, estimated at more than 800,000 million bolívars at an official exchange rate of 170:US$1).

By the end of 1994, many economic indicators had improved little since the 1950s. Real wages, after an important increase in the intervening decades, are now virtually identical, as is the unemployment rate. The intervening "good years" delivered little that is lasting.

SOCIAL IMPACTS ON THE LABOR MARKETS AND THE URBAN ENVIRONMENT

The impacts of the SAP and its accompanying compensatory social program are explored here through socioeconomic changes, with a special focus on poverty and social policies, the labor markets, and the urban environment.

Poverty and Social Policies

The CSPs, the *megaproyecto social*, became part of structural adjustment following the violent social revolt. The rationale was that the deterioration of real income among the vulnerable social sectors was temporary and that once growth was under way, the programs could be eliminated. A stronger impact was sought and money would be saved by targeting particular population sectors.

Program coverage and compensation levels rose rapidly from the initial lows of 1989 and generally achieved their goals in this regard. The real income of the vulnerable groups contracted 72 percent between 1989 and 1993, and the CSPs offset less than 12 percent of that loss at the outset, but a combination of lower inflation and rising nominal salaries raised this figure to 84 percent the following 2 years. Despite the rise, incomes are still about 12 percent lower than they were at the beginning of the period.

As part of the SAP, the state reduced its expenditures in several social areas, but it also introduced CSPs in an effort to deal with rising poverty and misery levels. The impacts of the overall decline in social budgets were quite serious, as summarized in Table 9.1.

Table 9.1 Impacts of Structural Adjustment on Social Conditions

Indicators	Trends, 1989-92
Health	Decline in number of medical consultations; decrease in number of hospital beds per capita; general decline in services delivery; increase in environment-related diseases (i.e., malaria and dengue); increase in infant mortality rates and low birth weight rates
Water supply	Growing number of households without water supply
Public education	Decrease in number of secondary and preschool places; resurgence of illiteracy; fewer resources, affecting quality of education
Nutrition	Rising proportion of income spent on food items (over 70 percent for many poor families in 1993); increased malnutrition among children under 15 years of age
General living conditions	Substantial increase in population with basic unmet needs (in 1990, 45 percent with basic unmet needs and 20 percent in critical poverty and, in 1993, 80 percent and 40 percent, respectively)

These impacts occurred in spite of the CSPs. As formulated in the antipoverty plan, the social programs would assist those most in need without providing blanket subsidies to a large number of people. The programs covered health, nutrition, education, social protection, housing and infrastructure, and employment and social security. Included were the Maternal-infant Assistance Program; the Food Grant, Milk Bonus and School Uniforms Program; the Child Care Center Program; the Promotion and Support for Popular Economy Program; the Pre-school Education Program; the Sociocultural Participation and Development Program; and the Consolidation of Marginal Areas Program.

The main instrument of the CSP is direct cash transfer; grants were the most significant, accounting for nearly one-half the total CSP budget in 1989-93. From a transitory measure, it slowly changed to a permanent program. The emphasis on food grants to fight declining living standards and poverty is criticized for several reasons. First, the approach is inadequate. Food grants are a relief measure; they do not touch the causes of poverty. Second, they do not meet their goal of alleviating poverty. Success in offsetting declining incomes and moving families to poverty-line levels of food expenditure is estimated at 10 percent for 1992. Further, the grants cover only about 37 percent of the target group.

In summary, it can be said that the slowdown in progress toward improvement in living conditions during the 1980s turned into stagnation and clear deterioration because of the economic adjustment. Social policy was incapable of reversing the trend, although it provided some relief through compensatory programs. As important as these programs are, emphasis on them undermined permanent public services. In some cases, services have collapsed. These growing deficiencies endanger social stability and give rise to daily violence, which transforms and restricts daily life.

Labor Markets

The labor markets are the main mechanism for making the adjustment policies work. But the policies have not led to comprehensive improvements in company and industry performance; rather, short-term competitive advantages for enterprises were achieved at the expense of the labor force. Unemployment continued to rise in 1989-92 despite a decline in the numbers seeking work, especially women.

The main impacts on the labor markets are summarized in Table 9.2.

A labor market survey shows that lower incomes have led to a more fragmented and impoverished society and to one that stigmatizes a portion of the population through short-term relief programs. The shift from rural to urban employment and the associated migration led to less population pressure on natural resources in rural areas but more pressures on the urban environment. The increased poverty that accompanies this transition leads to the conclusion that in addition to being the country's principal social problem, poverty is now its principal environmental problem, not only because it leads to the destruction of natural resources but also because biological and social reproduction for most of the population has been seriously weakened.

The Urban Environment

The expansion and intensification of poverty are increasing urban environmental damage. Squatter settlements have spread into areas

Table 9.2 Impacts of Structural Adjustment on the Labor Markets

Indicators	Trends, 1989-92
Rural-urban balance	Increased migration; decline of traditional/informal agricultural employment; more formal agricultural employment
Labor market employment	Small increase in index of precariousness concentrated in newly created jobs in the formal sector
Segmentation	Slow shrinkage of public sector employment (from 21.7 percent to 19.1 percent of the formal sector employment between 1989 and 1993); growing urban informal sector employment (now 32 percent of total employment)
Labor markets-poverty links	Declining numbers below minimum wage, mainly because of decline in purchasing power; percentage of households below the poverty line up from 72 percent in 1989 to 92 percent in 1993; overall inequality increase of about 5 percent; stronger growth of poverty in urban areas

formerly used for small-scale agriculture or as a protective belt for cities like Caracas (the city "eats" 1 hectare of agricultural land per day in this way). Within existing settlements, the increased population density leads to deficiencies in ventilation, a lack of open space, overused utilities, and health problems. This density increase is also associated with increased risks of building collapse during earthquakes and landslides.

Another aspect of the impacts of structural adjustment is the general decline in the quality of life in urban squatter settlements. The picture is the same for all cities in the more densely populated central regions of the country: water supply, waste collection, urban sanitation, street maintenance, public safety, and health—all are declining. Standards of living of the poor settler deteriorate year by year, and the problems of urban poverty and environmental degradation are self-reinforcing. The process, begun prior to the SAPs, was greatly intensified by them.

Some environmental impacts of the deteriorating urban situation are specific to the poor settlers, who have unequal access to water, sewerage, energy, land, stable soil, etc. No effort to reconcile environmental policies with economic and social policies within the urban environment has yet been made.

In sum, economic adjustment worsened social conditions for many Venezuelans despite the CSPs. Almost all the indicators have worsened. It is likely that they would have declined further in the absence of the CSPs, but this point is partly disputed; permanent public services may have been cut back to provide the CSPs, clouding the overall impacts. The ill effects of these changes are felt most in the urban environment; the rural environment may have benefitted. However, for the increasing number of urban dwellers (91 percent of the population), living conditions are now deteriorating at a faster rate.

The basic question is whether the situation can be turned around. If the adjustment package is successful and growth in employment and incomes takes place, it could be. Most of the urban environmental damages are more or less reversible. But if the economic crisis continues, there is a real danger that the social fabric will collapse.

THE ENVIRONMENT AND STRUCTURAL ADJUSTMENT

Venezuela's environmental policy dates back to the 1976 Organic Law on the Environment, which created the Ministry of the Environment and Renewable Natural Resources. A National Plan for the Ordering of the Territory exists, and the government has the conventional instruments for environmental regulation and enforcement—permits, fines, environmental impact assessments required prior to undertaking major changes in land use, national plans and strategies, education, and citizen participation. Notably missing, however, are economic instruments, such as fees, taxes and charges, tradable permits, etc. The eighth *Plan de la Nación* of 1990 affirmed the need for compatibility between the environment and development. In addition, although the Penal Law of the Environment was approved in 1992, it still lacks regulations needed for its application.

One result of the past 30 years' economic development is a concentration of population in the central-north region of the country, leading to a shortage of water and urban expansion onto scarce agricultural land. Urban conditions have been deteriorating for low-income households in step with urban migration. Certainly, the government paid little attention to the environment in its economic adjustment strategy despite the fact that economic growth was the single most important objective, with equity considerations a clear second.

Effects of Structural Adjustment Policies on the Environment

As is true of social policies, in any consideration of the SAPs' environmental impacts, it is difficult to differentiate the impacts of structural adjustment from the longer-term economic processes. Some of the policies were already in place prior to the Pérez administration, so many of the effects date back to the early 1980s. For this reason, many conclusions relating adjustment to observed environmental effects are only tentative. Detecting a clear and direct link between adjustment policy and environmental change is rare.

Three elements of relevance to the environment in relation to SAPs are important:

- a reduction in public spending, which led to a direct weakening of state institutions and programs (particularly those of the Ministry of the Environment, MARNR) and had indirect environmental impacts caused by the considerable increase in poverty.
- encouragement of foreign investment, which allows expansion of the oil, mining, and tourism industries; and
- relaxation of controls, which allows increased deregulated exploitation.

Environmental Indicators

The changes that took place during the SAP period were analyzed according to: (1) land use by sector (agriculture, forestry, conservation-protected areas, wetlands, and urban areas); (2) atmosphere (air pollution in Caracas: suspended particulates, lead in suspended particulates, carbon monoxide emissions, nitrous oxides emissions, sulfur dioxide emissions, greenhouse gas emissions, and ozone-depleting substances); (3) water (i.e., principal watersheds, beaches, and water supply for human use); (4) waste disposal (i.e., solid waste generation per capita, refuse collection, hazardous waste generation, waste disposal, and recycling); (5) biological resources (i.e., fish, wild fauna, and endangered species); (6) mineral resources (i.e., oil and gas, aluminum, coal, gold, and diamonds); and (7) environmental management structure (national environmental laws and regulations, other environmental regulations, participation in major international conventions, and overseas environmental assistance received).

It should be noted that the purpose of analyzing the environmental data and thus the environmental indicators was to facilitate quantitative comparisons among countries and moments in time. Here it must be stressed that, by themselves, quantitative data can often be misleading.

Institutions, the Environment, and Structural Adjustment Effects

This section discusses environmentally related institutions in the broad sense (e.g., laws and regulations, organization of a civil society, nongovernmental organizations (NGOs), some government bodies); it then discusses the national parks system in Venezuela. The latter is presented separately owing to its importance and relative success in the country's "affirmative" environmental policy.

Several points need to be made here in regard to Venezuela's regulatory framework. First, coordination among authorities dealing with the environment is poor. The oil industry in particular seems to operate independently of the environmental authorities despite the many oil spills and its other contributions to pollution. Second, during the structural adjustment period, even a lower priority was given to environmental factors. For example, the chemical industry abandoned most of its plans for environmental improvements. Third, the environmental legislative framework is full of ambiguities and loopholes and lacks definition; it needs to be tightened. Fourth, there is a real problem of information. Venezuela participates in many international agreements but does not have the baseline information to meet its obligations.

Environmental Organizations and Structural Adjustment
Many NGOs and conservation organizations are active in the country, dating back to the 1930s. Their roles vary from scientific research to lobbying for conservation and social and economic reform. But in the past few years, there has been a clear shift away from the more physical concerns with the environment to the socioeconomic dimensions of environmental problems both in urban and rural areas and in indigenous communities.

More than 8,000 neighborhood associations have played an important part in the environmental management of their communities. They have been successful in protecting natural areas from development, preventing hazardous waste from entering the country, etc. In recent years, however, their ability to act collectively has weakened. This change is attributed in part to the structural adjustment process. Other more pressing economic problems have emerged, and socioeconomic differences in communities have deepened the divisions among the members: cooperative action is being replaced by a struggle to obtain the scarce resources that the state is making available. If these associations continue to grow weaker, they will be a real loss to the goals of sustainable resource management in the country.

There are many environmental organizations and their number has been growing since 1985. Estimates range from 85 to 200. The income of some of them has suffered from the inflation of the past 2 years, but despite these difficulties, the large organizations have managed to maintain their real incomes. The stronger and more prestigious ones (e.g., Fudena) have not been affected directly in terms of funds availability, given their strong policy of fund raising, but the economic situation has affected those with a lower institutional profile and fund raising capacity, and some have already disappeared.

The economic reforms hit the MARNR hard. The ministry lost almost one-third of its payroll of 6,100 employees between 1989 and 1994, cutting the professional and technical staff in half. Real budgets in 1993 were just over one-half those in 1988. The ministry reacted by creating autonomous units that provide wildlife protection, forest management, regional environmental protection, and other services. These organizations, which can generate their own income by granting permits for development, resource exploitation, etc., were meant to relieve the ministry of some of its operating costs. But the MARNR still has to support their activities, and the need for support is growing. One must also question the environmental effectiveness of an organization whose income (and hence its survival) rely on granting licenses to exploit natural resources.

In accordance with the policies of decentralization of the state and privatization that accompanied the SAPs, responsibility for some services was shifted to lower levels of government or to the private sector. Water supply and sewerage in the Caracas area were transferred to local governments and thence to private companies. But like the autonomous services, they still depend on government funding in most cases, although there are signs that some are providing better service. With more experience, the shift can be expected to improve services further.

A third reaction of the ministry was increased cooperation with civil society, as organized by the NGOs. Although this is a desirable trend, there is no clear policy of joint management between the state and the NGOs. Indeed, much conflict exists: the NGOs claim that many activities that they are asked to support are driven by financial considerations and are not compatible with the conservation goals that they espouse. Despite these problems, developing cooperation is an important step forward.

The National Parks System

Venezuela's national parks system has been a principal mechanism for arresting the degradation of the natural environment. Forty-three parks cover 14 percent of the country. Recently, the focus of protection has shifted from watersheds, landscapes, and public recreation to larger concerns, including biodiversity protection. As in other countries, human activity other than recreation is not allowed in the parks except for indigenous communities already living there.

National parks are administered and owned by the National Institute of Parks (Inparques), a legal entity under the guidance of MARNR. It is also responsible for 70 recreational parks and 22 nature monuments. Since 1989, the institution has declared the conservation of national parks and nature monuments its primary goal.

Prior to the SAP, administration of the parks was underfunded: it lacked a high-level political commitment, and not only was staff turnover high, but staff lacked training. The designation of protected areas was not always accompanied by funds and authority for Inparques to manage the system adequately. Even physical demarcation of the boundaries was often lacking.

The effects of 5 years of structural adjustment are difficult to determine, but two are clear: a direct effect on the budget and an indirect effect on more external pressures on the park system. Real budget allocations increased until the end of fiscal year 1991. After that, they fell and in 1993 were below the 1989 level. But the effective resources per unit of area declined much more because the total area to be administered increased 50 percent between 1988 and 1994 and tourism in the parks grew tenfold. It may be that more funds are being provided for the national parks by reduced allocations to the recreational parks, but data were not available to verify this point.

The indirect effects of structural adjustment are viewed from evidence of increased economic activity that competes for national park resources.

It is possible that increasing agricultural encroachment and illegal fishing, hunting, removal of fauna, and logging are taking place in the national parks as a result of the growth of poverty. Further, pressure for commercial exploitation of mining and oil within the parks is growing. As the economic situation worsens, these pressures will be harder to resist.

Conclusions

The general conclusions regarding Venezuela's environment and structural adjustment are:

- Venezuela has extremely diverse and heterogeneous environmental systems that (thanks largely to a prosperous oil industry, obviates the need to exploit other resources) have survived more or less intact;
- although the effects of the 1989-93 adjustment program are difficult to disentangle from the trends that have earlier roots, it intensified the exploitation already under way; and
- the program diminished the possibility for long-term sustainable development by intensifying processes that have eroded natural resources and by reducing the capacity of the state to implement sustainable development policies.

EXPLORING FUTURE IMPACTS: SCENARIOS FOR THE ECONOMY AND THE ENVIRONMENT

Although Venezuela's environmental problems are not as acute as other countries', the situation appears to be rapidly changing, intensifying trends that suggest even further damage to environmental ecosystems. Thus analysis of these trends is important to identify what is in fact happening as well as to provide a basis for the justification and design of policies and actions oriented toward conservation of endangered ecosystems. These negative effects can and should be minimized through reorientation of structural adjustment policies. This section presents a prospective, longer-term approach to the economy-environment linkage by means of scenario analysis.

Macroeconomic Performance Modeled

The macroeconomic performance of the economy is tracked through a Centro de Estudios del Desarrollo (CENDES) simulation model (i.e., the

SEVEN Model, Simulation of the Venezuelan Economy, by Luis Mata Mollejas) that is post-Keynesian in spirit. The basic assumptions of the model are:

- Oil revenues and prices are externally determined, with the government share fixed.
- The consumption level is determined by wages and other real variables and by interest rates. Investment levels are affected by the profitability of enterprises as well as availability of credit. The levels of other real variables (e.g., government expenditure, exports, imports) are either exogenous (or determined by variables beyond government control) or are a function of domestic output. They are not influenced by either prices or, most important, changes in exchange rates. By virtue of the model's design, imbalances cannot be corrected by adjusting prices other than through passing the price changes on to enterprises, in turn affecting their profitability.
- Monetary markets are brought into equilibrium through institutional constraints and are not simply a function of interest rates.

The model is calibrated using historical data from 1950 to 1993 and then forecasts economic performance under three scenarios (understood as a set of economic policies): (1) the economy follows the liberal market reforms introduced in 1989-93, with freer trade, a crawling peg exchange rate, and increasing public spending; (2) the most recent policies, introduced in June 1994 and held in place for the next 10 years, include exchange controls, price regulation in some sectors, and stricter controls on public spending; and (3) this is the same as the second scenario, but policies would redistribute income to the poor at the expense of reducing profits.

Running the model under the three scenarios shows:

- The "free market" scenario (the first) results in continued capital flight, negative investment, and high inflation (about 35 percent per annum). Real GDP shows virtually no growth over the period. High fiscal deficits, high inflation, etc. point to the political unviability of this scenario.
- The "exchange control" scenario (the second) results in a slight revaluation of the bolívar as the economy grows at a moderate rate. It shows an increase in private consumption and a lower inflation rate (about 9 percent).

- The third scenario involves lowering the profit margins of enterprises. According to the model, this is the most effective measure in terms of increasing incomes, salaries, consumption, and profits. Inflation exceeds the rate under the second scenario.

The Environment and Structural Adjustment Scenarios

The methodology used for analyzing the linkages between structural adjustment and the environment involved the three scenarios described above: the free market scenario, the exchange control scenario, and exchange control with redistribution. Each was run for 1994-2003 using the CENDES model. The outputs of that model, which are macroeconomic variables, such as total income, exports, etc., were disaggregated into production sectors using an input-output matrix. This simulation gave the output by sector (e.g., agricultural crops, livestock, refining). The sectoral outputs were fed into an equation that linked economic and other indicators for each of the 38 subregions to a measure of environmental quality. The independent variables contributing to the environmental quality index are:

- environmental stability;
- the region's carrying capacity;
- population density;
- agricultural activity;
- forest activity;
- oil and gas production;
- mining activity; and
- manufacturing activity.

The first two variables relate to the natural environment, and they reflect the average resistance of each subregion to human activities. The economic variables were obtained from the macromodel and linked to the input-output matrix. The sectoral outputs had to be disaggregated to the subregional level, done by taking the 1989 spatial distribution.

Table 9.3 shows the subregional environmental state in 1993, along with the values of the independent variables. The dependent variable is "Envirom State." Using a scale in which 100 is the ideal environmental state, one can identify the regions where environmental pressures are greatest (e.g., Ciudad Bolívar, Valle de la Pascua) and where they are least (e.g., Guanare, Puerto Ayacucho). The table also shows where the biggest changes have occurred (e.g., Punto Fijo, Puerto Cabello).

The main results from analysis of each of the scenarios are:

- Wide variations in regional indices remain in all the scenarios. However, the neoliberal, or free market, scenario varies the most.
- Of the three, the environmentally most harmful is the free market scenario. The next is exchange control, the social scenario, followed by exchange control with distribution, the Caldera scenario.
- The causal chain in the model is mainly through a higher growth rate in general and activities of the more aggressive industries (e.g., mining, oil).

It is important to note that these impacts are calculated on the assumption that no further environmental measures are introduced to mitigate environmental impacts. Strengthening the regulatory framework or using directive policies to locate activities in less environmentally fragile areas could change the results substantially.

The research team intends to analyze the impacts of different environmental policies in the future.

Sustainable Development

Although sustainable development is a term now found in most official documents and some regions are promoting their sustainable development programs, economic policies and programs do not explicitly incorporate stronger environmental regulations. On the contrary, government decisions point toward giving priority to economic growth with few or no effective measures for considering possible environmental damage. At the same time, little is known about national leaders' (political, economic, religious, academic, etc.) opinions on environmental problems, which have not been a priority issue in national debates or the subject of academic studies. Given this situation, the research team explored the possibilities for a near-term conservation-oriented strategy for Venezuela.

Sociopolitical Feasibility Analysis

A sophisticated sociopolitical analysis model was used to assess the chances of obtaining a conservation-oriented strategy over the next 10 years and to determine what external factors would most influence those chances. Ten policy areas that are part of the SAP (i.e., the neoliberal scenario) were analyzed: privatization, price liberalization, interest rate

Table 9.3 Subregional Environmental State, 1993

No.	Subregions	Stability	Infra-structure	Population	Agriculture	Forestry	Oil and Gas	Mining	Manu-facturing	ENVIROM State	Difference percentage change since 1989	Difference 1989
1	San Rafael	2.49	3.18	15.4	2.1	0.1	0	69.2	7.8	45.23	-27.00	-35.07
2	Maracaibo	2.94	2.47	177.	2.1	0.1	0	69.2	26.0	42.87	-16.47	-24.78
3	Machiques	2.24	3.54	9.8	6.2	0.0	0	0.1	2.8	79.05	8.14	10.32
4	El Vigia	3.08	3.94	17.4	20.6	0.0	0	0.3	8.8	44.78	2.13	3.38
5	San Antonio	1.67	4.21	120.	0.7	0.0	0	0.0	1.4	93.07	2.61	2.85
6	San Cristobal	1.67	4.21	84.7	9.7	7.7	0	0.2	9.0	56.16	15.38	20.40
7	Merida	1.67	4.21	58.7	5.0	0.0	0	0.0	0.8	82.66	2.94	3.46
8	Valera	2.01	4.05	127.	1.4	0.0	0	0.1	3.5	88.71	0.08	-0.09
9	Trujillo	1.67	4.21	56.5	1.4	0.0	0	0.1	3.5	93.29	4.02	4.42
10	Ciudad Ojeda	2.68	2.58	22.8	1.1	0.0	205	0.1	3.3	-35.02	2.81	14.64
11	Cabimas	2.68	2.58	35.5	2.0	0.2	205	0.1	8.9	-38.68	3.31	19.86
12	Punto Fijo	2.78	2.34	35.3	1.4	0.3	0	0.0	8.3	55.28	-25.43	-33.72
13	Coro	2.22	3.16	27.4	5.9	1.3	0	0.1	36.0	75.43	16.73	23.81
14	Barquisimet	1.99	3.45	73.8	8.8	0.4	0	0.4	54.7	58.1	5.11	8.01
15	Barinas	2.55	3.88	16.1	6.8	10.6	0	1.3	14.2	75.41	-0.16	-0.19
16	Guanare	2.55	3.88	40.5	0.4	1.4	0	0.7	7.1	97.13	4.16	4.46
17	Acarigua	2.55	3.88	49.6	8.6	0.1	0	0.1	10.9	73.16	2.97	3.76
18	San Felipe	3.26	3.30	62.3	7.7	0.8	0	0.1	11.1	75.74	7.14	9.17

No.	Subregions	Stability	Infra-structure	Population	Agriculture	Forestry	Oil and Gas	Mining	Manu-facturing	ENVIROM State	Difference percentage change since 1989	Difference 1989
19	Puerto Cabello	1.43	3.71	147.7	2.3	0.3	0	0.7	71.3	54.05	-21.61	-30.18
20	Valencia	2.79	2.60	565.5	3.5	0.0	0	0.7	39.1	62.75	6.50	10.40
21	San Carlos	2.48	3.39	14.6	3.8	0.5	0	0.2	6.0	83.97	6.71	8.16
22	Guasdalito	3.34	4.02	4.7	6.9	1.2	0	0.0	1.2	80.33	-4.41	-4.87
23	San Fernando	3.05	3.98	4.7	8.6	0.4	0	0.0	3.1	77.13	-0.07	-0.08
24	Calabozo	2.92	2.50	9.4	7.5	0.2	0	0.0	4.2	68.56	11.63	17.01
25	San Juan	2.78	2.64	25.2	1.6	0.1	0	0.0	0.3	90.96	16.28	20.42
26	Maracay	2.11	3.15	221.8	1.6	0.0	0	0.3	93.5	66.52	3.76	5.60
27	Caracas	1.43	3.71	652.3	4.2	1.2	0	2.1	120.8	49.23	1.34	2.49
28	Valle Plascua	2.92	2.50	4.7	7.0	0.4	10	60.0	1.5	36.12	-12.84	-20.76
29	Barcelona	2.09	3.06	46.5	3.3	0.0	37	0.2	63.7	39.10	-12.95	-22.35
30	El Tigre	2.72	3.34	7.8	4.5	7.5	1	3.2	28.7	74.68	1.19	1.51
31	Cumana	1.57	3.79	117.4	3.1	0.0	0	0.2	4.9	84.41	7.73	9.51
32	Carupano	1.57	3.79	32.0	2.9	0.1	0	0.2	0.2	86.06	6.44	7.71
33	Maturin	2.72	3.34	18.3	4.7	0.5	49	0.1	2.1	44.26	-12.64	-18.69
34	Temblador	1.95	2.95	5.7	3.0	2.2	0	0.2	1.6	84.17	15.00	19.73
35	Tucupita	1.54	4.79	2.6	0.4	1.7	0	0.0	0.1	98.64	-1.04	-1.04
36	Ciudad Bolivar	2.92	2.50	6.1	4.2	8.5	1	191.2	39.5	10.71	-18.64	-34.75
37	Ciudad Guayana	2.91	2.30	6.1	1.1	17.0	0	523.6	148.7	-97.61	14.53	93.97
38	Puerto Ayacucno	2.92	2.50	0.3	0.1	0.2	0	0.1	0.1	96.55	18.10	22.10

liberalization, subsidy elimination, opening the economy to imports, opening the economy to private foreign investment, orientation of exports toward comparative advantage, tax increases, reductions in state control, and natural environment conservation. These are initially calibrated on a scale of 0-10 with 10 representing reasonable compliance with the policy.

Policy success is also determined by social peace, increases in oil income, institutional stability, pressure from the IMF, positive entrepreneurial responses to incentives, willingness of foreign investors to put money into the country, greater integration with other Latin American countries, availability of more conservationist technologies, and compliance with legal environmental reforms. These factors occur with certain probabilities, ranging from 0 to 1 in each of the years.

The model links the determinants to the policies, and by taking a range of values for the probabilities of the determinants, one can generate various scenarios, creating a set of final values of the policies. The revised values may exceed 10 if the policy is more than reasonably applied.

A number of the scenarios were selected for study of their implications. Table 9.4 shows those scenarios in which environmental conservation gains a high score. The figures are given for the year 2000. The last row gives the score for environmental conservation. For example, with the set of

Table 9.4 Most Probable Scenarios plus Structural Adjustment Policies' Average and Conservation Trend Values, Year 2000

Determinants																				

Determinants	Model Runs with 100 Scenarios Each[a]																			
	1	2	3	4	5	6	7	8	9	10	11	12	13	14	15	16	17	18	19	20
Social peace	0	0	94	0	0	0	0	0	0	94	0	0	0	94	0	0	0	94	0	0
Oil revenues	03	0	99	01	0	99	01	01	0	00	02	96	99	02	0	03	02	01	99	01
Institutional stability	0	95	94	0	0	0	0	02	01	0	0	0	0	95	0	0	00	0	99	0
IMF pressure	99	97	01	99	96	98	95	95	01	00	97	00	95	00	95	01	98	98	03	94
National capital flight	96	0	0	99	94	98	0	0	94	94	94	95	0	94	94	94	0	94	94	94
Entrepreneur attitude	02	94	96	95	03	02	99	98	96	96	99	98	96	02	97	01	03	97	00	95
Environmental laws compliance	0	0	0	0	0	0	0	0	0	02	0	0	98	0	03	96	03	0	0	0
Alternative technologies	0	0	0	0	0	0	0	0	0	0	0	02	0	03	0	97	0	0	0	0
Foreign capital	94	94	94	99	0	04	97	94	0	0	0	0	0	94	0	0	0	0	94	0
Integration	0	03	94	98	98	0	00	0	99	97	94	0	0	02	0	0	98	0	98	95
Structural adjustment average, year 2000	10	7	8	12	10	9	7	4	3	9	6	3	2	34	4	2	20	8	8	6
Conservation, year 2000	3	3	1	0	7	1	1	2	1	1	1	1	10	9	3	38	43	5	0	1

a. O=determinant does not occur during the period; other numbers indicate the year in which or before which the determinant occurs.

probabilities as given in run 1, the environmental conservation policy emerges with a score of 3. The row above that gives the average score for all the structural adjustment policies.

Table 9.5 selects the runs in which conservation is most likely to succeed. This table shows that, according to the assumptions built into the analysis:

- neither social peace nor the availability of alternative technology is critical to a successful conservation policy;
- institutional stability and pressure from the IMF do not emerge as relevant for conservation;
- oil revenue increases are important for conservation because they lead to increased levels of economic activity; and
- foreign capital inflows do affect conservation, and their higher levels result in less environmental conservation.

The free market scenario assesses policies in terms of their social value, institutional feasibility, de facto feasibility, soundness (solidity), and stability. These results are shown in Table 9.6. It should be noted that conservation as a policy is not included because it is not a part of this scenario. The assessments can be summarized as follows:

- All the policies have a high social value (i.e., they are of great interest to the population) and are institutionally and practically feasible.
- A policy is considered sound or solid if it can resist pressures to change it. Only movement of trade toward the export of goods with a comparative advantage falls clearly in this category.
- Only the elimination of subsidies presents low stability (i.e., its being maintained for the long term is unlikely). All others have medium to high stability.

The scenario analysis indicates that, during 1994-2000:

- There will be no social peace, institutional stability, or fulfillment of environmental laws; nor will alternative conservation technologies be available.
- The IMF will continue to press in favor of adjustment policies.
- National capital flight will likely continue.
- Foreign capital will likely enter the country.
- Integration with the rest of Latin America will continue.
- The economicist attitude of national entrepreneurs will continue.

Table 9.5 Environmentally Most Desirable Scenarios, plus Structural Adjustment Policies' Average and Conservation Trend Values, Year 2000

Model Runs with 100 Scenarios Each[a]

Determinant	1/	2/	3/10	4/	5/	6/	7/10	8/	9/	10/8	11/9	12/7	13/1	14/3	15/9	16/7	17/9	18/7	19/2	20/7
Social peace	0	0	94	0	0	0	0	95	0	95	94	0	0	0	0	94	0	0	0	0
Oil revenues	02	0	0	99	0	0	0	0	0	0	0	03	99	98	98	0	0	01	0	01
Institutional stability	03	96	97	02	0	0	0	0	0	97	01	0	0	99	99	0	94	94	0	94
IMF pressure	01	98	03	96	01	96	97	03	97	00	02	97	95	01	01	94	00	99	98	99
National capital flight	03	0	0	0	0	95	0	94	0	01	0	0	0	0	0	00	02	94	0	94
Entrepreneur attitude	03	02	03	02	03	99	03	00	03	00	03	99	96	00	00	01	02	01	00	01
Environmental laws obedience	03	0	98	02	0	95	01	98	97	99	0	98	98	99	99	99	96	97	0	97
Alternative technologies	0	95	0	0	0	96	97	0	0		0	98	0	0	0	0	0	98	0	98
Foreign capital	0	0	0	0	0	0	0	0	0	0	0	0	0	0	0	0	0	97	02	97
Integration	0	97	97	0	0	95	0	0	96	0	98	0	0	0	0	00	0	03	0	03
Structural adjustment average, year 2000	0	21	22	0	0	43	11	11	21	11	11	33	11	11	11	11	11	32	0	21
Conservation, year 2000	32	86	102	24	32	3	171	7	48	62	29	38	10	1	11	26	171	21	10	21

a. 0=determinant does not occur during the period; other numbers indicate the year in which or before which the determinant occurs.

Table 9.6 Structural Adjustment Policies' Sociopolitical Feasibility[a]

Structural Adjustment Policy	Social Value	Institutional Feasibility	Real Feasibility	Solidity	Stability
Privatization	0.67	1.00	1.00	0.55	0.87
Price liberation	0.67	0.92	0.86	0.35	0.58
Interest liberation	0.67	0.86	0.84	0.24	0.50
No subsidies	0.61	0.84	0.82	0.12	0.39
Open imports	0.67	0.86	0.85	0.25	0.49
Open foreign investment	0.88	0.91	0.90	0.59	0.77
Export competitive advantage	0.97	0.95	0.92	0.91	0.77
More taxes	0.93	0.76	0.74	0.15	0.77
Fewer controls	0.65	0.95	0.96	0.34	0.77

a. Estimated according to the Calcagno, Sainz, De Barbieri method.

CONCLUSIONS

Both the trends and effects analyzed correspond to a time that precedes the SAP, the package formally initiated in 1989. Thus the analysis is more in the before-after sense than with or without because disentangling the effects of new policies from early trends was not possible. But it is possible to extract some general conclusions:

- Venezuela's natural resources can amply support sustainable development. Nevertheless, environmental deterioration is acute and is rapidly growing.
- Over the past two decades, Venezuela has established specialized institutions and a strong legal base for protecting the environment. But application of the laws and regulations is undermined by ambiguities, loopholes, and the lack of precision.
- NGOs have been important in strengthening environmental awareness and in preventing environmental damage. Although economic conditions have adversely affected smaller organizations, others' participation is growing, and closer relations between the government and the private sector in regard to environmental management and conservation have developed.
- Official development assistance for environmental programs increased considerably during this period of structural adjustment, and it appears to be an important source of future support.

During 1989-1993, when the SAP was formally applied in a rather orthodox manner, the environment suffered significantly. This deterioration may be seen as linked to the free market development model accompanying the SAP, which implied:

- acceptance at government and entrepreneur decision levels that the main goal must be to increase production and productivity to achieve international competitiveness;
- impoverishment of the majority of the people under the promise of a better future, accenting the growth of urban marginal areas and rural activities (e.g., migrant agriculture, indiscriminant hunting);
- emphasis on exports based on comparative advantage at the international level: gold, oil, iron, aluminum, and tourism, which are highly aggressive vis-à-vis the environment;
- the freedom to import that has accelerated urban growth rather than examine other land use and spatial development alternatives within the country;
- weakening of government environmental controls as part of the tendency to increase economic freedom; and
- increase in violence and social unrest in a climate of growing personal insecurity.

10

CASE STUDY FOR PAKISTAN

This chapter is based on a study conducted by Sajjad Akhtar, Akhtar Hai, Haroon Jamal, Shaukat Ali, M.M. Sajid Manzoor, Mohammad Ilyas, S. Iqbal Ali, Wasim Akhtar, and Samina Khalil of the Applied Economics Research Centre, University of Karachi, with support of Jeffrey Vincent of the Harvard Institute for International Development. This summary was written by Sajjad Akhtar and Jeffrey Vincent.

INTRODUCTION

Pakistan's history since partition with India in 1947 has been marked by social and political turbulence. The geographical gap in the newly independent country, with East and West Pakistan at the opposite ends of hostile Indian territory, was the country's most striking feature, but less obvious divisions were more challenging. Its citizens shared a common religion, Islam, and a common legacy of struggle against British rule, but little else. The country's five major ethnic groups—Punjabis, Sindhis, Baluchis, Pushtuns, and Bengalis—had their own languages and long histories as political units. The coincidence of provincial boundaries and ethnic distribution added an ethnic overlay to the struggle for power between provincial governments and the central government. The ethnic mix was further complicated by the immigration of millions of refugees, or *mohajirs*, from India after partition. Many settled in Karachi, rapidly turning it into one of the world's largest cities.

The new country did not agree on a constitution until 1956, and even then the agreement was short lived: new constitutions were drawn up in 1962, 1973, and 1981. A spate of untimely deaths of key leaders repeatedly jolted the political scene. Pakistan's founder, Muhammad Ali Jinnah, died of natural causes one year after Independence, and its first prime minister, Liaquat Ali Khan, was assassinated just 3 years later. The country experienced two extended periods of military rule, from 1958 to 1971 and from 1977 to 1988. During periods of civilian rule, changes in government were frequent: four prime ministers lost office during 1956-58, and power changed hands four times in 1993. Pakistan went to war with India four times, and it fought a civil war in 1971 that resulted in East Pakistan's becoming independent Bangladesh. Ongoing tensions with India have precipitated a massive military build-up that is rumored to include nuclear weapons capability.

Considering the great number of destabilizing forces and events that have buffeted the country, its economic performance has been surprisingly strong. During 1970-80, its GDP grew at an average annual rate of 4.9 percent, almost one-half a percentage point above the average for low-income countries (according to categories used by the World Bank).[1] During 1980-91, the rate was even higher, 6.1 percent, which matched the average for the low-income group.

Despite the economy's strong performance, by the late 1970s and early 1980s, serious structural problems became evident. The country's savings rate was low by any standard. Gross domestic investment grew at rates well below the averages for low-income countries during both the 1970s and 1980s. The government was running persistent budget deficits, and the country faced repeated balance of payments problems. Moreover, the benefits of economic growth were dissipated by a population growth rate that was, and is, about 50 percent higher than the average for low-income countries.

In view of these problems, in the early 1980s and then again in the late 1980s and early 1990s, Pakistan entered into structural adjustment programs with the World Bank and the International Monetary Fund (IMF). The country received balance of payments support in return for agreeing to implement a far-reaching series of economic reforms.

Structural adjustment programs (SAPs) involve great changes in economic policies. It is their explicit intention to change the course of development. The question asked by this study is: "Is the development path that results from SAPs in Pakistan likely to be one that improves both economic performance and environmental quality, or are there likely to be trade-offs between the two?" If the latter is the case, what sorts of policies are appropriate for managing the trade-offs and ensuring that development does indeed generate ongoing welfare improvements in Pakistan, not simply increased economic growth?

The study is organized into three sections. The remainder of this section describes the country's economic development experience, highlighting events related to economic reforms, and the state of its environment. It closes by examining the extent to which SAPs in Pakistan have taken potential environmental and social impacts into account. The second section presents the results of four studies that examine particular aspects of the relationship between structural adjustment and the environment. Three studies are at the macro level, and the other is at the sectoral level. The sectoral study focuses on land degradation related to irrigated agriculture. The last section summarizes the main findings and discusses policy implications, particularly ones that are pertinent to the economic reform process.

Economic Development

Economic reforms in Pakistan are not limited to periods covered by the official SAPs of the 1980s and 1990s. Many policy changes in the 1960s contained reform elements, as did many in the late 1970s and early 1980s. Of principal interest here, however, are the reforms linked to World Bank and IMF SAPs initiated in the late 1980s, which called for the most comprehensive reforms.

1947-71: Industrialization and Inequality

Economic historians in Pakistan generally regard the 1950s as a period of economic stagnation and the 1960s as one of buoyant growth with inequitable distribution of economic rewards. Starting from an almost nonexistent industrial base, Pakistan, like many other newly independent countries in the postwar, postcolonial era, pursued an import substitution industrialization strategy. The proindustrial bias in resource allocation caused the agricultural sector to stagnate. Because agriculture was the dominant economic sector, per capita GDP hardly grew during the fifties. Imbalances developed on the fiscal side. The provision of basic services to 8.25 million refugees from India consumed a considerable amount of the government's meager resources. The commitment to strengthen the country's defense in view of border tensions with India had an even greater impact.

The political situation was unstable throughout the 1950s. But in October 1958, Ayub Khan declared martial law. The military regime is generally regarded as having practiced sounder economic management than the civilian government it replaced. Yet it continued to favor large-scale manufacturing, with investment depending largely on inflows of foreign aid. Social aspects of the regime's development policies undermined their sustainability. The growth strategy pursued in the 1960s relied on the doctrine of functional inequality, which advocated channeling resources to those classes that had a high savings rate. The single-minded pursuit of this strategy exacerbated class inequalities as the benefits of economic growth were captured disproportionately by a small group of industrialists and businessmen. The government grossly neglected social services. Class tensions began to surface in the mid-1960s, and they led to mass revolt against the regime in 1968. The 1971 civil war marked the end of this period of the country's development.

1972-77: Intervention and Erratic Growth
The economic agenda during 1971-77 was guided by the politicoeconomic ideology of Z.A. Bhutto's Pakistan People's Party (PPP). Reducing inequalities in income and in the concentration of wealth were two populist themes that helped Bhutto win the 1970 election in West Pakistan. Nationalization began in 1972 and continued in various stages until 1976. The initial takeovers of heavy and basic industrial units, commercial private banks, and insurance and shipping companies were in accord with the PPP manifesto. But nationalization was extended to enterprises owned by small and medium-size capitalists, and it was accompanied by additional interventionist policies. As a consequence, output and private investment stagnated, and inflation and strain on the government budget rose. Fiscal constraints limited the implementation of the PPP's health, education, and welfare programs.

1977-88: Growth with Structural Weaknesses
After a brief period of political and social unrest, the Bhutto government was dismissed in July 1977 by the military, led by General Zia-ul-Haq. The new government introduced a mix of fiscal and monetary incentives and institutional reforms (e.g., privatization) to restore the confidence of the private sector. In spite of these incentives, fixed investment fell from 18.7 percent of GNP in FY 77 to 14.8 percent in FY 83. Uncertainty regarding the fate of Bhutto and his party plus the Afghan crisis (from 1981) induced the private sector to seek more secure havens for its wealth. Investment picked up in FY 83, but it fell in the next year as the political

Figure 10.1 Pakistan

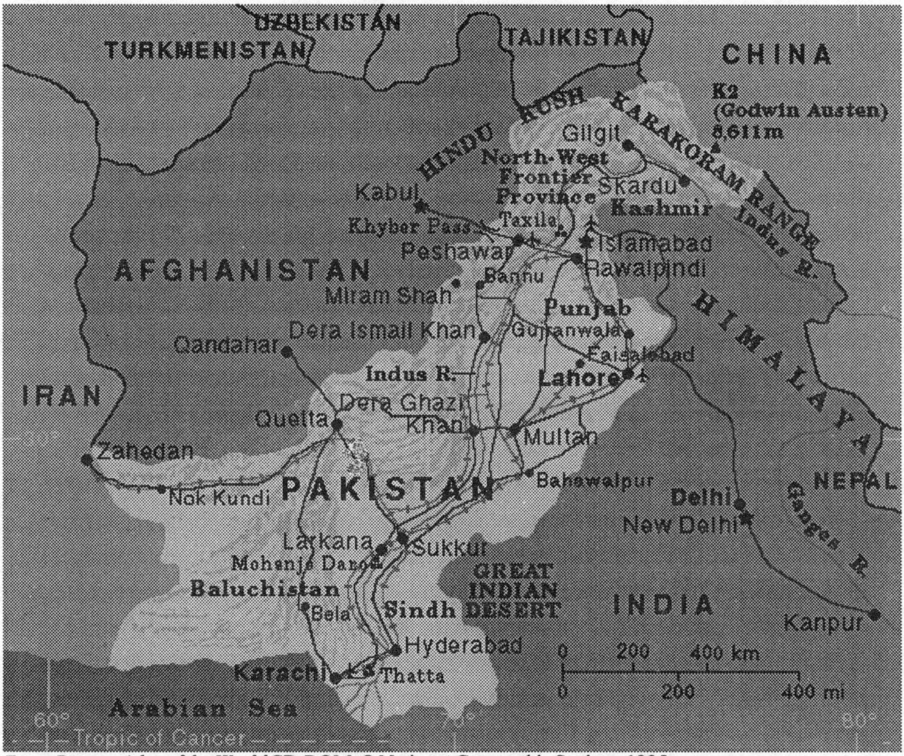

From *Picture Atlas of the World* CD-ROM, © National Geographic Society, 1995

situation deteriorated in Sindh. Inadequate and unreliable provision of electricity, gas, water, and telecommunications services also discouraged investment. Investment in utilities had been neglected in the 1970s in favor of heavy-industry projects.

The economy was also buffeted by several external shocks from the late 1970s to the mid-1980s. The second oil shock in 1979 and the ensuing world recession reduced aid flows. High international interest rates caused debt payments to escalate rapidly. By 1983, debt service was absorbing 70 percent of gross aid inflows. Fortunately, a dramatic rise in remittances helped stabilize the balance of payments and offset the country's sluggish export performance, which was hindered by slow progress in trade reforms. By 1984, remittances constituted the largest single source of foreign exchange earnings.

Because of fiscal constraints, only 70 percent of the Fifth Plan (1978-83) was implemented. No significant effort was made to increase revenues;

instead, expenditures, especially development expenditures, bore the brunt of relative fiscal restraint. On the other hand, both defense spending, which accounted for nearly 30 percent of central government expenditures, and debt service rose. Allocations to the social sectors particularly suffered at the expense of defense and debt service.

During 1980-83, shortfalls in the expected inflow of external resources compelled the government to seek relief from the Extended Fund Facility (EFF) of the IMF. It obtained additional funds from the World Bank under a structural adjustment loan (SAL) in 1982. The SAL involved no up-front conditionalities. M. Khan judged that reforms associated with the SAL were "unsuccessful in the two areas that . . . matter the most—fiscal reform and trade reform."[2] In fact, fiscal deterioration accelerated during the Sixth Plan (1983-88), when spending increased on defense, debt service, and after years of neglect, infrastructure and social programs. The plan placed little emphasis on measures to improve domestic resource mobilization to pay for the increased spending. Comprehensive measures to raise direct and indirect taxes were resisted by the country's economic-cum-political elites. The balance of payments remained sensitive to the underlying weaknesses of the external sector. The export base—mainly cotton and textiles—remained narrow, and foreign exchange earnings relied excessively on remittances. The current-account deficit tripled from FY 83 to FY 88. With the external sector out of balance, government borrowing in the domestic market to cover the deficit increased drastically.

1988-94: Structural Adjustment Amidst Political Instability
Military rule ended in 1988, following General Zia's death in a plane crash in August and elections in November. The elections were won by the PPP, led by Z.A. Bhutto's daughter Benazir. The civilian government inherited an economy whose structural problems—persistent budget and current-account deficits, unsustainable debt loads, deteriorating infrastructure, and poor social indicators—were partially masked by robust GNP growth. But the vulnerability of the economy to external shocks was exposed whenever aid flows and remittances faltered. In recognition of these circumstances, at the end of the Sixth Plan period, the government committed to accelerating the economic reform process under a 3-year (FY 89-FY 91) SAP supported by the World Bank. In return, it received balance of payments support from the Bank.

The SAP is described in a series of World Bank reports.[3] It recommended reforms in a number of areas; those receiving the most emphasis were the control of budget deficits, enhanced resource mobilization (i.e., higher national and government savings rates), liberalization of the trade regime, and financial sector reforms. The recommended reforms were more comprehensive than those associated with the IMF and Bank adjustment loans in the early 1980s. But implementation of the recommended reforms was slow and is far from complete, even today. The principal explanation is that the SAP period was characterized by extraordinary political instability. The country witnessed three elected governments during a short period of 4 years. In 1993 alone, control of the government changed hands four times. Political commitment, a necessary ingredient in successful economic reform, was always half-hearted. The lack of political will made it particularly hard to address the budget deficit. Given the slow progress, the SAP was extended 2 additional years (FY 92 and FY 93).

In drawing an overall conclusion, the World Bank commented: "In many respects, these reforms went significantly beyond what was originally envisaged," particularly ones targeted at increasing the role of the private sector.[4] But it highlighted insufficient savings and investment, excessively expansionary fiscal policy, and balance of payments constraints as three basic macroeconomic challenges the country continues to face. Table 10.1 shows that there has been no significant reallocation of current expenditures in the federal budget to social and environmental programs. The shares of budgetary resources allocated to such programs fluctuated considerably from year to year but were not significantly higher during 1989-93 than 1985-88. The shares actually fell for some programs, including land reclamation and population planning.

Given the unfinished business, in March 1994, the government, the World Bank, and the IMF agreed on a continuation of the SAP, with the IMF providing about $1.3 billion in balance-of-payments support from its Enhanced Structural Adjustment Facility (ESAF) and its EFF.[5] The support will be provided during FY 94-FY 96.

The Environment and Natural Resources

This section outlines the main characteristics of Pakistan's land and natural resources and briefly describes the environmental degradation that has occurred in the country.[6]

Table 10.1 Environmental Priorities in Development Plans: Current Expenditures

	Irrigation[a]	Land Reclamation[a]	Rural Development[a]	Forest[a]	Public Health Services[a]	Urban Town Planning and Regulatory Services[b]	Population Planning[b]
1984-85	1.72	0.25	0.12	0.24	0.29	45.00	0.50
1985-86	6.16	2.29	1.08	2.23	3.22	46.12	0.41
1986-87	9.96	2.96	1.84	2.66	3.83	38.34	0.38
1987-88	17.91	7.13	5.28	4.19	7.47	30.32	0.39
Average 1984-88	8.94	3.16	2.08	2.33	3.70	39.95	0.42
1988-89	1.50	0.70	0.45	0.42	0.71	53.00	0.29
1989-90	13.47	5.90	4.16	3.83	7.66	54.52	0.35
1990-91	13.07	4.47	4.14	3.81	7.53	74.68	0.36
1991-92	4.32	1.36	1.49	1.63	2.52	24.29	0.37
1992-93	1.72	0.61	0.72	0.866	1.26	31.25	0.37
Average 1989-93	6.82	2.61	2.19	2.11	3.94	47.58	0.35

a. Percentage of total current expenditures.
b. Percentage of total housing and physical planning expenditures.
c. Percentage of total health expenditure.

Status and Trends

Most of Pakistan is a dry country with a fragile environment that is sensitive to misuse. Of its 88 million hectares of land, 31 million (35 percent) are suitable for agriculture or forestry. About 20.4 million hectares are currently cultivated; the majority, 16.2 million hectares, are being irrigated. Irrigated land produces 90 percent of the total agricultural output. Forests cover only 4.6 million hectares and rangeland another 6.7 million hectares. Forest cover, just under 5 percent of the land, is among the lowest in Asia.

Degradation of natural resources is occurring in all parts of Pakistan. In the hills, large areas have been denuded of their protective vegetation by people in search of fuel and timber and by animals in search of fodder. In the process, the natural habitat of plants and animals indigenous to Pakistan has been reduced markedly. Although the government has established 7 national parks, 72 wildlife sanctuaries, and 7 game reserves during the past 23 years, many of these areas are protected more in name than in reality. In the nonirrigated semiarid and arid plains, overgrazing and inappropriate dryland farming techniques have caused sharp declines in production.

Irrigation has transformed the landscape in the Indus Valley, vastly increasing agricultural production. But poor water management has also led to serious waterlogging and salinity problems. Seepage from irrigation canals and inadequate drainage have raised the water table in many prime agricultural areas. When the water table is shallower than about 1 meter, capillary action moves excess soil water, which carries dissolved salts, to the surface.

In urban areas, major environmental problems relate to industrial pollution and inadequate provision of public services to urban households. An environmental conservation ethic does not exist in the industrial community in Pakistan. Although few studies have assessed the quantity and characteristics of industrial pollution, studies on industrial wastewater have shown high concentrations of toxic metals, metal salts, bacteria, acids, and oils. Leather tanning has created problems in several locations. At the time of Independence, 18 percent of Pakistan's population lived in urban settlements; by 1981 (the latest census year), the figure had risen to 28 percent. More than one-quarter of the urban population is living in illegal settlements, which lack piped water, sewerage, and drainage systems.

Population pressure is implicated in many of the country's environmental problems, most notably, land degradation, deforestation, and urbanization. Pakistan's population is growing at a rate of 3.1 percent per year. By the year 2000, it will reach some 150 million people, up from 84 million in 1981 and an estimated 124 million today. Nearly 77 percent of the population lives in the Indus Valley, which covers less than one-half the country. The government has tried, with little success, to reduce population growth through family planning programs. The country's extremely low level of female education, particularly in rural areas, appears to be the principal explanation for its stubbornly high fertility rates.

Legislation, Policies, and Institutions

Until the 1970s, the country's development policies focused on textbook strategies, such as expanding the industrial base to generate employment, maintaining agricultural growth to feed the growing population, and narrowing income inequalities. It was not until the Fifth Plan (1978-83) that the government noted the need "to relate development to larger ecological issues." In 1983, the government enacted the Pakistan Environmental Protection Ordinance to "provide for the control of pollution and the preservation of the living environment." The ordinance authorized the creation of an Environmental Protection Council and a national Environmental Protection Agency (EPA). The former has met just once, in August 1994. Although four provincial EPAs have been in existence since the late 1980s, the national EPA was never established.

The country's environmental policy framework into the mid-1980s was characterized by a piecemeal approach marked by incidental environmental laws and regulations, the establishment of new agencies without concomitant commitments of sufficient resources and political support, and limited integration of resource and environmental management into other activities in national development plans. Compared to earlier planning exercises, the Sixth (1983-88), Seventh (1988-93), and Prospective (1988-2003) Plans showed more evidence of recognizing the linkages among economic development, poverty alleviation, resource management, and environmental protection, but the gap between statement and action remained large.

The National Conservation Strategy (NCS) was an ambitious response to this situation. It was prepared through a collaborative effort of the Environment and Urban Affairs Division (EAUD) of the Ministry of Housing and Works and the International Union for Conservation of Nature and Natural Resources (IUCN).[7] It represents one of the most comprehensive environmental policy frameworks for any country in the world. Its general aim is to integrate environmental considerations into the "daily economic, social and physical decisions of households, communities, corporations and Government."[8] It suggests three approaches for achieving this aim: (1) incorporating environmental concerns into the planning and development process at both federal and provincial levels; (2) working through EAUD to ensure that implementation occurs; and (3) creating specialized institutions to develop policy recommendations, conduct studies, and provide training for government and nongovernmental organization staff. Donor support has been received for several program areas emphasized by the NCS.

Social and Environmental Elements in Structural Adjustment Programs

Issues related to social and environmental aspects of development are highlighted in all three World Bank reports on SAPs[9] as well as in the Policy Framework Paper for ESAF/EFF.[10] In all the documents, in fact, a primary justification offered for SAPs is that they are necessary for generating resources to finance social development. There is nowhere the sense that the motivation is growth for growth's sake. The documents recognize the limited objectives of adjustment programs and call for complementary programs to ensure progress on all development fronts, in particular, those related to social and environmental issues.

A sense that the Bank viewed economic reforms as a necessary but insufficient means to achieve broader development objectives is most evident in a 1993 World Bank report. Toward the beginning of the executive summary, a section on "Outstanding Adjustment Issues" states:

> Pakistan confronts major development tasks, including: (i) expanding and improving basic social services and accelerating efforts to reduce high population growth; (ii) diversifying and expanding the productive base in agriculture and industry; (iii) improving the management of natural resources, in particular, water; and (iv) overcoming severe infrastructural bottlenecks. Meeting these developments will require a significant increase in total investment . . . .[11]

The report discusses structural adjustment as a process that was broader than economic reform: "Pakistan's structural adjustment effort also aims at improving health care and education as well as reducing population growth."[12] It draws attention to the dominance of expenditures on the military, interest payments, and subsidies as an obstacle to implementation of programs to achieve these goals. It highlights the country's newly launched Social Action Program, which "aims at providing a coherent framework for the provision of basic social services—primary education, primary health care, family planning, and rural water supply and sanitation."[13] The ESAF/EFF Policy Framework Paper, which was leaked and published in the December 19, 1993 Karachi *Business Recorder*, contained similar language on social issues. It also included a separate section on the environment.

In both the World Bank's 1993 report and the ESAF/EFF Policy Framework Paper, there is some indication of a movement beyond complementarity toward a notion of structural adjustment in which economic reforms are just one element, albeit a vital one, in an integrated development program. But for the most part, the perception is one of equating structural adjustment with economic reform, with other programs bearing primary responsibility for actions related to social services and the environment. In no document is there discussion of the short- and long-run environmental impacts of SAPs relative to the impacts that would occur in the absence of the programs.

THE ENVIRONMENTAL AND SOCIAL IMPACTS OF REFORMS

Four related in-depth studies were conducted to analyze the impacts of economic reforms on the environment and society. The first three were at the macroeconomic level. The first was aimed at providing a rough long-run (50-year) picture of the relationships among economic growth, population growth, and environmental degradation in both the presence and absence of reforms. This study involved the construction of a simple long-run economic growth model. The second study complemented this analysis by providing more detail on the impacts of specific reforms upon individual sectors of the economy, still in a macroeconomic context. It involved construction of a computable general equilibrium (CGE) model. The third study addressed distributional impacts, focusing on the regressivity or progressivity of fiscal elements of reform programs. It made use of the Applied Economics Research Centre (AERC) tax policy simulation model. The fourth study focused on agriculture. It analyzed the impacts of economic reforms on cropping patterns, groundwater balances, and salinity for irrigated crops in the Indus Valley. It involved use of the Indus Basin model (revised), a linear programing model developed by the World Bank.

Long-run Projections

The long-run economic and environmental impacts of economic reforms were projected through a two-step procedure. First, construction of a simple economic growth model for the country made it possible to project long-run performance of the economy under three scenarios: without reforms, with reforms, and with reforms and population stabilization. Because of the simple structure of the model, "reforms" was defined simply as a 1 percentage point increase in the national savings rate. This figure is less than the impact forecast by the World Bank for SAPs but is about equal to the actual increase achieved during FY 89-93 compared to FY 84-87. An increase in the savings rate is not a reform per se, but as discussed above, it is increasingly recognized as the key change in economic behavior that adjustment programs in Pakistan must achieve. The mechanism for achieving population stabilization was not specified; it was simply assumed that exogenous factors (i.e., factors other than income growth) would cause the population growth rate to decline gradually to zero by 2038. Such factors might include efforts to boost female education and literacy. The magnitude of the exogenous decrease was 0.0333 percentage points per year.

Second, the projected trends in economic output and population were related to environmental impacts through the application of functional relationships drawn from previous cross-country studies. Several recent studies have investigated the relationship between income, as measured by per capita GDP, and environmental quality, as measured by ambient air or water quality or emissions of specific pollutants.[14] The studies found that some environmental indicators deteriorate as income rises, up to a threshold value or turning point, beyond which they improve. This relationship has been dubbed the "environmental Kuznets curve" after the famous relationship between income inequality and level of income proposed by Kuznets.[15] Environmental Kuznets curves imply that policy reforms that stimulate more rapid economic growth create a trade-off in environmental quality over time. On the positive side, they enable countries to reach the turning points more rapidly. On the negative side, more rapid growth means that the environmental deterioration associated with the first half of the curve (i.e., before the turning point is reached) will be more intense.

Table 10.2 summarizes the level of income turning points as determined by the studies. The estimates are reported in dollars at 1985 price levels. These reflect estimates of per capita GDP adjusted for differences in purchasing power across countries.[16] For comparison, Pakistan's per capita GDP in FY 88 at 1985 international prices was US$1,567.[17] If Pakistan's experience mirrors that of other countries, then economic growth since 1988 and into the future should be associated with rising percentages of the overall and urban populations having access to safe water and adequate sanitation, respectively, and with declining fecal coliform counts in rivers (of course, reflecting improved sanitation). For all other measures, however, environmental quality can be expected to deteriorate for many years.

The projections reported below should be considered no more than approximate. The growth model is simple. It does not include equations that model feedbacks from environmental quality to economic growth. If environmental degradation creates a drag on economic growth, then the model overstates the impacts of reforms on economic growth. The model also excludes policy instruments for mitigating environmental degradation. It is conceivable that well-designed policies to internalize environmental externalities could lead to improvements in environmental quality without appreciable sacrifices in economic growth.

Further, there is no guarantee that the functions relating income growth to environmental impacts provide good predictions of what will actually happen in Pakistan. The studies from which these functions are drawn estimated them using cross-country data covering just a few recent years. Most of the data pertain to developed countries. In sum, it is best to regard the projections as possible future scenarios for the country, not as forecasts. One should focus more on qualitative differences among the projections than on the magnitude of the differences.

Structure of the Growth Model

The core of the model consists of three econometrically estimated equations, which project GDP, the national savings rate, and population growth. The equations for GDP and the national savings rate were estimated using data for Pakistan; the equation for population growth used cross-country data. Five additional identities project capital stock, GNP, population, national savings, and investment.

Table 10.2 Per Capita GDP Turning Points Estimated by Cross-country Studies (Purchasing Power Parity Estimates, 1985 Price Levels)[a]

	Grossman and Krueger (1991)	Selden and Song (1993) US$/capita	Shafik and Bandyopadhyay (1992)
Air Quality			
Ambient SO$_2$	4,107		3,670
Ambient TSP	None[b]		3,280
Per capita SO$_2$ stocks		10,681	
Per capita TSP stocks		9,811	
Per capita No$_x$ stocks		12,041	
Per capita CO stocks		None[c]	
Water Quality			
Feel coliform count			1,375
Lack of access to safe water			465
Lack of access to sanitation			903
Dissolved oxygen concentration			None[c]
Other			
Per capita municipal waste			None[c]

Sources: G.M. Grossman and A.B. Krueger, "Environmental Impacts of a North American Free Trade Agreement," Working Paper No. 3914 (National Bureau of Economic Research, Cambridge, Mass., 1991); T.M. Selden and Daqing Song, "Environmental Quality and Development: Is There A Kuznets Curve for Air Pollution?" (Department of Economics, Syracuse University, New York, 1993); and N. Shafik and S. Bandyopadhyay, "Economic Growth and Environmental Quality: Time-series and Cross-country Evidence," World Development Report Working Paper WPS 904 (World Bank, Washington, D.C., 1992).

a. Pakistan's per capita GDP in purchasing power terms (1985 price levels) was US$1,567.

b. TSP level declines continuously with income.

c. Environmental indicator worsens continuously with income.

Environmental impacts are indicated by equations that project urban population, access to safe water for the entire population, access to adequate sanitation for the urban population, generation of municipal wastes, and emissions of three air pollutants: particulates, sulfur dioxide, and nitrogen oxides. The equation for urban population was econometrically estimated, and all the others were drawn from the studies discussed above. The projections are for the 50 years FY 89-FY 2038; FY 89 was the first year of the SAP.

Scenario Results

Table 10.3 compares the results of the three scenarios for key variables. Economic reform, both alone and with population stabilization, has a great impact on per capita GNP. In the "without" scenario, per capita GNP rises at an average annual rate of only 1.0 percent. In the "with" scenario, the rate of increase is 2.8 percentage points higher, at 3.8 percent; consequently, per capita GNP is four times higher in FY 2038. Stabilizing the population causes the average annual rate of increase to rise another 1.3 percentage points, to 5.1 percent. The positive impact of population stabilization reflects the fact that the population variable in the GDP equation shows diminishing returns. Capital must accumulate at a rapid rate to offset these diminishing returns and enable GDP to rise in per capita terms. The savings rate in the "without" scenario is barely high enough for this situation to occur.

In both the "without" and "with" scenarios, the country's population balloons to about four times its FY 89 level by FY 2038. The similarity of the trajectories indicates that on its own, a rising per capita GNP does not reduce population growth rapidly. The population growth rate in the "with" scenario is still high in FY 2038, at 2.1 percent per year. Even under the population stabilization scenario, the population in FY 2038 is still two and one-half times larger than the population in FY 89.

Economic reform increases the urban population, even when it is accompanied by population stabilization measures. The urbanization equation predicts that higher per capita GNP is always associated with a higher proportion of the population living in urban areas. This effect more than offsets the dampening effect of lower overall population growth in both the "with" and population stabilization scenarios.

Like the urbanization equation, the equations for water, sanitation, and waste are simple power functions of per capita GNP: there are no turning points. The first two are decreasing functions, and the third is an increasing function. Because per capita GNP rises in all scenarios, the percentage of the population without access to safe water and the percentage of the urban population without access to adequate sanitation fall in all scenarios, and per capita generation of municipal wastes rises. The results are more complicated when expressed in numbers of people. The number

**Table 10.3 Projections of Economic and Environmental Indicators
in 2038 under Alternative Scenarios**

	1989	2038 Scenarios		
		Without Reforms	With Reforms	With Reforms and Population Stabilization
Per capita GNP (1985 rupees)	5,590	9,285	36,506	68,319
Population (millions)	109	475	430	275
Population growth rate (%/yr)	3.1	3.0	2.1	0.0
Urban proportion (%)	34	41	68	85
Urban population (millions)	37	195	291	233
Safe water				
% without	45	32	14	10
No. without (millions)	49	154	61	26
Sanitation[a]				
% without	48	37	19	14
No. without (millions)	18	72	56	33
Municipal Waste				
Kg per capita	210	258	436	554
Billion kg	23	123	187	152
Particulates[b]				
Kg per capita		12	49	-22
Million kg		5,902	20,974	-6,143
Sulful Dioxide[b]				
Kg per capita		18	78	0
Million kg		8,521	33,547	-83
Nitrogen Oxides[b]				
Kg per capita		7	33	15
Million kg		3,216	14,118	4,203

a. Pertains to urban population only.
b. Impacts are relative to 1988 values.

of people without access to safe water and adequate sanitation is lowest in
the population stabilization scenario and highest in the "without" scenario
in all years. Hence reforms and population stabilization improve conditions,
according to these indicators. But the number of people without access to
safe water in FY 2038 is lower than in FY 89 only in the population
stabilization scenario (although a turning point is passed in FY 2021 in
the "with" scenario), and in no scenario do fewer people lack access to
adequate sanitation in FY 2038 than in FY 89 (although a turning point is
passed in FY 2030 in the population stabilization scenario). Large problems
remain. The aggregate volume of municipal waste is higher in all scenarios

in FY 2038, and no turning points are passed by that year. Moreover, the volumes are higher in the "with" and population stabilization scenarios than in the "without" scenario; reforms do not improve conditions, according to this indicator.

Per capita emissions of the three air pollutants rise over time in the "without" scenario as income rises but does not pass the turning points. They are even higher in the "with" scenario (although a turning point is passed in FY 2037 for particulates). In per capita terms, then, reforms alone increase emissions of air pollutants. The situation improves when population stabilization is added, but not until the end of the period; turning points are passed in FY 2032 for particulates, FY 2033 for sulfur dioxide, and FY 2034 for nitrogen oxides. Before these dates, per capita emissions are even higher than in the "with" scenario. The patterns for aggregate emissions loads are similar: economic reform alone increases aggregate emissions, and adding population stabilization reduces emissions below the "with" scenario levels, but not until nearly 50 years have passed.

Taken together, these findings point toward the following summary conclusions:

- Economic reforms that cause even small increases in the national savings rate are a powerful stimulus for economic growth.
- Population stabilization strengthens this growth stimulus.
- Economic reform reduces the number of people exposed to environmental risks associated with unsafe drinking water and inadequate sanitation, but it increases the urban population and the generation of municipal waste. The latter is true even when reforms are combined with population stabilization because the income effect dominates the effect of slower population growth.
- Economic reform increases aggregate emissions of air pollutants despite the existence of turning points for per capita emissions of air pollutants. The reason is that Pakistan's income level is far below the turning points. By accelerating income growth, population stabilization causes aggregate emissions to rise even more rapidly, at least for several decades.

Thus, unless corrective measures are taken, the income, water, and sanitation benefits of economic reforms will be offset by environmental degradation related to congestion, solid waste, and air pollution. Whether the environmental damage offsets the other benefits entirely or only partially cannot be determined by the analysis. Stabilizing the population helps the environment in some cases but not all, and in any event, it is not a sufficient policy response.

As with any modeling exercise, the final comment must be a reminder of the limitations of the analysis. The long-run growth model is obviously a highly simplified abstraction of the actual economy of Pakistan, not to mention actual relationships among economic development, population growth, and environmental quality. The individual equations make sense on the basis of theoretical principles, and their parameters are empirically derived, but obviously none offers anything near a complete representation of the economic behavior or economy-environment relationship it attempts to represent.

Equilibrium Analysis

The growth model treats the economic reform process simply as an increase in the national savings rate. Actual reforms associated with Pakistan's SAPs are much more diverse, ranging from price liberalization in particular sectors to tax, tariff, exchange rate, and other macroeconomic policies. The growth model provides a sketch of long-run possibilities, but it omits details relevant to economic policy decisions.

The CGE model was developed in response to these shortcomings of the growth model. The model is based on the 1984-85 social accounting matrix (SAM), which is the most recent one available. This fiscal year is a good one for these purposes because it is just a few years before the SAP began. Unlike the growth model, the CGE model does not project economic and environmental variables over time. In fact, it excludes entirely the two dynamic processes that are central to the growth model, capital accumulation and population growth. It takes the total stocks of capital and labor that existed in 1984-85 as fixed. It then predicts how these factors are allocated among competing sectors in response to policy shocks. It is designed to allocate the factors to achieve a competitive equilibrium in which the marginal return to each factor is equalized across competing sectors and aggregate output is maximized. It simultaneously predicts decisions by consumers regarding the allocation of income among purchases of different goods and services.

The CGE model sacrifices the dynamic features of the growth model in return for rich detail on policy instruments and the allocative decisions they affect. In one sense, it is a long-run model in that factors can move freely and completely among sectors, but it does not model the dynamic processes that, in reality, determine these movements and cause total factor stocks to change over time. It is best viewed as a framework for performing comparative statics experiments aimed at clarifying the equilibrium impacts of reforms implemented singly or jointly. As detailed as it is, it does not address all the important economic policy issues associated with economic reforms. For example, it is silent on issues of monetary policy because it is a model purely of the real economy.

Structure of the Computable General Equilibrium Model

The SAM includes 27 sectors divided between a current account (17 sectors) and a capital account (10 sectors). Because the intent was to build a CGE model of the real economy, much of the capital account is omitted. The revised SAM that was used as the basis for the CGE model includes 18 sectors.

Three principal limitations of the SAM that affect the CGE model must be noted. First, the SAM includes agriculture as a single highly aggregated sector. This feature severely limits the usefulness of the CGE model for analyzing reforms in the agricultural sector because the impacts of reforms are unlikely to be the same across major crops. Second, the SAM excludes the black economy (i.e., illegal activities) altogether and at best captures only part of the economic activity associated with the informal economy (i.e., legal but unrecorded and untaxed activities). Third, the SAM describes distributional aspects of the economy in an extremely limited way. It gives the allocation of factor payments between labor (i.e., wages, including salaries) and capital (i.e., gross profits, including land rents), but not by income class or rural and urban areas.

The revised SAM was converted to a CGE model using equations that predict the patterns of receipts and expenditures in the rows and columns of the SAM. The values of most parameters in these equations were determined through calibration of the equations to the values in the SAM. For example, it was assumed that production and utility functions had a Cobb-Douglas functional form, and the exponents in these functions (and in demand equations derived from them) were set equal to expenditure shares in the SAM. One would have more confidence in model results if functional forms and parameters were determined by econometric analysis, but doing so was not possible within the short time frame of the study. As in the case of the growth model, one should pay more attention to broad conclusions emerging from the analysis than to specific numerical results.

Definition of the Scenarios

The scenarios were run by: (1) solving the model at 1984-85 values of the parameters and exogenous variables to generate baseline (without reform) values of the endogenous variables; (2) changing the values of one or more policy parameters; (3) solving the model for the new equilibrium; and (4) comparing the new results to the baseline results. The policy changes investigated in the experiments do not duplicate the magnitude of actual reforms. They do, however, maintain the spirit and direction of actual reforms. Most parameters were altered by 1 percent (in relative, not absolute terms).

Because fiscal reform forms the core of SAPs in Pakistan, most of the experiments concern taxes and tariffs. The environmental implications of these reforms were investigated as follows. First, the environmental engineers associated with the study ranked the pollution impacts of 61 industrial subsectors on a scale from 1 (severe impact) to 5 (negligible impact). Four types of pollution were considered: air, water, biodegradable waste, and hazardous waste. Second, values for the major subsectors were averaged to derive aggregate values for the broader sectors included in the CGE model. To be consistent with an assumption that, *ceteris paribus*, more output means more pollution, the ranking system was reversed (i.e., a value of 1 was changed to 5, and 5 to 1). Further, the sectoral values for a given type of pollution were multiplied by corresponding percentage changes in sectoral output and then added across sectors to develop a bottom-line estimate of the economy-wide environmental impact for that pollutant.

Macroeconomic Performance of the Scenarios

Macroeconomic results of the scenarios are best understood comparing them one variable at a time. Given the highly detailed nature of model output and the study's concern with environmental implications, macroeconomic results are summarized verbally rather than numerically.

- GDP. As one would expect, reforms generally had a positive impact on GDP. The impact was less than proportionate for individual reforms except the 1 percent devaluation scenario. This result is not surprising because the exchange rate is an economy-wide policy variable.
- Industrial structure. In almost all cases, manufacturing GDP declined and agriculture and construction tended to benefit. Of the manufacturing sectors, only small-scale manufacturing tended to benefit, and then by smaller amounts than agriculture and construction.

- Resource allocation. Sectoral changes in labor and capital inputs mirrored changes in sectoral output. Two distributional impacts can be noted. First, because reforms tended to increase output in agriculture, they also tended to increase employment and investment in this sector. Second, reforms tended to raise the returns to labor relative to capital (although the change was small). Relatively more of the returns to the economic expansion were captured by labor.

- Government revenue. Revenue decreased by small amounts in two of the individual reform experiments and did not change in a third (i.e., a decrease in the deficit financing rate). These impacts are not surprising because the reforms involve either offsetting changes in fiscal instruments or offsetting changes in supply and demand for revenue. Government revenue increased in all other experiments, including all those with combined reforms. The biggest increase was seen when all reforms were enacted jointly.

- External sector. The net external impact of the reforms is given by the change in the balance of payments. With the exception of two experiments in which direct taxes and the deficit financing rate were changed, all reforms increased the balance of payments deficit, owing to an increase in imports. The implication is that the predicted increase in GDP depends on increased inflows of foreign capital. But this point reflects the structure of the model. Domestic savings by enterprises, government, and households are given by fixed proportions of income or revenue, depending on the case. An increase in income does not raise the savings rate as it does in the long-run growth model. The model also excludes some of the mechanisms (e.g., higher real interest rates) through which reforms would be expected to call forth higher levels of savings. The increased balance of payments deficits in the scenarios are therefore likely to be exaggerated. Nonetheless, they indicate that reforms that are not accompanied by fiscal restraint and measures to raise domestic savings rates will increase dependence on foreign capital instead of decreasing it.

- Savings. Total institutional savings (i.e., the sum of savings by enterprises, the government, households, and foreigners) rose in all experiments. The implication is that GDP would actually increase much more in the long run than the model indicates because the additional savings make increased investment possible.

Environmental Implications of the Scenarios

Although some of the most obvious polluters are large-scale manufacturers, by no means can the shift toward agriculture, construction, and small-scale manufacturing in most scenarios be assumed to be environmentally beneficial. Increased agricultural output could bring more waterlogging and salinization, as discussed below. Increased construction could bring more pollution of various types. The increase in small-scale manufacturing activity could be particularly damaging. First, with an increase in the number of manufacturing units, monitoring and enforcement of environmental regulations, already a problem in Pakistan, would be more difficult. Small-scale industries typically adhere less strictly to location and zoning laws. And because much of the informal economy consists of small-scale producers, reforms could boost activity in the segment of the economy that by definition is beyond regulation. Further, many small-scale producers lack access to technical know-how and capital for pollution abatement investments.

Table 10.4 shows the economy-wide estimates of environmental impacts for individual reforms and reform packages. Positive values indicate increases in pollution; negative values indicate decreases. The larger the value, the larger the impact. Results may be summarized as follows:

- Qualitatively, the patterns of impacts (whether the signs are negative or positive) are virtually identical regardless of the type of pollutant. A given reform or reform package either increases or decreases all types of pollution.
- Individually, three of the economy-wide reforms, changes in the structure of direct taxes, reduction in the deficit financing rate, and devaluation, increase pollution, as does the reduction in import tariffs on other large-scale manufacturing (except for hazardous waste). The results for the macroeconomic reforms are negative because these reforms lead to increased output without correcting distortions at the sector level.
- The remaining individual reforms, notably the removal of subsidies favoring textiles and energy and the increase in energy prices, and all four reform packages decrease pollution. The result for the reform packages is driven by the tariff and subsidy changes in one scenario that boosts agriculture, construction, and small-scale manufacturing relative to the more heavily polluting textile and leather sectors.

In contrast to the long-run growth model, the predicted impacts of economic reforms upon the environment are generally positive. This contradiction is more apparent than real. Results of the CGE model are static and reflect only the impacts of economic restructuring for 1984-85 stocks of labor and capital. The results suggest that improvements in economic efficiency stimulated by reform packages also lead to less pollution. The CGE model does not indicate the pollution impacts of increased levels of aggregate economic output brought about by capital accumulation and population growth. The dynamic relationship between

Table 10.4 Impacts of Economic Reforms on Pollution: CGE

Scenario	Air Pollution[a]	Water Pollution[a]	Biodegradable Waste[a]	Hazardous Waste[a]
S1[b]	+0.916	+0.728	+0.417	-0.139
S2[b]	-2.417	-2.205	-1.672	-2.343
S3[c]	+0.006	+0.005	+0.003	+0.004
S4[d]	-0.137	-0.242	-0.239	0.540
S5[e]	-0.165	-0.116	-0.104	-0.223
S6[f]	+0.004	+0.002	+0.001	+0.001
S7[g]	+0.257	+0.095	+0.043	+0.050
PPI[h]	-4.148	-4.135	-3.350	-5.527
PPII[h]	-2.014	-2.018	-1.634	-2.719
PPIII[h]	-2.014	-2.008	-1.634	-2.719
PPIV[h]	-2.683	-2.796	-2.294	-3.827

a. Positive values indicate increases in pollution; negative values indicate decreases.

b. Tariffs (S1 and S2): In S1, tariffs on imports that compete with products of the other large-scale manufacturing and mining sector were lowered 1 percent. In S2, tariffs on noncompetitive imports used as inputs by the other large-scale manufacturing and mining and the agriculture sectors were lowered 1 percent and subsidies (export rebates) in the large-scale textiles and large-scale leather sectors were eliminated.

c. Direct taxes (S3): The household income tax rate was raised 1 percent and the corporate tax rate lowered 1 percent.

d. Excise duties and sales taxes (S4): Excise duties and sales taxes were raised 1 percent in all sectors to which they applied in 1984-85 (i.e., all except agriculture and energy).

e. Energy pricing (S5): Excise duties and sales taxes in the energy sector were raised 1 percent.

f. Budget deficit (S6): The deficit financing rate (the percentage difference between revenues and expenditures) was reduced 1 percent.

g. Exchange rate (S7): The exchange rate was increased 1 percent to simulate devaluation.

h. Policy packages: The preceding individual policy shocks were also combined to study their joint effects. A tariff and domestic taxes package (PPI) combined S1 through S4. A second package added S5 (PPII), a third added S6 (PPIII), and a fourth added S7 (PPIV).

economic growth and pollution is what the results of the growth model indicate.

Social Implications of the Experiments

The CGE model suffers obvious limitations as a tool for exploring social impacts. The results do indicate, however, that reforms can be expected to raise wages both absolutely and relative to the return on capital. These effects are likely to be even stronger in reality: with capital accumulation (ignored by the model), the relative price of capital would fall even more and the marginal returns to labor inputs would rise (more capital per worker, hence higher productivity). Whether workers in Pakistan would actually reap the benefits of the increased value of their labor depends essentially on institutional factors. Consider the case of agriculture. The experiments indicate that reforms generally raised not only total payments to labor but also total payments to capital. In the model, payments to labor are based on labor's marginal product. In practice, the return to labor is part of the net surplus (revenue minus input costs) generated by farming. The allocation of this surplus between labor and agricultural capital, which is dominated by land, is easy to model but difficult to determine in the real world. Households that own the land they farm or that rent land in a competitive rental market are more likely to receive full compensation for their labor than those that rent land where there is a relatively small number of landowners. Unfortunately for tenant farmers, the latter describes the situation in much of Pakistan. There is therefore a real risk that the agricultural benefits of economic reforms could be captured disproportionately and inequitably by monopolistic landowners.

The scenarios generally predicted that reforms would lead to a reallocation of labor from manufacturing to agriculture. Superficially, this change suggests deurbanization and fewer problems related to congestion and strained municipal services. How can this implication be reconciled with the prediction of rising urban populations in all three scenarios of the long-run growth model? The apparent discrepancy reflects the fact that the CGE model is static. Even if rural-urban migration stopped, urban populations would continue to increase owing to population growth, which is excluded from the CGE model. Moreover, given the country's limited supply of arable land—which the model ignores—new investment opportunities are overwhelmingly in nonagricultural sectors. These sectors tend to be based in, or at least near, cities and towns. Investment in them will continue to draw migrants to urban areas.

Analysis of the Distributional Impacts

A major objective of fiscal reforms is to lower the budget deficit through enhanced resource mobilization. In the short run, however, these measures can put undue pressure on prices and adversely affect the real incomes of poor households. This situation can lead to social unrest and can undermine the sustainability of the reform process. The long-run growth model and the CGE model do not assess these distributional issues. The AERC tax policy simulation model (TPSM) was used to study the incidence of selected tax and tariff changes on various income brackets and price levels in the economy.

Structure of the Tax Policy Simulation Model

In June 1992, an AERC study was funded by the Central Board of Revenue to estimate the impacts of changes in tariffs and indirect domestic taxes upon nominal and effective tax revenues. For this purpose, the AERC surveyed 600 manufacturing units and 200 service units. It used information from the survey to construct a 77 x 77 industry-by-industry absorption matrix, which was then converted into an input-output table. The input-output table contains 11 agricultural sectors, including 7 crop sectors; 50 industrial sectors, including not just manufacturing but also mining and quarrying; and 16 service-related sectors. The AERC developed a similar matrix of input-demand coefficients for imported inputs.

Although it is primarily intended to simulate indirect tax regimes, the TPSM is fairly versatile in quantifying the first-round impacts of changes in various types and rates of taxes. Assuming that any change in taxes is shifted fully forward into prices, the increase in prices affects consumption levels through price elasticities. Because the model ensures that production always equals consumption, price and consumption changes can be translated into changes in nominal and effective revenues.

The TPSM contains income and expenditure profiles for representative households in different income classes. This information enables it to calculate tax burden as a percentage of either household income or household expenditure.

Simulation Results

Policy changes recommended by SAPs were simulated in the TPSM at their actual values, not by 1 percent, as in the CGE model. Broad findings include:

- Changes in customs policies and sales taxes generally have a greater impact on nominal and effective revenues than changes in excise duties. They also tend to have a bigger impact on food prices.
- Largely because of their impacts on food prices, changes in customs policies and sales taxes tend to be either regressive or initially regressive and then progressive (i.e., middle-income households benefit the most).
- Changes in excise duties tend to be progressive.

To the extent that the effects of changes in customs policies and sales taxes dominate those of changes in excise duties, the poor will be relatively worse off unless the additional revenue finances programs that benefit them or the reduction in fiscal imbalances stimulates economic growth that provides them with better employment opportunities.

The results of both the TPSM and the CGE model indicate that, in theory, anyway, fiscal reforms can loosen current fiscal constraints on public investment in social and environmental programs that improve the quality of life of the poor. The government's ability to match foreign funds with rupee resources is in fact essential for the smooth implementation of the 3-year social action program sponsored by the World Bank.

Given the country's three-tier system of government (i.e., federal, provincial, and local), however, increased revenues cannot be easily translated into investments in such programs. Constitutionally, local governments and civic bodies cannot claim any share of enlarged federal revenue receipts. On the other hand, they are solely responsible for managing municipal waste and sanitation. Proposed fiscal reforms mainly address the restructuring and broadening of federal taxes; they do not vigorously push local governments to reform the local tax system. Reforms at this level are sorely needed. For example, Karachi's property tax is still based on a comprehensive property value assessment survey taken in 1968-69. The coincidence of political power and economic power (usually based on property ownership) in Pakistan creates pressure on local governments and civic bodies to postpone updating property tax assessments.

Waterlogging and Salinization in Irrigated Agriculture

The CGE analysis generally indicates that economic reforms would benefit the agricultural sector. This sector is diverse, however, and one would expect that some crops and some farmers would benefit more than others. The CGE model does not include equations linking environmental impacts to the predicted changes in output levels and input purchases. Using a linear programing model of irrigated agriculture in the Indus Basin, the Indus Basin model (revised), the study team investigated the ways in which economic reforms, acting through input and output prices, affect cropping patterns, fertilizer use, groundwater levels, and salt balances.[18]

A Profile of the Agricultural Sector[19]

Despite its declining share in the economy over time, agriculture is still the single largest sector in the economy. Economic management of the sector has focused almost exclusively on short-run output levels, with little attention paid to the sustainability, stability, and equitability of the production systems employed. Pricing policies have imposed disguised taxes on the sector, thereby restricting the growth of investment funds at its disposal and undermining prospects for the introduction of more appropriate technologies. Policies have failed to provide incentives to improve the efficiency of use of inputs, particularly land and water.

Water is the most important agricultural input in Pakistan because most of the country is too dry to support rainfed agriculture. About 77 percent of the total cultivated area, 16.1 million hectares, is irrigated. Nearly all irrigated land is in the Indus Basin irrigation system, which is one of the oldest and largest contiguous gravity-flow irrigation systems in the world. Surface supplies of irrigation water are supplemented by groundwater, which is extracted by public and private tubewells. Tubewells not only enhance the supply of irrigation water but they also lower the water table and help prevent waterlogging and salinization.

In addition to cotton and rice, major crops include wheat and sugar cane. Nearly 90 percent of the area in these crops is in Punjab and Sindh, which form the major part of the Indus Basin. Cotton and rice are grown in *kharif* (summer: March-April to October-November), whereas wheat is grown in *rabi* (winter: November-December to February-March). Sugar cane is sown in September as well as in February. Cotton and wheat are usually grown in rotation, and rice is grown with or without wheat in *rabi*. Sugar cane is now a major substitute for the cotton-wheat combination, thanks to favorable pricing policies.

Economic Reforms in the Agricultural Sector

SAP objectives in the agricultural sector, as listed in World Bank documents, include improving the formulation of support prices, eliminating subsidies on fertilizers, providing incentives to farmers to improve the efficiency of resource utilization, and improving the efficiency of irrigation and drainage systems. Considerable progress was made toward achieving several of these objectives under the SAP. Domestic prices of cotton, rice, and in particular, wheat have risen. At present, they are near international levels. Subsidies on nitrogenous fertilizers have been eliminated, but subsidies for the purchase of phosphatic fertilizer are still in place. Subsidies on pesticides and seeds have been virtually eliminated, and subsidies on credit, tractors, and tubewells have been reduced significantly. On the other hand, irrigation water rates remain low, and they are based on irrigated area rather than on the volume of water used. Farmers still receive high subsidies for electricity.

The Indus Basin Model (Revised)

The recommended output and input price changes of the SAP can be expected to change crop areas, depending on how the reforms shift the relative profitability of different crops. With changes in the cropping pattern, aggregate input use will also change. These various changes have environmental implications related to fertilizer and pesticide runoff and the volume of water used, which affects the water table and thus waterlogging and salinity.

The Indus Basin model (revised) (IBMR) permits examination of these issues. It is a large-scale linear programing model of irrigated agriculture in the basin.[20] For given values of input prices and other parameters, it predicts the cropping patterns during *rabi* and *kharif* that maximize net social surplus (i.e., farm profits plus consumer surplus). It includes 18 crops and divides the basin into nine agroclimatic zones. The agroclimatic zones can be divided into fresh and saline areas. The proportion of land in each category is input provided to the model; that is, the model does not determine the saline area endogenously. It does, however, predict changes in groundwater balances and salt additions to groundwater, and this information can be used to infer impacts related to waterlogging and salinization.

Farm characteristics in each zone are based on the characteristics of the average farm in that zone in base year FY 88. The IBMR does not contain farms of varying sizes or with varying tenurial arrangements. Hence it cannot be used to assess the differential impacts of policy changes across categories of farmers. It also does not predict changes in input intensity resulting from changes in input prices because input demand is linked to cropped area by crop-specific input-demand coefficients. Hence it understates the response to changes in input prices.

The focus here was on two agroclimatic zones, PCW (Punjab cotton-wheat) and SRWN (Sindh rice-wheat North). Both are large agriculturally important zones. PCW covers 54 percent of the canal command area in Punjab. Cotton-wheat is the dominant crop rotation. SRWN covers 32 percent of the canal command area in Sindh. Rice-wheat is the dominant crop rotation. Both zones include significant areas classified as fresh (i.e., not saline) and saline. The water table tends to be lower in PCW, and therefore more of the PCW canal command area is fresh.

Definition of Simulations

Running simulations of the IBMR was analogous to running simulations of the CGE model. The model was solved at base-year values of exogenous variables and parameters, including policy parameters. The base year was FY 88, as noted above. Then one or more policy parameters were changed, and the model was solved again. These results were compared to the base-year results in terms of such aspects as cropping patterns, fertilizer use, groundwater balance, and salt additions. As in the CGE model, the simulations are static. The implicit assumption is that cropping patterns and input utilization can adjust immediately to the values that maximize farm profits. Simulations were run with both arbitrary changes of policy parameters (10 percent increases) and changes consistent with complete liberalization of the agricultural economy.

Results

As in the case of the CGE analysis, results of IBMR simulations are extremely detailed. Key findings can be summarized as follows:

- Significant changes occur only when prices were increased to market levels for all 18 agricultural commodities, water, and fertilizer. Agricultural variables are relatively insensitive to changes in individual policies. Comments below refer only to this scenario.
- Economic reforms tend to increase cropped area in fresh areas. Developed irrigated areas are used more completely, and farmers reap economic benefits.
- Economic reforms have little or no impact on cropped area in saline areas because existing land degradation (i.e., salinity) makes expansion

of cropped area unprofitable. This point suggests that land reclamation is economically more justified in the presence of reforms than in their absence because the opportunity cost is higher in the former case.

- If crop prices are brought up to world levels, water rates can be raised to levels that cover at least the operating and maintenance costs of the water system (i.e., tripled) without reducing cropped areas and agricultural output.
- Reforms tend to increase the aggregate application of fertilizer because increased cropped area outweighs the shift toward crops that require less fertilizer.
- Reforms tend to reduce the net groundwater balance, thereby slowing or even reversing the waterlogging process.
- Reforms tend to reduce salt additions to groundwater in fresh areas and drained saline areas, at least in the short run, but to increase additions in undrained saline areas. This finding suggests that investments in drainage should accompany economic reforms to reduce the risk that reforms will worsen salinity problems in saline areas and cause intrusion of saline water into fresh areas.

The likely impact of price-related economic reforms upon the agricultural sector seems positive in the short run. Higher output prices for agricultural commodities, particularly exportable ones, lead to higher production levels. This finding is consistent with simulation results from the CGE model. The increase in output occurs primarily through extensification of land use, although some changes in the crop mix occur. The increase in cultivated area implies increased employment in the agricultural sector and thus less rural-urban migration. This point too is consistent with the CGE results.

The impact of reforms is greater in fresh areas, where additional fresh groundwater resources can be tapped by private tubewells. Output increases are most likely to be sustained in areas with high water tables, where the additional water removals reduce the risk of waterlogging. Where water tables are lower, output increases could be undermined by increased intrusion of saline water. The improvement of drainage in saline areas is therefore critical to sustaining the benefits of economic reforms. Offering farmers higher prices for agricultural commodities without linking price liberalization to improvements in agricultural infrastructure could worsen the long-run degradation of agricultural land and groundwater resources.

Higher water rates would raise the revenue necessary for financing these improvements. Higher rates would also create an incentive for farmers to use water more efficiently, an improvement that would reduce waterlogging in the first place. Although the results for one scenario suggest that farmers would not respond to this incentive, the rate increase in this simulation was only 10 percent, and farmers' response in the model is limited to changing the cropping pattern. As an alternative to the government's setting water rates, it could promote the development of water markets by selling or granting water rights to farmers. Water prices would then be determined by the market, and the option to sell water would create a conservation incentive: the less water a farmer used, the more he could sell and profit from. Any effort to establish water rights would need to consider distributional impacts carefully. If water rights were linked to land ownership, the provision of water rights would accentuate the discrepancy in wealth between landowners and tenant farmers.

Summary and Conclusions

The four analyses reported in the preceding sections indicate that the environmental and social impacts of SAPs in Pakistan are complex and not unidirectional. Nevertheless, a reasonably coherent picture of these impacts emerges. The CGE analysis predicts that improvements in economic efficiency resulting from recommended adjustment programs provide net environmental benefits. They do so because the programs shift economic activity away from heavily protected and heavily polluting industries like textiles and leather and stimulate more efficient use of energy and other polluting inputs. However, individual reforms that do not address sectoral distortions, in particular some of the macroeconomic ones (e.g., devaluation, reduced deficit financing) can worsen environmental degradation. The overall structure of adjustment programs and the degree to which all the recommended reforms are indeed implemented are therefore of paramount importance.

The other three analyses help address three shortcomings of the CGE analysis: dynamics, distribution, and environmental feedbacks. The CGE analysis ignores the dynamic effects of adjustment programs. It considers only static efficiency, that is, the effects of economic reforms in an economy with labor and capital fixed at 1984-85 levels. The higher levels of investment predicted by the CGE model for reform scenarios suggest that reforms will indeed accelerate economic growth through higher levels of capital accumulation. The long-run growth model was used to investigate the environmental implications of this dynamic effect. The analysis predicts that reforms enable the country to attain more quickly a state of sustained improvements in many environmental indicators, but this state is several decades away. Outgrowing its environmental problems would take Pakistan a long time. In the absence of effective policy interventions, the more rapid economic growth triggered by reforms will intensify most forms of environmental degradation in the country in the short and medium terms.

The CGE analysis predicts that reforms can mobilize additional budgetary resources, which in principle could be used to support public sector environmental and social programs. This finding is confirmed by the TPSM. But the TPSM also reveals that these additional financial resources come at a social cost: many recommended fiscal reforms are regressive in that they impose a relatively heavier tax burden on low-income households. The CGE and growth models suggest that such households might be more than compensated in the long run by the additional employment and higher income generated by reforms. But in the short run, many of the recommended fiscal reforms cause the poor to lose out, at least in relative terms, and this fact could undermine public support for them.

Indeed, a feeling that the burden of reforms implemented to date is not being borne equitably is contributing to social and political tensions in Pakistan. Many of the rural and urban poor perceive that they are being forced to accept higher prices and a higher tax burden without a clear return or any form of compensation. They perceive that wealthier classes are succeeding in blocking reforms that might erode their own economic power. For example, fiscal reforms recommended by the World Bank and the IMF have generally steered clear of income collected by property owners, in particular those in the agricultural sector. This situation is considered by many observers as the price the international agencies are willing to pay to politically and economically dominant landowners for accepting remaining elements of reform packages. Even when potentially more progressive fiscal reforms manage to be introduced, as in the case of a recent tax on agricultural wealth, the actual impacts on wealthier classes tend to be nullified by pervasive and generous exemptions. A neutering of well-intended policies has long plagued economic reform efforts in Pakistan.

The CGE model, and for that matter, the growth model too, omit environmental feedbacks. Like social inequities, these threaten to undermine reform efforts by creating a drag on economic growth. The IBMR offers indirect information on some feedbacks in the agricultural sector as well as rich detail on the impacts of reforms in this important sector. It predicts that reforms will reduce waterlogging and salt additions to groundwater in freshwater areas and saline areas with drainage. Production and income in such areas are therefore more likely to be sustainable with reforms than without. In saline areas without drainage, however, reforms have no impact on salinization. This finding illustrates the importance of institutional factors in determining the success of reforms, in this case, the presence or absence of drainage and the willingness of government, landowners, and farmers to invest in it where it is not present.

In sum, the analyses indicate that although adjustment programs are necessary for enhancing long-run human well-being in Pakistan, they are not sufficient. Two aspects of adjustment programs require greater attention. First, their impacts on environmental quality must be more carefully considered and addressed during program design. Documents on adjustment programs in Pakistan evince increasing awareness by the World Bank and the IMF of the magnitude of environmental degradation in the country. Yet there is no evidence that these agencies have thought about whether the programs themselves improve or worsen the situation. This study indicates that the programs do indeed have significant short- and long-run environmental impacts. In some cases, such as the removal of energy subsidies, particular reforms provide environmental as well as economic and fiscal benefits and strengthen the rationale for reforms included in the programs. In other cases, when there is no such win-win prospect, modifying the programs to mitigate the degradation that certain reforms could cause would reduce the bill the country must pay in the long run. The World Bank already forecasts the short- and medium-term macroeconomic impacts of adjustment programs. A parallel effort should be made to identify the environmental impacts. The analyses in this study demonstrate that techniques exist for doing so, at least crudely. The techniques could undoubtedly be improved if the Bank committed some of its considerable human and fiscal resources to them. Recent publications indicate that it has begun the effort.[21]

But predicting impacts is not enough. When negative impacts are identified, reform packages should include appropriate policies to address them. The eventual environmental improvements predicted by environmental Kuznets curve studies and the long-run growth model are not automatic byproducts of economic growth; they reflect as well policy changes to prevent further environmental degradation and remedy damage that has already occurred. Documents on adjustment programs in Pakistan have increasingly highlighted the need to address environmental degradation in the country. Either implicitly or explicitly, the documents typically call for government programs that are complementary but separate initiatives, with adjustment programs being limited to purely macroeconomic or sectoral economic reforms (although the leaked ESAF/ EFF paper conveys a more integrated approach). This approach effectively absolves adjustment programs of any responsibility for their environmental impacts. It is clearly inadequate when the environmental programs assumed to accompany adjustment programs are underfunded or even nonexistent and are implemented by politically weak agencies.

A better approach would be to incorporate policies to safeguard the environment directly into adjustment programs. Identifying what these policies should be requires sector-specific analysis that is beyond the scope of this study, but the main guiding principle is readily identifiable: economic actors, whether they are individuals, households, firms, or government agencies, should pay the full price for any goods they purchase, consume, or use. The full price should reflect not just ordinary costs of production but also depletion costs and environmental costs. The reduction of subsidies on fertilizer represents an important step toward full-cost pricing that has already been taken in Pakistan under adjustment programs. Other reforms, such as higher water rates in agriculture, have been proposed. But in addition to subsidy reductions, full-cost pricing requires the imposition of additional charges that reflect nonmarket costs. These charges include fees on pollution emissions or polluting inputs (the polluter pays principle) and user fees that reflect the depletion costs of timber and minerals. Such fees can potentially provide an important source of government revenue while providing financial incentives to reduce environmental degradation and encourage resource conservation in the first place. The National Conservation Strategy identified such charges as one source of financing for its recommended environmental investment program.

To help ensure that environmental policies and programs do lead to environmental improvements, adjustment programs should include funding for ongoing monitoring of environmental conditions. Pakistan has a well-developed system for collecting and disseminating economic statistics. This makes it possible to monitor compliance with conditionalities attached to adjustment programs and to gauge program success. No such system exists for environmental statistics, particularly ones related to air and water pollution. Without such an information system, it would be impossible to determine the effectiveness of environmental activities incorporated in adjustment programs.

Distributional impacts are the second aspect of adjustment programs requiring greater attention. The sources of internal strife within Pakistan are highlighted at the beginning of this study, and some of the ways in which concerns about distribution have affected recent reform efforts are discussed above. Any economic reform effort in Pakistan can be sustained only if the benefits are spread widely and if a broad cross-section of the population in different ethnic groups and different regions feels that he/ she has a stake in continued reforms. The three recommendations for environmental impacts apply to distributional impacts as well: distributional impacts must be analyzed during program formulation, means of compensating those who are hurt must be considered, and an ongoing system for monitoring distributional impacts should be implemented. These recommendations obviously do not address the underlying political factors that, as discussed above, obstruct progressive reforms. However, better information would assist socially oriented reformers in making a stronger case for a more equitable and ultimately more sustainable reform process.

Addressing environmental and distributional impacts requires not just full-cost pricing and other policies to encourage sustainable private behavior but also public sector investments in environmental and social programs. Although the CGE model and the TPSM indicate that adjustment programs can be expected to increase revenue generation, these increases can be sustained only if the national savings rate rises. It is not going to happen overnight. In the short run, the need to spend more on environmental and social programs therefore conflicts with the need to reduce the budget deficit. The only way out of this dilemma is to change the current pattern of government expenditures, but this is dominated by spending on the powerful (in all senses) military sector. World Bank documents related to the country's adjustment programs emphasize the need to reallocate government expenditures to budget categories providing greater development benefits. The slow progress toward doing so indicates that domestic political will, not the quality of economic recommendations or the intentions of donors, is critical to a successful adjustment program.

ENDNOTES

1. See World Bank, *World Development Report* (Washington, D.C.: World Bank, various years).
2. M. Khan, Comment on W.A. McCleary, "Pakistan: Structural Adjustment and Economic Growth," in *Restructuring Economies in Distress*, ed. V. Thomas, A. Chibber, M. Dailami, and J. de Melo (New York: Oxford University Press, 1991), prepared for the World Bank.
3. World Bank, "Pakistan: Growth Through Adjustment," Rep. No. 7118-PAK (Europe, Middle East and North Africa [EMENA] Regional Office, 1988), "Pakistan: Medium-term Economic Policy Adjustment," Rep. No. 7691-PAK (EMENA Regional Office, 1989), and "Pakistan Country Economic Memorandum FY93: Progress under the Adjustment Program," Rep. No. 11590-PAK (Country Department III, South Asia Region, 1993).
4. World Bank, "Pakistan Economic Memorandum," op. cit., p. 36.
5. A. Furtado and S. Tareq, "Pakistan Steps Up Macroeconomic Adjustment and Structural Reforms," *IMF Survey*, March 7, 1994.
6. Information in this section is extracted primarily from the comprehensive *National Conservation Strategy* (Pakistan Ministry of Housing and Works, Environment and Urban Affairs Division, and International Union for Conservation of Nature and Natural Resources [IUCN]), *The Pakistan National Conservation Strategy* (Pakistan: Government of Pakistan/ Journalists' Resource Centre for the Environment-IUCN, 1992); and World Bank, "Pakistan: Environmental Protection and Resource Conservation Project," Staff Appraisal Rep. No. 9946-PAK (Country Department III, South Asia Region, 1992). Additional references on the environment in Pakistan include K. Mumtaz and M. Abidi-Habib, *Pakistan's Environment: A Historical Perspective and Selected Bibliography and Annotations* (Karachi: Journalists' Resource Centre for the Environment-IUCN, 1992); and F.K. Kahn, *A Geography of Pakistan: Environment, People, and Economy* (Karachi: Oxford University Press, 1991).
7. Ibid.
8. *Pakistan National Conservation Strategy*, op. cit., p. 140.
9. World Bank 1988, 1989, and 1993, op. cit.
10. Enhanced Structural Adjustment Facility, Extended Fund Facility, "Policy Framework Paper," *Business Recorder* (Karachi), December 19, 1993.
11. World Bank, 1993, op. cit., p. ii.
12. Ibid., p. iv.
13. Ibid.
14. G.M. Grossman and A.B. Krueger, "Environmental Impacts of a North American Free Trade Agreement," Working Paper No. 3914 (National Bureau of Economic Research, Cambridge, Mass., 1991); N. Shafik and S. Bandyopadhyay, "Economic Growth and Environmental Quality: Time-series and Cross-country Evidence," World Development Report Working Paper WPS 904 (World Bank, Washington, D.C., 1992); and T.M. Selden and Daqing Song, "Environmental Quality and Development: Is There a Kuznets Curve for Air Pollution?" (Department of Economics, Syracuse University, New York, 1993).

15. S. Kuznets, "Economic Growth and Income Inequality," *American Economic Review* 45(1):1-28 (1955).
16. R. Summers and A. Heston, "The Penn World Table (Mark 5): An Expanded Set of International Comparisons, 1950-1988," *Quarterly Journal of Economics* 61(2):327-68 (1991).
17. Ibid.
18. World Bank, Environmental Operations and Strategy Division, "Guide to the Indus Basin Model Revised" (January 1990).
19. Information in this section is drawn from Government of Pakistan, *Report of the National Commission on Agriculture* (Islamabad, 1988); A. Mahmood and F. Walters, *Pakistan Agriculture: A Description of Pakistan's Agricultural Economy* (Islamabad: Ministry of Food and Agriculture, Economic Analysis Network, 1990); and standard statistical sources.
20. World Bank, 1990, op. cit; and M. Ahmad and G.P. Kutcher, "Irrigation Planning with Environmental Considerations: A Case Study of Pakistan's Indus Basin," World Bank Technical Paper No. 166 (Washington, D.C., 1992). The study team expresses its deep gratitute to Masood Ahmad of the World Bank, who generously provided computer files and documentation for the IBMR and offered advice during the study. Any incorrect statements about the model or errors in interpreting its results are entirely the team's responsibility.
21. See, for example, World Bank, *Economywide Policies and the Environment: Emerging Lessons from Experience* (Washington, D.C.: World Bank, 1994).

11

CASE STUDY FOR VIETNAM

This chapter is based on a study carried out by the Institute for Long-term and Regional Planning under the coordination of Nguyen Quang Thai, with contributions by Lea Anh Son, Nguyen Van Thanh, Nguyen The Hien, Le Thi Kim Dung, Dang Huu Dao, Nguyen Van Vy, and Tran Kim Dong. Theodore Panayotou of the Harvard Institute for International Development and Nadeem Naqvi from the University of Georgia provided support to the research team and wrote this chapter.

During the 1980s, while many nations in the developing world were embarking upon stabilization and structural adjustment programs (SAPs) either to escape economic decline and indebtedness or to accelerate growth, the Socialist Republic of Vietnam was witnessing two profound economic phenomena near its shores. Both were indicative of the impending need for, indeed the desirability of, macroeconomic reform in Vietnam. One was a pull toward market reform: the neighboring Asian Tigers, most notably Hong Kong, Taiwan, and Thailand, were registering extraordinary growth in GDP, increasing standards of living, and rapid economic development. Vietnam did not share in this regional boom, experiencing low growth, mounting deficits, and little diversification or progress in its predominantly poor and agrarian economy. The other phenomenon was a push away from its centrally planned Soviet-satellite status. Vietnam's major benefactor, the Union of Soviet Socialist Republics (USSR), was poised for economic collapse and eventual dissolution, and quite drastically, its historically deep well of economic assistance to the Vietnamese ran dry. Meanwhile, Vietnam was suffering from runaway inflation, large budget and trade deficits, and a declining ability to address continued high levels of poverty and natural resource degradation. Thus a combination of internal and external forces obliged the country to pursue a new development strategy to meet its growing needs.

Since its unification in 1975, the Vietnamese government has been challenged with healing the social, political, economic, and ecological wounds of a long and destructive war. The obstacles of civil strife, crippled industry and infrastructure, and widespread environmental damage have not been minor. The government's stated mission throughout the past two decades has had the recurring theme of sustainable human development (long before the phrase was coined). Under a centrally planned economy, efforts toward such development have been expensive and largely inefficient, although not without some success in areas such as primary education and health care provision. (Although Vietnam ranks 153rd among 173 countries in terms of GNP per capita, on the Human Development Index, it climbs up 38 rank points to the 115th position.[1]) However, pre-1986 macroeconomic policy did not provide the appropriate institutions, infrastructure, and investment capital upon which sustained

Figure 11.1 Vietnam

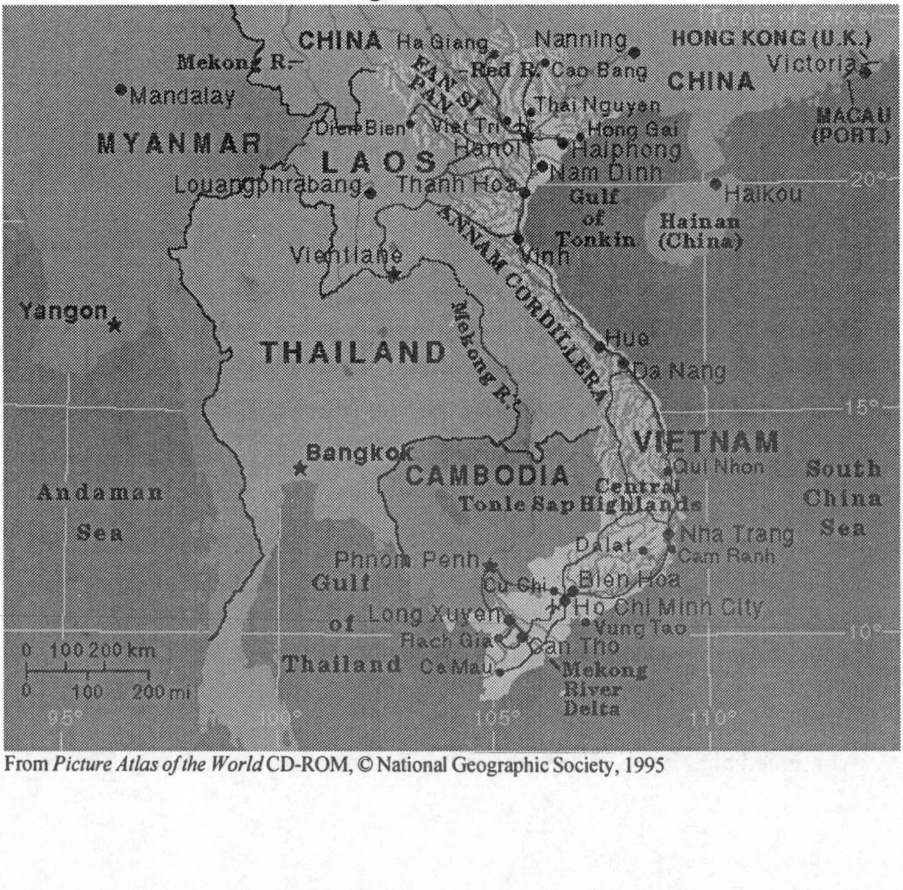

From *Picture Atlas of the World* CD-ROM, © National Geographic Society, 1995

growth in incomes, goods, and services depends. Neither did Vietnam's development prove *sustainable* in terms of alleviating widespread poverty and maintaining a healthy and productive natural capital base.

With the failures of past policy, the collapse of the former USSR (which provided not only the model but the major source of revenue for the government), and the enviable progress of neighboring countries' outward-looking development, the path to Vietnam's development goals seemed clear. Initially hesitant and gradual, Vietnam's macroeconomic adjustments have accelerated in recent years. The economy has stabilized notably from pre-1989 crisis conditions, and its structural adjustment efforts have been earnest, disciplined, and certainly painful in terms of its social goals.

What remains to be seen is whether Vietnam's macroeconomic policies will promote sustainable development, meeting the wants and needs of the present generation without compromising the ability of future generations to meet their own needs. Operationally, such development requires that the combined stock of natural, human, and man-made capital expand over time and is used with increasing efficiency to produce a growing national income and improve social welfare. Can Vietnam rely on macroeconomic reform to increase production, consumption, and social welfare drastically? Will the natural resource base sustain the unleashing of market forces, benefit from them, or suffer irreversible destruction for merely short-term economic gains?

To answer these questions, this study aims to (1) identify the major environmental issues facing the country, considering both resource supply and environmental quality, and examine the extent to which development policies have contributed to these issues; (2) explore the factors that affect the government's ability to integrate sustainable social and environmental policies into economic development strategies and the consequences on the country's well-being if sustainable development policies are not pursued in the future; (3) analyze the impacts of selected economic reforms on the country's natural resource base and environment and the effect of these impacts on the economy; and (4) recommend changes in the design and sequencing of reforms as well as parallel policies to promote integration of economic growth, poverty alleviation, and environmental sustainability. A comprehensive multisector computable general equilibrium (CGE) model of the Vietnamese economy was developed and used to test macroeconomic policy alternatives that may promote or impede sustainability.

A cursory and somewhat static examination of Vietnam's current development vector, observing only aggregate statistics, paints a bleak

picture in which drastic trade-offs among poverty alleviation, environmental integrity, and economic growth seem inevitable. Similarly, focusing
on natural resources alone might lead one to the conclusion that the country
is rapidly approaching environmental bankruptcy in many areas and that
rapid growth can only exacerbate the situation. However, after examining
economic realities and choices more dynamically, accounting for both
positive and negative externalities, and recognizing the vast potential for
institutional reform, particularly regarding property rights, this study finds
that sustainability, macroeconomic stability, and economic growth in
Vietnam can potentially be mutually reenforcing. Virtuous circles of
effective policy, reinvestment in human and natural capital, and rapid
growth are tenable and will require only moderate government intervention
in the market. Crucial to this effort are the promotion of environmentally
friendly, labor-intensive tourism and light industry sectors, secure property
rights, continued structural adjustment, and perhaps most important,
appropriate pricing policies to internalize both the positive and negative
externalities of production and consumption.

With a dynamic integration of economic, social, and environmental
goals and a strong commitment to reform, Vietnam and its external donors
can ensure not only an abatement of current economic and environmental
crises but a reversal.

The Economic Context of Reform

With the unification of Vietnam in 1975, the entire country came under
the control of a single socialist government, and the Vietnamese economy
was largely a command one. There did exist a household-level private
sector, but the bulk of the industrial economic activity (including
construction and energy) took place in state-owned and -operated
enterprises. From the time of unification up to 1989, Vietnam relied on
central planning, price setting by a government pricing board, collective
farming, and command and control measures to direct economic activity.
A large inefficient and expensive bureaucracy developed, and the state
dominated the formal labor market. Even in 1989, 70 percent of the
employed population over age 16 worked either in state-owned collectives
(55 percent) or directly for the state (15 percent).

When the US$1 billion in annual Soviet aid to Vietnam declined and
then abruptly ended in 1991 and the Council for Mutual Economic

Assistance (CMEA)-area trade collapsed, meeting the state-budget expenditure needs became a substantial financial burden for the Vietnamese government. This created the need both to develop a large tax base and to provide the opportunity for individuals to earn a livelihood on their own instead of looking to the state as the provider of all nonagricultural employment. In addition, fairly quick injection of foreign investment was needed because of the negligible private sector savings that resulted from the lack of incentives for accumulation by households. Indeed, as early as 1986, the Sixth Vietnam Communist Party Congress noted that domestic savings were meager and foreign assistance was inadequate for financing government expenditures; hence, the call for Doi Moi in 1986. Doi Moi— that is, the economic reform program—accelerated in 1989 primarily to meet the state payroll and to finance public expenditures either from mobilization of domestic savings or from the earnings of state enterprises.[2] Such a perspective is helpful in understanding the nature and magnitude of the government commitment to free-market reforms.[3] In the 3 years from 1991 to 1994, government revenue increased from 15 percent of GDP to almost 25 percent of a much larger GDP.[4] Thus on the one hand, Doi Moi has granted additional economic decisionmaking freedom in agriculture and in the household service sector but on the other hand has increased the government's role in the economy by appropriating a larger share of national income.

Major reforms in the 1986 Doi Moi include elimination of the cooperatives' monopoly on agriculture and forestry, introduction of short-term land use rights (up to 15 years for agriculture), currency devaluation, gradual liberalization of foreign investment, banking reform (including opening four commercial banks), and opening the floodgates of tourism.[5] Despite these reforms, the market-oriented transition was still too slow to fill the growing void of Soviet assistance, and some harsh macroeconomic lessons were yet to be learned. For example, a 1988 fourfold increase in domestic credit proved disastrous, fueling an inflation rate near 400 percent. The government chose to undertake a bolder economic stabilization program the following year, which included a more realistic devaluation of the dong, trade liberalization, removal of most price controls and subsidies, public expenditure and credit cutbacks, and higher interest rates.[6]

The 1989 reforms were effective in stabilizing the economy for the short run and in planting the seeds for future economic growth. In that year, inflation was slashed from 308 percent to 35 percent; banking deposits rose from under 1 percent to almost 4 percent, and the economy grew 8 percent (largely attributable to agriculture).[7] At the same time, the sharp growing pains of a market transition became evident, with massive reductions in public employment and social services, the collapse of inefficient industries, and a glaring lack of adequate infrastructure or capital (financial, physical, and natural).

The pace of reform and quest for ever higher growth rates has nonetheless been unabated. Vietnam's Socioeconomic Stabilization and Development Strategy of 1991 called for a doubling of GDP by the year 2000, which would have required an average annual growth rate of 7.2 percent, starting at about 5 percent. Successful macroeconomic reforms and external financing helped the economy to outstrip this goal initially and to accelerate to a real annual GDP growth rate of 8.43 percent since 1992[8]; 1994 GDP stood at US$15.48 billion, with an annual per capita income of $213. This is roughly the equivalent of US$1,573 in terms of purchasing power parity.[9] Given this unforeseen success, Vietnam's official development goals were upgraded, with a goal of doubling *per capita GDP* by the year 2000. With a current population of more than 71 million, increasing 2.33 percent per annum, this is indeed a lofty goal.[10]

There is no reason to assume a priori that such growth will be impossible or that it precludes sustainable development goals. However, severe natural, human, financial, and physical constraints are to be overcome, and there is every reason to assume that without appropriate attention to institutions, human welfare, and the environment, rapid and uncontrolled GDP growth could erode Vietnam's prospects for future growth and human development. These issues are explored in the two following sections.

CONSTRAINTS TO SUSTAINABLE GROWTH

As discussed earlier, there are real economic constraints to be faced in order for Vietnam to achieve sustainable economic growth, and some examples are provided below. These include the need, but not always the capability and/or resources, for large capital outlays, macroeconomic stabilization, and carefully planned liberalization of both domestic and international trade. Trade-offs among environment, human welfare, and economic growth are evident in every macroeconomic decision; thus the path to sustainability is not always a clear one.

Currently, 70 percent of the labor force is involved in agriculture and forestry, in which underemployment is commonplace and environmentally degrading techniques are often used.[11] The double-edged task of absorbing labor from these primary sectors while rapidly increasing productivity within them will require massive investment, public and private, in both the primary sector and the burgeoning secondary and tertiary sectors. The task is further complicated by a grossly inadequate infrastructure and the quality of domestic technical expertise.[12] Ensuring that investment eventually deepens the overall capital stock (including human and natural capital) presents a necessary yet formidable task.

In terms of man-made capital, Vietnam managed an impressive gross formation rate of 20.5 percent in 1993. To ensure continued savings that support such capital formation, however, the government must continue to fight inflation, which rose from 5.2 percent in 1993 to almost 15 percent in 1994. Because stabilization measures have already been rather drastic, this need presents a significant trade-off, exemplified by a choice between human capital formation (i.e., continued provision of social services) and physical capital development.

At present, human capital formation is threatened by population pressures and inadequate social services provision. Although 90 percent of the population has access to some form of health care, only 27 percent has access to safe drinking water and 18 percent to sanitation. Approximately 3.8 million children under the age of 5 are malnourished, and 37.6 million people live in absolute poverty. Mitigating these trends through family planning has proven ineffective: only about one-half the population has access to reliable birth control, and the average number of births per woman stands at 4 despite the fact that the average *desired* number of births is only 2.5.[13]

One option to provide the appropriate levels in both social services and capital investment is through export-oriented growth, similar to that of the Asian Tigers. Although trade liberalization measures have been accelerated sharply since 1989, the trade deficit nonetheless rose from US$443 million in 1993 to US$900 million in 1994.[14] This fact does not suggest that outward-looking development is untenable but that trade surpluses will require more time and more finely tuned macro policy.

Another option, undertaken by other Asian economies, would involve exploitation of existing natural resources to fuel investment in human and man-made productive assets. Unfortunately, though, Vietnam has neither the luxury of an extensive land frontier, as do Thailand and Indonesia, nor the benefit of a steady flow of investable surplus from resource extraction and export that Malaysia and Indonesia have enjoyed during the takeoff stages of their development. However, recent oil export development should help improve the situation. Vietnam will have to build all three stocks (i.e., natural, human, and man-made capital) simultaneously to ensure sustainable development; otherwise, with rapid population growth and a deteriorating resource base, gains in one stock may be offset by losses in another. This point is the fundamental reason environmental policy should be fully integrated with economic reforms if sustainable development is to be achieved.

MAJOR ENVIRONMENTAL ISSUES FACING VIETNAM

Natural resources, particularly land, forests, and fisheries, have been Vietnam's main productive assets, affording the Vietnamese people a modest but sustainable level of living for centuries. Destructive wars, rapid population growth, and neglect and mismanagement have left Vietnam with a smaller resource base and a more vulnerable environment to support a much larger population than at any other time in the country's 4,000 years. Although diversification away from the resource sectors is the only path to sustainable development, the latter cannot be accomplished without rehabilitation of the resource base and protection of the environment.

Land and Soil Resources

Vietnam has limited land and soil resources relative to its population of 70 million. The population density is 210 persons per square kilometer, which is comparable to that of the Philippines and twice that of Thailand. This comparison, however, understates the scarcity of land in Vietnam. Because only 21 percent of the total land area is cultivated, the average land-rural population ratio is only 0.14 hectares and in some areas such as the Red River delta is as low as 0.06 hectares, one of the lowest in the world.[15] Compounding land scarcity is the poor quality of the soils, which, with the notable exceptions of the Mekong and Red River deltas, suffer from chemical deficiencies or have other limiting factors. For example, most red and yellowish soils in Vietnam have high iron and aluminum content. Not only is three-quarters of the country mountainous or hilly with highly erodible slopes, but even flat areas have soil quality problems. In the river deltas, more than 3 million hectares are affected by salinization, alkalization, and inundation.[16] In the Red River delta alone, floods damage 240,000 hectares of crops, 40,000 of which yield no harvest.[17]

Land scarcity is increasing in Vietnam not only because the population is growing rapidly (over 2 percent per year) but also because land resources are deteriorating owing to uncontrolled soil erosion. Each year several hundred million tons of fertile soil are washed into the sea. The Red River alone is carrying sediment of 120 million tons and the Mekong 90 million tons annually.[18] At the same time, dams, reservoirs, irrigation canals, lakes, and harbors are losing their capacity rapidly as a result of sedimentation. For example, the Hoa Binh Dam's economic life for electricity generation has been reduced from 250 years to 50-100 years because of the Da River siltation.[19] According to one estimate, the nutrients of the alluvium soil lost each year are equal to 500,000 tons of nitrogen, 300,000 tons of phosphorous, and 300,000 tons of potassium,[20] for an economic loss of US$165 million (assuming a fertilizer price of US$150 per ton).

Vietnam suffers from high rates of erosion for several reasons. First, almost one-half the cultivated land is on slopes steeper than 15 degrees and one-third of this is on slopes steeper than 25 degrees. Observations at stations located in Huu Lung, Song Cau, Vinh Phu, and Tay Nguyen indicate that when the slope doubles, soil erosion quadruples.[21] Second, annual precipitation is high (averaging 1,500-2,000 millimeters annually) and is seasonal (i.e., 80-90 percent in the 5 months of the rainy season) and spatial; in the mountains of the Central Region, for example, rainfall reaches 3,000-4,000 millimeters. Third, the forest cover has been reduced drastically in the last three decades; in the Northwest, it occupies only 13 percent of the land area. There are 13.4 million hectares of barren hills, and more than one-third of the country is exposed to wind, rain, and solar energy. Bare land with a slope steeper than 25 degrees loses as much as 213 tons of soil per hectare per year.

A fourth major reason for the high soil erosion rates is the cultivation on slope land of groundnut, cassava, maize, and other crops that provide little canopy and root protection to the soil.[22] Reduced interception of the rainfall by groundcover results in higher surface flow. Evidence from Vietnam indicates that a two- to sixfold increase in surface flow results in a five and one-half to twentyfold increase in soil loss. Upland fields in the west plateau and in north hilly land planted to groundnut are reported to lose an average of 54 tons per hectare, compared to 9 tons per hectare for maize and cassava and 0.5 tons for a permanent coffee plantation.[23]

Forest Resources

Forest resources play a strategic role in both environmental protection and sustainable development. In addition to their direct economic value as a source of timber, fuelwood, and a variety of forest products, forests protect watersheds, control soil erosion, help maintain the capacity of irrigation and hydroelectric dams, lessen the severity of floods, provide habitat for wildlife, and act as a storehouse for biodiversity. The recorded direct contribution of forests to national income and employment is limited to 1.7 percent and 3.9 percent, respectively. But this does not include the collection of 22 million tons of fuelwood per year and a variety of forest products such as food and medicinal plants. About 20 million people are reported to live in Vietnam's forests, and they depend for part of their livelihood on forest products.[24] Yet far more critical to Vietnam's sustainable development is the forests' role in environmental protection. Although the direct contribution of Vietnam's forests to the economy will decline with industrialization and economic growth, their importance to the sustainability of growth and the quality of life will increase.

Out of the total land area of 33 million hectares, Vietnam had 22.2 million hectares of forests, with a coverage density of 67 percent in 1943. Today the forest covers a mere 9.6 million hectares, for a coverage density of 29 percent. The loss of 12.6 million hectares of forests over a half-century amounts to an average annual deforestation rate of 250,000 hectares. In 1994, the annual deforestation rate was about 2 percent. It should come as no surprise, therefore, that the northern parts of Vietnam have successively experienced flooding in the past 3 years (1992-94), with loss of life, the washing away of roads, and further destruction of plant and animal life. Although reliable estimates of loss of output and income caused by flooding in the North are not available, physical and natural capital damage is estimated at US$40-50 million for these 3 years.[25]

Deforestation has also continued in central and southern Vietnam. The 1994 floods in the Mekong delta have damaged about 3 percent of Vietnam's rice output, which is about 1.5 percent of its agricultural output or slightly less than 0.5 percent of GDP, amounting to $75 million in 1994. Keeping in mind that the per capita income is US$213 per annum in 1994 dollars, one can see how such crop damage has caused severe hardship for several hundred thousand households in the region. This loss is in addition to the approximately US$30 million of damage from the washing away of roads, schools, public buildings, and private property.

Because much of the deforestation responsible for flooding occurs outside the territorial boundaries of Vietnam, it is not clear whether this flooding problem can be handled by Vietnam alone. Some form of international cooperation involving the relevant countries may be the solution. This point is especially applicable to the Mekong delta.

Equally daunting is dealing with the social problems of 200,000 people living in and around national parks and 2 million people living in watershed areas. The government is resettling them, beginning with 200,000 households (1 million people) from 1,000 villages, by implementing 114 resettlement projects at a cost of 350 billion dong during 1991-95.

Water Resources

Vietnam's freshwater resources are critical to both economic development and environmental integrity. Surface water is abundant in Vietnam. Nine major river systems transect the country in addition to numerous lakes and wetlands. Groundwater is also plentiful in all but the most mountainous regions. But because of the seasonal rainfall pattern and geography, water resources are unevenly distributed. People in the mountainous areas often spend one-quarter of their working day collecting water, and communities in the coastal regions are forced to build earthen dams to store freshwater for the dry season, when rivers become highly saline.[26] Further, many surface water and shallow groundwater supplies are polluted by human and animal wastes, agrochemicals, industrial wastewater, and sediment.

As a result of Vietnam's focus on the agricultural sector, it accounts for over 80 percent of total water use. However, in most cases, farmers do not pay for the water they use for irrigation, leading to excessive water use and a disregard for water conservation.[27] Of the 6.6 million hectares of cultivated land, 2.5 million hectares (38 percent) are irrigated. Two-thirds of the irrigated land lies in the Mekong and Red River deltas. Because these deltas are the most productive agriculturally, cropping intensity is high and land area per capita is low (0.08 hectares); therefore some irrigation is necessary to maintain high yields on relatively small plots. But in the near future, larger volumes of water will be needed for industry and the growing population. Increasingly, there are conflicting demands for water for agriculture, industry, and domestic use.[28] Industry is expected to account for approximately 20 percent of water use by the year 2000.

Access to safe drinking water in urban and rural areas is low relative to other countries such as Thailand—48 and 45 percent coverage compared with 67 and 76 percent, respectively.

Further, Vietnam has just begun to exploit its hydroelectric power potential. Although water volume is not a concern—Vietnam currently uses only 1 percent of its water resources—pollution is rapidly depleting the supply of clean water.

Fishery Resources

Vietnam has an abundance of inland and marine fisheries, given its extensive system of rivers, lakes, and swamps and its long coastline. Further, because of the climate, geomorphology, and abundance of aquatic nutrients, the water bodies are suitable for fish production. Vietnam has 1 million hectares of inland surface water bodies and 900,000 hectares of brackish and marine water bodies.[29] Its coastline is 3,200 kilometers long. The two largest river systems, the Mekong and the Red River, contain 260 and 170 species of freshwater fish, respectively.[30]

Inland and marine fisheries are important as a source of both household income and nutrition. Many marine organisms (e.g., crabs, oysters, mollusks) have a high market value. In 1990, aquaculture production was more than 1 million tons. The export value of fish and fish products for 1990 was US$205 million, an increase of US$35 million from the preceding year. Vietnam's annual dietary fish intake averages 13 kilograms per capita, ranging from a few kilograms in the highlands to 27 kilograms in the Mekong delta.[31] Yet only a small part of the total surface water area is being used for aquaculture (12.5 percent of brackish water and 31 percent of freshwater) and productivity is low.[32] Between 1986 and 1993, the water surface used for aquaculture increased from 294,000 hectares to 347,000 hectares. Unlike agriculture, however, aquaculture production can grow through continued extensification rather than intensification.

Despite the apparent abundance of Vietnam's fish stocks, they are at risk from numerous sources of water pollution, overfishing, offshore oil exploration, and aquatic habitat destruction.

Biodiversity

Vietnam's biodiversity derives from a wide range of latitudes, land forms that vary from swampy deltas to high mountains, and a unique monsoon climate.[33] For a country its size, the flora and fauna are rich and diverse. Among the 8,000 known plant taxa in Vietnam, there is a high degree of endemism—10 percent of the total number of plants—indicating the uniqueness of many species. It has significantly more mammals and birds than the Philippines, a country of the same size.

The forests, which range from the rain forests in the South to evergreen forests in the North, contain the highest avian and primate diversity in mainland Southeast Asia. Four primate species are endemic to these forests. In addition, 7,000 of approximately 12,000 higher vascular plants used for medicine, wood, oil, and animal fodder grow there. Mangrove forests, also abundant in Vietnam, contain 35 species of genuine mangroves and 41 associated species. In 1950, they occupied 400,000 hectares of coastal area. By 1983, this area had been effectively halved to 252,000 hectares.[34]

The country's biodiversity is as vulnerable as it is rich, but it is rapidly declining owing to deforestation, watershed degradation, overhunting, and overfishing.[35] Deforestation, wetland conversion, and water pollution are destroying wildlife habitats and unique plant communities. Endemic flora are being eliminated from the genetic pool as forests, wetlands, and other unique ecosystems disappear with growing pressures on the land.

Vietnam has responded to the threat to its biodiversity in two ways. First, it inventoried the flora and fauna and developed a list of endangered species needing official protection. Currently, 54 mammals and 60 birds are on the list.[36] Second, Vietnam designated 1.1 million hectares (3 percent) of its land as nature reserves.[37] Although the total area is somewhat larger than that designated by China, the Philippines, and other countries, it is significantly less than Indonesia's and Thailand's. Further, there are 87 isolated reserves, so that any one reserve is too small to maintain viable flora and fauna populations.[38] Sixteen percent of Vietnam's protected areas have been declared "totally protected areas" by the International Union for Conservation of Nature and Natural Resources; the remainder are considered "partially protected areas," allowing recreation, tourism, and limited resource extraction.

These two steps, although promising, are not adequate to deal with the threat to biodiversity. Despite the existence of an endangered species list, monitoring the species and enforcing protection laws are nonexistent. Uncontrolled hunting and international trade in wildlife persist. Continuing deforestation and watershed degradation put more species at risk each day. In addition to reforestation and watershed management programs, future policies will need to strengthen both monitoring and enforcement, create more protected areas, and control hunting and wildlife trade.

Water Pollution

Of the country's 436 urban centers, only 100 have a piped water distribution system. These systems lack both proper chemical treatment and proper control equipment. As a result, the water is contaminated with iron, suspended solids, and germs, causing waterborne diseases. These distribution systems serve approximately 47 percent of the urban population; the other 53 percent uses water from rivers, streams, lakes, and ponds and therefore is also exposed to waterborne diseases and toxic chemicals.[39] The drainage systems in Ho Chi Minh City and Hanoi are badly damaged and are clogged by the sewage flowing into the pipes.

Vietnam has no treatment plant for its wastewater, domestic or industrial, in the entire country. The dumping of untreated sewage as well as industrial waste into lakes and rivers threatens both human life and aquatic ecosystems. Each year, an estimated 300 million cubic meters of wastewater flow into the country's major rivers, of which Hanoi is responsible for 120 million cubic meters.[40]

Although some large cities have underground sewerage systems, most are old and deteriorated; the majority of sewage flows through open street drains. Moreover, only 23 percent of the urban population is served by a waterborne sewerage system; the remainder uses septic systems or pit latrines, which contaminate groundwater.[41] The sewage is then discharged, often with little or no treatment, into the rivers. Surface water quality in the vicinity of these discharge points is poor. In both Hanoi and Ho Chi Minh City, the dissolved oxygen content is nearly always zero, and biological and biochemical oxygen demands are high, as is ammonia and bacteria content. In Ho Chi Minh City, pH has been as low as 4.0 in the dry season.[42] Industrial effluents also enter riverways untreated, releasing harmful levels of metals and toxics. Transportation adds to Vietnam's water pollution as the percentage of impermeable surface area increases, leading to high levels of storm runoff, which washes pollutants into water bodies.

In rural areas where the population is less concentrated, sanitation is less of a problem, although in some areas, water is contaminated by human and animal waste. The greatest threat to water quality in rural areas is pollution from agrochemicals. The practice of using human waste as fertilizer causes major health risks, especially during flooding.

Without improved water quality standards and development of an adequate sanitation infrastructure, the intensifying urbanization, industrialization, and agricultural intensification threaten to degrade Vietnam's extensive water resources seriously and to compound water pollution-related health risks and economic damages.

Air and Atmospheric Pollution

Air pollution is becoming a significant problem in Vietnam. The two major culprits are the industrial and transport sectors. Of the 63 industrial plants examined in a 1990 survey, 17 percent discharged lead, mercury, and benzene and had excessive dust emissions. Haphazard urbanization has caused many industrial centers to be located near densely populated areas,[43] for example, Thanh Xuan and Kim Giang in Hanoi and Xuan Nam in Ho Chi Minh City. As a result, pollutants such as carbon monoxide (CO), carbon dioxide (CO_2), sulfur dioxide, and various nitrogen oxides are several times higher than World Health Organization permissible levels in nearby urban centers. Hanoi's CO levels are almost twice the permissible level; nitrogen dioxide is up to 3 times and suspended particulates up to 10 times the permissible levels. Lead concentration in Hanoi was estimated at 0.001 to 0.002 milligrams per cubic meter in 1990. In Thuong Dinh, approximately 50 kilograms of sulfides and up to 60 kilograms of CO are released into the air every hour. The cement plant of Hai Phong covers much of the city in dust. This pollution is also evidenced by the fact that 27 percent of patients in three provinces suffered acute respiratory ailments.[44]

Another important source of air pollution is old vehicles manufactured before the advent of pollution control devices. Slow traffic, faulty engines, and narrow streets all exacerbate the effects of air pollution on the resident population.

The greatest source of greenhouse gas emissions in Vietnam is land use change—slash and burn agriculture, which releases large amounts of CO_2 into the atmosphere. In 1989, an estimated 150 million metric tons of CO_2 were released into the atmosphere as a result of land use change. Wet rice agriculture, which generates methane, is the second largest contributor to air pollution in rural areas.[45] However, compared with other countries, Vietnam is a relatively small contributor of greenhouse gas.

Many industries also release CO_2 into the environment, but their contribution is much smaller than that of land use change.

Solid Waste

Solid waste disposal, not a pressing issue in rural areas, is becoming a problem in crowded urban areas. There, one person generates 5 cubic meters of solid waste annually. Vietnam produces approximately 9,100 cubic meters of waste per day (Hanoi and Ho Chi Minh City account for one-third of this), 44 percent of which is collected and the rest thrown arbitrarily into lakes and ponds and on the ground. Most of the solid waste generated is from domestic activities, and only about 18 percent is generated by industry.[46] Based on data from Ho Chi Minh City, 80 percent of the solid waste generated in urban areas is organic material; the remainder is paper, metal, plastics, textiles, glass, and soil.[47] Disposal of solid waste in Vietnam is fairly unsophisticated. Landfills are untreated dump sites that leak into both surface- and groundwater sources. Incinerating plants and recycling programs are nonexistent. Ho Chi Minh City and Hanoi each have a small composting plant. However, of the roughly 1,500 tons of solid waste collected in Ho Chi Minh City per day, the composting plant can process only 40. In Hanoi, only one-half the solid waste generated (1,500 tons per day) is collected.

Hazardous Waste

Hazardous waste from industrial, agricultural, and domestic sources is a growing problem. Many of these wastes—in particular, toxic, metallic, and organic substances—are discharged into rivers and lakes or are released untreated into the atmosphere. In urban areas, more than 50 toxic and hazardous gases have been detected in the atmosphere.[48]

Inland and coastal waterways are polluted from industrial effluents, poisons used in fishing, and oil and hazardous substance spills. In rural areas, toxic agrochemicals pollute surface- and groundwater supplies. Agrochemical use in Vietnam is low compared to many countries; however, some pesticides that are banned in other countries because of their high toxicity are still used in Vietnam. Moreover, the majority of agrochemicals are used on rice and rice paddies, where the saturated environment creates a greater risk of contaminating groundwater or adjacent surface water.[49]

Industry discharges large amounts of toxic chemicals into the water supply. Monitoring is minimal. Viet Tri's textile, food, and chemical factories spew an estimated 35 million cubic meters of wastewater per year containing 100 tons of sulfuric acid, 4,000 tons of hydrochloric acid,

1,300 tons of sodium hydroxide, 300 tons of benzene, and 25 tons of pesticides. In the North, the Thai Nguyen industrial zone discharges 5 million cubic meters of wastewater per year. A major point source of hazardous waste is hospitals.[50]

One of the largest sources of toxic and hazardous wastes was the Vietnam War, in which the United States used herbicides and defoliants containing dioxin, a highly toxic substance. An estimated 550 kilograms of dioxin were released over South Vietnam during the war.[51] Because dioxin has a long half-life, Vietnam is still dealing with severe contamination of some water and land resources.

INTEGRATING DEVELOPMENT POLICIES AND THE ENVIRONMENT

To mitigate the aforementioned environmental problems, market policies will have to complement or be fully integrated with natural resource policies. The economic reforms under way in Vietnam since 1986 and the consequent increased reliance on the market as the principal mechanism for allocating resources have removed or lessened the influence of the command economy on the environment, thereby creating some preconditions for improved resource conservation and effective environmental management. The economic reforms implemented thus far, however, are incomplete or tentative, causing both a vacuum of authority and a climate of uncertainty that can be detrimental to both the conservation of the resource base and the protection of the environment. Moreover, economic reforms and a complete transition to a market economy are necessary but are not sufficient conditions for environmental improvement; conventional markets are least efficient in pricing and allocating natural resources and environmental assets because of ill-defined property rights, high transaction costs, public goods, myopia, uncertainty, and irreversibility. Thus in addition to and concurrent with economic reforms, an environmental policy for the emerging market economy formulated and integrated with these reforms is essential.

Trade liberalization and the devaluation of currency when it is overvalued are key policy reforms for export-oriented industrialization. However, if property rights over resources (e.g., land, forests, fisheries) are not well defined and secure and if environmental costs are not already internalized through some regulatory or economic mechanism, trade liberalization or currency devaluation may lead to a quantum increase in the export of natural resources and of pollution-intensive products. In such a case, resource depletion and environmental costs may offset the benefits from trade expansion.

The freeing of all prices to reach their market clearing levels is also necessary (but not sufficient) for efficient resource use and conservation. Artificially low prices for natural resources result in excessive and wasteful use, rapid depletion, and undue environmental pollution. Although with few exceptions (i.e., coal, electricity, fuel transport) prices since 1990 have been determined by markets, market prices do not fully reflect relative scarcities, much less relative environmental costs. Most distorted are the prices of resources (e.g., coal) or goods with a high natural resource content (e.g., electricity). The lack of clear and secure property rights and mechanisms to internalize environmental costs suggests underpricing of resource- and environment-intensive goods and services. In fact, the prices of coal and electricity are directly controlled by the state. Recently, the price of coal was only one-quarter of its opportunity cost (the world price), and state and residential electricity prices are below the long-run marginal supply costs. The results, of course, are excessive use of polluting coal and inefficient use of electricity, inadequate revenues for supply expansion, and impending electricity shortages even where there are now surpluses.

Efficient capital markets and availability of credit at competitive costs are also critical to the replacement of highly inefficient and heavily polluting production technologies and/or the introduction of pollution abatement technologies in compliance with environmental regulations. Similarly, access to credit is needed for investment in soil conservation, land development, crop intensification, and tree planting. In the absence of adequate capital, enterprises tend to face a more limited set of options for improvement of environmental performance. Until early 1993, state enterprises had some access to soft loans from the state although the terms became increasingly hard and credit difficult to obtain; now they are faced with inadequate credit. In the face of a credit crunch, environmental investments are usually the first to go.

The scarcity of credit funds for the private sector and for the semiautonomous state enterprises is caused partly by the underdevelopment of the capital markets and partly by the crowding-out effect of large state projects. The combined capital cost of these projects is a multiple of the annual national savings; yet their job creation potential is limited.

Capital-intensive projects with low return and low job creation per dollar invested have several implications for the environment and sustainable development: (1) such projects tend to have large-scale environmental impacts (sometimes of an unforeseen nature) as well as high maintenance costs; (2) high-return projects such as reforestation, soil conservation, and ecotourism development that have both economic and environmental benefits tend to be crowded out for lack of funds (based on the experience of Thailand and other countries); and (3) the absorption of most of the domestic savings and/or foreign assistance by large capital-intensive projects with minimal job creation means that many of the approximately 1 million new entrants into the labor force each year will not find employment in the formal sector and will instead put further pressure on the land, encroach on the remaining forest, or squat in the cities, creating a host of environmental and social problems.

The relationship between unemployment (or underemployment) and environmental degradation has another implication for the economic reforms under way. Firing a large number of workers in order to cut costs and rationalize overstaffed state enterprises may be good for the individual enterprise and even for short-term economic growth. However, if the displaced workers have no alternative employment, they are likely to encroach on public property or open-access resources with devastating effects in an environment as fragile and intensively exploited as Vietnam's (this situation occurred in Laos and is currently being experienced in Russia). On this count, the Vietnamese policy of choosing a middle ground between "shock therapy" and slow reform is a sensible one in light of equity and sustainability considerations. The companion policy that should be but is not yet as evident is rapid job creation in labor-intensive, export-oriented industry and active retraining of surplus workers in existing industries.

Agricultural Policy

Since 1988, there have been increased commercialization of the economy and increased market liberalization, allowing unrestricted buying and selling of products, including agricultural and forestry products. Whatever the long-term effects of the reforms, the immediate effect was increased pressure on the resource base of agriculture and forestry. Further, in 1988, the government of Vietnam relaxed its control on interprovincial migration. Although this change has led to relatively free movement of workers, it has also had some adverse environmental consequences. For example, between 1986 and 1992, 13,000 families settled on approximately 13,000 hectares of forest in the Dac Lac province. Such migration has been increasing slowly in the past few years, putting more valuable forest land at risk. Market incentives are necessary for growth, but they have to be fashioned so that such large risks to the environment are avoided or minimized.

In 1989 and 1990, under the renovation policy of Doi Moi, pesticide subsidies were removed. Pesticide use did decline[52]; however, the market forces that briefly effected that change were not the removal of these subsidies but a shortage of foreign exchange. This point can be further inferred from the case of fertilizer subsidies: their removal in 1991 did not cause a decline in the use of fertilizer because paddy prices increased more than the price of fertilizer.

Overuse of pesticides by Vietnamese farmers can be attributed basically to the lack of knowledge of appropriate use. Through the intercountry integrated pest management (IPM) program sponsored by the Food and Agriculture Organization of the United Nations, economic incentives are being offered to reduce the use of pesticides. However, IPM is not well known among the Vietnamese farmers and needs to be promoted more aggressively.

With regard to land tenure, although the new land law passed in July 1993 attempts to improve land tenure security, its benefits have not yet been realized. The reason is primarily that the leases are not yet indefinite in duration and are limited in use or transfer changes, provisions that would motivate farmers to engage in soil stabilization practices. And in part, too, there is a severe shortage of credit for land improvements. Clearly, formal land rights are needed. In an attempt to keep settlers from ravaging the forests, the Vietnamese government has allocated forest areas for protection under contract to the new settlers. This allocation has occurred in Dac Lac and Lam Dong (uplands) and Minh Hai and Ho Chi Minh City (low wetlands) and may prove to be a cost-efficient and effective means for protecting the forests. The protection of forests and improvement in long-term tenure rights with an emphasis on intensive cultivation will have to be implemented simultaneously for each to be effective.

Agricultural taxation is in the form of a presumptive productivity tax based on soil quality and land forms, with exemptions based on weather conditions and pest infestations. This form of taxation is difficult to integrate into environmental protection practices.

Forestry Policy

A Reforestation Fund was established by the government in 1980[53] and financed through the collection of registration fees for forest production and extraction ranging from 10 to 60 percent of the value of the extracted product. It provided rebates for those engaging in reforestation. This policy was hampered by the fact that the declared official prices of the products were low, leading to low rebates, as well as by the fact that the registration fee had to be paid before the rebates could be obtained. Deforestation continued unabated under this policy. In 1991 and 1992, a natural resource tax was introduced. Under this policy, the harvester and the user were separated for taxation purposes: the harvester paid 7-40 percent of the value of the harvested product, and the user paid a fee calculated as a percentage of the sales price in the local market. This approach worked well for those located in relatively healthy forest areas, but for those near degraded forests, the after-tax revenues were not enough to make it worth their while to engage in relatively costly harvesting in the degraded forests. Some of these degraded forests were left barren; the rest were turned into agricultural lands and put at risk for further degradation.

The price of timber increased steadily from 1980 to 1991 owing to the increasing demand from foreign markets, particularly for such species as *Dipterocarp* and *Fokienia*. But in 1991, the government banned the export of timber to protect its forests. Because of the export ban, local timber prices declined—with mixed results. On the one hand, low profits for loggers led to reduced logging; on the other hand, cheaper wood for fuel consumption increased the volume of wood demanded for this purpose. The net effect of these forces on the forests is ambiguous, and it will have to be evaluated. Perhaps planned agroforestry programs and forest conservation incentives will be more beneficial than an outright ban on logging.

Industrial Policy

The major issues here are the government's objectives in setting energy and water prices. In setting energy prices, the government has sought to generate enough funds not only to sustain the economic viability of the various energy sectors but to generate a surplus for future investment in the same industries. Petroleum is taxed with a view to providing funds for infrastructure development such as roads and bridges. Although the electricity prices have been doubled over the past 6 years, they do not cover actual production costs. They do not because the cost figures submitted to the government for determination of electricity prices are low owing to industry's undervaluation of fixed assets and low assumed depreciation rates for these assets.

Relative coal prices have declined because of improved coal quality (with regard to ignitability and other characteristics) and increased productivity. The Coal Consumers Association sets a minimum price for coal, but the market determines the price of fuelwood. And because lighting coal is difficult, there is a tendency to use more firewood than coal even though coal is somewhat cheaper.

Energy Policy

So far, the coal mining policy has not included control of dust pollution and topsoil damage. Mine pits are left open, and approximately 2,000 hectares of land have been despoiled with no efforts made to reclaim it. The cost of rectifying the indiscriminate piling over the years is estimated at US$150 million.[54]

Oil spills resulting from exploration pose a major environmental risk. Currently, approximately 1 percent of the oil extracted is spilled into the East Sea. Although Vietnam's annual per capita oil consumption of 40 kilograms per year is relatively low compared to South Korea and Hong Kong, which average 1,000 kilograms per year, increasing future consumption will pose greater risks to the environment. A major oil spill can have potentially hazardous consequences because, given the nature of the East Sea, the oil would flow back toward the Vietnamese shore.

Owing to its vast water resources, hydroelectric power is the major source of energy for Vietnam. Because hydropower plants are located downstream from watershed areas that are substantially deforested, erosion has led to siltation of reservoirs. The resulting flooding in 1992 led, for example, to the loss of 1,800 hectares of rice land, 700 hectares of cash crops, 200 hectares of fish ponds, 235 kilometers of roads, and 80,000 cubic meters of buildings in Hoa Binh. An estimated 4,000 displaced families, suffering from hardships and resentment owing to poorly planned relocation programs, have resorted to slashing and burning forests for their sustenance.[55] Since 1976, 3.92 million people have been moved from the Red River delta and northern midlands to the central highlands and other areas onto a land area totaling 0.75 million hectares.[56]

MODELING THE VIETNAMESE ECONOMY: PATHS TOWARD INTEGRATION

Many questions remain about the interactions among Vietnam's economic reform, environmental base, and various economic sectors. Answering them requires not only a dynamic intersectoral framework but also an account of total social costs and indirect effects. With such a general interdependence perspective in mind, this investigation of the Vietnamese economy's macroeconomic structural adjustment, its effect on the environment, and the consequent economic feedback effects was done in the framework of state-of-the-art CGE models. Capturing the feedback impact of environmental changes on the economy in a general equilibrium framework, with all indirect effects throughout the many sectors fully taken into account, is, in the authors' view, a novel feature not only of this study but also of the general methodology of CGE analysis.

In the framework of the CGE model, the following policy shocks are simulated and analyzed in terms of income, employment, and environmental effects:

- liberalizing commodity trade;
- subsidizing agriculture;
- securing property rights in agriculture and forestry;
- rechanneling some foreign direct investment into private sector light manufacturing and tourism;
- subsidizing reforestation through a logging tax; and
- subsidizing reforestation through an energy tax.

The Model

The research group used a theoretical general equilibrium model of an economy producing and consuming an arbitrary number of goods, with environmental externalities of a purely technological nature explicitly modeled.[57] This model forms the framework for evaluating the welfare effects of macroeconomic and other reforms under the Doi Moi program.

Policy Experiments

The first policy change scenario considered was one of complete liberalization of commodity trade undertaken in the framework of a 45-sector CGE model. For an idea of how restrictive a trade regime was in place prior to Doi Moi, the trade restrictive index (TRI) had a value of 0.788. A TRI value of 1 means completely free trade, and 0.788 is a substantial distortion.[58] Under a simulated commodity trade liberalization, the general equilibrium effect of a raise in the TRI value from 0.788 to TRI = 1 was to raise real income by US$81,504,896, which constitutes an increase of 0.8 percent. The employment coefficient for the country as a whole stood at 103,149 additional jobs for every 1 percent increase in real GDP.[59] This figure suggests that the commodity trade liberalization had the effect of creating 54,000 additional jobs. Given the rapid rate at which the labor force is growing, owing to both the high population growth rate and the increase in the participation ratio, the number of individuals entering the labor force far exceeded job growth effected by the liberalization policy. The implication is that unemployment-related forest encroachment may be reduced but not halted or reversed by trade liberalization alone. Vietnam will need to implement *complementary reforms* to create greater labor absorption and environmental sustainability.

The second scenario demonstrates the point that agricultural subsidization would not be an appropriate complementary reform; nor would it serve sustainable development interests in its own right. Simulating a 10 percent subsidy to agriculture recreated an earlier phase of Doi Moi in which fertilizer and pesticides were provided to farmers at a subsidized rate. The subsequent losses in income, employment, and environmental integrity are interpreted as the *gains* Vietnam achieves through the removal of these subsidies. Again, economy-to-environment and environment-to-economy links were employed in the general equilibrium model.

Based on several assumptions about deforestation, soil erosion, and opportunity costs, the study group concluded that if 1 additional hectare of land were brought under rice cultivation because of a subsidy (or for any reason), 1.4 hectares of deforestation would occur, leading to 168 tons of upland soil erosion. Ten percent of it would be captured by silt traps, and the remaining 150 tons would destroy approximately 0.03 hectares of lowland rice, which would cause a loss of US$6 per hectare per year. This feedback loop between economy and environment demonstrates clearly that a subsidy to agriculture leads to annual incremental productivity losses for every hectare of additional land brought under rice cultivation. With this relationship built into the general equilibrium model and combined with the factor demand equation for land, it was found that a 10 percent subsidy to agriculture reduced real income US$7.8 million. The lesson here is clear: although the government formerly subsidized agriculture for welfare reasons, trying to ensure that valuable foreign exchange would be spent on imports of rice, the net result for the economy actually reduced welfare by misallocating resources toward agriculture and away from other activities with greater marginal value. The distortion also hurt both the economy and the environment by increasing soil erosion, which in turn destroyed some lowland rice crops, and thus reducing primary factor income.

The third scenario simulated the clarification of property rights in agriculture, which is a consistent theme in Vietnamese adjustment reforms. A 3-sector CGE model was used, with agriculture and forestry constituting one sector; industry, energy, and construction the second sector; and services and miscellaneous the third. A vast literature in development economics shows that as tenurial laws create greater security of rights for the cultivators, more of them begin to undertake technological innovations, thereby raising productivity. Legal changes such as the promulgation of the Land Law of 1993 also engendered technological innovation. This enhanced productivity was integrated into the agricultural and forestry sector of the model, and it generated an overall (equivalent variation) real income increase of 0.32 percent for every 1 percent of increased productivity.

Although degrees of property rights security are difficult to quantify in productivity terms, this experiment demonstrates clearly that more secure property rights are a boon to both income and employment generation through increased productivity in land-based activities. They are also the most effective means to promote long time horizons for resource users, thus promoting more environmentally and economically sustainable practices. Although this aspect is not explicitly treated in the model, it would most certainly register even greater gains to the economy.

The fourth scenario considered a redirection of some investment toward labor-intensive light industry and services such as tourism instead of allowing the bulk of all investment to go into capital-intensive projects and industries, the current case. In 1994, Vietnam invested US$3.9 billion, of which US$1.2 billion was from foreign direct investment (FDI); US$1.4

billion was from the state sector, including US$0.4 billion from official development assistance (ODA); and the balance of US$1.3 billion was from the nonstate sector. Virtually the entire $1.4 billion of the state sector investment is being channeled into megaprojects such as upgrading national highways 1a, 5, and 80 and building 600-megawatt thermal power plants in Phailai and Phumy being financed by the Japanese government. Japan is also financing a feasibility study of the Cai Lau deep seaport in Quang Ninh province. In fact, in the Vietnam government's list of priority projects already funded or expected to be funded by ODA, only a few projects are aimed at such labor-intensive sectors as tourism and light manufacturing. Further, 99.6 percent of FDI commitments are to joint ventures with large state enterprises, with about two-thirds going to industry, oil, and natural gas and about one-third to services and tourism.

Simple calculations show that with a heavy industry or infrastructure ICOR (incremental capital output ratio) of 2.7 versus a tourism-light manufacturing industry ICOR of 1.5, the US$1.8 billion state sector investment made in 1994 would have generated additional real income worth US$0.93 billion in tourism-light industry, whereas the investment in heavy industry in 1994 actually generated only US$0.52 million of additional income. Based on an output-labor ratio of US$2,480 per worker for heavy industry and large-scale infrastructure and a ratio of US$970 for tourism and light manufacturing, 1.233 million additional jobs would have been created, whereas at best, only 269,179 could be generated in the heavy industry investment. Both environmental and economic reasoning seems to support such an investment rechanneling.

The principal objection to such rechanneling is that megaprojects generate substantial intersectoral gains because heavy industry, transportation infrastructure, etc. act as pivots on which much other economic activity hinges. As a check on the veracity of this claim, this state sector investment module was injected into the CGE model to capture the indirect general equilibrium effects. As expected, although infrastructure and heavy industries would generate large gains, in this case, US$449.15 million and 181,353 additional jobs, the tourism and light industries would generate far more—a US$790.33 million increase in real income and 812,331 additional jobs.

The potential losses from channeling the state sector investment (including ODA) into capital-intensive projects are further compounded by the fact that with 1 million workers entering the work force in 1994, light industry or tourism would have absorbed almost all of them, whereas the heavy industry bias of investment has meant that many of these workers will be left underemployed and will encroach on forest lands. As with the agricultural subsidy, the logic is intuitively obvious: to absorb labor and decrease unemployment-related pressure on quasi-open access natural resources, either biases against labor-intensive activities must be removed or the activities must be actively promoted to some extent. Further, promotion of any resource-intensive or environmentally degrading activity fuels the generation of its negative externalities, thus exacerbating the economic distortion.

The fifth scenario attempts to do just the reverse by taxing an activity with negative environmental externalities and simultaneously investing in a positive externality-generating activity. Specifically, a reforestation program financed entirely by a tax on logging is considered. Logging contributed US$396 million to Vietnamese GDP in 1992. A 20 percent tax on logging, with revenue-invested reforestation, was added. A prime example of a target area would be the Son La province. The total of forest saved and reforested is 204,000 hectares. The cost of the logging tax is a US$47.5 million decline in logging activity. However, the benefits are US$15.7 million from agriculture, US$3.5 million from reservoir use for power, and US$15.4 million from additional timber output (at a rate that preserves forest land). In a partial equilibrium framework, the result is a *net gain* in real income of US$125 million and a net employment gain of 24,000 jobs. The general equilibrium net gains are slightly less, at almost US$85 million in GDP growth and 19,500 jobs created.

As with previous experiments, it should be noted here that net gains might be greater if more external costs and benefits are considered. Examples would include the additional benefits of watershed protection, reduced flooding, and further reductions in deforestation owing to additional job growth. Thus further integration of environmental and social feedbacks to the economy bolsters the quantitatively based conclusion that appropriate taxation and investment policies (specifically, those that internalize socioecological costs and benefits) will lead to virtuous circles of economic growth and sustainability.

The sixth scenario builds upon this idea by exploring the effects of an intersectoral transfer of income, again with an aim to remove externality-induced distortions. The model includes a 20 percent surcharge on energy prices, with the proceeds used to finance reforestation in watershed areas. The surcharge resulted in a partial equilibrium cost of US$33 million or a general equilibrium cost to the economy of US$68.5 million. The tax revenue collected is US$101 million. The job loss to the economy owing to this tax is 44,000.

When this tax revenue is used to finance reforestation, however, the following outcomes are obtained: (1) 281,000 hectares are reforested, and US$67 million of additional real income in the forestry sector and 69,000 additional jobs in reforestation are created; (2) 6,700 hectares of lowland area under rice cultivation and 4,000 hectares under upland crops are saved (from the third year onward), and a net present value of increased agricultural income of $21 million is produced; (3) sedimentation, from the third year on, is reduced, leading to increased power generation at the Hoa Binh hydroplant, whose net present value is US$5 million; and (4) a sustainable timber output of US$22.5 million per year (or a net present value of US$225 million) is produced. Real income increases total US$250 million, or a general equilibrium increase of US$169 million. The employment increase owing to this energy surcharge to finance reforestation is 25,000 jobs in a partial equilibrium framework and 20,000 jobs under general equilibrium conditions.

Although both the energy and logging taxes, when reinvested in the natural capital base, produce remarkable gains in employment and national income, the intersectoral transfer (from energy to forestry) displays the greatest gains. One reason may be that the energy tax manages to capture further negative externalities while simultaneously providing a broader tax base. Both examples demonstrate the fact that deepening the natural capital base by reinvesting gains from resource use will provide growth today and secure it tomorrow. This point is the essence of sustainable development. The windfall gain of increased employment also feeds back into the economy and environment, forming a virtuous circle of sustainability.

Employment gains in the latter cases and in the investment reallocation scenario (the third) derive from the high labor intensity inherent in the activities they foster, such as reforestation, light manufacturing, and tourism and other services. This point dovetails well with Vietnam's dual development objectives of sustainable *human* development and doubling per capita income, for the constructive use of human resources is the key to improving human welfare. The same principle holds true for the environment in that appropriate stewardship and productive use will preserve natural resource integrity and future production potential. By employing a holistic and dynamic model to explore these interactions among economic growth and human and natural resources, each scenario offers strong evidence that sustainable development is possible for Vietnam and the potential for future real growth hinges on the policy integration of environment and economy.

CONCLUSIONS AND RECOMMENDATIONS

The preceding analysis answers two important questions regarding structural adjustment and the environment in Vietnam. First, it is entirely possible for Vietnam to shed the inefficiency, poverty, and environmental deterioration of the past and achieve sustainable growth. The push away from the Soviet-style central planning model and the pull toward the structural reform model of the Asian Tigers may indeed propel Vietnam toward greater prosperity. Second, however, the economy's propulsion must be guided appropriately to meet the government's goal of sustainable human development. Such guidance will be derived from a holistic integration of environmental and social costs and benefits with the more obvious economic objectives inherent in stabilization and structural adjustment programs.

Preconditions for Integration

For this integration to occur, certain preconditions must be met. Clearly necessary is a prudent, stable, and predictable macroeconomic policy. Money supply and inflation must remain under control, the exchange rate must be kept close to its market equilibrium value, and fiscal discipline must be exercised. Concurrently, enterprise reforms to increase the autonomy and responsibility of enterprises for their own profits and losses are a sine qua non condition for both economic competitiveness and response to economic incentives for sound environmental behavior. Defining and assigning secure property rights over resources such as land, forest, water, fisheries, pastures, and minerals are also a necessary condition for conservation and sustainable management of resources; only then is the depletion cost fully internalized and incorporated in the price of resource products.

Integration of environmental considerations in economic policy calls for less reliance on command and control regulations and more reliance on market-based instruments if growth and competitiveness are to be maintained. Yet during the transition period, when full-cost pricing cannot be fully instituted, tightening existing command and control standards and their enforcement might be necessary to avoid environmental deterioration during transition to a market economy. Similarly, privatization and trade liberalization without full internalization of environmental costs may lead to deterioration of environmental conditions and more intensive resource depletion. Thus enforcement of regulations in urban settings, fisheries, sensitive watersheds, and other areas would need to be strengthened at the same time that pollution taxes, effluent charges, user fees, and other economic instruments of environmental management are being phased in.

The Capital-theoretic Basis for Recommendations

The exploration of Vietnam's current environmental status indicates little margin of error for discerning macroeconomic policy effects on the stock of natural capital. Without the benefit of vast natural resources surpluses (in terms of either extractable resources or environmental absorptive capacity), the short-term gains from reform must be derived primarily from other factor inputs and reinvested in the land and people of Vietnam to ensure a balanced and welfare-enhancing productive base for the future.

The stock of human capital provides a logical comparative advantage for production. It is vast and has benefited in some ways from past policies. Capitalizing on its human resources, Vietnam can meet current demands for economic growth at the same time that it reduces unemployment- and poverty-related pressures on natural assets, for example, encroachment on forests and inefficient resource use from insecure tenure and short time horizons. Stemming excessive population growth and guaranteeing both civil and property rights to its populace are preconditions that are critical to human capital development in Vietnam.

Further, the man-made productive base, including infrastructure, embodied technology, and physical capital inputs, must grow through increased savings and investment, which can be achieved only through a commitment to stabilization and structural adjustment reforms. For this reason, the often hard-to-swallow medicine of price reform, devaluation, credit and expenditure reduction, and institutional reform are an absolute necessity for growth to occur.

Study recommendations reflect this necessity but emphatically qualify that macroeconomic policy provide not just *necessary* but also *sufficient* conditions for sustainable development in Vietnam. This policy, in turn, requires that external costs and benefits are internalized, property rights secured, and investment channeled to areas in which the greatest marginal welfare gains can be realized. With these overarching goals in mind, the more specific policy recommendations follow:

1. Vietnam should continue on an outward-looking development path to fuel GDP growth, typified by trade liberalization and export promotion, but the country cannot rely on this path alone to absorb labor and protect its land base sufficiently.

2. Given the external costs of underemployment and poverty (e.g., forest encroachment, high fertility, short-term resource overexploitation), labor-intensive activities such as tourism, services, and light manufacturing should be promoted, even beyond the level dictated by a free-market comparative advantage.

3. Some development assistance should be diverted from capital-intensive projects and industries (for which negative environmental externalities run high) to labor-intensive activities that have positive environmental externalities in the form of reduced pressure on the resource base, especially land and forests.

4. Perverse subsidies and other environmentally degrading price distortions should be eliminated, particularly in agricultural production, water provision, and energy supply. The elimination of agrochemical subsidies has had positive environmental and welfare impacts. Pressures to reinstitute such subsidies should be resisted, and subsidies on water and energy should be similarly phased out. Integrated pest management and irrigation water pricing should be more actively pursued.

5. Resource-extractive or -degrading activities should be taxed to reflect external costs, and revenue should be reinvested in productive assets with the highest social rate of return, such as natural capital (e.g., reforestation, surface water restoration) and human capital (e.g., technical training, primary education, health and reproductive services). The policy simulations attempted in this study indicate considerable scope for taxation of resource-extractive industries and use of the revenues to cross-subsidize resource conservation and rehabilitation activities to ensure the capture and reinvestment of resource rents created by the reforms and the reduction of associated environmental damage. In particular, the government should consider taxes on logging and energy consumption and use of the revenues to finance reforestation and protection of critical watersheds; for example,

labor-intensive activities have second generation beneficial environmental effects in the form of reductions in forest encroachment and cultivation of marginal lands.

6. Stabilization and structural reforms should be carefully sequenced and complemented with the establishment of preconditions for an efficient functioning market, such as property rights, access to credit, and capital mobility. Government intervention in the market should be optimized to correct distorted market signals and to mitigate unequal access to opportunity, credit, and productive capital.

7. Policy initiatives should be integrated or made complementary in terms of social, environmental, and economic objectives. Ex post facto remediation of inappropriate macro policies, such as those that sacrifice needed education or environmental integrity, is sometimes impossible (e.g., toxin-induced retardation, loss of genetic resources) and almost always more expensive (e.g., retraining an uneducated work force, treating pollution rather than preventing it).

In summary, drawing upon the modeling experiments and a comprehensive exploration of Vietnam's environmental, social, and economic conditions, the research group believes that the clearest path to success will require the integration of environmental and economic policy objectives and a sustained commitment to institutional and economic reform. The task ahead will be difficult in terms both of meeting the preconditions of integration and of capitalizing on the appropriate productive resources within the Vietnamese economy. But the rewards of a sustainable economy and higher living standards for Vietnamese citizens should prove well worth the pain and effort of structural transition.

ENDNOTES

1. United Nations Development Programme (UNDP), *Viet Nam: Technical Assistance in Transition* (Hanoi: UNDP, 1994).
2. David Dollar, "Vietnam: Successes and Failures of Macroeconomic Stabilization," in *The Challenge of Reform in Indochina*, ed. B. Ljunggren (Cambridge, Mass.: Harvard Institute for International Development, 1993).
3. The UNDP publication notes: "Vietnam today is a country on a sustainable and stable development path" (op. cit., p. 25). Vietnam continues to lose anywhere between 20,000 and 120,000 hectares of forests annually. With such deforestation still unchecked, it is

questionable whether the development path is indeed sustainable. A clear historical perspective does sometimes help avoid such careless observations as the one in this recent UNDP document.

4. General Statistical Office, *Statistical Yearbook 1993* (Hanoi: Statistical Publishing House, 1993); and State Planning Committee.
5. D. Dapice, J. Haughton, and D. Perkins, *In Search of the Dragon's Trail: Economic Reform in Vietnam* (Cambridge, Mass.: Harvard University Press, forthcoming).
6. James Riedel, "Vietnam: On the Trail of Tigers" (School of Advanced International Studies, Johns Hopkins Univesity, Washington, D.C., 1992).
7. Dapice et al., op. cit.
8. State Planning Committee estimates.
9. United Nations Development Programme, op. cit.
10. Cf. Judith Bannister, "Viet Nam Population Dynamics and Prospects" (Institute of East Asian Studies, University of California, Berkeley, 1993). On the basis of her analysis of the 1988-89 census, Bannister concludes that the annual population growth rate is 1.9 percent.
11. General Statistical Office, op. cit.
12. Tran Hoang Kim, *Economy of Vietnam: Reviews and Statistics* (Hanoi: Statistical Publishing House, 1994).
13. Bannister, op. cit.
14. State Planning Committee estimates.
15. World Bank, "Vietnam Transition to the Market: An Economic Report" (Washington, D.C., 1993).
16. "Vietnam National Report to the United Nations Conference on Environment and Development, Brazil 1992."
17. Ton That Chieu, "Soil Environment in Vietnam," in *Proceedings of the Seminar on Rational Usage of Soil Resources for Development and Environmental Protection* (Hanoi: Association of Soil Scientists of Vietnam, 1992).
18. World Bank, op. cit.
19. Ibid.
20. Nguyen Quang My, "Erosion of Hilly Land and Soil Environment in Vietnam," in *Proceedings of Seminar on Soil Resources*, op. cit.
21. Ibid.
22. Ibid.
23. Ibid.
24. Huang Ho, "The Role of Forestry for Sustainable Development in Vietnam" (Ministry of Forestry, Hanoi, n.d.).
25. State Planning Committee estimates.
26. International Health Program, "Assessment of Water Resources and Water Uses in the Socialist Republic of Vietnam" (Vietnam National Committee, Hanoi, 1992).
27. Nguen Gong Thanh, "Vietnam Environment Sector Study" (prepared for the Asian Development Bank, Manila, 1993).
28. Ibid.
29. International Health Program, op. cit.
30. United Nations Development Programme (UNDP), *Vietnam Water Supply and Sanitation Sector Study*, vol. 1 (Bankok: UNDP, 1990).
31. World Resources Institute, *World Resources 1992-93: Guide to the Global Environment—Toward Sustainable Development* (New York: Oxford University Press, 1992); and *Vietnam Water Supply and Sanitation Sector Study*, op. cit.
32. International Health Program, op. cit.
33. Vo Quy, "Environment and Development in Vietnam" (Center for Natural Resources Management and Environmental Studies, University of Hanoi, 1992).
34. World Bank, "Vietnam: National Environmental Action Plan" (Washington, D.C., draft, 1994).

35. United Nations Development Programme and Swedish International Development Agency, "Vietnam—National Plan for Environment and Sustainable Development 1991-2000, Framework for Action" (Hanoi, 1991).
36. Ibid.
37. World Resources Institute, op. cit.
38. "Vietnam—National Plan," op. cit.
39. Thanh, op. cit.
40. Ibid.
41. International Health Program, op. cit.
42. "Vietnam National Report to the United Nations," op. cit.
43. Thanh, op. cit.
44. Vietnam Ministry of Health, "Health Survey" (Hanoi, 1991).
45. World Resources Institute, op. cit.
46. Thanh, op. cit.
47. Le Van Khoa, "Pollution of Soil Environment," in *Proceedings of Seminar on Soil Resources*, op. cit.
48. "Vietnam National Report to the United Nations," op. cit.
49. Do Anh, "Fertilizers and Environment," in *Proceedings of Seminar on Soil Resources*, op. cit.
50. Thanh, op. cit.
51. "Vietnam National Report to the United Nations," op. cit.
52. Average imports declined from 20,000 to 9,550 tons. Total consumption data are not available.
53. Taxes had previously taken the form of stumpage fees on forest product extraction.
54. State Planning Committee estimates.
55. World Bank, op. cit.
56. Ibid.
57. In the theoretical model, the externalities are generally conceived, and they do not have to relate to the environment. For example, increasing returns to scale that are external to a firm but internal to an industry are captured by this model just as easily as environmental externalities. For more on this subject, see Nadeem Naqvi and Keith Weiner, "External Increasing Returns and the Shadow Price of Foreign Exchange," *Journal of International Economics* 30:177-84 (1991).
58. Anderson and Neary developed the trade restrictive index for measuring the true, theoretically sound distortion created by a set of tariffs and quantitative trade restrictions (James Anderson and Peter J. Neary, "Trade Reform with Quotes, Partial Rent Retention, and Tariffs," *Econometrica* 60, no. 1:57-76 [1992]). Their index does not suffer from the defects and inconsistencies inherent in other measures such as the average tariff or the tariff equivalent of nontariff barriers.
59. General Statistical Office, op. cit.

PART THREE

12

CONCLUSIONS: SHORT-TERM ENVIRONMENTAL IMPACTS OF STRUCTURAL ADJUSTMENT PROGRAMS

by David Reed

U pon completing the country summaries, the reader cannot help but recognize important differences in the economies of these nine countries: the causes of the economic crises giving rise to adjustment programs vary significantly, the incentive structures in place when adjustment programs began are particular to each country, and the processes and successes in implementing the structural reforms differ considerably.

Those differences, however, should not distract one from the nine countries' important commonalities. In many ways, they are conditions shared with other developing countries. First among those commonalities is their dependence on the export of either agricultural commodities or the extraction of natural resources, such as oil, copper, or timber, as their main productive sector and foreign currency earner. As a consequence, these economies depend on a small group of commodities, and their fortunes are closely tied to fluctuations in international commodities markets. Second, a large percentage of the population of the nine countries lives under difficult economic and social conditions and, excepting Vietnam, the ranks of the poor have grown in recent years. Third, with the exception of Jamaica, all countries have high population growth rates, reaching to 3 percent per annum in some countries. Fourth, with the exception of Venezuela, a high percentage, if not the majority, of the people live in rural areas and depend on agricultural production for their livelihoods and their survival. There is, consequently, a high degree of dependency of the rural poor on the productivity of the countries' natural resource base. Further, all countries have experienced serious environmental and natural resource degradation over recent years. Rapidly growing populations have intensified pressures on the natural resource base and have reinforced the cycle of poverty-induced environmental degradation.

It is perhaps the growing poverty that generated a common need, a common urgency, in implementing structural reforms in these countries. The growing numbers of poor increased social instability and weakened social cohesion as perhaps no other force could. Although these deteriorating conditions created an urgency to generate new employment opportunities and raise living standards, they also created a common risk in implementing the structural adjustment programs. If the reforms failed or if the "transitional costs of adjustment" were too high, the societies could experience economic problems and social dislocations capable of posing serious threats to the societies' manageability. Despite those risks, it was clear to national policymakers that failure to undertake structural reforms would condemn their societies to a downward economic cycle, if not collapse, for years to come. Not only have structural reforms been necessary, but they remain urgent in virtually all countries included in this study.

As the reader considers the conclusions presented below, an underlying dilemma will become apparent regarding the trade-offs between growth and environmental degradation. Certainly, failure to rekindle growth by undertaking fundamental economic reforms would continue to generate serious environmental damage, particularly as impoverished sectors of those societies increase pressure on natural resources to survive. Equally apparent is the fact that efforts to raise the countries to a higher economic growth rate through structural adjustment also entails trade-offs and environmental costs. It is important to clarify from the outset of these concluding chapters that the purpose here is not to question the urgency of stimulating growth in developing countries, including the extractive and agriculture-based countries studied. Rather, the analysis seeks, first of all, to clarify the environmental costs and benefits of the growth path promoted under structural adjustment for these kinds of economies. Thereafter, the analysis seeks to explain how those environmental costs and benefits are distributed among different sectors of adjusting societies.

The reader will also have to consider a second underlying dilemma that surfaces here. If taken in isolation of other factors, many price reforms associated with the adjustment process should lead to desirable economic and environmental outcomes. However, as the case studies reveal, overdue price corrections geared to increasing economic efficiency were often not accompanied by complementary policy reforms. Those reforms include full internalization of environmental costs, institutional and legal reforms, and strengthened local managerial capacity, among others. As a consequence, the price corrections effected through adjustment programs have often generated damaging environmental and social impacts that can offset the intended economic benefits. The intent is not to question the importance of correcting price distortions through economic reform. Rather, it is to highlight from the outset the intimate relationship between price corrections and policy reforms and to point out the additional responsibility that economic reform designers must take on in order to ensure that the process of "getting the prices right" leads to sustainable development strategies.

The conclusions[1] are organized in two chapters. This chapter summarizes the short-term impacts of structural adjustment on the environment of the nine countries. Chapter 13 examines the long-term impacts on the sustainability of the countries' respective development paths. Still a further word of clarification is in order.

The conclusions regarding the short-term environmental impacts cover two basic categories. The first relates to the ways that economic reforms have changed relative prices in adjusting countries and the ways that those price changes have altered patterns of production and consumption, changes that, in turn, affect use and pressure on natural resources. In this regard, the conclusions examine the impacts of reforms in exchange rate, trade, fiscal, and monetary policies on specific environmental problems. The second category of short-term impacts relates to the ways that the adjustment process has altered the social organization, the political structure, and the role of governments in adjusting countries. The discussion includes changes in class structure and social institutions, such as the functions of the state and the organization of civil society. How such changes in social structure alter the way society interacts with and uses environmental goods and services is a central focus of this chapter.[2]

Following this examination of the short-term environmental impacts, Chapter 13 examines the impacts of structural reforms on the sustainability of the countries' development paths. It uses the World Wide Fund for Nature's (WWF) normative statement on sustainable development (presented in Chapter 2) as the basis for assessing the longer-term impacts.

Point by point, Chapter 13 looks at the economic, social, and environmental components of sustainable development.

DIRECT ENVIRONMENTAL EFFECTS OF PRICE CORRECTIONS

Prices are changed through two basic adjustments. The first is adjustment of national prices to external price levels through exchange rate and trade policy reforms. Aligning national prices with international levels improves economic efficiency and facilitates the exchange of goods and services across national borders. The second major price adjustment uses fiscal and monetary policy reforms designed to bring aggregate expenditures in line with the national output level. Government action in regulating the money supply, changing tax policy, and setting government expenditure levels transmits new price signals and incentives throughout the economy.

In this section, both the positive and negative environmental impacts of changing relative prices are discussed. The price changes examined in the nine countries occurred primarily in the stabilization phase of the economic restructuring process and, consequently, the promised benefits of its supply-side response have not developed fully. Even so, employment gains and expansion of extractive industries, agricultural production, tourism, and some industrial production are documented in the nine studies. It is clear that economic growth has generated both positive and negative environmental impacts. Price changes being implemented during this transitional phase also influenced the breadth and depth of poverty in most countries included here. In turn, growing poverty placed greater pressures on the natural resource base of those countries, at times threatening their regenerative capacity, as the poor tried to find new ways of surviving in the face of harsh economic realities.

The detailed summary of how these environmental impacts occurred in the nine countries begins with external adjustments.

External Adjustments

Exchange Rate Policy
The correction of overvalued currencies was a long-overdue reform in the four African countries. For years, the exchange rate inflexibility of the franc zone in west and central Africa generated distortionary impacts on the agricultural and industrial sectors in Mali and Cameroon. East African

governments' reluctance to devalue their exchange rates caused similar economy-wide distortions, hurt export competitiveness, and maintained implicit subsidies for privileged sectors of society over many years. Exchange rate reforms were part of the restructuring programs in Asian and Latin American/Caribbean countries and, with the exception of Venezuela, devaluations tended to occur incrementally. For example, the Vietnamese devalued the dong on several occasions, just as the Jamaican and Pakistani governments did with their currencies. The El Salvadoran colon has appreciated steadily over recent years as foreign capital from worker remittances, development assistance, and private capital flows raised its value. In Venezuela, reeling under the effects of banking and financial crises, exchange rate reforms generated shocks as strong as those felt in the African countries.

The ways in which changed currency values are transmitted to the environment and natural resource base are complex. The underlying premise of devaluation and trade liberalization is that adjustments to external market conditions will provide incentives to increase international competitiveness of tradeable goods and shift production to export sectors. Over time, the supply response will increase productivity, expand employment opportunities, raise incomes, and as a consequence, alleviate poverty. Moreover, in the context of the African and other countries that maintained artificially high exchange rates for extended periods, it is assumed that exchange rate reform will also shift internal terms of trade in favor of farmers and away from urban consumers who have enjoyed subsidized imports. By creating employment opportunities, reducing the bias against the agricultural sector, stimulating on-farm investments, and reducing poverty, exchange rate policy changes are expected to have beneficial environmental impacts.

Some of these general assumptions about the positive environmental impacts have proven true in the countries included in the studies. There have been negative impacts as well. These mixed results can be explained in an examination of the production and substitution effects of changing relative prices through devaluation.

Production Effects. One positive economic and environmental effect of devaluation in Mali and Cameroon is the elimination of pressure that artificially high exchange rates placed on the industrial and agricultural export sectors. In both countries, the industrial sector languished, and agricultural products, such as Malian rice, were forced to compete against artificially low-priced imports. Devaluation provided an important, long-overdue correction to these price distortions and encouraged farmers to respond to new external incentives by increasing investment in the agricultural sector. A continued, albeit modest, increase in on-farm investment and farm incomes can be expected. Cameroon is a clear example of this positive economic and environmental outcome: the decade-long neglect of cocoa plantations is expected to be reversed now that devaluation has removed the penalty against agricultural exports. Intensified production will not only increase productivity and incomes but, in all probability, will improve management of tree stocks and soils.

Mali's main hard currency earner, cotton, remained profitable for farmers prior to and after devaluation largely because parastatals guaranteed markets for their crops and provided credit on a steady basis. Price corrections should encourage increased production and higher revenues in the short and perhaps medium terms. However, an important issue remains unresolved regarding the long-term economic impact of devaluation on cotton production and accompanying impacts on the environment. As the case study states, "If increased export earnings are passed through to farmers, existing trends toward unsustainable extensification and intensification are likely to continue." Devaluation, while correcting price distortions, will also provide new incentives that may encourage more farmers to produce cotton, a crop that is associated with serious long-term environmental damage in other regions. This situation poses difficult choices for Malian policymakers and individual farmers regarding the trade-offs between short-term economic benefits and the longer-term environmental and economic costs. With no easy solutions, it remains to be seen what the longer-term impacts of devaluation will be in the Malian context.

An important issue in assessing the impacts of price changes caused by devaluation is whether there is a shift from "erosive" to "nonerosive" crops and whether crops can be produced in more sustainable ways. As used in the case studies, erosiveness refers to the comparative impacts of crops on soil stability and watersheds. In Cameroon, for example, the profitability of traditional cash crops, such as coffee and cocoa, relative to food crops increased with the currency devaluation. These tree crops tend to be less erosive and, consequently, this shift in relative prices should have positive environmental impacts in the long term. However, Cameroon's devaluation also encouraged a shift from cocoa to nontraditional cash crops, such as potatoes, which tend to be more erosive. In addition to the direct effects of crop mix, certain crops generate negative environmental impacts because of their indirect effects, for example, during the processing stage after the crops are harvested. Tea and tobacco, which require fuelwood for drying and curing, illustrate these environmental impacts. In some countries, this processing stage has led to higher deforestation rates when cheaper alternative energy sources are not available. In sum, the environmental impacts of many shifts among crops require case-specific analysis and a longer period to calculate net effects. The calculation must consider a wide range of factors, including the benefits of reducing financial and environmental subsidies, the potential loss of man-made and human capital already invested in the sector, and social dislocations associated with changing production patterns. For some crops, such as tea and tobacco, the environmental impacts are quite predictable, and policy reforms affecting these commodities can include efforts designed to prevent or offset anticipated environmental problems.

Currency devaluation in Mali and Cameroon created an immediate upsurge in cattle sales to neighboring countries. By selling their cattle, farmers reduced short-term pressures on grazing land. But with rising incomes, the farmers are expected to increase their herds and, in the process, increase pressures on pastures. Concerns have been registered in both countries about the impacts of an anticipated growth in herd size and increased competition over land use that might even lead to range wars in Cameroon.

In a situation peculiar to Zambia among the nine countries, devaluation may have the positive impact of reducing the incentive to smuggle ivory and rhino horn across borders as a means of obtaining dollars that were not available inside the country prior to the adjustment program. This change will help stabilize population levels of these threatened species and thereby enhance the viability of the tourist industry in coming years.

Substitution Effects. In all four African countries, exchange rate reforms have raised the prices of imported agricultural inputs and machinery. In Mali, the price increases in farm inputs are sizable, and in the other three African countries, the price changes are serious enough to place agricultural inputs beyond the reach of many small farmers. Although the quality of such inputs has been questioned in some cases, farmers at the village level recognize the fact that their recent productivity gains are linked to chemical inputs. Studies in Cameroon and Tanzania point out that the use of improved seed varieties is lessened by rising seed prices and the shrinking government seed distribution programs. Without access to improved seeds, efforts to intensify agricultural production and increase yields in those countries have suffered.

To maintain their current level of farm income without those inputs, small farmers have expanded their agricultural holdings. This extensification has led to deforestation, as in Tanzania and Cameroon, as well as to cultivation of marginally productive lands. Several African cases studies also point out that where expanding the agricultural frontier is not possible, farmers reduce fallow periods between plantings, thus increasing demands on soils. All these impacts weaken the long-term productivity of the soil and accelerate deforestation. Use of organic fertilizers has increased in some areas, although it has not offset the impact of declining access to chemical fertilizers. One positive benefit of the price increases is to reduce the amount of pesticides used by farmers.

Rising input prices hurt small farmers most severely because they cannot shift to more profitable cash crops to offset the rising costs. Commercial farmers, in contrast, can respond to changing input and output prices more effectively. Yet the rising costs of fuel, machinery, and spare parts have led to a reduction in mechanized agriculture in several countries. Depending on the country and crop mix, commercial farmers' input prices have been offset by higher producer prices, allowing them to continue intensification of agricultural production. Small farmers, such as those in Tanzania, when faced with the rising costs of tractor use, revert to using animal traction and shift production to marginal soils that do not warrant mechanized cultivation.

The change in relative prices caused by devaluation, coupled with its inflationary consequences, has led to a wide range of substitution effects that caused environmental problems. As the price of both imported and formal sector goods increased following devaluation, urban and rural consumers substituted products made in the informal sector for the more expensive ones. As energy sources, notably kerosene and petrol, became more expensive, fuelwood extraction increased for both heating and cooking. Further, many families are pushed to consume forest products grown in the wild, frequently intensifying competition and conflict with other villagers and villages.

Trade Liberalization
Whereas the environmental impacts of devaluation tend to be most significant in the African countries, liberalization of trade policy has

generated environmental impacts in all the countries included in this study. Those impacts are diverse and tend to have longer-term cumulative environmental effects. Moreover, the environmental impacts are largely country specific in that they reflect specific linkages between a tradeable goods sector and world markets. It should be noted that liberalized trade policies have been accompanied in some countries by revised investment policies that changed conditions for profit repatriation, local reinvestment requirements, and investment guarantees.

Increased Direct Foreign Investment in the Extractive Sector. Tanzania, Zambia, Jamaica, and Venezuela experienced significant increases in foreign investment in the mining sector. In Tanzania, the result was a 19 percent increase in mining's contribution to GDP in the late 1980s. Although Zambia's reliance on copper continues to decline, investment in metals and semiprecious stones is increasing. With liberalization of its trade regime, Venezuela registered a significant influx of foreign firms investing in oil, alumina, iron, and gold. Many of those activities are in the relatively unexplored eastern and jungle areas of the country. Jamaica, which has relied heavily on mineral exports since independence, has experienced increased foreign investment in bauxite mining.

With few exceptions, these new mining activities brought immediate and at times widespread environmental degradation. Industrial gold mining, which has expanded in eastern Venezuela along the Amazon, is virtually unregulated. Bauxite mining in Jamaica, although formally subject to strict legal standards, continues to contaminate the waters and soils in surrounding areas. Environmental problems in both the extraction and reconversion of tailings and mined lands have increased in these four countries as a result of liberalized trade regimes. The Tanzania, Zambia, and Venezuela studies do not simply restate the established fact that mining and extractive industries usually generate highly damaging environmental impacts unless accompanied by strict mitigation measures. The point they make is that increased extractive activities have been accompanied by a weakening of government capacity to manage and regulate those industries so as to minimize the environmental costs. This point is examined in some detail in the section on institutional impacts. In short, however, the failure to pair price corrections and trade liberalization with adequate policy reforms and institutional strengthening is generating higher revenues on the one hand but, on the other, is creating higher environmental costs to be absorbed by the public in the future.

Impacts on Industrial Production. Trade liberalization in the industrial sector had mixed environmental results. First, trade liberalization, coupled with devaluation, provided new industrial incentives in several of the countries, although the reported modest industrial expansion seems to be occurring for somewhat different reasons. Tanzania's basic industrial policy of relying on import- and capital-intensive industrialization was not fundamentally revised under its adjustment program, but changing economic incentives stimulated a significant increase in its underutilized industrial capacity. In Vietnam, trade policy reform was a centerpiece of the transformation of the economy from a centralized to a market-driven one. Jamaica, strapped for hard currency earnings, built its adjustment program around increased exports that included expansion of cement production for export to the Caribbean region and beyond. In Venezuela, which relied ever more heavily on petroleum exports, petrochemical industries proliferated. Pakistan's reform program restructured trade policy to reduce tariffs on imports and increase competitiveness of Pakistani goods, including leather articles.

The country studies report an increase or an anticipated increase in the environmental damage related to industrial growth. It is expected to increase pollution from pulp and paper, cement, and fertilizer production in Tanzania; in Venezuela, it is expected to degrade Lakes Maracaibo from petrochemical contamination and Valencia from growing industrialization. The environmental impacts in Pakistan are not clear. That study indicated that "large-scale manufacturing sectors were far less efficient users of labor and capital than small-scale manufacturing" and that new trade incentives would stimulate production of small-scale enterprises. Given that large-scale industries are also among the country's worst polluters, the shift to small enterprises could have the net effect of improving environmental performance in the industrial sector. However, the lack of enforcement and monitoring capability, coupled with small firms' lack of technical know-how, could, in the aggregate, increase the environmental damage caused by small-scale producers of leather and other goods. In short, the net effect in Pakistan will become clearer in several years.

Vietnam poses a particularly difficult set of development options related to the choice between a labor- and technology-intensive industrialization process or one characterized by energy-intensive heavy industries. The net environmental consequences of these options will be reflected to a certain degree in the immediate environmental impacts but, perhaps even more important, in the ability of the industrialization process to absorb the rapidly growing population. Failure to create sufficient industrial employment will significantly intensify pressures on the agricultural and forestry sectors and thereby cause significant environmental degradation. Further, the Vietnam study states that unless institutional reforms accompany the pursuit of export-oriented growth, "trade liberalization or currency devaluation may lead to a quantum increase in the export of natural resources and of pollution-intensive products. In such a case, the country will face the challenge of ensuring that resource depletion and environmental costs do not offset the benefits from trade expansion." El Salvador shares a similar challenge.

As with extractive industries, the country studies do not question the potential economic benefits that increased industrial activity will bring about for their respective countries. The underlying issue is the failure to implement adequate mitigation measures, strengthen government managerial and regulatory capacity, and effect other institutional reforms that will enable the price corrections to lead to positive environmental outcomes rather than weakening the environmental fabric of the countries.

The Agricultural Sector. Liberalized trade regimes have mixed results in the agricultural sector in the short-to-medium term. Trade policy reforms provided new incentives for farmers to increase production of cocoa and coffee in Cameroon. They have led to diversified cash crops, such as sesame, soy beans, grapes, cardamom, and other nontraditional crops in Tanzania and have enhanced the returns on cotton and cattle in Mali. Sugarcane production increased in Jamaica, potato production in Cameroon, and banana exports in Venezuela. Vietnam is now the world's third largest exporter of rice, owing largely to its liberalized trade policy. The importance of these changes cannot be understated given their potential contribution to improving rural incomes, reducing rural poverty, and thereby reducing poverty-induced environmental degradation.

In Venezuela, the economic and environmental effects of trade liberalization are mixed in the short term. Strong external demand for coffee and bananas may encourage on-farm investments, with accompanying positive environmental effects, in a country that has neglected its agricultural sector for decades. Rising beef prices brought about by liberalization encouraged extensification and deforestation—with negative environmental impacts—to expand grazing land for cattle. Overall, however, dismantling protectionist barriers, coupled with the removal of agricultural subsidies, has led to a decline in the agricultural sector's contribution to the GDP. Moreover, the decline in output has increased reliance on food imports and weakened incentives to intensify agricultural production of other than a few commodities. As a result of these changes, small farmers tend to extensify agricultural holdings, causing deforestation and cultivation of marginally productive soils. Many small farmers, faced with declining incomes, have left their farms in search of work in urban centers. Although many of these short-term impacts seem to be negative, rising food prices may provide greater incentives for investment in the agricultural sector in the medium and long terms.

Among the Zambian government's priorities is increasing foreign investment in commercial agriculture, with the intention of significantly increasing that sector's contribution to GDP and replacing the mining sector as the country's economic mainstay. Although aggregate agricultural productivity may rise, this policy reform is also causing conflicts: "indigenous farmers are up in arms" as they struggle to survive the economic and social dislocations associated with the adjustment process. The Zambian study raises more general concerns about trade policy reform, asserting that the "haste and blind implementation . . . with which the import liberalization has been implemented, without achieving export neutrality, . . . has resulted in a continued decline in domestic productive capacity and massive job losses. In 1993, formal sector employment shrank by 4 percent and unemployment stood at a record high of 87 percent." The underlying issue raised by this study is how to combine price reforms with policy and institutional reforms that will increase aggregate income while strengthening social equity and environmental performance as well.

New price signals from liberalized trade regimes have provided incentives to which small farmers and commercial producers seem to have responded in different ways. Commercial farmers are able to shift crops, absorb increases in input prices, and adjust to new marketing arrangements tied to external markets far more effectively than small producers. Concerned primarily with their own food security, reluctant to invest in crops whose prices are uncertain, and faced with rising input prices, small farmers in many of the countries studied revert to producing food crops often by extensifying agricultural production, reducing fallow periods, and overtaxing marginal lands. Vietnam is an important exception to the general trend perceived among the other countries.

Impacts on the Forestry Sector. Trade liberalization reforms influence the forestry sector either through reforms targeted directly at this sector, as in Cameroon, or indirectly through substitution of imported goods. In Cameroon, whose forestry sector is larger than the other countries', the government identified this sector as a major source of foreign currency earnings. International pressure prompted the government to enact a new Forestry Code with explicit long-term sustainable management criteria at its core. The failure of its implementation, corruption, and the lack of administrative capacity have allowed rampant deforestation and the loss of anticipated resource rents. Further, adjustment and trade reforms have increased the profitability of logging relative to other export crops and thereby accelerated deforestation. Tanzania, although not a major world supplier, also experienced a significant increase in timber extraction as trade reforms increased the exporting companies' profitability.

Trade liberalization increased the relative prices of imported energy sources such as petrol and kerosene in Tanzania and Zambia. In response, urban and rural dwellers substituted fuelwood and charcoal for the more costly energy sources. The net effect was to increase the rate of land clearance and deforestation. The country studies raise the point to underline this environmental cost of the price correction, not as an argument against the price correction per se.

Impacts on the Tourist Sector. To one degree or another, many of the countries studied rely on foreign currency earnings from the tourist industry to service foreign debt obligations and finance imports. Consequently, governments project expansion of the tourist sector to strengthen their balance of payments positions and their financial stability. Zambia expects that tourism will help replace copper revenues in coming years. Since Tanzania's independence in 1963, tourism has played an important role in the economy, and its contribution is expected to increase. It is the largest source of foreign exchange earnings in Jamaica, and Vietnam anticipates a major increase in tourist trade in coming years.

In Zambia, the documented increase in poverty and the accelerated depletion of big game species during the adjustment period have placed the tourism industry under increased pressure. Reductions in public sector investment for the national parks further reduce the economic viability of expanding tourism in the country. Despite the importance of tourism, Tanzania's tourist infrastructure deteriorated as habitats and ecosystems were degraded by a combination of factors ranging from increased pressures on habitats from nearby communities to budgetary reductions. In Jamaica, where devaluation significantly increased tourist activity, environmental problems are also growing significantly. Tourist enclaves, degradation of the marine environment, and social conflicts have accelerated during the adjustment process. Vietnam's economic restructuring program calls for significant domestic and foreign investment in the tourist trade.

The country studies, not hesitating to identify the negative environmental impacts of rapidly expanding tourist activities, recognize the important potential contribution of the tourist sector in generating new employment opportunities and raising incomes. The issue they stress is the failure to couple the new growth opportunities brought about by the economic reforms with both application of adequate environmental performance standards for the tourist sector and maintenance of government enforcement capabilities. In this context, the studies underscore the long-term environmental costs of failing to put in place adequate mitigation measures to limit the negative impacts on coastal wetlands, fisheries, freshwater resources, and neighboring communities.

Impacts on the Transport Sector. Trade liberalization in at least five countries, Tanzania, Zambia, El Salvador, Jamaica, and Vietnam, opened the door to the import of used cars, buses, and motor bikes. The vehicles are not subject to emissions inspections and, consequently, even highly polluting vehicles, often in dilapidated condition, have been allowed entry. Increased urban air pollution is one result. The country studies point out that liberalized trade policies allowing for import of poorly maintained used vehicles have not been accompanied by regulations that would limit their negative effects on air quality.

Summary of the Environmental Impacts of External Adjustments
The countries included in this study are, to a large degree, still implementing stabilization measures and have yet to see the full range of promised benefits of the supply-side improvements. Both devaluation and trade liberalization have had important and immediate effects on their extractive and agricultural economies. In some cases, the growth impacts are clearly positive; for example, new agricultural incentives have stimulated expansion and diversification of tradeable crops and shifts to nontraditional commodities. The environmental impacts of those shifts are positive in that they have improved relative returns to the agricultural sector, raised

farm incomes for some producers, and thereby encouraged on-farm investments. Over time, these improvements may also encourage the introduction of new technologies and reduce poverty-induced environmental damage.

One of the key points raised in the foregoing conclusions is that the environmental impacts of the external adjustments are determined largely by the farmers' status in the adjusting countries. Commercial producers are able to respond to new price incentives from international markets by diversifying crops, intensifying production, and continuing to introduce new technological improvements. They are also able to absorb the rising costs of agricultural inputs without major difficulty. In short, the changing ratio of inputs to producer prices has either remained favorable to commercial farmers or their expanded production has overridden the negative effects of relative price changes.

Small farmers and rural workers with little or no land cannot absorb the increased costs of agricultural inputs, such as seed and fertilizer, as easily; nor have they been able to respond as effectively to the new price incentives offered by trade liberalization. Given their precarious situation, the small farmers' priority is to ensure their families' food security, often by extensifying food production, with all the attendant environmental problems. There are indications that the small farmers' situation has opened opportunities for commercial farmers to expand their commercial land holdings, thereby increasing their benefits from the emerging economic system. The full impact of the emerging economic changes on small farmers and rural populations will become more evident when the impacts of internal adjustment, including fiscal policy reform, are taken into account.

The extractive sectors, including forestry and mining, have responded quickly to the new economic incentives. Expansion in these sectors created environmental problems, and although some are already visible, the studies suggest that the long-term impacts may be more serious. This point also applies to the tourist sector. Local employment may increase as new hotels and facilities are built, but environmental problems are already in evidence and are expected to intensify. Expanded industrial production, coupled with expanded transport systems relying on poorly maintained used equipment, will lower the quality of urban environments through rising air pollution levels. These environmental costs are not immutable features of the adjustment programs implemented in the nine countries. They often result from disregard for the effects of price changes on the environment and from the lack of complementary policy reforms prior to or during the economic restructuring process.

The trade-offs between modernization and environmental degradation are also brought into focus in an examination of external adjustments' impacts. A more definitive assessment is made later in the analysis when the benefits of increased economic diversification and international competitiveness are weighed more accurately against the costs linked to high transitional costs, declining environmental quality, growing rural poverty, and governments' weakened capacity to manage their natural resource bases. It must be pointed out, however, that the reforms that increased the short-term expansion of commodity production and extraction of natural resources have not yet generated significant forward or backward linkages in the economy.

Internal Adjustments

Fiscal Policy

Structural reforms required a major reduction in the provision of public sector goods and services in all the countries studied except Vietnam. The unequal distribution of those cutbacks and their consequences for poorer social groups are similar across the countries, as are their subsequent impacts in weakening each country's natural resource base. This review of fiscal reform impacts is divided into four sections: the reduction of subsidies to specific economic sectors, the reduction in agricultural extension services, the reduction of government environmental institutions' managerial or regulatory capacity, and the cutbacks in the provision of social services.

The Reduction of Subsidies. Prior to adjustment programs, agricultural subsidies included support for fertilizer and pesticides in Cameroon, credit support for small farmers in Mali, price and input support in Zambia and Tanzania, and implicit subsidies for irrigation water in Pakistan and Vietnam. As governments removed subsidies in Mali, Cameroon, Zambia, and Tanzania, agricultural inputs and credit moved beyond the reach of many small farmers. On the one hand, removal of subsidies for pesticides has reduced the potential negative environmental impacts of their application. On the other hand, however, without support for fertilizers, small farmers have extensified agricultural production and in the process accelerated deforestation, overtaxed soils, and intensified use of marginal agricultural lands. Although these problems may be particular to the transitional period, their impacts on incomes and rural poverty are considerable. The governments of Pakistan, Vietnam, and Zambia have not used adjustment programs to remove water subsidies; nor have they used price reforms to help correct such problems as waterlogging and salinization that were associated with previous subsidy programs. The result of failing to remove the subsidies is continued misallocation and inefficient use of a scarce resource.

Fuel subsidies were widely used in Cameroon and Tanzania prior to adjustment reforms to encourage the use of kerosene, petrol, and coal as a way to forestall fuelwood consumption. Removing those subsidies has had the anticipated effect of encouraging the felling of trees as farmers seek alternative fuel sources. An obvious environmental benefit of removing these subsidies is reduced consumption of fossil fuels, which contribute to air pollution. In Vietnam, price reforms exempt coal, oil, and electricity, which continue to enjoy implicit government subsidies.

Reductions in Extension Services. In no country has the reduction in extension services been more acutely felt than in Cameroon. Withdrawal of government services that include technical advice, provision of inputs, and credit facilities is an important factor leading some cocoa growers to abandon their plantations, with a resulting decline in productivity. At the same time, small farmers' outputs fell as government extension support disappeared. In the forestry sector, wardens, stripped of their means of transportation and confined to their offices, remain unable to ensure logging companies' compliance with the terms of their concessions and to collect resource rents agreed upon in government contracts. El Salvador experienced a similar collapse in extension services that included watershed management and training in cultivation techniques.

In response to anticipated negative impacts of fiscal retrenchment, the Malian government encouraged more active participation of village associations and local groups in developing and overseeing land management regimes. Likewise, in Tanzania, the government encouraged village associations and local groups to participate in implementing afforestation programs. This effort in decentralization was widely accepted, and it has improved production regimes and resource management. The apparent success of encouraging broader ownership and managerial responsibilities holds lessons for reducing the social and environmental costs of the adjustment process.

Reductions in Environmental Services. Governments reduced expenditures for environmental goods and infrastructure in every country except Vietnam. In Zambia, Tanzania, and Cameroon, policymakers tried to protect government employees while cutting out the funds that would allow them to perform their jobs properly. In Venezuela, the environmental ministry lost one-half its professional staff. In El Salvador, environmental institutions were systematically gutted over the years. In virtually all countries, even prior to adjustment, environmental protection expenditures were but a small part of national budgets. Those admittedly weak environmental institutions limited the effectiveness of government efforts to control the negative environmental impacts of private sector activities. Even considering those institutional weaknesses, the cutbacks under adjustment programs led nonetheless to a noticeable, and often sharp, additional decline in those institutions' managerial and enforcement capacity.

Reductions in Social Services. With the exception of Vietnam, all countries seriously reduced the quality and scope of government-provided social services. The impacts of these reductions on the standard of living and the breadth and incidence of poverty in all countries range from serious to drastic. The rural poor and women in general suffered most severely from these cutbacks, although in the highly urbanized Venezuelan society, poor urban women have been the most directly affected. Programs in education, health care, and employment training were most regularly reduced. A more inclusive treatment of the issue is offered later in the discussion of indirect impacts.

Monetary Policy
With the exception of Venezuela, monetary policy reforms have had a comparatively minor impact on the environment in the nine countries under consideration. The Venezuelan case is somewhat unique in that the profound crisis in the financial sector, linked to changes in the exchange rate policy, jeopardized the nation's economic stability and ultimately required sweeping financial reforms. This broader economic instability generated significant indirect environmental effects because of the impact on the declining standard of living of the lower- and middle-income sectors. Access by small farmers to credit is documented in several countries, including Cameroon. Unavailability of credit is caused not so much by rising interest rates but more by the dismantling of local cooperative and other credit institutions to which farmers had previously had easy access. Without credit,

farmers have cut back on purchasing inputs, farm machinery, and traction animals and have tried to maintain their income levels by expanding the area cultivated. The end result is a push toward deforestation and a tendency to overtax marginal agricultural lands.

Privatization

Privatization has taken quite different forms and has led to economic effects of varying importance in the countries studied. In the African countries of Zambia, Mali, and Tanzania, privatization involved downsizing or dismantling state marketing boards for agricultural products and divesting transportation systems to the private sector. In Venezuela, divestiture of state-owned companies included but was not limited to airports, hotels, agroindustries, telephone systems, banks, and construction companies. In Pakistan, privatization of similar magnitude was initiated during the 1980s and expanded in the early 1990s. In Vietnam, basic changes in land use rights were a pillar of the country's economic reform program. The state still owns all land, but under the 1993 Land Law, the "right to use, exchange, inherit, cultivate and build on land has now been granted to households. For agricultural cultivation, the land grant is given for 20 years and for perennial crops for a period of 50 years."

Among all these countries, the net environmental impact of privatization varies. For example, none of the African studies questioned the urgency of privatizing the agricultural marketing boards and transportation systems in those countries given that their state-run enterprises had been frequent sources of corruption and financial mismanagement for decades. The studies do point out, however, that one of the short-term effects of changing ownership is a significant disruption of marketing systems. Lack of confidence in the new, as yet patchwork, marketing and transportation systems discouraged investment in cash crops and has led to a decline in farmers' incomes. The net short-term result is extensification of agricultural production, with the attendant negative environmental impacts. These transitional costs were apparently not taken into account in planning the privatization process. Another common experience is that higher product prices were not passed on to producers and thus increased the merchants' and transport companies' profit margins. The expectation remains, nonetheless, that more efficient and competitive marketing and transportation systems will evolve over time as the government's direct economic interventions are reduced. If returns to producers increase as anticipated, there are grounds to expect that new economic opportunities and incentives will lead to an increase in on-farm investment, the introduction of new production technologies, and the implementation of more environmentally sound agricultural practices.

The Venezuelan study did not examine the environmental effects of privatizing the scores of state-owned companies. The study recognizes that "a massive privatization program" is "indispensable" to improving the country's economic situation. However, the study also raises basic concerns about carrying out a sweeping privatization process "without a strategic definition of policy regarding the public sector's participation in the new economic structure taking shape." The Pakistan study did not cover the environmental impacts of privatization.

The clarification of land use rights in Vietnam is expected to generate considerable environmental benefits in both the immediate and long terms in that property rights will be secure, enforceable, and transferrable.

Summary of the Direct Environmental Impacts of Internal Adjustments

Internal adjustment measures have had broad environmental impacts. When subsidies are removed, the impacts are direct and often immediate. The studies generally recognize the need to withdraw price supports and subsidies in order to increase efficient allocation of resources and reduce the drain on national budgets. But the studies take issue with the process followed in these countries: some subsidies were removed while others were not, and maintenance of some subsidies benefited the wealthy while removal of other subsidies fell on the more vulnerable. They also question the net impact of subsidy removal when transitional compensatory or mitigation actions are not taken to ensure maintenance of living standards of the poor, particularly the small farmers.

As regards reductions in agricultural extension activities and social services, the impacts fall decisively on the poor, and most directly on the rural poor and women. The cutbacks not only weakened social services and survival safety nets but led governments to withdraw goods and services that contributed to increasing the long-term productivity of the rural populations, often the poorest in the nine societies. The impacts of these fiscal reductions on the poorest sectors have further weakened small farmers' ability to respond to the new economic incentives emanating from the export-oriented growth strategy. Loss of credit for agricultural inputs, such as hybrid seeds and fertilizer, the reduction of agricultural extension services to encourage intensification of production, and the disruption of marketing systems caused by privatization are among the most direct effects of internal economic adjustments on rural populations. These changes generated downward pressure on the living standards of the poor and, in the process, accelerated the most intractable environmental problem facing many countries—that is, poverty-induced environmental degradation.

The country studies affirm the need for extensive privatization programs. The positive effects of reducing fiscal deficits, increasing efficiency, rooting out corruption, and ultimately creating new employment have to be balanced against the short-term dislocations and negative social impacts, including widespread layoffs and disruption of marketing systems. The environmental impacts of privatization vary from industry to industry and country to country; consequently, they must be assessed on a case-by-case basis. In addition, those impacts must be assessed over time to ensure that long-term benefits are weighed against short-term costs.

INDIRECT ENVIRONMENTAL IMPACTS OF ECONOMIC REFORMS

The preceding section focused on the direct linkages between macroeconomic instruments and specific environmental problems. This section examines how those same macroeconomic instruments affected functions of the state, social structure, and social institutions. Moreover, it examines how those social changes alter the ways that the state and various social groups use and manage the country's natural resources. The conclusions about these indirect impacts describe how the adjustment process influences a society's human and institutional capital and, in turn, how those changes affect use of the country's natural capital.

Social Impacts

An understanding of how adjustment changes social structures and thus the environment requires consideration of the impacts on the breadth and depth of poverty in the adjusting countries. There are two main considerations here: first, the impacts of adjustment on labor markets and, in particular, on "informalization of the economy" and second, the effects of changes in social services on poverty. Taken together, these changes' influence on the patterns and intensity of environmental pressures is assessed.

Impacts on Labor Markets

Realignment of labor markets took place through several complementary processes in the nine adjusting countries. For example, the recessions that accompanied the stabilization stage of adjustment programs placed a strong downward pressure on wages in many countries. Government layoffs in both the public sector enterprises and government agencies were particularly influential in this regard in Cameroon, Mali, Tanzania, Zambia, Jamaica, Venezuela, and Vietnam. Sharp economic contraction in Venezuela during the adjustment period led to layoffs in many private firms, adding to the growing ranks of the unemployed. In Tanzania, trade liberalization and increased competition from international markets contributed to the collapse of small and medium-size businesses. During the adjustment process in Jamaica, labor markets were affected by the reduced share of income distributed to workers relative to capital.

These and many other changes in formal sector employment opportunities and the supply cost of labor led to informalization of the economy in many countries. Contraction of the formal sector often predated but then continued or accelerated during the adjustment process. Formal sector employment in Zambia, for example, declined from 24 percent to 10 percent during the 1980s and then shrank another 4 percent between 1990 and 1993. Cameroon's experience was similar.

Without employment prospects in the formal sector, unemployed workers pursue activities in the informal sector to ensure their survival. Urban vendors, artisans, and microentrepreneurs have proliferated. In periurban areas of some countries, many underemployed families began cultivating food crops. In rural areas, families turned to using natural resources to survive through producing charcoal, capturing wildlife, and brewing home beer.

Migration accompanied informalization of the economy through different combinations of push-pull factors. In Cameroon and Zambia, at least initially, the policy seems to have sparked a return to rural areas, particularly among unemployed government workers. As pointed out in the Cameroon study, new farmers have begun to appear in the villages, thereby increasing pressures on local natural resources. In Mali and Tanzania, increasingly difficult conditions in the countryside seem to have strengthened movement toward urban areas. With little cultivable land available on steep hillsides in Jamaica, rural families have opted to move to the cities. In Venezuela, failure of the adjustment program to stimulate economic opportunities for small farmers accelerated rural-to-urban

A NEW WAY OF SEEING OUR ENVIRONMENT

Earthscan Publications Ltd

120 Pentonville Road, London N1 9JN   Tel (44) 171 278 0433   Fax (44) 171 278 1142   E-mail earthinfo@earthscan.co.uk

Photo © Maggie Murray/Format Photographers, London

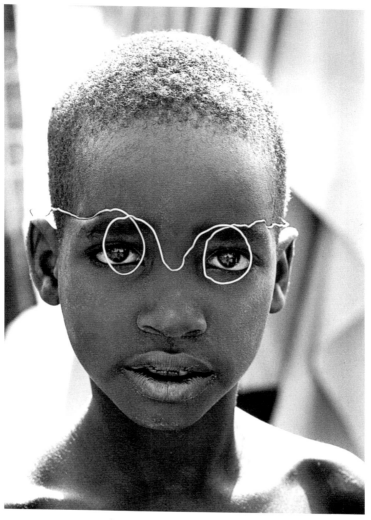

http://www.earthscan.co.uk

migration, significantly increasing pressure on sanitation and water facilities. Pakistan and Vietnam face similar migratory trends. In El Salvador, the growth spurt, based on commerce, industry, services, and other urban economic activities, has encouraged rural-to-urban migration, particularly as rural economic activity remains depressed.

Not all research teams examined in detail the impacts of adjustment on their countries' respective labor markets. All did, however, recognize the important changes that have taken place in the status of workers, be it through employment instability, informalization of the economy, loss of benefits, or a decline in real purchasing power. Individually and in the aggregate, those changes leave the working sectors of adjusting societies in more precarious and unstable living conditions. The studies of Venezuela, Tanzania, and Jamaica indicate that the elites have been able to consolidate if not improve their economic standing as the reforms have taken hold. The experience in El Salvador confirms the point that adjustment has allowed the elites to shift their resources to the financial and commercial sectors of the economy, with few benefits accruing to the rural poor.

Reductions in Social Services

Provision of basic social services goes hand in hand with creation of employment opportunities as requisites for maintaining the living standards of the poor and most vulnerable sectors of adjusting societies. By and large, the country studies did not concentrate on social services but offered overall statistics and summary statements regarding the relative changes in social services delivery under their respective adjustment programs. Reductions in seven of the nine countries, El Salvador and Vietnam excepted, ranged from serious to drastic in the quality and/or quantity of social services provided by the government to the most vulnerable sectors of society. Education and health are among the areas frequently identified as receiving most serious cutbacks. These reductions are integral to bringing government expenditures in line with revenues.

All those reductions take different forms, but all ultimately contribute to a decline in the living standard of the poorer sectors of the seven countries. In Cameroon, for example, delivery of the already limited education and health services has declined significantly, particularly in rural areas. At the rural-community level, budgetary cutbacks range from one-half to two-thirds the previous allocations. Consequently, the number of doctors, health workers, teachers, and educators providing services to the poor has plummeted. Similar experiences are documented in Tanzania,

Zambia, and Mali, leading to lower school attendance rates, higher dropout rates, higher child mortality rates, and increased cases of diseases associated with malnutrition and inadequate sanitary facilities. Decreases are often hard to measure with absolute certainty, but the local case studies provide adequate examples of these changes and their impacts on the social fabric and well-being of local communities.

The Jamaica study points out the steady trend of reducing various social expenditure components since the 1980s. The trend in cutting government expenditures continued during the adjustment period. The Pakistan study asserts that long-standing social inequalities and neglect of social services for the impoverished has left Pakistan with some of the worst social indicators in the world. The study states that a basic objective of structural reform has been to increase resources available for development relative to the demands of the military and to external debt servicing. That objective has not been accomplished under the structural adjustment process, leaving basic social services out of reach of many Pakistan citizens. The Venezuela study provides a comprehensive analysis of the decline, often the collapse, of social services under the adjustment program. The decreasing availability of social services is best documented in urban areas but is applicable to the rural sector as well. The analysis further asserts that the compensatory antipoverty plan implemented as part of the adjustment program, by gaining public attention and generating short-term improvements, has allowed the government to reduce basic social services that formed the backbone of traditional government programs.

Incidence of Poverty

Changed labor markets and reduced delivery of social services converge to influence the breadth and depth of poverty in these adjusting countries. It is the overall impact on poverty, rural and urban, that results in major changes in rates and patterns of use of natural resources and environmental services. As pointed out at the beginning of this chapter, all countries included in the study have faced structural poverty for decades, and most, in fact, have experienced the deepening grip of poverty on their societies within the past decade.

Despite efforts to isolate environmental impacts of adjustment from existing trends, it is clearly impossible to make that separation absolute. This methodological difficulty pertains to the issue of poverty as well and thus underscores the importance of recognizing that all the impacts of poverty-induced environmental degradation occurring under adjustment in these nine countries cannot be ascribed exclusively to the adjustment process per se. However, what can be said unequivocally is that poverty has increased during the adjustment process in seven of the nine countries and in some countries has worsened sharply. In El Salvador, rural poverty remains pervasive; the collapse of rural livelihoods that occurred prior to the adjustment process has not been reversed. Vietnam is an exception to the trend documented in the other countries.

The inability to earn stable incomes through the formal labor market, coupled with the decline if not disappearance of social services in many communities, has forced individuals, families, and communities in the four African countries to rely increasingly on natural resources and environmental goods, which tend to be "free and available," for survival. Unemployed civil servants have returned to the countryside despite the shrinking limits of the external agricultural frontier. Rural farmers expanded their agricultural lands by cutting down forests. They substituted forest resources and vegetative cover for fossil fuels. They supplemented their agricultural produce with nuts, berries, and game from surrounding forests and steppes. They mined streambeds for gold and semiprecious stones. They embarked on business activities based on using natural resources in hunting, exporting animal species, producing charcoal, and brewing home beer. Each of these steps seeking to ensure their survival has come at the expense of consuming or straining the productivity of natural resources.

The poorest, most vulnerable sectors of the five other countries have much in common with the African experience in their efforts to survive. In Venezuela, the rural poor have mined gold in tributaries of the Amazon and have captured lizards in protected areas for export to American and European markets. In Jamaica, farmers have expanded coffee production to ever-steeper hillsides. In El Salvador, farmers have denuded hillsides at even the highest elevations. In Vietnam, with farms already subdivided into minuscule parcels, the growing rural population has moved into and cleared tens of thousands of hectares of forests in protected areas to expand agricultural lands.

In addition, the impacts of poverty on the environment in the non-African countries have spilled over to the urban areas, where the rural poor often migrate to escape their destitution. Rural-to-urban migration has accelerated in Venezuela, where new arrivals build shacks on steep outlying areas in new shanty towns. As urban population density increases, pressures on hygienic facilities increase proportionately and the urban environment becomes more polluted and unsanitary. As in Venezuela, rising urban population densities in Jamaica are accompanied by worsening pollution and contamination problems, increased crime, and social disintegration. Urban sprawl in Karachi, fueled by the arrival of hundreds of thousands during the past decade, has overwhelmed the limited and outdated water, sanitation, and environmental infrastructure, not to mention the forces of law and order.

A major problem identified in the majority of the studies is that women bear the brunt of downward pressures on living standards. Women carry responsibilities not only as householders but also as farmers, fuelwood collectors, and water bearers in all countries. The pressures to secure means for their families' survival in the face of diminished social services, declining agricultural productivity, and inadequate educational opportunities and family planning possibilities have intensified. Women's disproportionate burden, it should be noted, is clearly not limited to the adjustment experience alone.

Institutional Impacts

The conclusions regarding the adjustment programs' institutional impacts and their subsequent environmental effects are divided into two main sections. The first summarizes the governments' ability to manage natural resources and regulate activities that generate social costs. The second concerns social institutions, that is, institutions of civil society, through which the public has tried to improve management of its environmental patrimony.

Government Institutional Capacity

Seven of the nine countries, Vietnam and Pakistan excepted, report significant or Draconian reductions in their respective government's ability to manage pressing environmental matters. (The Pakistan study does not cover changes in fiscal policy.) The norm among those countries is cutbacks so severe that basic resource management functions have been gutted or paralyzed. In Cameroon, cuts in the forestry service budget resulted in failure to police logging concessions to ensure compliance with sustainable forest management and collect resource rents agreed upon in contracts between private logging firms and the government. In Tanzania, although foreign direct investment in the extractive sector has increased, government allocations for monitoring those activities have declined. In Mali, severe fiscal constraints have led to a reduction of extension services and natural resource management. One positive response to the decrease in central government expenditures is decentralization of decisionmaking, giving local communities greater responsibility in planning agricultural production and natural resource management.

In the non-African countries, cutbacks are equally important. For example, the Jamaican government planned a 50 percent cut in environmental expenditures that was halted only by external donors, who tied their financial support to restoring environmental protection programs. In Venezuela, institutional fragmentation of environmental functions has worsened within the government since adjustment began in 1989, and it has been aggravated by a 40 percent reduction in real budgetary allocations for personnel in the Ministry of the Environment. Prior government plans to strengthen the monitoring of environmental impacts of petroleum and petrochemical companies' activities have been abandoned.

In no country have institutional impacts been so severe as in El Salvador. Under the call for fiscal discipline, adjustment programs have "eliminated budgets that held together the institutions directly related to natural resource management, forcing their collapse and the dispersion of national technical capacity." The national managerial capability has been removed and the regional and local functions allowed to decline. As the adjustment process proceeded in that country, national-level institutions were put in place. However, the environmental interests they are to promote have garnered only minimal interest and support throughout operational institutions, thus leaving them with ceremonial and diplomatic functions, including responsibility for responding to external donors.

Capacity of Civil Society

The Venezuela case study opens new ground in understanding the impacts of adjustment programs on civil institutions that address environmental problems. In examining the impacts on the approximately 200 environmental nongovernmental organizations (NGOs) (out of a total of 8,000 community-based organizations concerned with a wide range of social issues), the researchers documented the fact that the declining living standards of both the middle- and low-income sectors weakened their ability to sustain community-based organizations. In light of the precarious economic and social conditions, the very survival of organizations based in low-income areas is placed at risk. Moreover, whereas cooperation among organizations from the different social strata was commonplace prior to adjustment, after adjustment the two sectors have competed against each other as they sought to gain access to a smaller pool of funding and programs. In short, adjustment not only weakened the ability of the groups to deal with such issues as local contamination and toxic waste dumping, water sanitation, and resource management, but it has also allowed social disintegration and antagonism to replace cooperation and joint management efforts.

Summary of the Indirect Environmental Impacts of Economic Reforms

Only Vietnam has experienced a significant decline in poverty as a result of its adjustment program, and this improvement is expected to continue. Poverty has deepened in seven of the nine countries, and it continues to be pervasive in El Salvador. In these countries, the "informalization of the economy," declining agricultural productivity in many areas, diminishing access to agricultural inputs and technical advice, and increasing population pressures have converged to lower living standards, particularly among the rural poor. Cutbacks in social services have weakened the survival systems of the most vulnerable. The poor respond to their falling standards of living by migrating and by increasing their reliance on natural resources. Depending on conditions in each country, the direction of migration varies: in some African countries, the poor tend to move back to the land; in El Salvador, Jamaica, and Venezuela, they move to urban areas. Jamaicans often emigrate from the island to the United States and Canada. Those who remain survive through agricultural extensification, deforestation, intensified use of marginal lands, and a wide range of informal productive activities ranging from brewing home beer to catching animal species for export. The decline in living standards has been accompanied by a weakening of institutions of both the government and civil society involved in managing and protecting the environment. The institutional decline resulted in the loss of resource rents, weakened control over natural resource management, and increased extraction of natural capital. In short, the social and institutional impacts of adjustment measures transmitted to the environment are profound, and they may have long-term consequences.

GENERAL SUMMARY

Traditional measures of macroeconomic performance provide ample evidence that adjustment programs are having their desired effects.

Aggregate production and per capita GDP are up in most countries studied. Agricultural exports have increased and are now somewhat more diversified in most of the countries. If this trend continues as economic reforms deepen, agricultural incomes are likely to rise, possibly encouraging intensified production. Revenues from timber, fossil fuel, mineral, semiprecious stone, and other extractive industries have risen, and fledgling industrial sectors have new market opportunities and incentives in some countries. Budget deficits have declined and inflation brought under control in many countries. These economic gains often accrued during the stabilization phase of the adjustment programs, indicating that anticipated supply-side response will bring greater economic benefits in the future.

The improvement in traditional economic indicators seems to contrast with the broader social and environmental impacts described in the country studies. This imbalance raises questions about the trade-offs policymakers must consider when designing and implementing comprehensive economic reforms. As regards the social dimension, for example, there are consistent and disturbing trends in the deepening of poverty in rural and urban areas in virtually all countries included in the study. The structural poor in many countries have been joined by the new poor, who lost employment, social services, and other support systems during the adjustment process. Not only have the ranks of the poor grown, but distributional inequalities have also increased in most of the countries studied, and at this stage of the adjustment process, they show no signs of improving.

The environmental impacts of the adjustment process are mixed. Some price reforms have positive environmental impacts, for example, by intensifying commercial agricultural production, promoting less-erosive crop mixes, and reducing subsidies for agricultural inputs. Others have negative outcomes, as exemplified by widespread extensification of subsistence farming, acceleration of deforestation, and overtaxing of soil productivity. Downward pressures on living standards and informalization of the economy have obliged many urban and rural poor to increase their reliance and pressures on natural resources and environmental services just to survive.

Presented below are five general conclusions that help explain the complexity of the outcomes of the adjustment process on the economic, social, and environmental aspects of life in the adjusting countries.

1. As stated in the introductory chapters, the nine studies confirm the fact that the structural adjustment programs facilitated integration of the

countries' economies into the emerging global market system by adopting a development strategy based on:

- promotion of outward-oriented growth;
- expansion of the private sector's role as the growth process's driving force;
- removal of barriers to international capital flows;
- diminution of the state's economic role; and
- deregulation and restructuring of domestic labor markets.

The adjustment programs differ from the emerging export-oriented economic model only in that these programmatic instruments compress and accelerate economic reforms to help countries adjust more rapidly to international market conditions. Thus the applicability and relevance of the accompanying conclusions regarding environmental impacts can be extended beyond adjustment programs per se to the emerging economic order more generally.

2. Integration of the nine countries into the emerging market system by changing relative prices—that is, by "getting the prices right"—has generated mixed environmental impacts. The direct linkages between macroeconomic instruments, whether external adjustments accomplished through exchange rate and trade policy reforms or internal corrections using fiscal and monetary policy reforms, and specific environmental problems vary significantly among countries. Environmental effects depend on specific components of the reform packages, the incentive structure in place prior to adjustment, and the institutional medium through which the reforms are implemented.

The studies found that many price corrections associated with adjustment programs hold the potential for effecting positive economic *and* environmental outcomes. But they often do not realize this potential because price corrections are not accompanied by complementary policy and institutional reforms. The removal of some but not all subsidies, an unwillingness to internalize environmental costs, the failure to correct legal and land tenure problems, and the omission of transitional and mitigation programs are among the consistently disregarded policy reforms that would strengthen the positive effects of price corrections. This mixed environmental record reflects the lack of intentionality to use the adjustment process to strengthen national environmental performance as a vital component of a country's long-term economic growth.

3. The environmental impacts of structural adjustment programs differ according to the kind of economy undergoing reform, that is, whether they are extractive, agricultural, manufacturing, or information/service economies. The nine countries included in this study are predominantly extractive and agricultural economies.

- A principal response of extractive economies to structural adjustment programs was to expand and intensify extraction of natural resources to be traded on international markets. This is consistent with the types of policy changes applied, including removing barriers to capital flows, encouraging expansion of the export sector, and reducing the state's regulatory capacity as regards natural resource management. Under these conditions, the environmental impacts have been quite damaging, and indications are that these negative effects will be cumulative.

- In agricultural economies, the commercial and subsistence sectors have reacted quite differently to new price signals. Commercial farmers responded to the new price signals transmitted from the outward-oriented growth model by expanding and often diversifying production. The ability of medium-size to large commercial farmers to respond to new prices, to work within emerging marketing conditions, and to use inputs more efficiently often enabled them to absorb the deteriorating ratio of input-producer product prices experienced in some countries. There have been some positive environmental improvements associated with these changes, and their intensified agricultural production should strengthen those positive impacts over time. Whether those improvements materialize will depend largely on the strength of the government's environmental managerial capabilities and the market-based incentives integrated into the economic system.

    In contrast, subsistence farmers extensified production in response to deteriorating economic and social conditions, leading to major environmental damage. In some countries, farmers are confronted by both internal and external agricultural frontiers. Rural families with little or no land have no alternative but to intensify pressure on marginally productive agricultural areas or enter the growing ranks of informal workers in urban centers. The mutually reinforcing character of deepening poverty and environmental degradation in broad areas of some countries indicates that environmental problems will worsen in coming years.

The overall response and environmental impacts depend largely on the relative size and the economic and social conditions of those two sectors.

- The previous WWF study included two diversified manufacturing economies, Mexico and Thailand. Their manufacturing sectors underwent major changes as they adjusted to intensified international competition, reduced government subsidies, and privatization programs. Their reforms' environmental impacts ranged from more efficient use of increasingly scarce natural resources to higher levels of pollution caused by increased, albeit more efficient, industrial production. The potential environmental gains were frequently offset by the failure to implement complementary policy and institutional reforms.

  It should be pointed out that those two economies also had important extractive and agricultural sectors whose response to deeper integration into international markets was quite similar to the experience of the nine countries studied, as summarized above. That response included increased opportunities for commercial farmers coupled with downward pressure on wages and living standards of the poor, particularly the rural poor. As in the nine countries, the poor intensified pressure on available but often marginal agricultural lands, and they mined natural resources in order to survive. When they exhausted those limited, often short-term opportunities, the rural poor spilled into urban areas to be absorbed into the informal sector associated with the manufacturing economy.

- Neither the current nor the previous study examined the environmental impacts on information/service economies.

4. Structural adjustment programs affect social classes and groups to varying degrees and in distinct ways; moreover, adjustment effects different changes in the ways those social groups interact with and rely on the country's environment and natural resources.

- In the stabilization phase, the benefits of the adjustment programs have accrued more consistently to the wealthy, the export-oriented producers and merchants, the commercial farmers, and the investors in extractive industries. The environmental impacts of these more dynamic, better-off, or dominant social sectors as they respond to new market conditions differ, sometimes improving environmental performance, sometimes weakening the country's environmental fabric. A main factor in determining the environmental impacts of economic agents is the effectiveness of national regulatory and management regimes and the scope of complementary government policies.

- To date, many adjustment program costs have been shouldered by landless and subsistence farmers, workers in the rural and urban informal sectors, urban consumers, redundant employees, and women. Their standard of living has declined owing largely to the combined effects of price corrections, government fiscal policy reforms, and changes in functions of the state. Although some migrate, the dominant response of the poor to downward pressure on their living standards is to increase pressure on the environment and natural resources in order to survive. This poverty-induced environmental degradation is often characterized by irreversible impacts on natural resources and services provided by the environment.

- Economic and social inequalities between these groups have grown during adjustment. Although better-off groups can respond more efficiently to new price incentives, the more vulnerable groups often exhaust their productive assets to survive. Failure to implement corrective social policy to address the growing social inequities also undermines the potential positive economic and environmental outcomes of price corrections.

5. The changing role of the state has had significant environmental effects. Reducing the state's role as an economic agent is a major contribution of adjustment programs in helping to reduce government mismanagement and correct fiscal imbalances. The country studies point out the role of predatory and feudal governments having little accountability to broader civil society prior to and during adjustment. In many countries, the adjustment process has brought to light the deleterious economic and social effects of state actions.

Accompanying this positive change, however, was the widespread and detrimental weakening and dismantling of government institutions that have undermined economic reforms, jeopardized social stability, and weakened environmental sustainability. Fiscal reductions diminished government agencies' ability to manage and protect natural resources, internalize the environmental costs of expanded economic activity, develop sorely needed environmental infrastructure, and provide basic public goods and services.

The cutbacks reduced—often drastically—social services, extension services, and other programs that were core elements of government's redistributive function and its role as guarantor of basic conditions of social equity.

Moreover, in reducing government capacity on many levels, the policy and institutional reforms that should complement price corrections were not formulated. Were they to be developed, the countries would have a weakened capacity to implement them. Paradoxically, it may now be more difficult for the market forces being strengthened through adjustment to work effectively because the governments' ability to correct market and policy failures has been diminished. With the disappearance of the state as provider of fundamental services and equitable societal conditions, future social development is much at the mercy of the changing demands and requirements of the international marketplace.

In sum, the studies confirm the contributions of structural reforms to improving aggregate economic indicators, but they also pose challenges to some of the adjustment programs' operative assumptions in these nine countries. They affirm the positive impacts of expanding and diversifying agricultural production, correcting some government policy failures, and removing major structural impediments and inefficiencies. At the same time, the studies question whether the traditional macroeconomic reform prescription for "getting the prices right" is adequate to address the economic, not to mention the social and environmental, needs of these countries.

The country studies highlight the costs of implementing adjustment programs that fail to take into account the type of economy undergoing adjustment, social structures, the relative size of the formal and informal sectors of the adjusting economies, and the breadth, depth, and characteristics of poverty. In particular, the studies document the fact that reform program benefits often accrue to the relatively better-off sectors of the societies while the costs associated with the restructuring process often fall on those social sectors least able to absorb them. The studies thus bring into focus important economic, social, and environmental trends that will shape these countries as they deepen their integration into the emerging international economic order.

ENDNOTES

1. The full country studies were the basis for the conclusions presented in Chapters 12 and 13.
2. I would like to acknowledge the contributions of AIDEnvironment (Amsterdam) in interpreting the impacts of adjustment programs on water, soil, and forests in the nine countries included in this study. See T.T. Verkuyl, *Structural Adjustment and Natural Resources: Life Support Systems under Pressure* (Washington, D.C.: WWF-International, 1996).

13

CONCLUSIONS: IMPACTS OF STRUCTURAL ADJUSTMENT ON THE SUSTAINABILITY OF DEVELOPING COUNTRIES

by David Reed

The nine case studies illustrate the difficulties facing policymakers of developing countries in providing minimal conditions of survival and well-being for their populations. Each country examined has been beset by crises, sometimes short-term, other times deeply rooted and structural, that threaten the viability of its economic foundations, its social structures, and the integrity of its natural resource base.

The content of adjustment programs does not differ in any fundamental way from the emerging development paradigm based on outward-oriented growth, a diminished role of the state, greater influence of private sector funds, and restructured labor markets. In fact, structural adjustment has been the programmatic means of helping countries become integrated into that rapidly changing international market system.

Structural adjustment programs designed to pull the economies out of crisis and raise them to higher growth rates have not explicitly considered their environmental impacts. The preceding analysis shows that the environmental impacts caused by changing relative prices are mixed— that is, they are sometimes positive, sometimes negative, depending on prior economic conditions and the specific reforms being implemented. The environmental impacts caused by changes in social structures and institutions under adjustment programs are often more serious and widespread than the direct effects of price changes. None of the reform programs explicitly considered the impacts that the restructuring of the economies might have on societies' long-term sustainability. That is the issue addressed below.

Chapter 2 sets forth a normative definition of sustainable development, stating that sustainable development means improving the quality of human life while living within the carrying capacity of supporting ecosystems. The objective of sustainable development is to improve the quality of human life, and the condition for reaching that objective is to respect the earth's ecosystems. That definition affirms the fact that there are three basic pillars of sustainability—the social, environmental, and economic—and given that these three components are intimately interrelated, efforts to promote sustainability must support all three components. That normative statement concluded by affirming that together these three components "should converge in such a way as to generate a steady stream of income, ensure social equity, pursue socially agreed upon population levels, maintain human-generated and natural capital stocks, and protect the life-giving services of the environment."

Assessing the impacts of structural adjustment and the emerging development model on the sustainability of the development paths pursued by the nine countries is based on this statement on sustainable development. The discussion begins by reviewing the specific elements of the economic component of sustainable development and then proceeding to points under the social and environmental components of sustainability. Following from that summary, several general issues are raised regarding the challenges of promoting the transition to sustainable development in the context of the emerging export-oriented development model.

It should be made clear from the outset that the standard used in this assessment is not whether the adjustment process has actually placed the countries on a sustainable development path. None of the countries was on a sustainable path before adjustment, and given the crisis conditions facing each country, it is unrealistic to expect that economic restructuring actually accomplished such a societal transformation or radical change in development strategy. Rather, the question is one of direction and tendency. Has adjustment to international economic conditions helped move countries toward a more sustainable development path by creating conditions through which long-term improvements in the countries' economies, social systems, and natural resources can take place? Or to the contrary, has the adjustment process created economic conditions, social relations, and environmental problems that will hinder pursuit of sustainable development in the long run? The assessment offered below is seldom definitive and, in many cases, can only pose questions whose answers will become apparent as the contours of the emerging global economy sharpen in coming years.

The Economic Dimension of Sustainable Development

The main issue in assessing the economic dimension of sustainable development is whether the adjustment process will help countries generate a steady stream of income as they are integrated more intimately into the global market system. A central feature of this assessment is understanding the degree to which the economic structures being put in place will strengthen the long-term productive capacity of the country, diversify its economic base, and strengthen its ability to respond to negative external conditions.

Sound Macroeconomic Management

With few exceptions, the adjustment programs have helped the countries improve, albeit modestly, traditional macroeconomic indicators through increasing aggregate productivity, improving current account balances, and lowering fiscal deficits. International capital flows have improved as a result of the adjustment programs in countries such as El Salvador and Vietnam, but they have been much slower to materialize in other countries, particularly in Africa, except for private investments in extractive industries. With the exception of El Salvador, major debt overhang continues to limit the resources available to domestic economies for development activities.

These improvements represent important steps toward pursuing sustainable development strategies. They indicate the commitment of governments to exercise financial discipline and to live within the countries' income levels. They demonstrate a willingness to undertake major economic reforms to increase efficiency and to abandon development approaches that are no longer in keeping with emerging economic conditions.

Two basic challenges regarding sound macroeconomic management and stability warrant attention in most countries. The first relates to the prospects of obtaining debt relief from international creditors, including multilateral lenders. No amount of fiscal discipline or more efficient use of resources will spawn sustained economic growth unless the debt burden is significantly reduced, particularly for highly indebted low-income countries. Second, sound macroeconomic management does not ensure integration of these extractive and agricultural economies into international markets on terms that will promote stability, access to markets, or fair terms of trade. Sound macroeconomic management promoted through adjustment measures can enhance the resilience of these small economies but cannot ensure their longer-term viability or sustainability when they face adverse external conditions in an export-oriented world economy.

Poverty-alleviating Growth

The stabilization phase of the adjustment process has had a net negative impact in generating employment opportunities for the poor, most vulnerable sectors of those societies. Recessions and economic dislocations associated with the implementation of adjustment programs have expanded the ranks of the under- and unemployed, worsened working conditions, and led to expansion of the informal sector in the majority of the nine countries. The short-term costs of stabilization, resulting from environmental damage, loss of extension services, and weakened delivery of health and education services, may inhibit the countries' longer-term ability to expand productivity and employment opportunities, particularly for small and medium-size producers.

As the supply-side response has evolved in various countries, some success in promoting poverty-alleviating growth has been registered. In El Salvador, expansion of the urban economy has created job opportunities for the urban poor, although the rural poor, representing roughly one-half the population, largely remain locked in poverty. Modeling simulations for Pakistan indicate that employment in the agricultural sector should improve steadily over coming years as a result of the reforms, but distribution of those anticipated economic benefits to the rural poor is not certain. Vietnam's structural reforms have given priority to absorbing the underemployed, largely rural population into the expanding industrial, service, and tourist sectors and thus give ample reason to expect that living standards among many of the country's poor will rise.

Except in Vietnam, as mentioned above, the adjustment programs have not given priority to creating conditions expressly conducive to the expansion of small farms and small businesses. Some adjustment programs have included compensatory components aimed at stimulating development of small-scale enterprises among the poor. Given that those compensatory activities have been slow to materialize and have experienced serious implementation problems, their overall contribution to poverty reduction remains inconclusive. However, several research teams raised concerns about whether those components were designed with a political intent of counteracting public discontent with the adjustment process rather than seeking to generate long-term economic opportunities for the poor.

In the medium to long term, adjustment seeks to rekindle growth that will not only counter the negative employment impacts of the stabilization phase but also raise the country to a higher growth path, thereby creating more broadly based employment. The underlying assumption of this approach is that the economic growth process per se will pull the poor out of poverty through trickle-down economics, providing both more employment and social benefits to the poor. In East Asia, for example, that strategy for pursuing higher growth rates has led to substantial poverty reduction. However, eight of the nine country studies provide little evidence that a widespread outcome of this kind can be counted on. Future, more definitive assessments will determine which sectors of developing societies are benefiting from export-oriented growth strategies and which sectors remain at the margin of the export-led development process.

Agricultural Production

One of the most important economic contributions of adjustment programs is the removal of distortions that prejudiced the agricultural sector for many years. Commercial agricultural production expanded and diversified in many countries as trade and exchange rate reforms opened new market opportunities for commercial producers. Distortionary subsidies have been removed, and more efficient marketing arrangements are evolving as government-controlled marketing boards, although still in place in some countries, are being dismantled. In no country have the benefits been as immediate and direct, even for small producers, as in Vietnam. Although growth in the agricultural sector is the central requirement for putting countries on a more sustainable development path, it should be pointed out that the environmental costs of commercial agriculture are also raised in the Pakistan, El Salvador, and Venezuela studies.

Even more fundamental, however, are the uncertainties raised by the country studies as to whether the benefits of the new economic regime will reach the small farmers and rural families with little or no land. For example, will small farmers be able to respond to potential market opportunities unless credit arrangements, extension programs, and marketing systems are restored? Will targeted economic reforms and external support be available to help small farmers intensify production rather than relying on extensified production to survive? To what degree will the increased economic difficulties facing the rural poor oblige them to increase reliance on natural resources to survive, thus generating irreversible damage to soils, watersheds, and forests during the transitional period and in the long run? Will population stabilization programs be made available to the rural poor so as to halt the demographic pressure on diminishing resource bases? Further, will the current restructuring process accelerate the concentration of land ownership, further reducing economic assets and productive opportunities of the rural poor? Answering these questions would be highly speculative at this time, but the current trends identified in the country studies are not encouraging.

The Role of the State

The functions of the state are an important area of analysis in the country studies. The scope of government activities in the nine countries, as well as their ability to carry out those functions, varies significantly. In some countries, governments have been abusive, acquiring characteristics of the predatory state's sapping business and civil society of their vitality and independence. In one country, the national government remains beholden to a small group of landed aristocrats, assuming characteristics of a feudal state. In another, the government has a major role in redistributing natural resource rents to broad sectors of the population through a wide range of social programs. To give adequate attention to the impacts of adjustment programs on government activities, the following section analyzes three separate functions of the state.

The State as an Economic Agent

The adjustment programs implemented in the majority of the countries made important inroads in reducing the state's role as an economic agent in areas in which it has performed less efficiently than the private sector. Although privatization reforms are still incomplete in several African countries, Venezuela, Pakistan, and Vietnam, decisive steps have been taken toward reducing the governments' economic role there. That change not only helped reduce fiscal imbalances but it also improved the prospects of generating new private sector employment and of increasing productivity over the medium and long terms. Whereas many state-owned enterprises have not been economically viable or sustainable, transfer to private ownership has clearly improved the prospects of their making long-term contributions to the economy.

Several studies expressed concern about the long-term development implications of privatization. None of the studies challenged the need for divestiture of state-owned enterprises, although researchers question whether privatization should move forward with what the Venezuelan study calls the lack of "a strategic vision of the state's role in a modern economy." Given the countries' different stages of development, that strategic economic function would necessarily vary. However, in the present ideological climate, economic functions of the state have been discredited and swept aside as an outdated concept altogether. When this period of economic restructuring is assessed in coming years, the longer-term impacts of eliminating the state's economic functions in many of the countries will have to be a focus of the analysis.

The State's Administrative and Managerial Functions
The economic reform process has encouraged strengthening of government regulatory functions in the financial sector to ensure transparent and stable conditions for foreign capital to participate in national markets. The success of this enhanced regulatory function is reflected, for example, in the growing foreign investment in the extractive and other sectors and, to a more limited degree, in the creation of local capital markets.

On the other hand, the ability of the state to regulate the social costs of economic activities has declined significantly under the aegis of structural adjustment. This change is most apparent in the relaxation and at times the dismantling of environmental regulations and standards designed to protect society from the negative environmental impacts generated by the private sector. Without such standards and regulatory mechanisms firmly in place, the social costs will be borne by society as a whole and passed on to future generations through reduced development options.

The State's Role in Guiding Social Development
The diminution of the economic role and regulatory functions of the state are accompanied by a more general delegitimization of the state's role in guiding social development. Social policies geared toward promoting distributional equity and providing basic standards of living have been

discredited and abandoned under the adjustment process. The role of government in providing basic social goods and services has also been weakened and challenged in most countries.

This delegitimization of the state stems not only from the current ideology accompanying structural adjustment and the emerging development model; it has grown, as well, from years of government mismanagement, corruption, and abuse. As a consequence, it is difficult to isolate the effects of that negative legacy from the current ideology. What is indisputable, however, is that the role of the government as a provider of social goods and implementer of social and environmental policy is significantly diminished. This fact poses an important challenge to promoting sustainable development in that a higher economic growth path brought about by adjustment policies does not address the current trend toward growing economic and social inequalities. Without redistributive mechanisms through government programs, the prospects of unequal social development resulting from the economic reforms remain high.

Cost Internalization

Cost internalization is good economics as well as an integral part of getting the prices right. Internalization of economic activities' social and environmental costs has been set back in virtually all countries included in this study during the adjustment period. Regulatory activities were relaxed, capture of resource rents fell, and enforcement programs were cut back or eliminated. No efforts seem to have been made to integrate full-cost pricing into the adjustment programs' cost-benefit calculations. No measures were enacted to reflect environmental costs in pricing goods traded on international markets.

The difficult financial conditions besetting adjusting countries encouraged governments to reduce or remove "disincentives" for potential investors. Such disincentives include reduction or removal of environmental protections that might increase the short-term costs of extracting resources, building infrastructure, or installing industrial plants. Although many companies have taken advantage of relaxed environmental standards to gain competitive advantage, some foreign corporations maintain standards higher than the host governments' so as to reduce environmental damage and potential liabilities. However, the fact that governments have relaxed regulatory constraints and accepted externalization of the environmental costs of development is clearly a setback for promoting sustainable development strategies.

Failure to internalize environmental costs cannot be attributed to adjustment programs per se because establishing national environmental policies and enforcement agencies is the main vehicle for correcting this policy failure. However, to the degree that adjustment programs facilitate integration of resource-dependent economies into the global marketplace on terms that might seriously weaken their natural resource base, strengthening environmental regulations and enforcement capability and implementing complementary policy reforms should receive particular attention in designing adjustment policies.

THE SOCIAL DIMENSION OF SUSTAINABLE DEVELOPMENT

Equity is the fundamental concern of sustainability's social dimension. The standard used in assessing social sustainability is whether society is providing all citizens the opportunity to have access to minimum standards of security, human rights, and social benefits, including food, health, and education. Included in those opportunities must be ensuring that all people can make productive, justly remunerated contributions to society and that the benefits of their contributions are distributed broadly and fairly.

Distributional Equity

Distributional equity worsened in the majority of countries included in this study. Increased income disparities are expected as liberalization of Vietnam's economy benefits different sectors of society unequally. While urban dwellers in El Salvador have benefited from the reform process, the relative incomes of the rural poor have declined. Perhaps nowhere have distributional inequities grown as sharply or as rapidly as under the Venezuelan reform. Jamaica, Pakistan, Tanzania, and Zambia have also registered growing income disparities. In short, the poor, particularly the rural poor, women, and small-business owners seem to be among the short-term losers in the adjustment process; medium-size and large farmers, entrepreneurs in the export sector, investors in the extractive industries, and some manufacturing firms figure among the winners.

This relatively uniform experience of worsening income inequality reflects the difficulty, or at times, the indifference, of societies to redistributing wealth and productive assets or creating new productive opportunities for the economically weak and vulnerable. Economic liberalization programs weakened existing redistributive mechanisms in Tanzania, Zambia, and Venezuela and imparted greater influence to market forces in determining the welfare of individuals and social sectors. The long-term consequences of that social and institutional change will largely depend on whether the economic benefits of structural adjustment are enduring, which sectors of the adjusting societies participate in the promised economic growth, and whether redistributive social programs are put back into place if income inequalities continue to grow.

Social Services

The short-term negative impacts of fiscal retrenchment on delivery of social services have fallen largely on those social groups, including the rural and urban poor, women, and the uneducated, that are least able to maintain their living standards during the dislocations caused by the adjustment process. The long-term impacts of adjustment on social services provision, however, are not so clear. It is conceivable, as development agencies claim, that stronger macroeconomic performance may create economic conditions that will lead to more efficient, comprehensive social services delivery. Moreover, downsizing and reforming current social services institutions, which often have bloated bureaucracies and inefficient performance records, may hold potential for improving social services delivery in the long run.

But even if macroeconomic performance improves steadily in the future, improved social services are not guaranteed. The dismantling of many social services over the past years has created an institutional vacuum in some countries, making expanded and improved services more difficult and costly. It is clear that if current trends in social services delivery continue, their negative impacts on poverty will increase. In turn, continued poverty increases can only worsen the existing environmental problems documented in the country studies. Such trends would not promote sustainability.

Gender Equity

The four African and Venezuelan case studies affirmed the fact that adjustment costs have fallen disproportionately on women. The impacts are felt through the disproportionate loss of employment by women and the loss of social services on which women rely for health and child-rearing support. The impacts are immediate and they may have long-term implications as well. For example, studies demonstrate that cutbacks in educational services directly affect women's income-generating opportunities, access to social and productive activities, and family size. Consequently, the unequal burdens placed on women through the adjustment process have medium- and long-term effects on the sustainability of development paths not only by reducing their incomes but also by denying them opportunities for human development and by denying them the option of controlling fertility. (The remaining four studies did not address the distribution of adjustment's costs and benefits along gender lines.)

Population Stabilization

The country studies recognize the unrelenting strain that growing population and high fertility rates place on the countries' resources. In several cases, including Mali, Cameroon, and Tanzania, growing populations prevent increased productivity from generating higher per capita incomes. However, with the exception of noting the uneven distribution of adjustment costs on women, none of the studies examined the impacts of adjustment on the provision of social programs specifically designed to provide family planning services. It should be noted that the more general decline in education and health care, documented in the studies, remains an important determinant of birth rates.

The loss of opportunity for women and continued high population growth rates, when considered together, seriously challenge the long-term sustainability of all the countries' development paths. Improved economic productivity will be of little benefit if it is exceeded by population growth and mounting population pressures on fragile environmental resources.

Political Participation

The general process used by governments in designing and implementing adjustment programs can be characterized as vertical, imposed from above. By and large, decisions have been made by policymakers at the highest level of government, usually in finance ministries, transmitted through various government agencies, and then implemented without public consultation.

Venezuela and Zambia experienced social upheavals when stabilization programs were first implemented, forcing those governments to recognize the importance of public education and management of public opinion in carrying out further economic reforms. With few exceptions, genuine public consultation and input from civil society into the design and implementation of the stabilization and adjustment process have not been part of the reform process. Rather than using the opportunity to strengthen civil society's participation, adjustment is too frequently a test of what the elites can impose without involving the wider public. Concomitantly, adjustment has become a test of how much of the adjustment burden can be placed on the poor while the privileged often take advantage of the reform process.

The structural adjustment programs seem to reinforce the prevailing political economy in the adjusting societies as regards elites and popular sectors of society. Overall, this political experience has weakened, not strengthened, the participatory mechanisms of adjusting societies and does not provide any indication that governments will be able to work more closely with civil society to manage their resources more effectively over the long term.

Two notable exceptions are Mali and Tanzania: those governments, in recognizing their weakened administrative capacity, have encouraged broader local participation in resource and agricultural management activities in the context of structural adjustment programs. These efforts merit further review so that positive aspects of their experience can be shared more broadly.

THE ENVIRONMENTAL DIMENSION OF SUSTAINABLE DEVELOPMENT

The main concern in assessing the environmental dimension of sustainability is maintaining the integrity of a country's environmental infrastructure and life-support systems. Environmental goods and services must be used in such a way as to maintain the productivity of nature and the overall contribution of environmental goods and services to human welfare.

Consumption of Renewable Natural Resources

The nine countries in the study have experienced loss of renewable natural resources through deforestation, soil degradation, and watershed disruption during the adjustment period. The country studies vary in their ability to establish causal relationships between adjustment and its environmental impacts. In some cases, environmental trends worsened under adjustment; in others, preestablished trends continued. But the trend of unsustainable use of natural resources and environmental services is clearly established in both circumstances. Within the relatively short time frame of these studies, it is difficult to ascertain the degree to which those losses are irreversible. Loss of biodiversity, destruction of habitats, and disruption of water catchment systems, for example, have not always been quantified by the research institutes. Without exception, however, the studies affirm the fact that the current environmental impact trends are serious, have long-term implications, and in many cases, show signs of irreversible damage. Of equal concern is the fact that the adjustment process's new economic incentives have prompted the conversion and intensified use of those resources without providing new sources of those environmental goods and services to match rising consumption rates. Nor has the adjustment process put in place stronger environmental management agencies capable of addressing the new conditions and challenges that threaten the countries' resource bases.

Consumption of Nonrenewable Resources

One of the principal effects of adjustment is expanded extraction of nonrenewable resources, including petroleum, semiprecious stones, gypsum, alumina, gold, diamonds, copper, and other ores. Adjustment programs created conditions facilitating this expansion. Exporting countries rely heavily on those resources to earn hard currency.

One concern related to resource extraction is the failure to reinvest the rents and revenues derived in economic activities that will diversify the economic base and generate a long-term stream of income benefits for the nation. In most cases, rents and revenues are used to correct fiscal imbalances. In regard to two resources, alumina in Jamaica and copper in Zambia, the governments established reinvestment schemes years ago. However, prior to implementing the adjustment process, revenues from those nonrenewable resources were mismanaged, used for other purposes, and therefore did not contribute to generating a long-term stream of income. Adjustment programs have not created such funds because priority attention was given to addressing immediate balance of payments problems and improving fiscal deficits.

Sink Functions

Expanded extractive activities, expanded industrial production, and increased numbers of heavily polluting vehicles have contributed to growing pressures on the sink functions of the adjusting countries' environments. Whatever regulatory standards were in place prior to adjustment, the general tendency has been to relax them so as to reduce private enterprise's short-term economic costs. In El Salvador, industrial pollution and urban sewage further stress already strained surface- and groundwaters. In Tanzania, where industrial production is modest, and in countries where industrial expansion is anticipated, pollution standards and enforcement capacity are admittedly weak; the research teams caution that pressures on sink functions will increase in coming years. Trade-offs will have to be made as the industrialization process accelerates. Current signals regarding the weakening managerial and enforcement capacity indicate that the environmental costs of economic development will be higher than necessary.

Natural Capital

Consumption of natural capital to finance macroeconomic imbalances is a central part of the adjustment programs in Venezuela, Tanzania, Zambia, and Cameroon. Natural capital is drawn down as well by the poor, who have used natural resources to survive. Conversion of natural capital stocks has not been accompanied by investment of rents or other revenues in productive enterprises or by programs to maintain or rebuild natural capital stocks. Prior to implementation, adjustment programs did not consider the impacts of the economic reforms on natural capital stocks; nor did they establish accounting or monitoring mechanisms to analyze the impacts. Thus the country studies provide no grounds for affirming that this dimension of the adjustment process has moved the countries to a more sustainable development path.

Precautionary Principle

The precautionary principle requires that agents refrain from carrying out activities whose potential negative environmental impacts are not known owing to limited current knowledge. The environmental impacts of the economic restructuring process were not considered in the design or appraisal of the lending operations. Potentially negative environmental impacts were not identified in adjustment programs or mitigation or precautionary measures implemented. Potential irreversibilities and their accompanying long-term negative impacts on the sustainability of the country's development process have been uniformly overlooked.

Institutional Framework

With the exception of Vietnam, all countries experienced a serious decline in the institutional capability of natural resource departments. Staffs were reduced, operational budgets cut, and mandates more narrowly defined. Enforcement capabilities were cut back, regulatory standards were ignored, and national environmental strategies were pushed aside in the face of pressing financial needs.

Weakening and dismantling institutions designed to protect the environment will have far-reaching impacts because of the difficulty in obtaining the services of highly qualified professionals; the complexity of establishing viable, dynamic relationships among central institutions, local offices, and communities; and the time required to integrate environmental agencies' experience, views, and recommendations into the operations of other government agencies. The hard-earned achievements in effective environmental management realized earlier, often in the face of government disregard, will be even harder to reestablish after qualified personnel have left, confidence has been broken, and private economic agents have learned to ignore regulations. The weakening of environmental institutions represents a major setback in moving countries toward sustainable development paths.

IN CONCLUSION

This assessment of whether structural adjustment has helped to place developing economies on a more sustainable development path is premised on recognizing that any process of economic change entails trade-offs between what is given up or foregone and what is to be gained. This chapter of conclusions highlights the benefits to be gained by adjusting to an export-driven development model in relation to the accompanying social and environmental costs. Given that the integrated global character of the international market system is still taking form, the choice was made here to err on the side of tentativeness in the foregoing assessment. Often questions are posed rather than assertions made with regard to what will be lost and gained by different social groups and countries as a result of the economic restructuring process.

This caution notwithstanding, three issues, summarized below, rise to the fore from the evidence presented above.

1. The nine countries studied are primarily resource-based economies with important extractive and agricultural sectors. All nine opened their borders to international capital flows as an integral part of the adjustment process. The weakening of government managerial and regulatory functions further encouraged placing natural resources more directly under the control of the international market system. Some governments facilitated the wholesale transfer of once nationally owned natural resource assets to private interests; other governments opened up areas of their countries to private concerns seeking to identify and exploit marketable natural resources. As a result, price signals from international markets, not development strategies that consider both social needs and opportunity costs, are now preeminent in defining the rates and conditions under which those resources are used as well as who the beneficiaries will be.

The concern this change in control of natural resources raises is whether the new economic regime will encourage countries to use their natural resources and environmental services in a way that will generate returns to those societies on an enduring basis. Prior to adjustment, many of the countries did not have the financial, managerial, or enforcement capabilities to see that drawing down natural capital would create a long-term stream of income for the country's welfare. Environmental strategies were often not in place, economic incentives worked against sustainable resource management, and institutions were either underfinanced or relegated to the margins of policymaking. With the added pressures of debt overhang, coupled with the weakening of state managerial capabilities, indications are that adjustment and deeper integration into the global marketplace have accelerated the drawing down and overuse of natural capital and environmental services. This trend is reinforced by the weakening of environmental institutions responsible for managing the countries' natural resources.

If indeed this is the case, as the results of this study indicate, what then will be the economic foundations of extractive economies once those resources are depleted or degraded? What forward and backward economic linkages are these economic relations creating that can lead to more diversified, stable economies in the future? Adjustment programs have assumed that "getting the prices right" will address these broader policy issues. Although "getting the prices right" may correct short-term market inefficiencies from a global perspective, they do not offer satisfactory options for those countries as regards their economic security or place in the future world economy. Nor do they promise to provide a means of generating sustainable incomes for the majority of the citizens of these extractive societies in the long run.

2. As with extractive economies, questions need to be raised about the viability of agriculture-based economies in the new international division of labor. Over past decades, the export value of primary commodities declined relative to the export value of manufactures, providing evidence that those countries with diversified manufacturing economies have benefited and will continue to benefit more than others in the context of the export-oriented development model. As an International Monetary Fund study states, "Since their short-lived recovery in 1984, real non-oil commodity prices have fallen by about 45 percent, translating into a sharp deterioration in the terms of trade for most commodity-dependent exporters."[1] If this trend continues, as indeed all signs indicate, are not agricultural economies being relegated to a decreasing relative share in global economic wealth? Further, are not agriculture-based economies, under the conditions signaled in this study, using up their productive capacity at an unsustainable rate? Under these conditions, how can diversification of these resource-dependent economies be financed? In short, is this development path increasing the risks of mortgaging the economic futures of the countries for the prospects of gaining greater access to global markets in the short term?

Additional questions need to be raised about the long-term viability of the restructuring process taking place in many of these agricultural countries. Structural adjustment programs have sought to increase the productivity and contribution of the agricultural sector to national income. The removal of distortions, the freeing up of markets, and the opening of borders to trade have offered new incentives for expanding and diversifying agricultural production. The studies show that some farmers, mainly large and medium-size commercial farmers, have responded efficiently and flexibly to the new opportunities offered by recently opened international markets. The studies indicate that during the transitional period, the majority of small farmers, in contrast, have not been able to respond to the new price incentives and market opportunities. Further, the absence of functioning markets, the lack of credit and information, unstable marketing arrangements, and a host of other political, economic, and social factors weigh heavily against small farmers' being able to respond to the new economic conditions and derive enduring benefits. In fact, many face a daily struggle to survive that forces them to overtax their resources and weaken their own productive capacity. The studies show that this survival response has accelerated the drawing down of natural capital, including forests, wildlife, and mineral wealth, while also overtaxing the productivity and regenerative capacity of soils, watersheds, and woodlands.

Perhaps in the long run, the benefits of the emerging economic regime will lead to higher incomes that will be distributed equitably among all farmers, large and small. However, current trends identified in the country studies indicate that inequalities are growing in the agricultural sector. Are the adjustment process and the export-led development strategy an acceptable approach if they continue to generate inequalities and reinforce structures that give rise to such inequality? The answer is particularly vital to societies where poverty is pervasive, where population growth rates exceed gains in productivity, and where the rural poor face external and/ or internal frontiers of agricultural production. Further, what institutional force will mitigate and reverse the trend toward growing inequality and poverty-induced environmental degradation if the ability of governments to promote basic standards of equity and decency has been weakened? The promise of improving traditional macroeconomic indicators through economic adjustment does not address many of these fundamental social and environmental issues on which sustainable development strategies must be built.

3. The conclusions focus on economic restructuring and their environmental and social impacts on a national level. This concluding concern pertains to the global environmental impacts of the current economic restructuring process. An assumption of the adjustment process is that negative environmental "externalities" on a national level can be addressed by government action to correct policy failures, strengthen institutions, and establish market-based incentives to protect the environment. This assumption seems to have proven faulty because the institutional capacity and influence of national government, the main agent for internalizing environmental costs and correcting policy failures, have declined under the adjustment process. As a result, market failures that affect the environment, including unpriced environmental services and externalization of costs, will generate greater negative impacts with their attendant problems for many levels of national life.

Failure to correct these problems on a national level accentuates concern for addressing market failures and "externalities" on a global level. What mechanisms exist to internalize environmental costs as the scope and influence of market relations deepen their embrace of natural resources around the world? Will consumption of resources on a global scale lead to environmental irreversibilities before growing relative scarcity is reflected in the prices of natural resources? What international institutions and incentives will monitor and address problems associated with a growing absolute scarcity of natural resources? In short, what system of international environmental management will ensure that the planet's resources are managed sustainably?

If the designers of structural adjustment programs gave little thought to national-level environmental impacts of economic restructuring, they certainly gave no consideration to the global implications. Yet the process of economic reform and the integration of economies into the global market have immediate and profound global implications for the environment. Unless responsive yet flexible systems of governance are put in place to address these issues, the market economy will impose its own solutions, with rather disquieting costs to individuals, nations, and the world community.

The international market system may improve allocation of scarce resources in the short term and, in doing so, may stimulate economic growth in many quarters of the world. However, the three issues raised in this final section underscore the fact that the market mechanism does not address basic questions of unequal development among different economies and societies, the concentration of wealth and growing income inequalities among social sectors, and the finite set of natural resources the human community has inherited from the planet. Although expanded growth associated with globalization of the world economy may provide partial short-term solutions to growing poverty and inequality, these issues underscore the fact that the new economic paradigm has postponed addressing many of the underlying requisites of forging a sustainable human society.

ENDNOTE

1. Eduardo Borensztein, Mohsin S. Khan, Carmen M. Reinhart, and Peter Wickham, *The Behavior of Non-oil Commodity Prices* (Washington, D.C.: International Monetary Fund, 1994), p. 1.

14

RECOMMENDATIONS

by David Reed

S tructural adjustment programs differ little, if at all, from the emerging
economic paradigm that is predicated on a globalized world economy.
Basic features of that model include strong export orientation,
flexible exchange rates, commercial bank finance and private sector
expansion, reduced economic intervention by governments, government
regulation focused on controlling inflation and fiscal deficits, and decontrol
of labor markets. In fact, structural adjustment programs, coupled with
new trade regimes, have been the main programmatic vehicle responsible
for accelerating the integration and globalization of the world economy.
During no other historical period has such a uniform set of policy
prescriptions—including privatization, diminution of the state's role,
liberalization and export promotion, and decontrol of labor markets—been
applied in so many countries, in such a short time, with such sweeping
results.

In many countries, notably middle-income countries with a diversified
economic base, the structural adjustment process has generated
demonstrable economic improvements. The distribution of economic
benefits has been fairly even in some middle-income countries, but social
inequities and environmental problems have intensified in others. Although
rising GDP and GDP per capita should make more resources available to
address underlying social and environmental problems, these areas have
often been overlooked in allocating resources among competing priorities.

In many low-income countries, the impacts of adjustment policies
remain highly controversial. Chapters 12 and 13 highlight the fact that
resource-dependent and agricultural economies responded differently from
manufacturing economies, often generating outcomes not anticipated by

adjustment program designers. A defining response of extractive resource-dependent economies to structural adjustment programs is a significant increase in resource extraction as new price signals become operative. The predominant response in agricultural economies to adjustment programs is intensified pressures on the natural resource base, both to spur economic expansion in tradeable agricultural goods and to address the urgent survival needs of the rural poor. For economies that are both extractive and agricultural, the outcome of economic restructuring as currently experienced does not appear to be sustainable.

These study results indicate that basic changes should take place regarding the objectives and content of structural reforms in extractive and agricultural economies and also in diversified economies with large agricultural or extractive sectors. The results also indicate that basic changes should be made in the development strategies of those economies to ensure their long-term economic, social, and environmental viability in the emerging world economy.

The recommendations presented below are predicated on the view that structural reforms are central to improving the long-term productivity and stability of many developing countries. The underlying theme of these recommendations is not to diminish the importance of implementing economic reforms but to ensure a change in how the costs and benefits of adjustment—and of the emerging development model—are distributed. Specifically, they seek to ensure that costs and benefits are distributed more equitably and that social and environmental costs are built into the calculus of development strategies. To this end, the recommendations are essentially prescriptions that call for changes in the priorities of development strategies and a shift in function among the actors in the development process.

INTEGRATING ENVIRONMENTAL ISSUES INTO MACROECONOMIC REFORMS

Simply correcting economic distortions and improving efficiency are not a sufficient basis for designing and implementing adjustment programs. Restructuring economies through policy reforms should be guided by a long-term strategy based on each country's needs as well as on the potential position it could occupy in the emerging international market system. The country's natural resource base and environment should be central in shaping that strategic vision.

1. All macroeconomic reforms, including structural adjustment, should differentiate economies according to the functions they serve in the current international division of labor, for example, whether they are:

- extractive economies;
- agricultural economies;
- manufacturing economies; or
- information and high-tech economies.

Design of adjustment programs must address the different place these economies occupy in the world economy and ensure that the economic stability and sustainability of those economies are fully considered.

2. To this end, strategic environmental assessments should be applied to all countries undergoing macroeconomic reform.[1] The basic purpose of strategic environmental assessment is to:

- identify trends and causalities of the country's major environmental problems;
- identify the functions expected of the environment and natural resources in the country's proposed development strategy;
- in the context of the proposed development strategy and accompanying environmental profile, assess the impacts of structural adjustment programs on the rate and composition of natural resource use and on environmental services;
- assess the impacts of macroeconomic and sectoral reforms on the social structure and institutions of the adjusting country and, thereafter, the impacts of those social changes on the country's natural resource base;
- identify policy corrections and mitigation measures that will ensure that adjustment measures generate positive environmental outcomes; and
- identify complementary policy and institutional reforms to be implemented before or during the adjustment process to ensure that price corrections lead to positive environmental outcomes.

Although further research is needed, it is now becoming more feasible to anticipate the impacts of price changes on the rates and composition of natural resource use in countries undertaking adjustment programs.[2] Social and institutional changes brought about by adjustment programs can also be anticipated in general terms, as can the subsequent impacts on the country's natural resource base. The overriding concern of this analysis should be to ensure that poverty-induced environmental damage is minimized.

3. In extractive and agricultural economies, a clear strategic vision, not just "getting the prices right," should be articulated regarding how those sectors will drive the countries' economic development. Moreover, in those economies, basic measures must be taken to ensure sustainability.

In extractive economies:

- National economic accounts should be established that register depletion and degradation of natural resources; these accounts should be made part of the public record and should be integrated into national development planning.
- Extraction of nonrenewables should be coupled with plans to reinvest rents and profits in long-term income-generating activities. In particular, income should be invested in sustainable economic activities that will diversify the country's economic base.
- Information should be made available to the public regarding the capture of resource rents and the structure of government subsidies, in short, how the benefits of resource extraction are being used for public or private gain.
- National trade policies should be established that will promote long-term sustainability in the country; a central requirement of promoting sustainable trade policies is analyzing and making public their environmental costs.

In agricultural economies:

- National economic accounts should be established that integrate depletion of forest resources and degradation of agricultural lands and watersheds into the calculation of economic performance.
- Indicators and mechanisms should be established for monitoring productivity of agricultural lands, expansion of the agricultural frontier, and conversion of forests into agricultural lands.
- Priority attention should be given to using structural reforms to increase the productivity of farmers, particularly small farmers, through measures that include:

  o maintaining agricultural extension services;
  o providing credit for inputs and technology improvements; and
  o maintaining subsidies on inputs and farm implements until productivity gains and increased savings allow for gradual removal.

4. Transformation of extractive and agricultural economies into diversified manufacturing economies remains the primary objective of most developing countries today. Such structural change generates new social and environmental impacts and entails redistribution of costs and benefits to different social groups and geographic areas. During and after such change, however, economies remain dependent, to varying degrees, on the productivity of the agricultural and extractive sectors. In addition to creating the managerial and regulatory institutions to address the largely urban environmental problems associated with this economic transformation, measures should be taken to ensure sustainability of the country's natural resource base:

- A strategic vision should be articulated regarding the role of natural resources and environmental goods and services in the transformation process and in sustaining the manufacturing economy.
- A natural capital investment plan should be articulated and made public to ensure the long-term productivity of natural resources required for maintaining the manufacturing economy. This plan should include both information on the role of natural resources in subsidizing the industrialization process and details on the transitional process through which environmental costs would be internalized.
- Such information should be used to establish national economic accounts that register depletion and degradation of natural resources; in parallel, national sustainability indicators should be established to monitor economic, social, and environmental performance.

POVERTY

One of the underlying justifications of adjustment programs is to remove biases against the poor, particularly the rural poor, through expansion of the agricultural and tradeable goods sectors. Many small farmers are not able to respond to new price incentives in a timely manner, and faced with disruptions in marketing systems, credit institutions, and supply of inputs, they respond by overtaxing their productive assets in order to survive. To reverse this trend:

1. Adjustment programs should ensure that government mechanisms are put in place to provide input, credit, and extension supports during the transitional period from government to private ownership of marketing, transportation, and credit systems.

2. During the transitional period, adjustment programs should also establish information mechanisms to help small farmers respond effectively to the new price structures, to learn how to shift crop mixes, and to market their produce until more stable marketing and distribution mechanisms are in place.

In addition, the following society-wide measures should be implemented to maintain and thereafter improve living standards of the poor:

1. Social services, education, and health care should be maintained, given their central role in supporting the survival of the rural and urban poor.

2. Particular emphasis should be placed on providing services and income-generating opportunities for women. Of central importance is providing small-scale lending facilities to stimulate microenterprise development by women.

3. Programs and mechanisms for promoting distributional equity should be reintroduced as a central objective of the adjustment process. The tendency for income distribution to worsen in many countries highlights the importance of including equity targets and employment generation opportunities as key aspects of the adjustment process. In addition, measures should be taken to ensure that social mitigation and safety nets actually reach the poor and are not captured by the middle classes.

4. Transitional employment and training programs and targeted food-assistance programs should be strengthened in all adjustment exercises. These programs should be included in the original design of the adjustment program, not grafted on as the costs of social dislocations become more apparent. Moreover, these programs cannot be implemented at the expense of dismantling established social services programs.

THE ROLE OF THE STATE

A different understanding of the state's role in the context of the emerging global economy is required to provide goods and services for which neither civil society nor the private sector can or will assume responsibility. The change implies a reversal of current ideology as well as a departure from the abusive, predatory behavior of governments in many countries. The change will also require developing a strategic vision of the state's role in each country. This need is particularly important for countries in which the state previously played a major economic role: simply privatizing state-owned enterprises, dismantling state marketing boards and transport systems, and declaring markets' existence are elements of an inadequate approach. Transition strategies should be put in place, particularly in agriculture-based, low-income countries to ensure continuity in production and distribution systems and to strengthen the ability of the most vulnerable social sectors to respond to new price incentives and economic regimes.

Adjustment programs should be designed not only from an economic point of view but also from a political economy point of view, that is, designers of adjustment programs must create reform programs that are politically feasible over the short and long terms. This perspective requires addressing short- and medium-term needs of the broadest sectors of society, not just the elites. Further, in order to enhance the ownership of adjustment programs in countries with weak governments, sustained institutional development programs must be undertaken with support from international donors.

The state is responsible for, among other functions, developing trade policies that are consistent with sustainable development given the fact that the international marketplace seeks only short-term profit, not long-term sustainability. National-level transparency of social and environmental impacts of trade regimes is the only guarantee of sustainable trade practices.

More specific state functions should:

1. Identify areas in which its role as economic agent is needed until the private sector can fulfill the same role. These functions, whether as equity holders in development activities or guarantors of private sector initiatives, must be both transitional and tailored to country conditions.

2. Strengthen the government's managerial and administrative capacity in the environmental sector: improve pollution monitoring capability, enforce regulations as regards urban pollution and extractive industries, and establish a market-based system of environmental incentives.

3. Identify and promote responsibilities of the state as a producer of social and environmental goods and services. These range from providing basic social services in health and education, to developing environmental infrastructure for water, sanitation, and soil management, to gathering and disseminating environmental data.

4. Strengthen fiscal and regulatory means to ensure full-cost pricing so that prices include extraction, production, depletion, and other environmental costs.

5. Improve national planning capacity, ensuring the integration of economic growth and environmental management strategies. This integrated economic and environmental strategy must be included in agreements with the international donor community. Moreover, integrated development strategies should include monitoring and evaluation of the environmental impacts of macroeconomic and trade policies.

NATIONAL INSTITUTIONAL REFORMS

Closely tied to strengthening the role of the state is addressing institutional constraints, particularly in low-income countries. The dislocations and problems associated with the adjustment process draw attention not only to policy and market failures but to institutional problems as well. Among them are issues of uncertain property rights, population planning policies and programs, environmental data collection and monitoring systems, difficulties in integrating national environmental action plans into macroeconomic development strategies, and a weakened capacity to enforce existing environmental laws and regulations. Through strategic environmental assessment, adjustment programs should identify the areas in which institution building must occur so that integration into the global economy is managed on a sustainable basis. Further, designers of adjustment programs should identify the areas in which economic reforms must be preceded by institutional reforms and strengthening to ensure that the economic benefits of adjustment are not offset by institutional and policy failures.

THE ROLE OF CIVIL SOCIETY

The importance of local groups has grown and will continue to grow in response to the inability of governments and the private sector to deliver many services to broad sectors of citizens. Adjustment programs should be used as an opportunity to:

1. Deepen education and dialogue with communities to solicit input on adjustment objectives and priorities, mobilize support for the requisite economic reforms, and encourage public debate about future development options.

2. Expand the role of community groups and nongovernmental organizations in administering social and environmental mitigation programs, increase their responsibilities for delivering social services, and broaden their contributions to formulating local development plans.

3. Expand the scope of community groups to address growing environmental challenges, identify development activities' costs and benefits, and mobilize support for long-term environmental protection activities.

REFORM OF INTERNATIONAL FINANCIAL INSTITUTIONS

Globalization of the world economy, reflecting the new role of private capital, is significantly changing international financial institutions' contributions to the development process. To respond to the new demands and challenges, changes will inevitably take place in the priorities and operations of multilateral institutions, most importantly, of the World Bank. Regardless of future institutional arrangements, some basic reforms should be made, including those listed below:

1. Operations designed to carry out policy and structural reforms will remain an important part of international institutions' lending portfolios, particularly in light of the rapid changes if not volatility of the world economy. Rethinking the current approach to policy lending consistent with the needs of different kinds of economies in the international division of labor will improve multilateral lenders' overall operational effectiveness. An important feature of rethinking the current approach is expanding the axiom of "getting the prices right" to include "getting long-term social and environmental strategies right," particularly in extractive and agricultural countries. This more inclusive approach should become the foundation for the World Bank's country assistance strategies (CASs).

2. This refocusing should give priority to strengthening the capacity of government institutions, particularly in low-income countries, to plan and manage their respective functions in providing public goods and services.

3. Lending priorities should shift away from financing projects for which private sector funds can be used and toward developing the public goods sectors to which private sector funds will not flow. This shift includes improving efficiency in delivering social services, building and maintaining environmental infrastructure, and strengthening resource management capacity.

4. A centralized function of the World Bank, one to be carried out in conjunction with all multilateral development banks, should be to strengthen monitoring and analysis of data pertaining to development trends, providing analysis and assistance in strategy formulation to developing countries and sharing information with governments and civil society.

5. International Monetary Fund (IMF) stabilization programs should be redesigned to protect government managerial and administrative capacity in adjusting countries. Attention must be given to protecting governments' ability to provide environmental and social services on which the long-term productivity of countries depends. In addition, the IMF should pay greater attention to the differential impacts of fiscal reductions on various sectors of adjusting countries, thereby protecting the most vulnerable sectors of those societies.

Decentralization of activities and operations to national and regional offices should be undertaken to enhance accountability to local stakeholders and civil society in recipient countries.

REFORM OF INTERNATIONAL INSTITUTIONS

Whereas monitoring and regulatory capacities may exist on the national level to ensure compliance with environmental laws and promote social objectives, no such mechanisms exist on a global level. In the context of globalization of the world economy, such monitoring and regulatory mechanisms should be established. Initial steps in developing those functions should include:

1. Reform the system of national accounts[3]: All countries and international agencies should use national accounting systems that reflect environmental values. Accounting approaches must be adjusted to reflect specific environmental problems in extractive, agricultural, and manufacturing economies. Similar accounting methods must be adopted across the board by multilateral lenders and the IMF to reflect more accurately real productivity gains of the economy rather than distorting these figures by including consumption of natural capital and defensive expenditures.

2. Establish sustainability indicators[4]: The impacts of structural adjustment should be monitored through application of sustainability indicators that reflect changes in economic, social, and environmental conditions. International institutions, including the United Nations Commission on Sustainable Development, the World Bank, and the United Nations Development Programme, should integrate their parallel efforts to establish a common framework of indicators for assessing sustainability of countries' development paths on comparative and absolute terms. On the national level, governments should establish sustainability indicators that reflect their specific conditions and development priorities. The main purpose of using both sets of indicators is to guide the formulation of national development strategies. In addition, those indicators should be used to compare previous and current development strategies and to assess government compliance with international obligations.

3. Reform the international trade system: Participation in international trade regimes requires that governments enact laws to protect intellectual property rights. So too should international trade regimes require that participating governments:

- have in place a minimal environmental regulatory enforcement capacity to encourage internalization of environmental costs;
- conduct assessments and monitor environmental costs and benefits of various trade regimes;
- guarantee public transparency of environmental impacts of the trade regimes in which the country participates; and

- reform international trade rules to ensure their compatibility with rigorous national and international environmental standards.

ENDNOTES

1. Robert Goodland was most helpful in developing these ideas. For a more inclusive discussion of his perspective, see Robert Goodland and Gus Tillman, "Strategic Environmental Assessment: Strengthening the Environmental Assessment Process" (Washington, D.C., 1995).

2. The following studies exemplify the progress being made in analyzing the linkages between macroeconomics and the environment in developing countries: Arlene Alpha, *Etude "Ajustement Structurel et Environnement": Cas de la Côte d'Ivoire* (Paris: Développement des Investigations sur Ajustement à Long Terme, 1994); Elizabeth Cromwell and James Winpenny, "Does Economic Reform Harm the Environment? A Review of Structural Adjustment in Malawi," *Journal of International Development* 5(1993):623-49; P.J. Darling, *Etude "Ajustement Structurel et Environnement": Cas du Mali* (Paris: Développement des Investigations sur Ajustement à Long Terme, 1994); Antonio Garcia Lizana, *Etude "Ajustement Structurel et Environnement": Cas de la Guinee Equatoriale* (Paris: Développement des Investigations sur Ajustement à Long Terme, 1994); Ramón López, *Evaluating Economy-wide Policies in the Presence of Agricultural Environmental Externalities: The Case of Ghana*, rev. ed. (College Park: University of Maryland, 1994); Julie A. Richardson, ed., *Structural Adjustment and Environmental Linkages: A Case Study of Kenya* (London: Overseas Development Institute, 1993); Julie A. Richardson, *Etude "Ajustement Structurel et Environnement": Cas du Kenya* (Paris: Développement des Investigations sur Ajustement à Long Terme, 1994); World Bank, *Economywide Policies and the Environment: Emerging Lessons from Experience* (Washington, D.C.: World Bank, 1994); and Wilfredo Cruz and Robert Repetto, *The Environmental Effects of Stabilization and Structural Adjustment Programs: The Philippines Case* (Washington, D.C.: World Resources Institute, 1992).

3. After more than a decade, the intellectual work of Salah El-Serafy, Ernst Lutz, Michael Ward, Yusuf Ahmad, Rueffie Heuting, Robert Goodland, and Robert Repetto, among many others, in promoting national accounting system reforms of the system of national accounts is being tested and applied. Some 20 countries, including Mexico, India, the Philippines, South Africa, Sweden, and the Netherlands, have instituted important reforms in their economic information systems. WWF's efforts, including international conferences, research, and public education, have helped translate these technical advances and proposals into realistic reform programs. See Fulai Sheng, *Real Value for Nature* (Gland, Switzerland: World Wide Fund for Nature-International, 1995).

4. During the past decade, numerous international organizations, NGOs, and specialized development groups undertook programs to develop sustainability indicators. Two main weaknesses characterize those initiatives: the proposals lack policy relevance and applicability, and the efforts are driven by specialists who fail to consider the concerns and priorities of civil society. Development of an integrated system of indicators should build commonalities among the partner institutions. The end product should acquire greater usefulness for policymakers and reflect the perspectives of the informed public.

BIBLIOGRAPHY

Adam, Christopher, William Cavendish, and Percy S. Mistry. *Adjusting Privatization: Case Studies from Developing Countries.* London: James Curray, 1992.

Adams, W.M. *Green Development: Environment and Sustainability in the Third World.* London: Routledge, 1992.

Alpha, Arlene. *Etude "Ajustement Structurel et Environment": Cas de la Côte d'Ivoire.* Paris: Développement des Investigations sur Ajustement à Long Terme, 1994.

Antrobus, Peggy. "The Impact of Structural Adjustment Policies on Women: The Experience of Caribbean Countries." Quoted in Pamela Starr, "Banking on Women: Where Do We Go from Here?" In *Mortgaging Women's Lives: Feminist Critiques of Structural Adjustment,* edited by Pamela Starr. New York: Zed Books, 1994.

Ascher, William, and Robert Healy. *Natural Resource Policymaking in Developing Countries.* Durham, N.C.: Duke University Press, 1990.

Barbier, Edward B. *New Approaches in Environmental and Resource Economics: Toward an Economics of Sustainable Development.* London: International Institute for Environment and Development, 1988.

Barbier, Edward B., and Anil Markandya. *The Conditions for Achieving Environmentally Sustainable Development.* London: International Institute for Environment and Development, 1989.

Barker, Ernest, ed. *Social Contract: Essays by Locke, Hume, and Rousseau.* London: Oxford University Press, 1969.

Bello, Walden, with Shea Cunningham and Bill Rau. *Dark Victory: The United States, Structural Adjustment, and Global Poverty.* London: Pluto Press, with Food First and Transnational Institute, 1994.

Bergquist, Charles, ed. *Labor in the Capitalist World-Economy.* London: Sage Publications, 1984.

Borensztein, Eduardo, Mohsin S. Khan, Cormen M. Reinhart, and Peter Wickham. *The Behavior of Non-oil Commodity Prices.* Washington, D.C.: International Monetary Fund, 1994.

Boulding, Kenneth E. *Beyond Economics: Essays on Society, Religion and Ethics.* Ann Arbor: University of Michigan Press, 1970.

Bourguignon, François, Jaime de Melo, and Christian Morrisson, eds. *World Development* 19, no. 11 (1991). (Special issue. *Adjustment with Growth and Equity.*)

Bretton, Tony. *The Greening of Machiavelli: The Evolution of International Environmental Politics.* London: Earthscan, 1994.

Carson, Rachel. *Silent Spring.* Boston: Houghton Mifflin, 1962.

Cline, William R., and Sidney Weintraub, eds. *Economic Stabilization in Developing Countries*. Washington, D.C.: Brookings Institution, 1981.

Comeliau, Christian. *Les Relations Nord-Sud*. Paris: Éditions la Découverte, 1991.

Commission on Global Governance. *Our Global Neighborhood: The Report of the Commission on Global Governance*. Oxford: Oxford University Press, 1995.

Corbo, Vittorio, Stanley Fischer, and Steven B. Webb, eds. *Adjustment Lending Revisited: Policies to Restore Growth*. Washington, D.C.: World Bank, 1992.

Cornia, Giovanni Andrea, Richard Jolly, and Frances Stewart. *Adjustment with a Human Face*. Vol. 1, *Protecting the Vulnerable and Promoting Growth*. Oxford: Clarendon Press, 1987.

Cromwell, Elizabeth, and James Winpenny. "Does Economic Reform Harm the Environment? A Review of Structural Adjustment in Malawi." *Journal of International Development* 5 (1993):623-49.

Cruz, Wilfredo, and Robert Repetto. *The Environmental Effects of Stabilization and Structural Adjustment Programs: The Philippines Case*. Washington, D.C.: World Resources Institute, 1992.

Daly, Herman E. *Ecological Economics and Sustainable Development*. Washington, D.C.: World Bank, 1990.

———. 1991. *Steady-state Economics*. Washington, D.C.: Island Press, 1991.

———. "The Perils of Free Trade." *Scientific American* (November 1993):50.

Daly, Herman E., and John B. Cobb, Jr. *For the Common Good: Redirecting the Economy Toward Community, the Environment, and a Sustainable Future*. Boston: Beacon Press, 1989.

Darling, P.J. *Etude "Ajustement Structurel et Environnement": Cas du Mali*. Paris: Développement des Investigations sur Ajustement à Long Terme, 1994.

Demery, Lionel, and Tony Addison. *The Alleviation of Poverty under Structural Adjustment*. Washington, D.C.: World Bank, 1987.

Diaz-Bonilla, Eugenio. *Structural Adjustment Programs and Economic Stabilization in Central America*. Washington, D.C.: World Bank, 1990.

Erhlich, Paul. *The Population Bomb*. New York: Ballantine Books, 1990.

French, Hillary. *Costly Trade-offs: Trade and the Environment*. Washington, D.C.: World Watch, 1993.

Frieden, Jeffry A., and David A. Lake. *International Political Economy: Perspectives on Global Power and Wealth*. New York: St. Martin's Press, 1991.

Georgescu-Roegen, Nicolas. *The Entropy Law and the Economic Process*. Cambridge, Mass.: Harvard University Press, 1971.

Gill, Stephen, and David Law. *The Global Political Economy: Perspectives, Problems and Policies*. Baltimore: John Hopkins University Press, 1988.

Gilpin, Robert. *The Political Economy of International Relations*. Princeton, N.J.: Princeton University Press, 1987.

Goldin, Ian, Odin Knudsen, and Dominique van der Mensbrugghe. *Trade Liberalisation: Global Economic Implications*. Paris: Organisation for Economic Co-operation and Development and World Bank, 1993.

Goodland, Robert, and Herman E. Daly. "Ten Reasons Why Northern Income Growth Is Not the Solution to Southern Poverty." In *Population, Technology, and Lifestyle*, edited by Robert Goodland, Herman E. Daly, and Salah el Serafy. Washington, D.C.: Island Press, 1992.

Goodland, Robert, Herman E. Daly, and Salah El Serafy, eds. *Population, Technology, and Lifestyle: The Transition to Sustainability*. Washington, D.C.: Island Press, 1992.

Goodland, Robert, and Gus Tillman. "Strategic Environmental Assessment: Strengthening the Environmental Assessment Process." Discussion draft, World Bank, Washington, D.C., 1995.

Gosovic, Branislav. *The Quest for World Environmental Cooperation: The Case of the UN Global Environment Monitoring System*. London: Routledge, 1992.

Holmberg, Johan, Koy Thomson, and Lloyd Timberlake. *Facing the Future*. London: Earthscan, 1993.

Honey, Martha. *Hostile Acts: U.S. Policy in Costa Rica in the 1980s*. Gainesville: University Press of Florida, 1994.

International Union for Conservation of Nature and Natural Resources (IUCN), United Nations Environment Programme (UNEP), World Wide Fund for Nature-International (WWF-I). *World Conservation Strategy*. Geneva: IUCN, 1980.

———. *Caring for the Earth*. Gland, Switzerland: IUCN, UNEP, and WWF-I, 1991.

Jannson, AnnMari, Monica Hammer, Carl Folke, and Robert Constanza. *Investing in Natural Capital: The Ecological Economics Approach to Sustainability*. Washington, D.C.: Island Press, 1994.

Kaimowitz, David. "*La Economia Politica de la Gestion Ambiental en America Latina*." Catalina, Costa Rica, 1993.

Kapp, K. William. *Towards a Science of Man: A Positive Approach to the Integration of Social Knowledge*. The Hague: Matinus Mijhoff, 1961.

———. *The Social Costs of Private Enterprise*. New York: Schocken Books, 1971.

———. *Social Costs, Economic Development and Environmental Disruption*, edited by John Ullman. Lanham, Md.: University Press of America, 1983.

Keohane, Robert O., and Joseph S. Nye. *Power and Interdependence.* Harper Collins, 1989.

Killick, Tony. *The Quest for Economic Stabilisation: The IMF and the Third World.* London: Heinemann Educational Books, 1984.

King, Robert E., and Helena Tang. *International Macroeconomic Adjustment, 1907-92: A World Model Approach.* Washington, D.C.: World Bank, 1989.

Kolko, Joyce. *Restructuring the World Economy.* New York: Pantheon Books, 1988.

Korten, Alicia. "A Bitter Pill: Structural Adjustment in Costa Rica." Development Report No. 7. Oakland, Calif.: Institute for Food and Development Policy, 1995.

Lipschutz, Ronnie D., and Ken Conca, eds. *The State and Social Power in Global Environmental Politics.* New York: Columbia University Press, 1993.

Lizana, Antonio Garcia. *Etude "Ajustement Structurel et Environnement": Cas de la Guinee Equatoriale.* Paris: Développement des Investigations sur Ajustement à Long Terme, 1994.

López, Ramón. *Evaluating Economy-wide Policies in the Presence of Agricultural Environmental Externalities: The Case of Ghana.* Rev. ed. College Park: University of Maryland, 1994.

Low, Patrick, ed. *International Trade and the Environment.* Washington, D.C.: World Bank, 1992.

Maasland, Anne, and Jacques van der Gaag. "World Bank-supported Adjustment Programs and Living Conditions." In *Adjustment Lending Revisited,* edited by Vittorio Corbo, Stanley Fischer, and Steven B. Webb. Washington, D.C.: World Bank, 1992.

McCormick, J. *The Global Environmental Movement.* London: Bellhaven Press, 1989.

McGraw, Daniel, ed. *NAFTA & the Environment: Substance and Progress.* Chicago: American Bar Association, 1995.

Maddison, Angus. *The World Economy in the 20th Century.* Paris: Development Centre, Organisation for Economic Co-operation and Development, 1989.

Marglin, S.A., and J. Schor, eds. *The End of the Golden Age.* Oxford: Clarendon Press, 1990.

Meadows, Donella, Dennis Meadows, Jorgen Randers, and William W. Behrens III. *Limits to Growth.* New York: Universe Books, 1972.

Mosley, Paul, Jane Harrigan, and John Tage. *Aid and Power: The World Bank and Policy-based Lending.* Vol. 1, *Analysis and Policy Proposals.* London: Routledge, 1991.

Nellis, John R. "Reform of Public Enterprises." In *Restructuring Economies in Distress: Policy Reform and the World Bank,* edited by Vinod Thomas, Ajay Chhiber, Mansoor Dailami, and Jaime de Melo. New York: Oxford University Press, 1991.

Nelson, Joan M. *Economic Crisis and Policy Choice: The Politics of Adjustment in the Third World.* Princeton, N.J.: Princeton University Press, 1990.

Organisation for Economic Co-operation and Development (OECD). *Integration of Developing Countries into the International Trading System.* Paris: OECD, 1992.

Palmer, Ingrid. *Gender and Population in the Adjustment of African Economies: Planning for Change.* Geneva: International Labour Office, 1991.

Panel of Experts Convened by the Secretary-General of the United Nations Conference on the Human Environment. *Environment and Development: The Founex Report on Development and Environment.* New York: Carnegie Endowment for International Peace, 1972.

Pearce, David W., ed. *Sustainable Development and Cost Benefit Analysis.* London: International Institute for Environment and Development, 1988.

Pearce, David W., and R. Kerry Turner. *Economics of Natural Resources and the Environment.* Baltimore: Johns Hopkins University Press, 1990.

Polanyi, Karl. *The Great Transformation: The Political and Economic Origins of Our Time.* Boston: Beacon Hill Press, 1944.

Porter, Gareth, and Janet Brown. *Global Environmental Politics.* Boulder, Colo.: Westview Press, 1991.

Redclift, Michael. *Development and the Environmental Crisis: Red or Green Alternatives?* London: Routledge, 1984.

———. *Sustainable Development: Exploring the Contradictions.* London: Routledge, 1987.

Reed, David. "The Global Environment Facility and Non-governmental Organizations." *American University Journal of International Law and Policy* (Fall 1993):191-213.

———. "Review of *World Development Report 1992.*" *International Environmental Affairs* 4 (1992):367-71.

———. *The European Bank for Reconstruction and Development: An Environmental Opportunity.* Washington, D.C.: World Wide Fund for Nature-International, 1991.

Richardson, Julie A. *Etude "Ajustement Structurel et Environnement":* Cas du Kenya. Paris: Développement des Investigations sur Ajustement à Long Terme, 1994.

————, ed. *Structural Adjustment and Environmental Linkages: A Case Study of Kenya*. London: Overseas Development Institute, 1993.

Rohrlich, George F. *Environmental Management: Economic and Social Dimensions*. Cambridge, Mass.: Ballinger, 1974.

Scientific American 261, no. 3 (September 1989), *Managing Planet Earth*. (Special issue.)

Sheng, Fulai. *Real Value for Nature*. Gland, Switzerland: World Wide Fund for Nature-International, 1995.

Sparr, Pamela. *Mortgaging Women's Lives: Feminist Critiques of Structural Adjustment*. London: Zed Books, 1994.

Standing, Guy, "Adjustment and Labour Market Policies." In Guy Standing and Victor Tokman, eds. *Towards Social Adjustment: Labour Market Issues in Structural Adjustment*. Geneva: International Labour Office, 1991.

Stedman, Pamela. *Setting a New Mandate for the Bretton Woods Institutions: Meeting the Challenges of Sustainable Development in a Changing Global Economy*. Washington, D.C.: World Wide Fund for Nature-International, 1995.

Steppacher, Rolf, Brigitte Zogg-Walz, and Hermann Hatzfeldt. *Economics in Institutional Perspective*. Lexington, Mass.: Lexington Books, 1977.

Stern, Ernest. "Evaluation and Lessons of Adjustment Lending." In *Restructuring Economies in Distress*, edited by Vinod Thomas, Ajay Chhiber, Mansoor Dailami, and Jaime de Melo. New York: Oxford University Press, 1991.

Stockholm Conference. *Only One Earth: An Introduction to the Politics of Survival*. London: Earth Island, 1972.

Stonich, Susan C. "The Promotion of Non-traditional Agricultural Exports in Honduras: Issues of Equity, Environment and Natural Resource Management" Development and Change22 (1991)725-55.

Szentes, Tamas. *The Transformation of the World Economy: New Directions and New Interests*. London: Zed Books, 1988.

Thomas, Vinod, Ajay Chhibber, Mansoor Dailami, Jaime de Melo, eds. *Restructuring Economies in Distress: Policy Reform and the World Bank*. Oxford: Oxford University Press, 1991.

Thrupp, Lori Ann. *Challenges in Latin America's Recent Agroexport Boom*. Washington, D.C.: World Resources Institute, 1995.

Thrupp, Lori Ann, with Gilles Bergeron and William F. Waters. *Bittersweet Harvests for Global Supermarkets: Challenges in Latin America's Agricultural Export Boom*. Washington, D.C.: World Resources Institute, 1995.

Torres Zorrilla, Jorge A. *Agricultural Modernization and Resource Deterioration in Latin América*. San Jose, Costa Rica: Inter-American Institute for Cooperation on Agriculture, 1994.

United Nations. *Agenda 21: Programme of Action for Sustainable Development*. New York: United Nations, 1992.

United Nations, Conference on Trade and Development. *Trade and Development Report, 1990*. New York: United Nations, 1980.

United Nations Development Programme. *Human Development Report 1992*. New York: Oxford University Press, 1992.

———. *Human Development Report 1994*. New York: Oxford University Press, 1994.

Wilber, Charles K., and Kenneth P. Jameson. *The Political Economy of Development and Underdevelopment*. New York: McGraw-Hill, 1992.

Williamson, John. *The Political Economy of Policy Reform*. Washington, D.C.: Institute for International Economics, 1994.

Wolfensohn, James. Address to the Board of Governors of the World Bank Group. Washington, D.C., October 10, 1995, mimeograph.

World Bank. *World Development Report 1980*. Washington, D.C.: World Bank, 1980.

———. Operational Manual Statement No. 3.58, Annex II. Washington, D.C., 1982.

———. *Structural Adjustment Lending: A First Review of Experience*. Washington, D.C.: World Bank, 1986.

———. *Adjustment Lending: An Evaluation of Ten Years of Experience*. Washington, D.C.: World Bank, 1988.

———. *Adjustment Lending: Policies for Sustainable Growth*. Washington, D.C.: World Bank, 1990.

———. *Structural Adjustment and Poverty: A Conceptual, Empirical, and Policy Framework*. Washington, D.C.: World Bank, 1990.

———. *The Third Report on Adjustment Lending: Private and Public Resources for Growth*. Washington, D.C.: World Bank, 1992.

———. *World Development Report 1992: Development and the Environment*. Washington, D.C.: World Bank, 1992.

———. "Implementing the Bank's Poverty Reduction Strategy: Progress and Challenges." Washington, D.C., 1993.

———. "Summary of Discussions at the Meeting of the Executive Directors of the Bank and IDA, January 26, 1993." Washington, D.C., 1993.

———. *Economywide Policies and the Environment: Emerging Lessons from Experience*. Washington, D.C.: World Bank, 1994.

———. *World Development Report 1994: Infrastructure for Development*. New York: Oxford University Press, 1994.

World Bank, Development Committee. "Social Security Reforms and Social Safety Nets in Reforming and Transforming Economies." Washington, D.C., 1993.

World Commission on Environment and Development. *Our Common Future*. Oxford: Oxford University Press, 1987.

ACRONYMS AND ABBREVIATIONS

ACP	Africa, the Caribbean, and Pacific
ADMADE	Administrative Management Design program [Zambia]
AERC	Applied Economics Research Centre
AVs	village associations [Mali]
BWI	Bretton Woods institutions
CACM	Central American Common Market
CAS	country assistance strategy [World Bank]
CCAD	Central American Commission on Environment and Development
CCC	Carib Cement Company [Jamaica]
CCM	Chama Cha Mapinduzi [Tanzania]
CEM	country economic memorandum [World Bank]
CENDES	Centro de Estudios del Desarrollo [Venezuela]
CENTA	Agricultural Research and Extension Center [El Salvador]
CFDT	Compagnie Française pour le Developpement des Textiles [Mali]
CGE	computable general equilibrium
CITES	Convention on International Trade in Endangered Species of Wild Flora and Fauna
CMDT	Compagnie Malienne pour le Developpement des Textiles [Mali]
CMEA	Council for Mutual Economic Assistance
CO	carbon monoxide
CO_2	carbon dioxide
CONAMA	National Commission for Environment [El Salvador]
CSD	Commission on Sustainable Development [United Nations]
CSP	compensatory social program [Venezuela]
DGRN	Directorate for Renewable Natural Resources [El Salvador]
EAUD	Environment and Urban Affairs Division [Pakistan]
EFF	Extended Fund Facility [International Monetary Fund]
EPA	Environmental Protection Agency [United States]
ERP	Economic Recovery Program [Tanzania]
ESAF	Enhanced Structural Adjustment Facility [International Monetary Fund]
ESAP	Economic and Social Action Program [Tanzania]
FAO	Food and Agriculture Organization of the United Nations

FDI	foreign direct investment
FONADER	National Fund for Rural Development [Cameroon]
FY	fiscal year
GATT	General Agreement on Tariffs and Trade
GDP	gross domestic product
GEF	Global Environment Facility
GNP	gross national product
HIID	Harvard Institute for International Development
IBMR	Indus Basin model (revised) [Pakistan]
ICOR	incremental capital output ratio
IDB	Inter-American Development Bank
IER	Institut d'Economie Rurale [Mali]
ILO	International Labour Organization
IMF	International Monetary Fund
IPM	integrated pest management
ITTO	International Timber Trade Organisation
IUCN	International Union for Conservation of Nature and Natural Resources
KSAC	Kingston and St. Andrew Corporation [Jamaica]
MARNR	Ministry of the Environment and Renewable Natural Resources [Venezuela]
MENR	Ministry of the Environment and Natural Resources [Zambia]
MIDENO	North-West Development Authority [Cameroon]
MINEF	Ministry of the Environment and Forests [Cameroon]
MMD	Movement for Multi-party Democracy [Zambia]
NATCOM	National Commission on the Environment [Cameroon]
NCS	National Conservation Strategy [Zambia]
NEMC	National Environmental Management Council [Tanzania]
NGO	Nongovernmental organization
NIEO	New International Economic Order
NRCA	National Resources Conservation Authority [Jamaica]
OAS	Organization of American States
ODI	Overseas Development Institute
ODA	official development assistance
OECD	Organisation for Economic Co-operation and Development
ON	Office du Niger [Mali]
PPP	Pakistan People's Party
PUSH	Programme Urban Self-Help [Zambia]
R&D	research and development
SAL	structural adjustment loan
SAM	social accounting matrix

SAP	structural adjustment program
SEMA	Executive Secretariat for the Environment [El Salvador]
SODECOTON	National Cotton Development Authority [Cameroon]
SSMA	San Salvador Metropolitan Area
TFAP	Tropical Forest Action Plan [Cameroon]
TPSM	tax policy simulation model
TRI	trade restrictive index
USAID	United States Agency for International Development
UNCED	United Nations Conference on Environment and Development
UNDP	United Nations Development Programme
UNEP	United Nations Environment Programme
UNIP	United National Independence Party [Zambia]
UNICEF	United Nations Children's Fund
USAID	United States Agency for International Development
USSR	Union of Soviet Socialist Republics
WCED	World Commission on Environment and Development
WCS	World Conservation Strategy
WWF-I	World Wide Fund for Nature-International

INDEX

Index compiled by Indexing Specialists, UK.